Signs of the Cross:
The Search for the
Historical Jesus

Signs of the Cross: The Search for the Historical Jesus From A Jewish Perspective

And

The Recovery of the True Origin of the New Testament

Andrew Gabriel Roth

Copyright © 1997, 2001 by Andrew Gabriel Roth.

Library of Congress Number: 2001116844
ISBN #:   Hardcover   0-7388-9980-1
           Softcover   0-7388-9981-X

All rights reserved. No part of this book may be reproduced or transmitted in any form or by any means, electronic or mechanical, including photocopying, recording, or by any information storage and retrieval system, without permission in writing from the copyright owner.

This book was printed in the United States of America.

To order additional copies of this book, contact:
Xlibris Corporation
1-888-795-4274
www.Xlibris.com
Orders@Xlibris.com

Contents

Acknowledgements: 11

Prelude: 13

In the Beginning: Y'shua the Rabbi 17

Part One:

Determining the Time of Nativity 47

Part Two:

The Six Sides Of The Messiah 107

Part Three:

Recovering The Semitic Linguistics Of
The New Testament 179

Part Four:

Y'shua Year By Year And Beyond 375

Bibliography

Bibles: 493

Bible Reference: 495

Other Books, Magazines and Journals: 496

Picture Credits: 503

Endnotes 504

*For my loving wife Jaye,
and to all the martyrs for the true Gospel
past and present,
this book is humbly dedicated.*

ACKNOWLEDGMENTS:

The author is indebted to the many members of his family, friends and Aramaic colleagues who have assisted him in vital decisions regarding the scope, content and focus of this book. To my parents Jane and Robert Roth, I am very grateful and humbled for your unfailing enthusiasm and support of this project from its inception. Also a hearty thank you to Paul Younan and Victor Alexander, both of whose ongoing research and translation work is a source of continued inspiration to me. To Dr. James Scott Trimm, founder of the Society for the Advancement of Nazarene Judaism, I wish you the best of everything and thank you for showing me a lot of this evidence and encouraging me to investigate it thoroughly for myself. And though it was some time ago, a special thanks to John Mosely, Director of the Griffith Observatory, Los Angeles, California. John's timely and gracious assistance with the astronomical portions of this book gave a much needed scientific edge to this field of inquiry.

And of course, once again, to my wife Jaye, who is first, last and always in my heart: Thank you for being there and making this work not only possible, but worthwhile.

PRELUDE:

The Masks of Christ

Jesus Christ.

Whether you believe in him or not, no matter who you are or what part of the world you are from, those two words have a resonance and a meaning in your life. We mark time based on his birth and, even after two millennia, we are still unable to free ourselves from the ramifications of his death. In essence, our niche in Western spiritual thought, is cast by the shadow he left behind.

In the spring of the common year 30, before dying a horrific death asphyxiating on a Roman cross, he told us in no uncertain terms:

> "Heaven and earth will pass away, but my words will never pass away."
>
> Matthew 24:35

So far, in the twenty centuries that followed, he has been proven correct. This one man, more than any other before or since, has completely defined the Western spiritual experience.

Nor is the Eastern half of the world immune from these two words.

Hindus and Buddhists have referred to Christ as an "avatar," or great teacher, or as an incarnation of Vishnu, the god who brings spiritual wisdom to men. There are many who believe Christ journeyed to Northern Japan after taking on his Palestinian Ministry, with stories and documents that date back almost two thousand years. Similar tales are found across Asia, and have even extended to our own Continent, with the Mormon Church claiming Christ ministered to American Indians. It is not my purpose to examine the historicity of these claims. Rather, I only wish to show how they reflect the fame and power of this Jewish carpenter, who came seemingly out of nowhere, and left the world forever changed afterwards.

As we sift through the minefield of controversy regarding Jesus' life, it is my considerable task to scrub off two millennia of cultural accretions that have diluted the original image of Jesus the man. Even using the word "Jesus" is a compromise to the current state of affairs, for it is a pale Greek substitute of a majestic Semitic name. My personal preferences run more along the lines of either *Y'shua Ha Moshiack* (Hebrew: "Y'shua the Messiah") or *Maran Eshoo Meshikha* (Aramaic: "LORD Eshoo [the] Messiah"). Therefore, so the reader may begin to get a flavor for this paradigm early on, I will be referring to the Messiah directly by his Hebrew name and title for the duration of this book.

However, so that I am not misunderstood, let me say for the record that I have no intention of espousing exclusive sacred name doctrine. Nor should it be taken that I will put myself in the unenviable position of telling a billion plus *goyim* that their prayers are in vain because they go to the "wrong name" a la Acts 4:12. However, a very strong *suggestion* is definitely intended to show that honoring the Messiah in his original name and language certainly shows a great amount of respect. In fact, to *never* do so I find to be a sort of reverse cultural arrogance. Furthermore, the reason for this view, not suprisingly, can be directly traced to my culture and upbringing. As a Jewish believer in the Messiah, I have generations of ancestors who have always venerated Scripture in its original Hebrew regardless as to their location or vernacular.

With Christianity however certain linguistic issues have, over the centuries, made it more difficult to ascertain an original scriptural language for the New Testament.

On the other hand, that is the main issue I intend to address and correct in this book. I also freely admit to another agenda as well. Put simply, if only a small fraction of the Messiah's Gentile followers would undertake even a minor study of his native language, the continued survival of Aramaic would be guaranteed forever. Unfortunately, as of this writing, it teeters on the brink of extinction; a precious and ancient voice about to fade away from the world.

It is only then, when Aramaic is reclaimed for the whole world of believers that follow him, that the masks of Christ can at last fall off.

IN THE BEGINNING: Y'SHUA THE RABBI

So where do we begin? Well, perhaps no source summarizes the development of Jewish thought in the last two millennia better than the collection of biblical commentaries known as the *Talmud*. While the official compilation of this work began in the second century, a good amount of its teachings easily hark back to the time of the Messiah, whereas other highly regarded teachers found fame in the Middle Ages. Either way, what we see is that the Rabbi from Nazareth—far from feeling ostracized by his brethren as so often has been supposed—would have instead felt quitecomfortable in terms of his ideas and analysis as a moderate and mostly Pharisaic-Rabbinic teacher.

As proof of this assertion, I offer the following parallels[1]:

> "There is nothing concealed that will not be disclosed, or hidden that will not be made known."
>
> Matthew 10:26
>
> Hillel says, "... do not say anything which cannot be heard, for in the end, it will be heard."
>
> Mishnah, Pirke Avot 2:4

Now a man came up to Y'shua and asked, "Teacher, what good thing must I do to get eternal life?"

"Why do you ask me about what is good?" Y'shua replied. "There is only One who is good. If you want to enter life, obey the commandments."

Matthew 19:16-17

[Hillel] would say, " . . . [If] he has gotten teachings of Torah, he has gotten for himself life eternal.]

Mishnah, Pirke Avot 2:7

"And why worry about a speck in your friend's eye when you have a log in your own? How can you think of saying, 'Let me help you get rid of that speck in your eye,' when you can't see past the log in your own eye? Hypocrite! First get rid of the log from your own eye; then perhaps you will see well enough to deal with the speck in your friend's eye."

Matthew 7:3-5

"Take that toothpick from between your teeth!" and the defendant would, retort, " First take that beam from between your eyes!"

Baba Bartha 15b

"And when you pray, do not keep on babbling like pagans, for they think they will be heard because of their many words. Do not be like them, for your Father knows what you need before you ask him."

Matthew 6:7-8

R. Simeon says, "Be meticulous in the recitation of the shema and the Prayer. And when you pray, don't treat your praying as a matter of routine. But let it be a [plea for] mercy and supplication before the Omnipresent, blessed be he."

Mishnah, Pirke Avot 2:13

"Again, I tell you that if two of you on earth agree about anything you ask for, it will be done for you by my Father in heaven. For where two or three come together in my name, there am I with them."

Matthew 18:20

R. Hananiah b. Teradion says, "[If] two sit together and between them do not pass teachings of Torah, lo, this is a seat of the scornful (Ps. 1:1). But two who are sitting, and words of Torah do pass between them—the Presence is with them, as it is said. Then they that feared the LORD spoke with one another, and the LORD hearkened and heard, and a book of remembrance was written before him, for them that feared the LORD and gave thought to His name (Mal. 3:16). I know that this applies to two.

Mishnah, Pirke Avot 3:2

"Come to me, all you who are weary and burdened, and I will give you rest. Take my yoke upon you and learn from me, for I am gentle and humble in heart, and you will find rest for your souls. For my yoke is easy and my burden is light."

Matthew 11:28-30

R. Nehunya b. Haqqaneh says, "From whomever accepts upon himself the yoke of the Torah do they remove the yoke of the state and the yoke of hard labor."

Mishnah, Pirke Avot, 3:5

The Sabbath was made for man, not man for the Sabbath.

Mark 2:27

R. Jonathan b. Joseph said: . . . [the Sabbath] is committed to your hands, not you to its hands.

Yoma 85b

The Sabbath is given over to you, and not you to the Sabbath.

Mekilta on Exodus 31:13 (109b), cited in *The New Testament Background*, C.K. Barret

"Which is lawful to do on the Sabbath, to do good or to do evil, to save life, or to kill?

Mark 3:4

Signs of the Cross: The Search for the Historical Jesus

R. Ishmael, R. Akiba and R. Eleazar b. Azariah were once on a journey, with Levi ha-Saddar and R. Ishmael son of R. Eleazar b. Azariah following them. Then this question was asked of them: Whence do we know that in the case of danger to human life the laws of the Sabbath are suspended? — R. Ishmael answered and said: If a thief be found breaking in. Now if in the case of this one it is doubtful whether he has come to take money or life; and although the shedding of blood pollutes the land, so that the Shechinah departs from Israel, yet it is lawful to save oneself at the cost of his life — how much more may one suspend the laws of the Sabbath to save human life! R. Akiba answered and said: If a man come presumptuously upon his neighbour etc. thou shalt take him from My altar, that he may die.22 i.e., only off the altar, but not down from the altar.23 And in connection therewith Rabbah b. Bar Hana said in the name of R. Johanan: That was taught only when one's life is to be forfeited,but to save life one may take one down even from the altar. Now if in the case of this one, where it is doubtful whether there is any substance in his words or not, yet [he interrupts] the service in the Temple [which is important enough to] suspend the Sabbath, how much more should the saving of human life suspend the Sabbath laws!

Talmud—Mas. Yoma 85a-b

Y'shua said to them, "I did one miracle and you are all astonished. Yet, because Moses gave you circumcision (though actually it did not come from Moses, but from the patriarchs), you circumcise a child on the Sabbath. Now if a child can be circumcised on the Sabbath so that the law of Moses may not be broken, why are you angry with me for healing the whole man on the Sabbath? Stop judging be mere appearances and make a right judgement."

John 7:21-24

R. Eleazar answered and said: If circumcision, which attaches to one only of the two hundred and forty-eight members of the human body, suspends the Sabbath, how much more shall [the saving of] the whole body suspend the Sabbath!

Yoma 85b

"Therefore everyone who hears these words of mine and puts them into practice is like a wise man who built his house on the rock. The rain came down, the streams rose, and the winds blew and beat against that house; yet it did not fall, because it had its foundation on the rock. But everyone who hears these words of mine and does not put them into practice is like a foolish man who built his house on sand. The rain came down, the streams rose, and the winds blew and beat against that house, and it fell with a great crash."

Matthew 7:24-27

R. Eleazar ben Azariah: "One whose wisdom exceeds his deeds unto what is he compared? Unto a tree [which] the branches thereof are many and the roots few, so that when the wind comes, it uproots it and overturns it upon its face, as it is said, for he shall be like a tamarisk in the desert and shall not see when good comes, but shall inhabit the parched places in the wilderness, a salt land and not inhabited. But one whose deeds exceed his wisdom, unto what is he compared? Unto a tree the branches therefore are few, and the roots many, so that even if all the winds in the world come and blow upon it, they do not move it from its place, as it is said, for he shall be as a tree planted by the waters and that spreads its roots by the river, and shall not see when heat comes, but its foliage shall be luxuriant, and shall not be anxious in the year of drought, neither shall cease from yielding fruit.

Mishnah, Pirke Avot 3:17

"The kingdom of heaven is like a king who prepared a wedding banquet for his son . . ." Matthew 22:2

And:

"What shall we say the kingdom of God is like, or what parable shall we use to describe it?"

Mark 4:30, Cf. Luke 13:18, 20

R. Judah ha-Nasi: "To what may this be likened? To a king who made a banquet . . ."

"He sent his servants to those who had been invited to the banquet to tell them to come . . ."

Matthew 22:3

R. Judah ha-Nasi: "... a king ... made a banquet to which he invited guests ..."

"He sent his servants to those who had been invited to the banquet to tell them to come ..."

Matthew 22:3

R. Judah ha-Nasi: "He said to them, 'Go, wash yourselves, brush up your clothes, anoint yourselves with oil, wash your garments, and prepare yourselves for the banquet ..."

"Therefore keep watch, because you do not know the day or the hour."

Matthew 25:13

R. Judah ha-Nasi: "[The king] fixed no time when they were to come to [the banquet] ..."

"The wise, however, took oil in jars along with their lamps."

Matthew 25:4

R. Judah ha-Nasi: "The wise among them walked about by the entrance of the king's palace, saying, ' Does the king's palace lack anything?'

"Then [the king] sent some more servants and said, `Tell those who have been invited that I have prepared my dinner: My oxen and fattened cattle have been butchered, and everything is ready. Come to the wedding banquet.'

Matthew 22:4

R. Judah ha-Nasi: "The foolish among them paid no regard or attention to the king's command. They said, 'We will in due course notice when the king's banquet is to take place, because can there be a banquet without labour [to prepare it] and company?'

"But they paid no attention and went off—one to his field, another to his business."

Matthew 22:5

R. Judah ha-Nasi: The foolish among them paid no regard or attention to the king's command. So the plasterer went to his plaster, the potter to his clay, the smith to his charcoal, the washer to his laundry.

"The bridegroom was a long time in coming, and they all became drowsy and fell asleep. "At midnight the cry rang out: `Here's the bridegroom! Come out to meet him!' "Then all the virgins woke up and trimmed their lamps. The foolish ones said to the wise, `Give us some of your oil; our lamps are going out.' "`No,' they replied, `there may not be enough for both us and you. Instead, go to those who sell oil and buy some for yourselves.' "But while they were on their way to buy the oil, the bridegroom arrived. The virgins who were ready went in with him to the wedding banquet. And the door was shut."

Matthew 25:5-10

R. Judah ha-Nasi: "Suddenly the king ordered, ' Let them all come to the banquet.' They hurried the guests, so that some came in their splendid attire and others came in their dirty garments. "

"But they paid no attention and went off—one to his field, another to his business. The rest seized his servants, mistreated them and killed them. The king was enraged. He sent his army and destroyed those murderers and burned their city . . ."But when the king came in to see the guests, he noticed a man there who was not wearing wedding clothes. `Friend,' he asked, `how did you get in here without wedding clothes?' The man was speechless. "Then the king told the attendants, `Tie him hand and foot, and throw him outside, into the darkness, where there will be weeping and gnashing of teeth.'

"For many are invited, but few are chosen."

Matthew 22:5-14

R. Judah ha Nasi: The king was pleased with the wise ones who had obeyed his command, and also because they had shown honour to the king's palace. He was angry with the fools who had neglected his command and disgraced his palace. The king said, ' Let those who have prepared themselves for the banquet come and eat of the king's meal, but those who have not prepared themselves shall not partake of it.'

Y'shua, Rav Shaul (Paul) and Hillel the Great

Another connection that is often overlooked in the development of early Christian thought resides in the provenance of first century pre-talmudic rabbinicism. In particular, during Y'shua's early years, two influential teachers vied for dominance in Jewish thought. The first was a former engineer turned rabbi named Shammai, who was known for his strict letter of the law views. His opponent was the legendary Hillel the First, who was known for a more spirit of the law approach.

In most cases, Hillel's view prevailed to the point where legends were crafted showing this rabbi's superior insights. In one of them, a scoffer of God goes first to Shammai and asks provocatively if he could be taught the Torah while standing on one foot. The old man, furious at the disrespect, drove the infidel away with his measuring rod. Then, some time later, this same man came to Hillel and asked the fateful question a second time. Hillel is then said to have replied, "Whatever is hateful to you, do not do to your neighbor. That is the whole Torah; the rest is commentary", and the man reportedly converted.[2]

If that sounds familiar, it should:

> So in everything, do to others what you would have them do to you, for this sums up the Law and the Prophets.
>
> Matthew 7:12 (NIV)

Similarly, Hillel is credited with writing down seven of the most ancient and important rules for analyzing the Torah and the Hebrew Bible as a whole. Additionally, as was shown at the beginning of the previous section, Hillel and Y'shua shared a lot of common ground.

However, what is not commonly known is the greater linkage to the man who wrote almost half of what would become the New Testament.

After the death of Rabbi Hillel, his school and mission became the responsibility of his son, Simeon. Then, some years later, Simeon also died and the mantle was passed to Hillel's grandson, Gamaliel. This rabbi, as it turns out, had a very promising student:

> "Brothers and fathers, listen now to my defense." When they heard him speak to them in Aramaic, they became very quiet. Then Paul said: "I am a Jew, born in Tarsus of Cilicia, but brought up in this city. Under Gamaliel I was thoroughly trained in the law of our fathers and was just as zealous for God as any of you are today.
>
> Acts 22:1-3

Therefore, what follows is an analysis of how these rules codified by Hillel influenced both the most important subject and the most prolific writer of the New Testament.[3]

Rule #1: Light and Heavy (Kol v'khomer)

This rule, simply stated, can be reduced to an equation:

If statement B is greater than statement A, and statement C is greater than statement B, then statement C must be much greater than A. (If B>A and C>B, then C>A.)

Of all the techniques out there, this is by far Y'shua's favorite. It is, in fact, his main method for explanation in the Sermon on the Mount. Let us take a quick look at how one verse in Genesis is used several times.

> So God created man in his own image, in the image of God he created him; male and female he

created them. God blessed them and said to them, "Be fruitful and increase in number; fill the earth and subdue it. Rule over the fish of the sea and the birds of the air and over every living creature that moves on the ground." Then God said, "I give you every seed-bearing plant on the face of the whole earth and every tree that has fruit with seed in it. They will be yours for food. And to all the beasts of the earth and all the birds of the air and all the creatures that move on the ground—everything that has the breath of life in it—I give every green plant for food." And it was so.

Genesis 1:27-30

This core concept, that man is greater than animals and plants, is the final destination of the argument. However, how our Rabbi gets there is a bit odd:

STATEMENT A:

"Therefore I tell you, do not worry about your life, what you will eat or drink; or about your body, what you will wear. Is not life more important than food, and the body more important than clothes?

STATEMENT B (remembering Genesis 1:27-30):

Look at the birds of the air; they do not sow or reap or store away in barns, and yet your heavenly Father feeds them.

STATEMENT C:

Are you not much more valuable than they?

And:

STATEMENT A

Who of you by worrying can add a single hour to his life? "And why do you worry about clothes?

STATEMENT B

See how the lilies of the field grow. They do not labor or spin. Yet I tell you that not even Solomon in all his splendor was dressed like one of these.

STATEMENT C

If that is how God clothes the grass of the field, which is here today and tomorrow is thrown into the fire, will he not much more clothe you, O you of little faith? So do not worry, saying, 'What shall we eat?' or 'What shall we drink?' or 'What shall we wear?' For the pagans run after all these things, and your heavenly Father knows that you need them. But seek first his kingdom and his righteousness, and all these things will be given to you as well. Therefore do not worry about tomorrow, for tomorrow will worry about itself. Each day has enough trouble of its own.

Matthew 6:25-34

Another example of *kol v'khomer* has to do with healing on the Sabbath day and comes up in several places:

STATEMENT A:

> Y'shua said to them, "I did one miracle, and you are all astonished. Yet, because Moses gave you circumcision (though actually it did not come from Moses, but from the patriarchs), you circumcise a child on the Sabbath.

STATEMENT B:

> Now if a child can be circumcised on the Sabbath so that the law of Moses may not be broken . . .

STATEMENT C:

> . . . why are you angry with me for healing the whole man on the Sabbath? Stop judging by mere appearances, and make a right judgment."

John 7:21-24

In this situation, the "lighter weight" is setting aside the Sabbath commandment to rest in order to perform circumcision, which applies to a small part of the body. Y'shua's argument is therefore that his healing of the entire body is the "greater weight" and that if the Sabbath can be set aside for the light, it must also be done so for the heavy.

One more example, a short version of the same idea:

> He said to them, "If any of you has a sheep and it falls into a pit on the Sabbath, will you not take

hold of it and lift it out? How much more valuable is a man than a sheep! Therefore it is lawful to do good on the Sabbath."

Matthew 12:11-12

In this case, Statement A is implied, and ends up being a combination of Genesis 1:27-30, as well as various Scriptures commanding the Sabbath as a day of rest. However, the rest flows as before. Statement B contrasts the general rule with the real world problem of an animal falling into a pit and needing rescue. As is recorded both by Y'shua and the Talmud, most in Israel would in fact rescue the livestock, although the Qumran Essenes, according to the Dead Sea Scrolls, would not.[4] Even so, it is clear what the expectation is, and we pick it up again with Y'shua saying basically: "You would rescue a sheep on the Sabbath, whereas I am trying to rescue a man, who is more important. Therefore, my deed again outweighs Sabbath regulations."

This pattern pervades the entire Sermon, most of the time being revealed by the simple phrase, "how much more". It is also one of the least understood aspects as far as Gentile scholarship is concerned, since the myth that Y'shua opposed or changed the Sabbath persists even to this day. The truth is that Y'shua simply *interpreted Sabbath practice differently*, but never suggested an abolition of the practice as a whole.

Furthermore, in the wider context of Jewish culture, *the Pharisees did not even agree on proper Sabbath practice themselves!* Remembering the schools of Hillel and Shammai again, both men would have been considered Pharisees, and both would have held to a list of thirty-nine forbidden activities. However, the tests these two men used to determine if something fit into one of those categories varied widely, and this does not even count their disputes with the Sadducees and the Essenes, the latter of whom had a list twice as long of Sabbath prohibitions than anyone else!

Therefore, to take these very natural disputes which are part of Jewish culture and somehow try to use Y'shua's participation in them as a reason to set the entire cultural view aside is, at minimum, the height of scholarly myopia.

Other examples of *kol v'khomer* with Y'shua are:

> Matthew 6:26,30=Luke 12:24,28
> Matthew 7:11=Luke 11:13
> Matthew 10:25
> Matthew 12:12
> John 7:23
> John 15:18-20

Paul uses the same concept in these passages:

> Romans 5:8-10,15,17; 11:12,24
> 1 Corinthians 9:11-12; 12:22
> 2 Corinthians 3:7-9,11
> Philippians 1:16
> Hebrews 2:2-3; 9-13; 10:28-29; 12:9,25

Rule #2: Equivalence of expressions (G'zerah shavah)

Two separate texts are compared on the basis of a common root, phrase or word. Here is a great example of this technique in the book of Hebrews:

> But Messiah is faithful as a son over God's house. And we are his house, if we hold on to our courage and the hope of which we boast. So, as the Holy Spirit says: "Today, if you hear his voice, do not harden your hearts as you did in the rebellion, during the time of testing in the desert, where

your fathers tested and tried me and for forty years saw what I did. That is why I was angry with that generation, and I said, 'Their hearts are always going astray, and they have not known my ways.'

So I declared on oath in my anger, 'They shall never enter my **rest**.'

Hebrews 3:6-11 (NIV)

. . . For he is our God and we are the people of his pasture, the flock under his care. Today, if you hear his voice, do not harden your hearts as you did at Meribah, as you did that day at Massah in the desert, where your fathers tested and tried me, though they had seen what I did. For forty years I was angry with that generation; I said, "They are a people whose hearts go astray, and they have not known my ways."

So I declared on oath in my anger, "They shall never enter my **rest**."

Psalms 95:7-11 (NIV)

Then Paul compares these to two other citations:

"By the seventh day God had finished the work he had been doing; so on the seventh day he **rested** from all his work."

Genesis 2:2 (NIV)

And:

> For somewhere he has spoken about the seventh day in these words: "And on the seventh day God **rested** from all his work."

Hebrews 4:4 (NIV)

So now, finally, we get to the conclusion with Paul comparing all these references to days and Sabbaths:

> Therefore God again set a certain day, calling it Today, when a long time later he spoke through David, as was said before: "Today, if you hear his voice, do not harden your hearts."
>
> For if Joshua had given them rest, God would not have spoken later about another day.
>
> There remains, then, a Sabbath-rest for the people of God; for anyone who enters God's rest also rests from his own work, just as God did from his. Let us, therefore, make every effort to enter that rest, so that no one will fall by following their example of disobedience. For the word of God is living and active. Sharper than any double-edged sword, it penetrates even to dividing soul and spirit, joints and marrow; it judges the thoughts and attitudes of the heart. Nothing in all creation is hidden from God's sight. Everything is uncovered and laid bare before the eyes of him to whom we must give account.

Hebrews 4:7-13 (NIV)

Rule #3: Building the "father" from one text (Binyan ab mikathub echad)

In this third rule of Hillel, one passage serves as the "father", or the guide for all the similar passages and situations. For example, again going from Hebrews:

> When Messiah came as high priest of the good things that are already here, he went through the greater and more perfect tabernacle that is not man-made, that is to say, not a part of this creation. He did not enter by means of the blood of goats and calves; but he entered the Most Holy Place once for all by his own blood, having obtained eternal redemption. The blood of goats and bulls and the ashes of a heifer sprinkled on those who are ceremonially unclean sanctify them so that they are outwardly clean. How much more, then, will the blood of Messiah, who through the eternal Spirit offered himself unblemished to God, cleanse our consciences from acts that lead to death, so that we may serve the living God![5] For this reason Messiah is the mediator of a new covenant, that those who are called may receive the promised eternal inheritance—now that he has died as a ransom to set them free from the sins committed under the first covenant. In the case of a will, it is necessary to prove the death of the one who made it, because a will is in force only when somebody has died; it never takes effect while the one who made it is living. This is why even the first covenant was not put into effect without blood. When Moses had proclaimed every commandment of the law to all the people, he took the blood of calves,

> together with water, scarlet wool and branches of hyssop, and sprinkled the scroll and all the people. He said, "This is the blood of the covenant, which God has commanded you to keep."
>
> In the same way, he sprinkled with the blood both the tabernacle and everything used in its ceremonies.
>
> In fact, the law requires that nearly everything be cleansed with blood, and without the shedding of blood there is no forgiveness.
>
> Hebrews 9:11-22 (NIV)

This key teaching then takes all sorts of examples and brings them together under the root concept of the atoning power of blood, including passages like this one:

> Moses then took the blood, sprinkled it on the people and said, "This is the blood of the covenant that the LORD has made with you in accordance with all these words."
>
> Exodus 24:8

Rule #4: Building the father from two or more texts (Binyab ab mishene kethubim)

This time, two separate texts build the foundation for all other similar concepts.
So this text . . .

> Psalms 2:7: I will proclaim the decree of the LORD:

> He said to me, "You are my Son; today I have become your Father.

... combined with this one ...

> 2 Samuel 7:14: I will be his father, and he will be my son. When he does wrong, I will punish him with the rod of men, with floggings inflicted by men.

... result in this guiding principle or "father" text:

> Hebrews 1:5: For to which of the angels did God ever say, "You are my Son; today I have become your Father"? Or again, "I will be his Father, and he will be my Son"?

Here's one more example:
"CHILDREN":

> Deuteronomy 32:43: Rejoice, O nations, with his people, for he will avenge the blood of his servants; he will take vengeance on his enemies and make atonement for his land and people.

> Psalms 97:7: All who worship images are put to shame, those who boast in idols— worship him, all you gods!

"FATHER":

> Hebrews 1:6: And again, when God brings his firstborn into the world, he says, "Let all God's angels worship him."

Rule #5: The general and the particular (Kelal uferat)

In this discipline a general statement is offered and then it is shortly followed by a brief remark that specifies its parameters. Here's a great example:

> For if the dead are not raised, then Messiah has not been raised either. And if Messiah has not been raised either. And if Messiah has not been raised, your faith is futile; you are still in your sins. Then those who have also fallen asleep in Messiah are lost. If only for this life we have hope in Messiah, then we are to be pitied more than all men. But Messiah has indeed been raised from the dead, the firstfruits of those who have fallen asleep. For since death came from a man, the resurrection of the dead also comes from a man. For as in Adam we all die, so in Messiah will all be made alive."

> 1 Corinthians 15:16-22

Rule #6: Analogy made from another passage (Kayotze bo mimekom akhar)

This is probably my favorite one. In it, two passages appear to conflict, but a third one resolves the issue. For example, how do you reconcile this . . .

> "The just shall live by faith."[6]

> Romans 1:17=Habakkuk 2:4

. . . with this . . .

"There is none righteous, no, not one."

Romans 3:10=Psalm 14:1-3=Psalm 53:1-3

. . . and this. . . .

(God) will render to each one according to his deeds.

Romans 2:6=Psalm 62:12

. . . with this. . . ?

"Blessed are those whose lawless deeds are forgiven and whose sins are covered; blessed is the man whom YHWH shall not impute sin."

Romans 4:7-8=Psalm 32:1-2

These seem contradictory, but the answer is elsewhere:

"Abraham believed God, and it was accounted to him for righteousness."

Romans 4:3,22=Genesis 15:6

Rule #7: Explanation obtained from context (Davar hilmad me'anino)

Simply stated, this last rule is simply an admonition to look at the whole breadth of Scripture and not just pulling isolated verses out of context. This, the most far sweeping rule of them all, is very succinctly referred to in a few places:

> "Do your best to present yourselves before God as one approved, a workman who does not need to be ashamed and who correctly handles the word of truth."

2 Timothy 2:15

> "All Scripture is God breathed and is useful for teaching, rebuking, correcting and training in righteousness, so that the man of God may be thoroughly equipped for every good work."

2 Timothy 3:16-17

> "Test everything. Hold on to the good. Avoid every kind of evil."

1 Thessalonians 5:21-22

The Unmasking Begins

As for the unmasking process itself, the following must be added:

Since there have been literally thousands of books in recent years that study the life of Y'shua of Nazareth from the perspective of Greek based texts, I felt strongly that a new approach was needed for this book. Put simply, we have near unanimous agreement that *complete* NT codices go back to roughly the fourth century in both Aramaic and Greek. Therefore, it should be easily agreeable by both Hellenistic and Semitic NT scholars that a complete understanding of the way the Messiah thought and taught is not possible by relying only on Greek based texts. The very fact also that 95% of all Christian scholars do not have a grasp on the native language of their subject should, at the very least, point to the fact that a something is clearly wanting.

However, my new methodology goes far beyond just picking different translations and lining them up side by side. Instead, the Greek texts are put through a rigorous series of external and internal analysis that, quite honestly, has not been done at this level previously.

Granted, just using Aramaic based translations to the extent that the Greek ones were exclusively employed can create its own series of problems, and there is no other credible way to uncover a lot of these textual distortions without comparing both. However, what makes this new methodology truly different is that the Greek texts are looked at in a way that goes far deeper than just the quality of the prose. In fact, one of the main points of this book is that some redactors are obviously going to do a better job at conveying ideas in the receiving language than others. Therefore, in my view, a high level of Greek prose, such as that used in Luke, is a bit of a red herring, because even the best Greek in the NT has Semitic patterns beneath the text that testify to its true origins.

So, with these ideas in mind, I have utilized four well-known Greek based translations. They are, in order of frequency of use, The New International Version (NIV), The Ryrie Study Bible New American Standard Version (RSB-NASV), and the new and conventional King James Versions (NKJV, KJV).

Additionally, these works are all compared with three Aramaic based translations. Since these may be less familiar to the reader, a little background information is offered.

The first, and by far my favorite, is that of my colleague Paul Younan (Younan Peshitta Interlinear Version—YPIV). Mr. Younan has taken the rather unusual and groundbreaking step of showing the original Aramaic script side by side with a word for word English translation below. His literal approach is stunningly accurate, and in almost all cases I prefer his readings to any other.

However, using this translation also must come with a few clarifying points. First, as of this writing, Mr. Younan has neither completed nor published his translation. He has instead made it graciously available as a work in progress to both myself or any other interested party via his website *(www.peshitta.org)*, but he and I both believe it will be published in book form in the foreseeable future.

Second, because the word order is exactly as it appears in Aramaic, the English can come out sounding awkward or stilted (i.e. "spoke Y'shua to disciples"). Therefore, whenever I quote from him, I will put the word order into a more English-friendly syntax. In no cases are any of his English words changed by me.

Third, the reader must be made aware of the source of this and the other translations used. Called "Peshitta"—the Aramaic word meaning "straight, true"—the Assyrian Church of the East (hereafter referred to as the "ACOE") has a clear historical and liturgical link to the first century apostles. Contained in their traditions are vital details about how the apostles both founded their church in about the year 40 and brought up 22 original Aramaic NT documents to their door. It is fair pointing out that I find their claims to be highly credible and persuasive, but will make every attempt to establish this position from known historical and linguistic evidence. Meanwhile, with regards to the minimum position on the need of Aramaic for a balanced picture, the methodology demands that I say without ambiguity that no authorized English translation of the Peshitta NT currently exists. However, unlike the other two works that I will describe shortly, Paul Younan's work does have a reasonable chance of being at least tolerated as a study aid by the ACOE, of which he is a life long member.

Fourth, as Paul himself goes to great lengths to state, no translation is perfect, and it cannot be stressed strongly enough that only the Aramaic Peshitta itself is sacred. Everything else is merely a translation of the sacred, and translations have errors in them.

The second source used here is more complete than Mr. Younan's but still not done entirely. Victor Alexander, another native Aramaic speaker and member of the ACOE, has provided a translation of many Peshitta books also available online *(www.v-a.com/bible)* and in book form, (Victor Alexander Aramaic Translation Project—VA-ATP). Alexander's work with recording Aramaic idioms is outstanding and in many cases the text reads just beautifully in English. I am therefore proud to include his contribution in this project in books that Mr. Younan has not yet had an opportunity to translate.

However, as with Mr. Younan, there are issues here as well. Victor has, in a few places, taken a more liberal approach than either myself or Mr. Younan would otherwise prefer. It is these liberties, coupled with the fact that Victor also translates five disputed books not in the ACOE canon, which will guarantee that his work will never be sanctioned at any level by the ACOE. On the other, hand, for those same disputed books, I feel very comfortable comparing Alexander's Aramaic renderings to the more familiar Greek and drawing the conclusion that where they agree a high degree reliability exists.

The third and final source is that of George Lamsa who, by 1940, had translated all the Aramaic books of both Old and New Testaments into English, (The Modern New Testament from the Aramaic, 1998 Revised Edition). In many respects, this is an admirable collection. However, Lamsa, unfortunately to an even greater degree than Victor did, has taken major liberties also, and it is my opinion that these are serious enough to be of doctrinal importance. Therefore, Lamsa's quotes and methods, while somewhat useful when neither of the other two have translated a given a book, will be kept to a minimum in this work. Although, overall, when Lamsa does not let his liberal theological tendencies sway his judgment, it is quite adequate.

Furthermore, a disclaimer should also be offered. The reader should be aware that, just because a certain translation is used in the body of the text does not mean it was not checked against others for clarity prior to its inclusion. In many cases, the needs of the topic dictate which version is chosen, and the emphasis will be, as we go forward, in showing those areas that point strongly to the original nature of the texts themselves. Otherwise, it is proper to assume that no major variations or distortions exist from one version to another.

Finally for Old Testament citations the situation is much easier as there are only two translations worth considering. The first is the Jewish Publication Society 1955 translation (JPS-1955) which, except for a very few instances that I will refer to later, is an outstanding representation of the original Hebrew. I have also found it particularly effective to examine this translation along with the excellent exegesis done in *The Torah: A Modern Commentary, 1981 edition*, which is also done by the JPS. The second Old Testament translation that I find most useful is, without question, the NIV. The rendering of the OT into a more modern English prose that is both liturgically reverent and highly accurate is, in a word, stunning. In many areas, this is really my translation of choice. However, because I am aware of accusations of Christian tampering that are sometimes alleged by conventional Jews, I have tempered this preference with a generous use of the JPS to show what they have in common and what they do not.

As for the way my new paradigm plays throughout the structure of this book, it manifests in several ways. One section deals with messianic prophecies in the Hebrew Bible, as well as the ancient Jewish mystical tradition, which proves that many aspects of mainline Christianity are in fact rooted in Jewish—and not pagan—thought as has often been supposed. There is also considerable attention to recovering actual days of many events in the life of the Messiah, as well as scriptural evidence on his location during the so-called "lost years" which has not previously been dealt with. And, finally, there is the heart of the work, a new Semitic based compositional theory that affirms both Aramaic primacy and the historical accreditation of the New Testament to genuine first century apostles.

PART ONE:

Determining the Time of Nativity

But first, before all these other bold expeditions can begin, I have the privilege of sharing the results of a remarkable detective story. With the discovery of the true astronomical cause of the Star of Bethlehem, along with critical linguistic and internal textual clues in the Gospels, we can finally give the most famous man who ever lived a genuine historical birthday. We begin our search where we must, from the Gospels themselves:

> "In those days Caesar Augustus issued a decree that a census should be taken of the entire Roman world. (This was the first census which took place while Quirinius was governor of Syria) . . . So Joseph went up to the town of Nazareth in Galilee to Bethlehem, the town of David, because he belonged to house and line of David . . ."

Luke 2:1-2, 4 (NIV)

> " . . . Y'shua was born in Bethlehem during the time of King Herod . . ."

Matthew 2:1 (NIV)

For now, we can start by addressing certain diffilcuties with the way the ancients kept track of time. Then, once this is accomplished, we can find out what the historical record has to say about Herod the Great and Quirinius, the governor of Syria.

The Jewish Calendar

The Jewish system uses a *compound calendar*, or one based on both lunar and solar cycles.[7] The 12 months are moon based, consisting of 29 or 30 days each. However, because this gives us a total of only 354 days, the shortfall frequently caused harvest festivals to occur out of season. To fix this problem, a 19 year cycle was developed in which the last month, Adar, was followed by a leap month known as second Adar, and this kept the moon and sun cycles synchronized.

The years in the cycle where second Adar happens are the 3rd, 6th, 8th, 11th, 14th, 17th and 19th.

The names of the Jewish months are: Nisan, Iyar, Sivan, Tamuz, Av, Elul, Tishri, Heshvan, Kislev, Tevet, Shevat, and Adar, all running on a spring to spring cycle.

Also, because Genesis says, "And it was evening and it was morning, the first day," the Jewish day runs from sundown to sundown, not midnight to midnight as we do. The daylight hours are reckoned starting with 6 AM as the first hour.

The Roman Calendar

The Roman Empire had two different calendars used during its long history. The first one commemorated the Empire's legendary founding, and was known as the *Anno Urbis*, or year of the city. In modern parlance, this time translated to 753 BCE.[8] From the Anno Urbis, the times were measured by the reigns of various emperors.

Then, in 248 CE, the Emperor Diacletion introduced a radical innovation that we have come to know as a New Year's Day.

The Julian Calendar

Three centuries later, a monk named Dionyssus Exigius, or Dennis the Little, was given the task of creating the first Christian, or Julian calendar. Unfortunately, Dennis was lacking in a few necessary facts.

First, at this time there was no concept of zero in the west. The Hindus were the most probable inventors of the idea, and they passed it on to Arabs along well traveled trading routes throughout the Middle and Far East. So when Dennis fixed the year of Messiah's birth, he called it 1 Anno Domini, the year of our LORD, and the year before it was 1 BC or Before Messiah.

Added to this problem was the fact that, when Dennis went to cross reference AD 1 with Roman records, he neglected to include four years of Augustus' reign, counting "Octavian" as a separate ruler. This calculation also threw off the proper timing of Tiberius' fifteenth year, which Luke says was the time of the Baptism.

After this, Dennis made one more critical error in Bible interpretation. He didn't realize that *none of the Gospel writers knew Messiah's true age and at best they give estimates.* Luke 3:23 says that Y'shua was *about thirty.* Taking this figure as gospel, if you'll forgive the pun, Dennis subtracted exactly thirty years from his (wrong) calculation of Tiberius' fifteenth year to arrive at Anno Domini 1 or 753 Anno Urbis. Therefore, what we have is an error of at least five years, which is why Messiah was born "BC".[9]

At this juncture it is important to note that most modern scholars do not use the terms "BC" and "AD", because they invite cultural and religious offense. That is the reason also why I have, for the duration of this work, adopted the terms BCE (Before the Common Era) and CE (Era Commonly Accepted).[10]

Back to our story. When Dennis was finished he presented his findings to the Pope, who later sanctioned it for use throughout all Christendom. However, since it was nothing more than Diacletions' calendar given a Christian façade, errors from that emperor's time continued to accrue, resulting in one day being lost every 128 years.[11]

The Gregorian Calendar

Centuries piled on, one after the other, and by 1582 something had to be done. In that year Pope Gregory reviewed all the data and concluded that eleven days had been "misplaced", so he added them back in. Unfortunately, the calendar wasn't right even then.

One solar cycle takes 365 days *and six hours*. So every four years, an extra day was needed to compensate, hence the leap year day of February 29th.

In the end then, once all these adjustments were implemented, the result is that when we turn to Jewish/Gregorian conversion tables, we can be sure that a day has not been lost from Messiah's time to our own.

The Problem with Quirinius

According to Luke, the reason Joseph and Mary returned to Bethlehem was to register for "the first census which occurred while Quirinius was governor of Syria." Since records from this time are fairly complete, one would suspect that identifying such a huge undertaking would be relatively easy. Unfortunately, this is not the case, for even though strong historical evidence points to a census being taken in the closing years of Herod's reign, the year in question had another man governing Syria.

Is this a contradiction? Is Luke just plain wrong? At least two scenarios have emerged in modern times that more than account for this alleged discrepancy. The first is that Quirinius was considered a kind of military co-regent:

> "For a long time it seemed as though St. Luke had made a mistake. It was only when a fragment of a Roman inscription was found at Antioch that the surprising fact emerged that Quirinius had been the Emperor's legate in Syria on a previous occa-

> sion, in the days of Saturnius the Proconsul. At that time his assignment had been purely military. He led a campaign against the Homanadenses, a tribe in the Taurus Mountains in Asia Minor. Quirinius established his seat of government as well as his headquarters in Syria between 10 and 7 BC."
>
> The Bible as History, p. 344

In fact, we have a Syrian coin depicting Quirinius and dated to 11 BCE.[12] And, another census, conducted in the Syrians' "backyard" is also recorded at that time:

> IUSSU QUIRINI CENSUM EGI APAMENAE CIVITATUS MILLIUM HOMINUM CIVIUM CXVII. IDEM MISSU QUIRINI ADVERSUS ITRURAEOS IN LIBANO MONTE CASTELLUM EORUM CEPI.
>
> Translation: On command of Quirinius I have carried out the census in Apamea, a city-state of one hundred and seventeen thousand citizens. Likewise I was sent by Quirinius to march against the Itrureans, and conquered their citadel on Lebanon mountain.
>
> Lapis Venetus Inscription, from *Corpus Inscriptorum Latinum*, 3rd Supplement 6687. English translation from Stauffer, *Jesus and His Story*, p. 28.

Apamea was a city state just north of Israel, and Quirinius' role is widely believed to have been as a kind of military enforcer given title and power to make sure taxation ran smoothly. Furthermore, the word

Luke chooses in the Greek, the title *hegemon,* has a much looser interpretation than the English "governor" implies. The term can actually mean "regional leader", which Quirinius is clearly acting as with this title:

> C. CARISTA(NIO) C.F. SER. FRONT(ONI)
> CAESIANO IULI(O) PRAEF(ECTO) FAB(RUM)
> PONT(IFICI) SACERDOTI PRAEFECTO **P.**
> **SULPICI QUIRINI DUUMV(IRI) PRAERECTA**
> M. SERVILI HUIC PRIMO OMNIUM PUBLICE
> D(ECURIONUM) D(ECRETO) STATUA POSITA
> EST.
>
> Inscription from the base of statue at Pisidian Antioch, recorded by Ramsay, *Bearing of Recent Discovery,* p. 235.

The title *duumviri praerfecta* can also easily be interpreted as "regional leader" without having the formality and rigidity of the way "governor" sounds in English and very much in keeping with the way *hegemon* reads in Greek. Technically speaking, Quirinius *appointed a citizen to serve as prefect.* However, in Egypt the prefect was actually IN CHARGE of the census there. Such a scenario clearly then bears out the power that Quirinius had, if not it title, then in actual practice.

The question then arises, do we have any evidence from the archaeological record of anyone holding a leadership position of Syria twice?

Surprisingly, the answer is yes.

> (BELLUM GESSIT CUM GENTE
> HOMONADENSIM QUAE INTERFECERAT
> AMYNTAM R)EGUM QUA REDACTA IN
> POT(ESTATEM IMP. CAESARIS) AUGUSTI
> POPULIQUE ROMANI SENATU(S DIS

IMMORTALIBUS) SUPPLICATIONES BINAS OB RES PROSP(ERE AB EO GESTAS ET) IPSI ORNAMENTA TRIUMPH(ALIA DECRUIT) PRO CONSUL ASIAM PROVINCIAM OP(TINUIT PR. PR.) DIVI AUGUSTI (I)TERUM SYRIAM ET PH(OENICEN OPTINUIT).

Inscription "Lapis Tiburtinus", from *Corpus Inscriptorum Latinum* 14:3613. See Schurer, *History of the Jewish People* I;1, p. 354. Text restored by Mommsen with conjectures in parentheses.

While some of this text is, admittedly, corrupted, most scholars agree this depicts someone as *pro praetor* of Syria twice. And, while the name of the officer is unfortunately missing, there does not seem to be anyone other than Quirinius acting in this capacity as co-regent and dealing with taxation issues in the right place at the right time.

As for the Roman censuses, we know a great deal about how they were conducted. Under the reign of Augustus, massive reforms were enacted:

> ... the gradual disappearance of the tax-farming companies who levied the direct and indirect taxes. Their place was taken by the imperial officials or procurators, who were employed in the Emperor's name in all the provinces, both imperial and senatorial. These men, except those filling the highest positions, were almost all either imperial slaves or imperial freedmen. They had offices for collecting the taxes in the chief town of the province and branch offices elsewhere; and all the threads of this network of finance were gathered up in the personal treasury of the Emperor at Rome. Thus the financial administration of the Empire was

gradually converted into an elaborate bureaucratlc machine, governed from the centre by the Emperors.

Michael Rostovzeff, *Rome* (New York: Oxford, 1960), p. 202.

After these reforms, we have census documents—or evidence of the censuses themselves— showing up in the historical record. Josephus recalls a revolt at one census in the common year 6, and this is confirmed by statement by Luke as well, (Antiquities 18.1.1, Acts 5:36-37). From there, we have the actual edicts from the years 20, 34, 48 and 62, or fourteen year intervals. In one of these—for the year 48, we find this interesting fact:

> "I Thermoutharion along with Apollonius, my guardian, swear by Tiberius Claudius Caesar Augustus Germanicus Emperor that the preceding document gives an accurate account of those returning, who live in my household, and that there is no one else living with me, neither a foreigner, nor an Alexandrian, nor a freedman, nor a Roman citizen, nor an Egyptian. If I am telling the truth, may it be well with me, but if falsely, the reverse. In the ninth year of Tiberius Claudius Augustus Germanicus Emperor."

Oxyrhynchus papyrus 255

So this document at least appears to imply that people had to leave for their places of origin in order to register. In another edict, from the year 104, this is stated directly:

Gaius Vibius Maximus, the Prefect of Egypt, declares: The census by household having begun, it is essential that all those who are away from their nomes [administrative districts] be summoned to return to their own hearths so that they may perform the customary business of registration and apply themselves to the cultivation which concerns them. Knowing, however, that some of the people from the countryside are required by our city, I desire all those who think they have a satisfactory reason for remaining here to register themselves before . . . Festus, the Calvary Commander, whom I have appointed for this purpose, from whom those who have shown their presence to be necessary shall receive signed permits in accordance with this edict up to the 30th of the present month E . .

Select Papyri. Vol. 2: *Non-Literary Papyri; Public Documents.* Loeb Classical Library, 282. Cambridge: Harvard Univ. Press, 1934, p. 108. (Translation supplied by K.C. Hanson)

So, if Josephus and Luke are both recording a registration and census in the common year 6, the fourteen year cycle would suggest a previous census was held in the area around 7 BCE. This was also the year that Quirinius subdued new territories in the region for Rome. In the wake of that victory, it was also a common practice to begin a counting process immediately as a way to figure out the wealth and situation of a recently vanquished enemy—especially when it coincided with the commencement of the regular fourteen year cycle anyway.

However, a common criticism of such a scenario is that it is often alleged that Herod was considered "A Friend of Rome", and his kingdom was semi-autonomous, outside the boundaries of the Empire, and thus immune from taxation.

This simply was not true. Rome preferred to rule from a distance through local puppet kings as a matter of political expediency. When those kings became ineffective, they were deposed and replaced by a Roman governor. This happened in 6 CE when Herod's son, Archaleus, was booted out of power.[13] Since those "kings" serve at Rome's pleasure, their level of autonomy is seriously in question. And if they are under Roman rule, they must pay Roman taxes.[14]

Furthermore, even if Herod was exempt before, Josephus tells us he made the mistake of quarreling with the Emperor. Augustus was then so angry that he warned Herod: "You are no longer Rome's friend, but her subject."[15] Subjects, by definition, are taxed, and the timing of the argument was again around 7 BCE.

Now to be fair, Josephus also tells us Herod reconciled with Augustus a short time later. My point is, did he have a choice? Probably the only reason Herod swallowed his pride was so that he could hold on to power, not to mention his life.[16] Augustus, having spared the monarch, would not be likely then to repeal a tax jurisdiction after it had been established.

Besides, one need only look to our own Internal Revenue Service and wonder how likely it would be for them to say: "You know all that money we were going to make from that tax? Well, we decided it was too much. Unfair. So we're going to forget the whole thing!"

Finally, while Josephus does not mention a 7 BCE census directly, he may have come close to implying that one happened. In Antiquities 17.2.4, Herod puts to death thousands of Pharisees because they had refused to swear an oath of allegiance to Caesar. If this statement is to be taken in concert with the "Rome's subject" quote by Augustus, then the executions make deadly sense. The reason is, of course, that oaths of allegiance were very commonly demanded when new territories came under taxable status for the census.

We also need to look at what "autonomy" really meant from a practical standpoint of governance. We know, for example, that Herod could only mint copper or bronze coins.[17] By contrast, another nearby independent principality, known as Nabatea, had permission from

Rome to mint silver. And yet, the Nabateans paid regular taxes and were far from independent when it came to their Roman masters.[18]

Apamea in Syria was also granted "autonomy", but as was previously demonstrated with the Lapis Venetus inscription, that freedom did not extend to being free from taxation either.

Finally, there is the issue of logistics to consider. Up until now, we have been talking about the registration phase of the census (in Greek, *apographe*). However, there was another part that also needs discussing. After all the property had been catalogued, a suitable period of time ensued between that and the actual payment for said property, or *apotimosis*. The interval between these two stages varied widely depending on location. Wars in Gaul once delayed payment for forty years, whereas a well run place like Egypt would typically take five years to discharge their duties.

That being said, two possibilities emerge. Either the time that Mary gave birth (around 5 BCE) could easily fit within the registration's time frame that began only two years previously, or Luke is thinking about this process in another way.

Now over the years, a lot of futile harmonization attempts focused on a linguistic solution. Some scholars suggested, quite erroneously, that Luke's use of the word PROTOS could mean "before Quirinius was governor of Syria" instead of "first census", which it actually does. The Aramaic is even clearer on this point by the way, so it need not be spelled out here. However, it may also be that linguistics do play a part, but that scholars looked in the wrong place.

In order to see why more clearly, let us assume the skeptics are correct. We will now suppose that there is no hard evidence of Quirinius having a prior governorship of Syria and, as a result, that there is only one census recorded under his tutelage, in 6 CE.

If that is the case, then the 6 CE uprising could be an *apotimosis* from a previous registration WHICH JUST HAPPENS TO COINCIDE WITH THE COMMENCEMENT OF THE NEXT REGISTRATION. In other words, owing to the fact that Egypt (5 years) and Gaul (40 years) are extremes in the time frame between the registration and collection of funds, it is quite easy to fit Israel's collection process into the middle of that range. Additionally, the annexation of new territories which had not been previously taxed could also take that long to complete. Therefore, taking into account all this evidence, it is easy to see how the payment due for the last census could occur around the same time as the registration of the next one. Finally, we can also understand how riots might be more likely to occur upon payment as opposed to merely recording one's property.

This scenario also plays into the linguistic evidence, since the language in the Gospel is worded in a way that Luke could easily mean: "This was the first census *completed* under Quirinius." That is to say, Luke is thinking in terms of the result, not the start of the process. So in 7 BCE Augustus says, "I want a list of all the property in Judea that can be taxed." Then, at the end of the fourteen years, Quirinius compiles the data, figures out the bill and says, "Here is the list you asked for, Your Majesty." Such would be done, in spite of the use of the Greek *apographe* ("registration") because Luke is telscoping the entire process into that one term.

In response however some have said that if Luke meant "completed" why didn't he say so? The answer may simply come down to a matter of writing style. In Greek, as well as English, the use of "occurred" to mean "completed" is very natural. In fact, the scenarios in which "occurred" takes on the "completed" meaning are identical in both cases, each of which involve complex, long term results. Here is how Strong's Concordance puts it:

> Ghinomay (#1096—verb). Definitions: 1) to become, i.e., to come into existence; 2) to become, i.e., to come to pass, happen, (a) of events; 3) to arise, to appear in history, come upon the stage; (a) men appearing in public; 4) to be made, finished; (a) of miracles, to be performed, wrought; 5) to become, be made.

Similarly, the Aramaic word also has this kind of *happened versus completed* flexibility to it, and has been translated alternatively as "took place", "happened" and "was done". So, in the final analysis, there are a number of compelling possible scenarios that more than account for this alleged problem, and the bottom line is that Luke is not seriously contradicted in any particular detail that he chooses to relate to us.

However, starting with the next section, the rest of the Nativity evidence will revolve around seven major historical clue—what I like to call "anchors"—*that are represented by italic script.*

The Problem with King Herod the Great

Our first historical anchor is the death of Herod the Great.

As the Gospels clearly tell us, Y'shua was most definitely born prior to this, and fixing this time is the single most important facet for recovering the birth.

In spite of the strides of modern scholarship, the tides of tradition pull very strong. Those who have not accepted the Gregorian System continue to assert that Herod must have died around 1 BCE, because it is closer to their ancient viewpoint.[19]

To support this contention, they point to an Empire wide census initiated by Augustus in 2 BCE, and administered in part by Quirinius later. According to this theory, the logistics involved with getting everyone to return to their ancestral homes would have taken a year or more, and so Joseph and Mary's arrival in Bethlehem would have coincided roughly with Herod's death at that time.[20]

Also, again according to Josephus, Herod died shortly before Passover, and just before that there was a lunar eclipse.[21] This is very significant, because it is the only time in Josephus' vast collection of history that he even refers to a celestial event to fix a date. A quick look at astronomical tables confirms that a lunar eclipse did occur around Passover in the year 1 BCE.

However, in spite of all of this, the vast majority of scholars have rejected the 1 BCE date in favor of a 4 BCE date for the following reasons:

1) The error of Dennis the Little encompasses at least a five year period.[22]

2) Josephus tells us that Herod died 37 years after the Romans declared him King, and 34 years from the time he actually became King. Both dates will bring us to 4 BCE.[23]

3) The 2 BCE census, while a seemingly strong piece of evidence at first glance, appears to be a kind of special occasion to give extra tribute and not a true census at all. In addition to the fact that it is occurring outside the fourteen year cycle that Augustus himself had partly developed or at least sanctioned a continuance of, two other issues play into this scenario. First, it was the 750th anniversary of Rome's birth. Second, it was also Augustus' "Silver Jubilee", his 25th anniversary in power![24] As the greatest Emperor Rome had ever seen, bending the rules to celebrate two great institutions would have hardly been beneath the Romans. Further evidence of this even comes from the words of the monarch himself:

> When I administered my thirteenth consulate (2 B.C.E.), the senate and Equestrian order and Roman people all called me father of the country, and voted that the same be inscribed in the vestibule of my temple, in the Julian senate-house, and in the forum of Augustus under the chario which had been placed there for me by a decision of the senate. When I wrote this I was seventy-six years old.
>
> Deeds of the Divine Augustus 1.35

And the historian Seutonius adds:

> **LVIII.** The whole body of citizens with a sudden unanimous impulse proffered him the title of *Pater Patriae* ["Father of his Country"]; first the commons, by a deputation sent to Antium, and then, because he declined it, again at Rome as he entered the theatre, which they attended in throngs, all wearing laurel wreaths; the Senate afterwards in the House, not by a decree or by acclamation, but through Valerius Messala. He, speaking for the whole body, said: "Good fortune and divine favour attend you and your house, Caesar Augustus; for thus we feel that we are praying for lasting prosperity for our country and happiness for our city. The Senate in accord with the people of Rome hails you *Father of your Country*." Then Augustus with tears in his eyes replied as follows (and I have given his exact words, as I did those of Messala): "Having attained my highest hopes, Fathers of the Senate, what more have I to ask of the immortal gods than that I may retain this same unanimous approval of yours to the very end of my life."
>
> Suetonius, *De Vita Caesarum*, 2 Vols., trans. J. C. Rolfe (Cambridge, Mass.: Harvard University Press, 1920), pp. 123-287.

As we can see, this is hardly a formal census! In fact, the only time Seutonius even mentions a census in connection with Augustus is when the monarch reformed the system as previously stated. Odd then that it should not come up here as well!

4) We're on a much firmer footing dating the start of the ruling times of Herod's children, and it is certain that Herod Antipas, Philip and Herod Archaleus all begin their respective reigns around 4 BCE. Other historical signs point to a vigorous and paranoid monarch who would kill even his family on the mere rumor of conspiracy. Both factors also virtually guarantee that the king would never cede all his lands to his progeny three years before his death if it happened in 1 BCE.[25]

5) It just so happens a lunar eclipse also occurred on March 13th, 4 BCE, and Passover would have happened around April 11th, less than a month later.[26]

Therefore, not only do the vast majority of Bible scholars feel they have a "lock" on the month Herod died, most can even reliably date it to the proper week, because his funeral occurred just seven days before Passover in that year.[27]

The 4 BCE date also fits well into the next topic we are about to discuss:

What was the *Star of Bethlehem*?

Where the Natural Meets the Supernatural

When dealing with great issues of faith, fitting spiritual events into a physical context can sometimes be very problematic. Such is the case with the *Star of Bethlehem*, which a great many people view as a completely supernatural phenomenon. A radical few might even look at any scientific inquiry on the subject as being akin to a magician telling the audience how a trick is done. For those of you who share these beliefs, I ask you to put them aside for the moment, and consider a different kind of miracle: A natural event with supernatural ramifications.

The first question about the *Star of Bethlehem* that needs to be asked is simply this: Why did no one see it except the Magi?

Signs of the Cross: The Search for the Historical Jesus

A careful reading of the Nativity accounts reveals that neither the shepherds, nor Joseph and Mary—nor even Herod himself—saw it over Bethlehem. While it is true that astrology was forbidden to most Jews as a divination practice, the Levites and priests did keep a careful watch on the heavens, especially when it came to observing the motions of the moon.[28] A moving star, hovering like modern day aircraft over a city, would most certainly have attracted more attention. And if it did, wouldn't it then be a simple matter for Herod to follow the star, find the child, and kill him?

Most historians also agree that the Magi were, as Matthew states, professional astrologers. They probably came either from Persia or Babylon, or what is today modern day Iran and Iraq, respectively.[29]

If they were from Babylon, there is a good chance they would have been familiar with messianic prophecies, since there was a very strong Jewish community there at the time. Babylon also boasted one of the finest astronomical schools in the world, at Sippar, which actually tracked the celestial event we are about to discuss.

As for Persia, these astrologers would have another great reason to watch the skies which, ironically, dovetails with their Zoroastrian faith regarding their version of the birth of a world savior.[30]

> "The legend of the Magi-Kings was embellished in apocryphal books and Christian folklore. The *Protogospel of James* and the *Chronicle of Zuqnin* describe the birth of the Saviour. Like the god Mithra, the divine child is consubstantial with celestial light and was born in a mountain cave on December 25. Such imagery of the Nativity of Messiah and the symbolism of the royal visitors may originally have descended from Iranian accounts of the birth of the cosmic saviour, for the accounts seem to owe a great deal to Iranian theologies of light. But the themes have been recast in Christian terms. The *Opus imperfectum in Matthaeum* relates that 12 Magi-

Kings lived near the Mountain of Victories, which they climbed every year in the hope of finding the messiah in a cave on the mountaintop. Each year they entered the cave and prayed for three days, waiting for the promised star to appear. Adam had revealed this location and the secret promises to his son Seth. Seth transmitted the mysteries to his sons, who passed the information from generation to generation. Eventually the Magi, sons of kings, entered the cave to find a star of unspeakable brightness, glowing more than many suns together. The star and its bright light led to, or became, the Holy Child, the son of the Light, who redeems the world."

> Encyclopedia Britannica, "The Magi and the Child of Wondrous Light"

It also may not be coincidental that high-ranking Zorastrians were actually called "magi".

Also, interestingly enough, a journey from either Persia or Babylon would take roughly the same amount of time on well established eastern trading routes—about four months. Ezra made just such a journey during the spring from Babylon to Jerusalem and would have traveled in a class similar to the Magi, (Ezra 7:8-9).

The same can be shown with Nehemiah from the Persian capital of Susa. According to his own account, Nehemiah left Persia in early April and, three days after he arrived in Jerusalem, work began on rebuilding the walls, which were completed on October 2. Since Nehemiah also tells us this work took fifty-two days to complete (Nehemiah 2:1,11-20, 6:15), we can deduce that he arrived in Jerusalem fifty-five days before that, or around August 5. Once again a four-month journey is recorded and, once again the traveler is, like the Magi, going in style. So, regardless of which nation the Magi came from, their travel time is well fixed. We also cannot discount the possibility that they may be a mixed group from both countries!

As for the miracle in question, it had to be something pregnant with mystical meaning to those who watched the skies, but at the same time something ordinary enough that it could be missed if you didn't know to look for it. Can science give us an answer?

The First Sign:
Triple Conjunction, What's Your Function?

Around the time of Messiah's birth, the system we call *the Zodiac* had long been in place and, along with it, a practice of assigning stars and planets to a given geographical area or people. In the case of Israel and Syria, the sign that represented them was Pisces.[31] Also during this time, large parts of Syria were a part of Israel's ancient borders, a fact that has created strife in that region of the world even to this day.

In addition, the planet Saturn was traditionally viewed as the Protector or Savior of the Jewish people, and the planet Jupiter, as one would expect by its name, was the King of all planets.[32]

On May 29th, 7 BCE, Jupiter and Saturn had a conjunction, or appeared to merge, in the constellation of Pisces. Now this may not seem that out of the ordinary, except for the fact that it happened two more times that year, October 3rd and December 4th. A triple conjunction of those planets in that region of the sky occurs only once every 1400 years.[33] And, if the Magi were from Babylon, the date of the second conjunction would have really caught their attention. In 7 BCE, October 3rd was Yom Kippur, the holiest day on the Jewish calendar.[34] Therefore, to the ancient mind, the sky was doing far more than just foretelling the birth of a great king in Israel. It was shouting it.

The Second Sign: The Massing

So imagine for a moment you are one of the Magi. The signs in the sky have definitely captured your interest, but maybe you're not quite motivated to go through the long hassle of a trip to Israel just yet. There are logistical considerations: Food, provisions, the best route to take — and also the time of year — play heavily in your mind. Right now it's early December, the rainy season, and not the best time of year for a long journey if you can help it. So you wait.[35]

Three months later, in February of 6 BCE, another stunning celestial event occurs in the constellation of Pisces.

Jupiter and Saturn are joined by a third planet, Mars, in what is now known as a "massing". This is somewhat different than a conjunction, where the two heavenly bodies appear to merge. Instead, a *massing* has the planets getting very close together, in this case within 8 degrees, but they can still be discerned separately. It too is a rare event, occurring only once every 800 years.[36]

As we will see later, the most compelling reasons against the Magi leaving during the triple conjunction have to do with linguistic clues. However, apart from that argument, if you are one of the Magi, three other characteristics tell you that a trip to Israel now would be a disaster:

First, the addition of Mars, the Greek God of War, may indicate that the new king is destined to rule in dangerous times.

Second, the star you have been tracking, the one symbolizing the king, has disappeared behind the sun. A review of astronomical tables reveals it will not rise again (i.e. be born) for at least another year. The King, apparently, is not ready to come just yet.[37]

The third characteristic has to do with next sign we are about to discuss.

The Third Sign:
Comet/Nova, "The Wake-up Call"

For more than a year, the skies have been silent, and what the Magi have seen up until now has been the equivalent of a "coming soon" promotion. With King Jupiter hidden behind the sun, the signs seem incomplete.

Then, in March 5 BCE, another celestial object was observed. Some have theorized that it was a nova, but descriptions of it in Chinese records make it more likely to be a comet.[38] Regardless as to what it was, both novae and comets have the reputation of predicting major future events.[39] To the Magi, seeing the comet, which first was in Capricorn, and then did the astronomical equivalent of a loop-de-loop to get into Pisces, must have been like the heavens screaming at them, "Wake up! It's almost time!"

The Fourth Sign:
"Follow the King"

Put yourself back in the Magi's place once again. Two signs have told you the event: The birth of a great king, and two signs have told you where: Israel. The comet or nova has also told you when: very soon. Now a trip is looking more likely. Perhaps you've discussed these great heavenly occurrences with some of your astrologer friends, and they agree: Something big is about to go down. Then one of your friends asks: "But where in Israel will it happen?" You think for a minute. Perhaps, if you're familiar with Jewish scriptures, you remember the prophecy in Micah and reply: "In Bethlehem." If not, the next best choice is Jerusalem, only five miles northward, where the kings were known to live. Either way, you've got your itinerary down.

Two months pass, and now it's May. You and your friends feel the time to go is right, if only there were one more sign to guide you. Then, as if returning home from a triumphant battle, King Jupiter emerges from the other side of the sun. Saturn and Mars, his loyal subjects, quickly fall back. The King catches up and passes them, and is now leading way out in front. The motion is provocative, and there can be no doubt where the King is headed: West, towards Israel.[40] Now you know this is it. Time to grab the frankincense and go!

About four months later, as you follow King Jupiter west, the planet appears to stop in its tracks just as you and your friends arrive in the area of Jerusalem and Bethlehem.[41] For the Jews in your midst, nothing out of the ordinary has happened in the night sky. For you, however, the heavens have been guiding your steps, bringing you inexorably to this time and place.

So, our second historical anchor is the first of three conjunctions of Jupiter and Saturn, as seen in the constellation of Pisces. On this point more than 90% of historians are in agreement, and so this brings us to our first range of possible dates for the birth: May 29th, 7 BCE to late March, 4 BCE.

A Matter of Linguistics, Part 1[42]

> "Now after Y'shua was born in Bethlehem of Judea in the days of Herod the king, behold, Magi came from the east arrived in Jerusalem, saying, 'Where is he who has been born King of the Jews, for we saw his star (when it rose) in the east and have come to worship him."
>
> Matthew 2:1-2 (NIV)

Many scholars have assaulted Matthew for being too general in his description of the word "star". The word he uses is "aster", which is the singular form of the word.[43] Critics are eager to point out that more specific terms exist in Greek, such as "planes aster" for a single planet, and "planete" for more than one planet.[44]

However, there are a few facts to also keep in mind. First, the term "planes aster" literally means "wandering star", and therefore the ancients considered planets a kind of star as well. If the Magi followed Jupiter only, as opposed to a massing where three distinct planets are involved, then the term "aster" is perfectly appropriate.[45] The same delineation also exists in the Aramaic versions.

Alternatively, for those who wish to match the Magi's departure with the triple conjunction, linguistic rules tend not to favor their scenarios. As Robert Rodman points out in his *Planetarian* article *A Linguistic Note on the Christmas Star*:

> "Ronald Oriti meets this objection (that "aster" must be singular) by claiming the word for star in the New Testament Greek could mean one star or several stars, just as the word for fish in English can mean one fish or several fish.
>
> The word fish is unusual in that it is spelled the same in singular or plural, just like sheep, deer, et cetera. This is not true of star in Greek, however, which has a distinct plural spelling **asteres** . . .
>
> In the four occurrences of **aster** in Matthew 2:2, 7, 9, 10, it is used in the singular.
>
> Although Oritis' linguistic explanation is incorrect, there remains the possibility that aster was used as we use the "collective noun" **enemy**. The singular form of **enemy** may refer to several individuals. (Cf. The enemy are at the gates.) Unfortunately, there is evidence such is not the case. The most comprehensive Greek-English lexicon available makes no mention of the possibility that **aster** could have a collective meaning.[46] Moreover, Ancient Greek actually had a word **astron**, "constellation," which comes closer in meaning to "conjunction of planets" than **aster**."

The Star Also Rises

As for Matthew 2:1-2, the words in parentheses "when it rose" represent a variant reading inserted by the editors of the New International Version of the Bible. They are not intended to change the meaning of the sentence, but add new information. It is clear that the *Star of Bethlehem* was sighted in the East by astrologers who were from the East. It is also clear that this is a new star *which they saw rise in the East and which prompted their journey*.[47]

Also notice that the Magi call it "his star", or the one belonging to the king. Many stars are associated with kingship, but, beyond simple rising and setting as regular stars do to "going out before them" as Matthew says, only a planet like Jupiter can move in this manner.[48]

Matthew also uses the vague word "above" to describe the star's location. So, if we are to believe it literally pointed to the exact spot of the birth then—once again—Herod could find Messiah without the Magi's help. The Magi, for their part, still needed to ask for directions when they first arrived in Jerusalem. Assuming Herod didn't know what the star looked like, professional astrologers who were tracking it for months certainly would. And, if the star pointed directly over the birth spot, why would the Magi have been lost to begin with?

What we are looking for then is a phenomenon that appears to be contradictory in many respects. It moves—yet remains stationary—and covers a broad area "above", while pointing to or eclipsing a given spot. Can all these assertions be true, even if they seem diametrically opposed?

Reverend Phil Greetham points out that there is a very logical explanation for describing what the wise men saw. In his article, "The Magi and King Herod" he writes the following:

> "I remember something similar happening to me while moving from our house in Barnsley when I had to attend theological college at Lincoln. Having safely dispatched my family and goods to our

new house, I was left to load the car with the few things I left behind and then set off for Lincoln.

"By this time it had got dark and a bright star (actually Saturn), low down in the south east seemed to hang over the general direction I was going. All the way down the A1 it was right in front of me. I then had to zig zag my way through the countryside, the star apparently moving left or right constantly reminding me of the direction I had to go. It was easy to think of it as a guiding star going on ahead of me, and the star in front of the Magi would have behaved in much the same way . . .

"Going back to my journey to Lincoln, I eventually turned south on to the A15, a straight Roman road. Saturn was now also due south. From my position in the car, Saturn was no longer moving but stood over the city where I was going. Its position remained constant over the city because I was now heading straight for the city in an exact straight line with Saturn. As I got closer, the star appeared to descend upon the city, eventually being eclipsed by one particular building . . .

"Perhaps this is what Matthew is trying to describe in his gospel."

Greetham is also quick to point out that the odds that the "right" structure being the one eclipsed by the planet is, no pun intended, astronomical. However, a far more basic and commonplace mechanism may also be at work.

Consider for a moment that the Earth and various planets are moving through the heavens at different speeds. As a result, from our perspective, a planet can appear to race ahead of us and then later slow down, stop and go backwards. This phenomenon is extremely common, and is known as *retrograde motion*. Such a pattern with Jupiter was detected just prior to Messiah's birth and fits the seemingly conflicting descriptions that the Star moved **and** remained stationary over the birth spot. In summing up the findings of the noted astronomer Ivor Bulmer Thomas, the author of *The Star of Bethlehem: An Astronomical Perspective* writes:[49]

> "Ivor Bulmer-Thomas proposes that the Bethlehem Star was simply Jupiter passing through a stationary point in its trek across the sky. When a planet undergoes retrograde motion, it makes a loop against the stars. The planet appears to be stationary at the end of the loop for about a week to the naked eye. Babylonian astronomers had a keen interest in retrograde motions and the wise men may have been in Bethlehem when Jupiter was at a stationary point. In Bulmer-Thomas' theory the 7 BCE triple conjunction and the near-conjunction of Mars, Jupiter and Saturn in 6 BCE, would have alerted the wise men to look for a further sign in the sky. If they followed Jupiter from the time it emerged from behind the sun in May 5 BCE, they would have seen Jupiter pass through a stationary point four months later (about the length of their journey)."[49]

So the most probable explanation is that a combination of both phenomena took place. Like Saturn, Jupiter could appear to shift, stop and descend over a general area. However, if Jupiter did not eclipse the exact Nativity spot as described by Greetham, it could very easily have done the same thing during its retrograde cycle. In other words, "Greetham's Law" happens as the Magi *approach the city*, and the retrograde cycle guides the Magi to exact spot some time later. Notice also that the retrograde motion allows us to date precisely the time of the Magi's arrival, mid September of 5 BCE, the time when the stationary period at the end of the loop happened.

The Jewish Response and Kepler

Perhaps the most compelling evidence in identifying the *Star of Bethlehem* has to do with how Jewish authorities were said to interpret the triple conjunction itself. Renowned German scholar Werner Keller explains what happened when the famed astronomer Johannes Kepler viewed this same phenomenon:

> "Shortly before Christmas 1603, on December 17 . . . Johannes Kepler . . . was observing with his modest telescope the approach of two planets . . . That night Saturn and Jupiter had a rendezvous in space within the constellation of Pisces.
>
> "Looking through his notes later, Kepler suddenly remembered something he had read in the rabbinic writings of Abarbanel, referring to an unusual influence that Jewish astrologers were said to have ascribed to this same constellation. Messiah would appear when there was a conjunction of Saturn and Jupiter in the constellation of Pisces.[50]
>
> "Could it have been the same conjunction at the time of the birth of Messiah as Kepler had observed at Christmastide in 1603? Kepler checked his calculations again and again . . . The result was a threefold conjunction within the space of a year. Astronomical calculations gave the year as 7 BC."

The Bible as History, p. 347-8.

However, as many liberal critics eagerly point out, Kepler fell into disrepute for a few centuries because of a later fascination with mysticism and the more traditional astrology of his day. In response to this charge, Werner Keller explains how a combination of archaeological and scientific discoveries rescued Kepler from the ash heap of history:

> "Consequently, Kepler's hypotheses were for a long time rejected and finally disregarded. It was not until the nineteenth century that astronomers remembered them again. But even then it was impossible to produce clear scientific proof.
>
> "Science has provided it in our own day. In 1925 the German scholar P. Schnabel deciphered 'papers' in Neo-Babylonian cuneiform of a famous professional institute in the ancient world, the School of Astrology at Sippar in Babylonia. Among the endless series of prosaic dates of observations he came across a note about the position of the planets in the constellation of Pisces. Jupiter and Saturn are carefully marked in over a period of five months. Reckoned in our calendar the year was 7 BC!
>
> ". . . Mathematical calculations established further that this threefold conjunction of the planets was particularly visible in the Mediterranean area."
>
> The Bible as History, p. 349.

A Matter of Linguistics, Part 2

Also keep in mind that since "aster"[51] refers to a singular star, the Magi could not have set out on their journey during the triple conjunction of 7 BCE, which they knew involved more than one planet.

The same is true for the massing in 6 BCE. As for the comet/nova of 5 BCE, it was first sighted in Capricorn, not Pisces, so its significance was probably a minor one.

However, when Jupiter emerges from behind the sun, it is literally *rising in the exact manner the Magi describe*. Therefore, it presents the most straightforward, astronomical explanation available.

So why didn't Matthew avoid all the confusion and be more specific by modifying the word "aster" with the adjective "planes"?[52] Two reasons: First, since he is already describing the motion of the star, Matthew might have felt the use of the word "planes" redundant, or akin to saying "the moving star moved". Second, there is the tremendous influence of tradition. Matthew quotes from the Old Testament about 128 times and is by far the most Jewish centered of all the Gospel writers. Neither the Hebrew original nor the *Septuagint*[53] ever use the equivalent words for *planet*. However, the word for *star* is very common, occurring 24 times.[54]

Plus, we have the advantage of knowing what the Magi did not, for as Matthew tells us:

> "Now when they (the Magi) had departed, behold, an angel of the LORD appeared to Joseph in a dream, saying, 'Arise and take the child and his mother, and flee to Egypt, and remain there until I tell you, for Herod is going to search for the child to destroy him.'"
>
> Matthew 2:13 (NIV)

So you see, they almost missed the whole thing!

Therefore, our third historical anchor is May 5 BCE, the earliest the Magi could leave. So, from a range of almost three years, the window for the birth is now cut by two thirds, from May of 5 BCE, until Herod's death in March of 4 BCE.

Andrew Gabriel Roth

The Shepherd's Tale

> "And there were shepherds living out in the fields nearby, keeping watch over their flocks at night. An angel of the LORD appeared to them, and the glory of the LORD shone around them, and they were terrified. But the angel said to them, 'Do not be afraid. I bring you good news of great joy that will be for all people. Today in the town of David a Savior has been born to you; he is Messiah the LORD.'"
>
> Luke 2:8-11

This small statement from Luke is one the best clues available for narrowing the range of the birth, and it is given particular clarity with the advent of excellent modern translations, such as the NIV. Furthermore, our understanding of Koine Greek, its depth and nuance, has undergone a radical transformation in the last four decades.[55]

When we look then at the picture conveyed by the NIV regarding Luke 2:8-11, new scholarship confirms the literal meaning of the verse. The shepherds, according to every linguistic convention in the Greek, *literally live out in the fields at night without any shelter whatsoever.* Luke therefore says what he means, and means what he says, and any attempts to "stretch" the verse have no foundation for acceptance.[56]

Once we understand this, modern scientific observations, coupled with reliable ancient testimonies, effectively resolve the issue. Once again I quote from Professor Keller:

> "Meteorologists have made exact recordings of the temperature at Hebron. This spot in the southern part of the highlands of Judah exhibits the same climatic conditions of Bethlehem, which is not far distant ... According to all existing information the climate of Palestine has not changed apprecia-

bly in the last 2,000 years; consequently modern accurate meteorological observations can be taken as a basis.

"At Christmastime, Bethlehem is in the grip of frost, and in the Promised Land no cattle would have been in the fields at that temperature. This fact is borne out by a remark in the Talmud to the effect that in that neighborhood the flocks were put out to grass in March and brought in again at the beginning of November. They remained out in the open for almost eight months. Around Christmastime nowadays both animals and shepherds are under cover in Palestine."

The Bible as History, p. 354.

Therefore, our fourth historical anchor trims the previous range by half, because the birth could not have taken place past the middle of November. The range is now cut to 6 months, **from mid May to mid November, 5 BCE.**

The Holy Order

From here it is necessary to look at another key detail: The Baptist's father, a priest named Zacharias', had a vision in the Temple while he was on duty. If we can then figure out when his priestly course of Abijah actually served, we will be much closer to finding the actual time of the Nativity.

Now our search for priestly cycles starts in the book of Numbers, chapters 7 and 8. At that time, God is having Moses set up the tabernacle. During the last 2 weeks of Adar, each of the 12 tribal leaders contributes gifts to the altar. Then, in Numbers 9, we enter the first month of Nisan, when God commands the priests to purify themselves, minister to the tabernacle and prepare for the second Passover. Thus we see priestly service beginning on or very near 1 Nisan.

In Leviticus 8, we get some added details. In that account, God commands Aaron and his sons to serve as priests. At that time Aaron had four sons, but two of them die because they did not offer a sacrifice properly. Furthermore, because both were childless, all future priests were descended from the remaining sons, Eleazar and Ithamar.

Four centuries later David codified Aaron's tradition in the following manner:

> "These were the divisions of the sons of Aaron: The sons of Aaron were Nadab, Abihu, Eleazar and Ithamar. But Nadab and Abihu died before their father did, and they had no sons; so Eleazar and Ithamar served as the priests. With the help of Zadok a descendant of Eleazar and Ahimelech a descendant of Ithamar, David separated them into divisions for their appointed order of ministering. A larger number of leaders were found among Eleazar's descendants than among Ithamar's, and they were divided accordingly: sixteen heads of families from Eleazar's descendants and eight heads of families from Ithamar's descendants. They divided them impartially by drawing lots, for there were officials of the sanctuary and officials of God among the descendants of both Eleazar and Ithamar.
>
> The scribe Shemaiah son of Nethanel, a Levite, recorded their names in the presence of the king and of the officials: Zadok the priest, Ahimelech son of Abiathar and the heads of families of the priests and of the Levites—one family being taken from Eleazar and then one from Ithamar. The first lot fell to Jehoiarib, the second to Jedaiah, the third to Harim, the fourth to Seorim, the fifth to Malkijah, the sixth to Mijamin, the seventh to

Hakkoz, **the eighth to Abijah**, the ninth to Jeshua, the tenth to Shecaniah, the eleventh to Eliashib, the twelfth to Jakim, the thirteenth to Huppah, the fourteenth to Jeshebeab, the fifteenth to Bilgah, the sixteenth to Immer, the seventeenth to Hezir, the eighteenth to Happizzez, the nineteenth to Pethahiah, the twentieth to Jehezkel, the twenty-first to Jakin, the twenty-second to Gamul, the twenty-third to Delaiah and the twenty-fourth to Maaziah.

This was their appointed order of ministering when they entered the temple of the LORD, according to the regulations prescribed for them by their forefather Aaron, as the LORD, the God of Israel, had commanded him.

1 Chronicles 24:1-20 (NIV)

Additionally, the Jewish historian Josephus records the same event this way:

But David, being desirous of ordaining his son king of all the people, called together their rulers to Jerusalem, with the priests and the Levites; and having first numbered the Levites, he found them to be thirty-eight thousand, from thirty years old to fifty; out of which he appointed twenty-three thousand to take care of the building of the temple, and out of the same, six thousand to be judges of the people and scribes, four thousand for porters to the house of God, and as many for singers, to sing to the instruments which David had prepared, as we have said already. He divided them also into

> courses: and when he had separated the priests from them, he found of these priests twenty-four courses, sixteen of the house of Eleazar, and eight of that of Ithamar; **and he ordained that one course should minister to God eight days, from sabbath to sabbath**. And thus were the courses distributed by lot, in the presence of David, and Zadok and Abiathar the high priests, and of all the rulers; and that course which came up first was written down as the first, and accordingly the second, and so on to the twenty-fourth; and this partition hath remained to this day. He also made twenty-four parts of the tribe of Levi; and when they cast lots, they came up in the same manner for their courses of eight days. He also honored the posterity of Moses, and made them the keepers of the treasures of God, and of the donations which the kings dedicated. He also ordained that all the tribe of Levi, as well as the priests, should serve God night and day, as Moses had enjoined them.
>
> Antiquities 7.4.7

Now we have a few critical details. There are 24 courses that serve "from Sabbath to Sabbath", and all 24 had to be present during the three great feasts. Also, since Abijah serves 8th, we know their first service period would hit around May-June and the second almost six months later. However, services rendered during the Three Great Feasts are not in our calculations because Luke tells us Zacharias was burning incense, and this act could only be done when a particular course was scheduled to serve. Or, to put it another way:

> As stated in a previous chapter, all the twenty-four courses, into which the priests were arranged, min-

> istered in the temple on this, as on the other great festivals, and they distributed among themselves alike what fell to them of the festive sacrifices and the shewbread. But the course which, in its proper order, was on duty for the week, alone offered all votive, and voluntary, and the public sacrifices for the whole congregation, such as those of the morning and the evening (Succah v. 7).
>
> Alfred Edersheim, The Temple: It's Ministry and Services

However, while this system was fine for David, how did it hold up throughout the following centuries? Well first, under his son Solomon, we have this:

> On the altar of the LORD that he had built in front of the portico, Solomon sacrificed burnt offerings to the LORD, according to the daily requirement for offerings commanded by Moses for Sabbaths, New Moons and the three annual feasts—the Feast of Unleavened Bread, the Feast of Weeks and the Feast of Tabernacles. In keeping with the ordinance of his father David, he appointed the divisions of the priests for their duties, and the Levites to lead the praise and to assist the priests according to each day's requirement. He also appointed the gatekeepers by divisions for the various gates, because this was what David the man of God had ordered. They did not deviate from the king's commands to the priests or to the Levites in any matter, including that of the treasuries.
>
> 2 Chronicles 8:12-15

Then there is the great reformer, Josiah, almost 300 years later:

> Josiah celebrated the Passover to the LORD in Jerusalem, and the Passover lamb was slaughtered on the fourteenth day of the first month. He appointed the priests to their duties and encouraged them in the service of the LORD's temple. He said to the Levites, who instructed all Israel and who had been consecrated to the LORD: "Put the sacred ark in the temple that Solomon son of David king of Israel built. It is not to be carried about on your shoulders. Now serve the LORD your God and his people Israel. Prepare yourselves by families in your divisions, according to the directions written by David king of Israel and by his son Solomon. "Stand in the holy place with a group of Levites for each subdivision of the families of your fellow countrymen, the lay people. Slaughter the Passover lambs, consecrate yourselves and prepare [the lambs] for your fellow countrymen, doing what the LORD commanded through Moses."
>
> 2 Chronicles 35:1-6

And after the Captivity, Ezra tells us the following:

> For the dedication of this house of God they offered a hundred bulls, two hundred rams, four hundred male lambs and, as a sin offering for all Israel, twelve male goats, one for each of the tribes of Israel. And they installed the priests in their divisions and the Levites in their groups for the service of God at Jerusalem, according to what is written in the Book of Moses. On the fourteenth day

> of the first month, the exiles celebrated the Passover.
>
> The priests and Levites had purified themselves and were all ceremonially clean. The Levites slaughtered the Passover lamb for all the exiles, for their brothers the priests and for themselves.
>
> So the Israelites who had returned from the exile ate it, together with all who had separated themselves from the unclean practices of their Gentile neighbors in order to seek the LORD, the God of Israel.
>
> For seven days they celebrated with joy the Feast of Unleavened Bread, because the LORD had filled them with joy by changing the attitude of the king of Assyria, so that he assisted them in the work on the house of God, the God of Israel.
>
> Ezra 6:17-22

On the other hand, there was at least one notable "bump in the road"—such as when Antiochus Epiphanes defiled the Temple for a few years and prevented any Jewish worship there. Obviously then priestly services would not apply to that time.

However, the Temple was subsequently re-dedicated in 164 BCE, and there is no indication from any of the primary sources on the subject (Josephus, 1 and 2 Maccabees) that any change in priestly service was implemented. Certainly such a change after a thousand plus years of tradition would have been mentioned if it had in fact occurred.

Other Considerations

Now a few final bits and pieces will help tie the whole picture together. Since Luke tells us Elizabeth was 6 months pregnant at the time Mary conceived, it should be a simple matter to prove that a total of 15 months passed between Elizabeth's conception and Messiah's birth.

Additionally, Joseph and Mary also had to stay in the area for another 6 weeks in order that Mary might undergo proper purification and present him to the Temple, (comp Luke 2:21-40 and Leviticus 12:1-8).

As for how Herod may have spent his time while Mary was getting purified, Scripture gives us a hint:

> "When King Herod heard this he was disturbed, and all Jerusalem with him. When he had called together all the chief priests and teachers of the law, he asked them where the Messiah was to be born. 'In Bethlehem, in Judea', they replied, 'for this is what the prophet has written . . . Then Herod called the Magi secretly and found out from them the exact time the star had appeared and said, 'Go and make a careful search for the child. As soon as you find him, report to me, so that I too may go and worship him.'"

Matthew 2:3-5, 7-8 (NIV)

The reason for King Herod being troubled is obvious. A sign has occurred proclaiming the birth of a new "King of the Jews". For our study, however, the most significant part is that Herod asked the Magi when the star appeared.

As stated earlier, conjunctions of Jupiter and Saturn occur once every 19 years. Therefore, when the first one happened, it probably did not even rate much above an astronomical yawn in the Magi's eyes.

That is why Herod probably didn't ask when the first conjunction happened, since he was not a star watcher to begin with. The better question would be: "*When did you notice something unusual about the star that is currently overhead?*"

The Magi, believing Herod to be Jewish[57], would have honestly answered October 3rd, 7 BCE, *or Yom Kippur exactly two years earlier.* In this context then, Herod's command to kill all infants two years old and under, makes deadly sense. As for the Magi, their reply was very accurate, because if a rare celestial event happened to hit the Jewish Sign on the Jewish Holy Day, this must have more than met Herod's criteria.[58]

Connecting the Evidence

As we've seen previously, "aster" must be a singular star. As a result, the Magi could not leave until May of 5 BCE at the earliest, because the conjunctions and massings involved multiple planets which are better covered by the Greek *astropov.*[59] That leaves the comet or nova of March 5 BCE to consider, and while either phenomenon could have been could have been designated as *aster,* two facts rule against it as a credible candidate. First, the prevailing assumption is that these phenomena presaged *evil omens.* Therefore, its appearance in the night sky, combined with that of Mars—the god of war—would not have been received by the Magi as an incentive to travel. Second, and even more critically, this particular phenomenon *did not begin in Pisces but in Capricorn!* True, it did eventually get into Pisces and it is likely the sign was read as general harbinger of great change, but the important point is that it would not be read as saying, "You've got to get up and travel there right now". As stated before, the real "King's star"—Jupiter—had disappeared behind the sun, and there would be no reason to go before it returned.

The retrograde motion of Jupiter is also positively dated to mid

September of 5 BCE, which is clearly the time that the Magi consulted with Herod.

As for Joseph and Mary, they certainly knew that Herod was after their child and they probably risked their lives to hide their son for 6 weeks prior to presenting him to the Temple. Other clues in the Gospels, as well as common sense, tell us that the family then departed for Egypt the very night that the Magi left, (Matthew 2:13).

Therefore, if the earliest time of the birth is May, and the latest September, that purification period and the departure immediately after it simply adds 6 weeks to the range. So, that is why the earliest possible time for the Egyptian sojourn must be July and the latest mid November.

Therefore, the Egyptian stay itself is our fifth historical anchor, and we now know the minimum time it could last, mid November to late March when Herod died, or four and a half months!

So let's add up all the time that has been retrieved so far:

From Elizabeth's conception to Mary's conception .... 24 weeks
From Mary's conception to the Nativity .... 36 weeks
From the Nativity to the end of the purification period, including the Magi visit .... 6 weeks
From the end of the purification period to the end of the Egyptian sojourn .... 18 weeks
Herod dies in March 4 BCE
TOTAL TIME: 84 WEEKS (21 MONTHS)

The only other time period to be accounted for then is the gap between Zacharias' vision and the onset of his wife's pregnancy. In that case, the only salient question that emerges is this: Is it likely that Zacharias would wait more than 6 months to do what God commanded? This is relevant because, again, he only served twice a year, and would therefore have to delay compliance with those instructions for more than that time to shift into a later service date. Not suprisingly, all of the evidence in the Gospel record would say no because:

- Zacharias has been pining for a son for many years, and Elizabeth felt ashamed and isolated because she could not provide one, (Luke 1:25).
- Zacharias and Elizabeth lived very near Jerusalem (Luke 1:39).
- Although elderly, God has opened Elizabeth's womb. As a result, we can expect a quick pregnancy, (Luke 1:13).
- The sooner Zacharias starts, the sooner he will regain his ability to speak, (Luke 1:20).

That brings us to one, and only one, possible service cycle, the one approximately in June of 6 BCE, our sixth historical anchor. As a result, the next range for the birth is 15-16 months later than this, or early September to early October 5 BCE.

Our next section then deals with the challenges associated with this time of year.

The Burden of the Law or, "What is a manger?"

There is a lot of confusion about the true details regarding the Nativity. Some of it has to do with early Christian tradition and other facets are based on a lack of understanding of the appropriate Hebrew, Aramaic, and Greek terms. However, most of it is due to the convenient (and sloppy) "telescoping" of events in Matthew and Luke.

With the Magi's arrival dated to the stationary position of Jupiter in mid September, there are now two powerful reasons for record breaking crowds to swell throughout the Jerusalem/Bethlehem area. The census, as stated before, required all Jews to register their property or lose their rights to it. As if that wasn't bad enough, the Romans had scheduled this census at a time when they could also control crowds coming up for the Feast of Tabernacles[60]. In so doing, the Romans wisely minimized the times they needed to bring in troops, getting two occasions for the price of one.

Furthermore, a massive migration and registration, such as this one, was much more cost effective if conducted before the rainy season began in November.[61] Therefore, to do so later on, as the 1 BCE camp contends, would have been the height of folly.[62] The Eastern provinces were contentious enough when the weather was good. Also, if the 2 BCE tribute is any indication of a traditional time for payment because it was when Rome was born—with Augustus' Jubilee just being a happy coincidence for them—then the Romans would begin collection during the Spring.

Unfortunately for Joseph, this Roman "efficiency" also guaranteed that every inn along the way would be stacked to the bare walls. What's a righteous carpenter to do?

In order to figure that out, we must return to our starting question: What *is* a manger anyway?

According to Strong's Concordance, word 5356, "manger" (Greek "phatnay") means "a stall for animals or a crib". However, the roots of the word are even more specific, since *phatnay* is derived from the Greek word *pateomai* which means "to eat". Thus, most scholars have included the words "feeding trough for animals" in this definition.[63] This would also bring the Greek more in line with the Hebrew equivalent.[64]

Some have stated that a "manger" is nothing more than an open stable, but this is not the case at all. Rather, a "manger" is a "trough", which can be a part of a stable, but not necessarily.

In the past, scholars have tried to piece together the birth site by suggesting that the "manger" was a stall cut out of stone from natural cave formations that populate the area.[65] It is for this reason that a very early tradition arose that Messiah was born in a cave, but this finds no support within the Biblical record.[66]

As for the exact kind of shelter the innkeeper had in mind, Scripture presents a very likely candidate at this time of year:

> "So beginning with the fifteenth day of the seventh month, after you have gathered the crops of the land, celebrate the festival to the LORD for

> seven days... Live in booths for seven days: All native born Israelites are to live in booths so your descendants will know that I had the Israelites live in booths when I brought them out of Egypt."
>
> Leviticus 23:39, 42-43

The first logical question to ask is simply: Would a booth like this provide enough shelter for the family? To answer this, I quote from Alfred Erdesheim:

> "The Mishnah gives most minute details as to the height and construction of these 'booths,' the main object being to prevent any invasion of the law. Thus it must be a real booth, and constructed of boughs of living trees, and solely for the purposes of this festival. Hence it must be high enough, yet not too high—at least ten handbreadths, but not more than thirty feet; three of its walls must be of boughs; it must be fairly covered with boughs, yet not so shaded as not to admit sunshine, nor yet so open as to have not sufficient shade, the object in each case being neither sunshine nor shade, but that it should be a real booth of boughs of trees. It is needless to enter into further details, except to say that these booths, and not their houses, were to be the regular dwelling of all in Israel during the week, and that, except in very heavy rain, they were to eat, sleep, pray, study—in short, entirely to live in them."
>
> The Temple: Its Ministry and Services, Chapter 14

It is also helpful that tradition strictly dictated when it had to be built and torn down. For the former, we turn to Nehemiah:

> "**On the second day of the month,** the heads of all the families, along with the priests and Levites, gathered around Ezra the scribe to give attention to the words of the Law, which the LORD had commanded through Moses, that the Israelites were to live in booths **during the feast of the seventh month** and that they should proclaim throughout their towns and Jerusalem: 'Go out to the hill country and bring back branches from olive and wild olive trees, and from myrtles, palms and shade trees, to make booths—as it is written.' So the people went out and brought back the branches and built themselves booths on their own roofs, in their courtyards, in the courts of the House of God and in the square by the Water Gate and the one by the Gate of Ephraim."

Nehemiah 8:13-16

The second day of Tishri in 5 BCE, translated to September 1st. Then, by the last day of the Feast (22 Tishri, September 21st), they were torn down:

> "We can now with some measure realize the event recorded in John 7:37. The festivities of the Week of Tabernacles were drawing to a close. 'It was the last day, that great day of the feast.' It obtained this name, although it was not of 'holy convocation' partly because it closed the feast and partly from the circumstances which procured it from Rabbinical writings the designations of 'Day of the Great

Hosanna' and 'Day of Willows' and 'Day of Beating the Branches', **because all the leaves were shaken off the willow boughs, and the palm branches were beaten in pieces by the side of the altar."**

The Temple: Its Ministry and Services, Chapter 14

That gives us three weeks for the holy family to seek shelter beneath the *sukkah*, the last space available in Israel. *This range also represents our seventh, and last, historical anchor.*

However, even this range can be narrowed, because while the *sukkah* could have gone up on September 1st · the stationary portion of Jupiter's retrograde cycle would not happen for another week. Therefore, the next possible range is cut to 11 days, **or September 10th through the 21st.**[67]

We are now almost at the very limit of what can be recovered. For the last piece, we need to look at the nature of the holiday in question. Since all the Israelites had to dwell in booths for the week, it therefore stands to reason that the inns are packed because the holiday has not started yet! When the inn is full, Joseph then either decides to build the sukkah himself or else borrows the innkeeper's unused one. In either case it does not matter, because both scenarios zero in on the last four days between Jupiter's retrograde cycle and the start of Tabernacles itself— **or September 10th through the 13th, 5 BCE.**

As for the final arrangements, Joseph begins his work, probably procuring a few cheap linens from the innkeeper. Some of it is cut into strips to wrap the infant when he comes, (Luke 2:7) but the bulk of it must have went to form a makeshift partition around the *sukkah*, so that Mary could be afforded some measure of privacy. Joseph then enters the nearby stable and sees a small feeding trough shaped remarkably like a crib. He then fills it with hay and takes it back to his son.

So while Y'shua was laid IN A MANGER, he did not SHELTER

BENEATH ONE. This is a critical distinction. Neither Mary nor Joseph were "in" a manger either, but rather, beside one.

Jewish custom then fills in the remaining gaps regarding the Nativity. First, a midwife is called to assist during labor.[68] When this is completed, the umbilical cord is cut and Y'shua is washed with water and then anointed with special salts. Then the newborn is wrapped tightly in the linen strips so that he cannot move his limbs. This procedure was due to a folk belief that the limbs would not grow straight unless they were immobilized for the first 6 months of life.[69] Thus we find all the direct and indirect evidence strongly pointing to an early Fall birth.

Finally, it may or may not be coincidental that a birth at Sukkot would mean a conception during Hanukkah, which is known as the "Festival of Lights". This leads us inexorably then to a tantalizing detail in John's Gospel:

> "In him was life, and that life was the light of men. The light shines in the darkness but the darkness has not understood it. There came a man who was sent from God; his name was John. He came as a witness to testify concerning that light. He himself was not the light; he came only as a witness to that light. The true light that gives light to every man was coming into the world."

> John 1:4-9 (NIV)

Could this be John's way of describing the Nativity in a brief but highly allegorical way? Might it even be a clue about the time of the birth? Furthermore, is it coincidental that Hanukkah commemorates the re-purification of the Temple that until the Messiah's advent was the vehicle for forgiving sin? We may never know, but this next line certainly raises some intriguing possibilities:

> "The Word became flesh and dwelled among us. We have seen his glory, the glory of the one and only Son, who came from the Father full of grace and truth."
>
> John 1:14 (NIV)

In Hebrew, a synonym for *dwell* is "sukkot"—tabernacle, because the Israelites had to dwell in booths to commemorate their time in the wilderness. In John's mind then, the "wilderness" could be symbolic also of the longing for the Messiah since the time of Moses. The Spirit of God also, as is recorded in the Torah, "dwelled" with THE TABERNACLE in the wilderness.

So, if true, where did John get this information? Well, his Gospel shows certain information that none of the others have. When Y'shua is clearly alone with his family, John still manages to record an intimate discussion, (John 7:1-7). These details, and others like it, probably came from him taking care of Y'shua's mother after the crucifixion, where all the things that she "treasured in her heart" could finally be opened, (Luke 2:20, John 19:27).

What about December 25th?

There is a very old story. A man from the Middle East goes on a spiritual journey, faces many hardships and dies a violent death. Afterwards, he is reborn and many proclaim him to be a god. This man was also born, according to long-standing tradition, by a virgin on December 25th. Is this Y'shua? No, not by a long shot.

Remarkably, I am describing the story of Mithras, a deity of Persian origin. In the first couple of centuries of the common era, the cult bearing his name was at its peak in power and influence. Mithras was worshipped almost universally by the Roman army, and his followers were representative of all classes in the Empire.[70]

Now Rome was very tolerant of other religions, as long as they were pagan.[71] The official Roman pantheon of gods, derived from myths first told by the Greeks, was supposed to be a tie binding all the different nationalities under its control. One could worship any deity they desired, so long as they paid minimal lip service to Jupiter or Jove, the supreme Roman god. If you believe in a dozen gods, what's one more if it'll keep peace between you and the rulers of the world?[72]

However, for Jews and Christians, belief in Almighty God excluded even the slightest acknowledgment of Jupiter.[73] On the other hand, the fact that Mithras was born on December 25th would have made the day ideal to celebrate Messiah's birth also.

By commemorating a December 25th "divine birthday" Christians then were seen as good citizens. Moreover, since the Roman soldiers who enforced the religious rules were also Mithraists, Christians could hardly have made a better choice to celebrate the birth of their LORD. At the same time, another winter solstice festival, a drunken orgy known as the *Saturnalia*, was also going on. [74]. If anyone else had felt the urge to persecute Christians at that point, chances were the wine they consumed would have dulled their fever. This was critical to the survival of the early Church, which faced continuous persecution for most of the next 300 years. [75]

To be fair, however, it should be noted that officially sanctioned Christmas celebrations *that we are aware of* did not take place until the fourth century. Because of this, some scholars have downplayed the Saturnalia/Christmas connection. However, they forget that Christianity was an underground movement throughout the Roman Empire and that much of its early practices were shrouded in mystery.[76] In this context and circumstance, having a "backup" plan in case they were caught would be perfectly understandable.[77]

In 275 CE, Mithras was officially recognized as the Roman deity Invictus, and an official feast on December 25th was ordered.[78]

Then, just a few decades later, a breakthrough occurred. The Emperor Constantine, after seeing a cross in the sky and praying to Y'shua for a hard won victory, converted to the new faith. First the religion was granted toleration and then, some years later, it became the official religion of the Empire. The carpenter they crucified was now their Supreme God! The earliest official Christmas celebrations then began showing up around the year 335, and from that point on the practice spread throughout the world.[79]

At this point then, little else need be said, except to show how all these linguistic and historical clues fit together. It is for that reason that I offer the first of what will be three "Gospel Harmonies", or a study of a given topic derived from combining two or more accounts. Obviously neither this nor any other such study is intended to replace the originals, but I do think putting a lot of this information together in one place will facilitate a study of those four intimate portraits we call Gospels.

So what follows then is a full reconstruction of the Nativity as told by both Matthew and Luke. Additionally, the reader should note that parentheses ( ) indicate my words have been inserted either for the purposes of sentence flow when we switch from one account to the other, or else to supply the historical information in its proper context. In no way should either be construed as an attempt to change that which is already sacred. Finally, the text of these harmonies are based on the New International Version of the New Testament, but also is different from the NIV. Their footnotes have not been retained and neither do my emendations appear in their text. Also Aramaic information will be brought into this NIV shell texts where appropriate.

Gospel Harmony Study #1: The Nativity

(Mark 1:1)

The beginning of the gospel about Y'shua Ha Moshiack, the Son of God.

(Luke 1:1-4)

Many have undertaken to draw up an account of the things that have been fulfilled among us, just as they were handed down to us by those who from the first were eyewitnesses and servants of the word.

Therefore, since I myself have carefully investigated everything from the beginning, it seemed good also to me to write an orderly account for you, most excellent Theophilus, so that you may know the certainty of the things you have been taught.

(John 1:1-5)

In the beginning there was the Word, and the Word was with God, and the Word was God. He was with God in the beginning.

Through him all things were made; without him nothing was made that has been made. In him was life, and that life was the light of men. The light shines in the darkness, but the darkness has not understood it.

(Luke 1:5-25)
June 2-9, 6 BCE

In the time of Herod the King of Judea , there was a priest named Zacharias, who belonged to the priestly division of Abijah; his wife Elizabeth was also a descendant of Aaron. Both of them were upright in the sight of God, observing all the LORD's commandments and regulations blamelessly. But they had no children, because Elizabeth was barren; and they were both well along in years.

Once when Zacharias' division on duty and he was serving as priest before God, he was chosen by lot, according to the custom of the priesthood, to go into the Temple of the LORD and burn incense. And when the time for the burning of incense came, all the assembled worshippers were praying outside.

Then an angel of the LORD appeared to him, standing at the right side of the altar of incense. When Zacharias saw him, he startled and gripped with fear. But the angel said to him: "Do not be afraid, Zacharias; your prayer has been heard. Your wife Elizabeth will bear you a son, and you are to name him John. He will be a joy and a delight to you, and many will rejoice because of his birth, for he will be great in the sight of the LORD. He is never to take any wine or other fermented drink, and he will be filled with the Holy Spirit even from birth. Many of the people of Israel will he bring back to the LORD their God. And he will go on before the LORD, in the spirit and power of Elijah, to turn the hearts of the fathers to their children and the disobedient to the righteous – to make ready a people prepared for the LORD."

Zacharias asked the angel, "How can I be sure of this? I am an old man and my wife is well along in years."

The angel answered, "I am Gabriel. I stand in the presence of God, and I have been sent to speak to you and to tell you this good news. And now you will be silent and will not be able to speak until the day this happens, because you did not believe my words, which will come true at their proper time."

Meanwhile, the people were waiting for Zacharias and wondering why he stayed so long in the Temple. When he came out, he could not speak to them. They realized he had seen a vision in the Temple, for he kept making signs to them but remained unable to speak.

When his time of service was completed, he returned home. After this his wife Elizabeth became pregnant and for five months remained in seclusion. "The LORD has done this for me," she said. "In these days he has taken away my disgrace among the people."

(Matthew 1:18)
 (Now) this is how the birth of Y'shua Ha Moshiack came about:

October, 6 BCE
(Luke 1:26)
 In the sixth month, God sent the angel Gabriel to Nazareth, a town in Galilee,

(Luke 1:27, Matthew 1:18 (b))
to a virgin pledged to be married to man named Joseph, a descendant of David. The virgin's name was Mary

(Matthew 1:18 (c))

But before they came together, she was found to be with child through the Holy Spirit (because)

(Luke 1:28-56)
the angel went to her and said, "Greetings you who are highly favored! The LORD is with you."

Mary was greatly troubled at his words and wondered what kind of greeting this might be. But the angel said to her, "Do not be afraid, Mary, you have found favor with God. You will be with child and give birth to a son, and you are to give him the name Y'shua. He will be called Son of the Most High. The LORD God will give him the throne of his father David, and he will reign over the house of Jacob forever; his kingdom will never end."

"How will this be," Mary asked the angel, "since I am a virgin?"

The angel answered, "The Holy Spirit will come upon you and the power of the Most High will overshadow you. So the holy one to be born will be called the Son of God. Even Elizabeth your relative is going to have a child in her old age, and she who was said to be barren in her sixth month. For nothing is impossible without God."

"I am the LORD's servant," Mary answered. "May it be to me as you have said." Then the angel left her.

At that time Mary got ready and hurried to a town in the hill country of Judah, where she entered Zacharias' home and greeted Elizabeth. When Elizabeth heard Mary's greeting, the baby leaped in her womb, and Elizabeth was filled with the Holy Spirit. In a loud voice she exclaimed: "Blessed are you among women, and blessed is the child you bear! But why am I so favored, that the mother of the LORD should come to me? As soon as the sound of your greeting reached my ears, the baby in my womb leaped for joy. Blessed is she who believed what the LORD said to her will be accomplished!"

And Mary said: "My soul praises the LORD and my spirit rejoices in God my Savior, for he has been mindful of the humble state of his servant. From now on all generations will call me blessed, for the Might One has done great things for me– holy is his name. His mercy extends to those who fear him, from generation to generation. He has performed might deeds with his arm; he has scattered those who are proud in their inmost thoughts. He has brought down rulers from their thrones but has lifted up the humble. He has filled the hungry with good things but has sent the rich away empty. He has helped his servant Israel, remembering to be merciful to Abraham and his descendants forever, even as he said to our fathers." Mary stayed with Elizabeth for about three months and then returned home.

March, 5 BCE

When it was time for Elizabeth to have her baby, she gave birth to a son. Her neighbors and relatives heard that the LORD had shown her great mercy, and they shared her joy.

On the eighth day they came to circumcise the child, and they were going to name him after his father Zacharias, but his mother spoke up and said, "No! He is to be called John."

They said to her, "There is no one among your relatives who has that name."

Then they made signs to his father, to find out what he would like to name the child. He asked for a writing tablet, and to everyone's astonishment he wrote, "His name is John." Immediately his mouth was opened and his tongue was loosed, and he began to speak, praising God. The neighbors were all filled with awe, and throughout the country of Judea people were talking about all these things. Everyone who had heard this wondered about it, asking, "What then is this child going to be?" For the LORD's hand was with him.

His father Zacharias was filled with the Holy Spirit and prophesied: "Praise be to the LORD God of Israel, because he has come and redeemed his people. He has raised up a horn of salvation for us in the house of his servant David as he said through his holy prophets of long ago, salvation from our enemies and from the hand of all who hate us – to show mercy to our fathers and to remember his holy covenant, the oath he swore to our father Abraham: To rescue us from the hand of our enemies, and to enable us to serve him without fear in holiness and righteousness before him al our days. And you, my child, will be called a prophet of the Most High; for you will go on before the LORD to prepare the way for him, to give his people the knowledge of salvation through the forgiveness of their sins, because the tender mercy of our God, by which the rising sun will come to us from heaven to shine on those living in darkness and in the shadow of death, to guide our feet into the path of peace."

And the child grew and became strong in spirit; and he lived in the desert until he appeared publicly to Israel.

(Matthew 1:19-25)
(Meanwhile), because Joseph her husband was a righteous man and did not want to expose her to public disgrace, he had in mind to divorce her quietly.

But after he had considered this, an angel of the LORD appeared to him in a dream and said, "Joseph, son of David, do not be afraid to take Mary home as your wife, because what is conceived in her is from the Holy Spirit. She will give birth to a son and you are to name him Y'shua, because he will save his people from their sins."

All this took place to fulfill what the LORD had said through the prophet: "The virgin will be with child and will give birth to son, and they will call him Immanuel" - which means "God with us."

When Joseph woke up, he did what the LORD commanded him and took Mary home as his wife. But he had no union with her until she gave birth to a son,

(Luke 2:1-20)
(which happened during the time) that Caesar Augustus issued the decree that a census should be taken of the entire Roman world. This was the first census which took place (from 7 BCE and was completed in 6 CE) while Quirinius was governor of Syria. And everyone went to his own town to register. So Joseph also went up from the town of Nazareth in Galilee to Judea, to Bethlehem, because he belonged to

the hose and the line of David. He went there to register with Mary, who was pledged to be married to him and was expecting a child.

September 10-13, 5 BCE

While they were there, the time came for the baby to be born, and she gave birth to her first born, a son. She wrapped him in strips of cloth and placed him in a manger, because there was no room for them in the inn.

And there were shepherds living out in the fields nearby, keeping watch over their flocks at night. An angel of the LORD appeared to them, and the glory of the LORD shone around them, and they were terrified. But he angel said to them, "Do not be afraid. I bring you good news of great joy that will be for all people. Today in the town of David a Savior has been born to you; he is Messiah the LORD. This will be a sign to you: You will find the baby wrapped in strips of cloth and laying in a manger."

Suddenly a great company of heavenly host appeared with the angel, praising God and saying, "Glory to God in the highest, and on earth peace to men on whom his favor rests."

When the angels had left them and gone into heaven, the shepherds said to one another, "Let's go to Bethlehem and see this thing that has happened, which the LORD has told us about."

So they hurried off and found Mary and Joseph, and the baby, who was lying in the manger. When they had seen him, they spread the word concerning what had been told them about this child, and all who heard it were amazed at what the shepherds said to them. But Mary treasured up all these things and pondered them in her heart. The shepherds returned, glorifying and praising God for all the things they had heard and seen, which were just as they had been told.

On the eighth day, when it was time to circumcise him, he was named Y'shua, the name the angel had given him before he had been conceived.

Late October, 5 BCE

When the time of their purification according to the Law of Moses had been completed, Joseph and Mary took him to Jerusalem to present him to the LORD, as it was written in the Law of the LORD, "Every firstborn male is to be consecrated to the LORD", and to offer a sacrifice in keeping with what is said In the Law of the LORD: "a pair of doves or two young pigeons."

Now there was a man in Jerusalem called Simeon, who was righteous and devout. He was waiting for the consolation of Israel, and the Holy Spirit was upon him. It had been revealed to him by the Holy Spirit that he would not die before he had seen the LORD's Messiah. Moved by the Spirit, he went into the Temple courts. When the parents brought in the child Y'shua to do for him what the custom of the Law required, Simeon took him in his arms and praised God, saying:

"Sovereign LORD, as you have promised, you now dismiss your servant in peace. For my eyes have seen your salvation, which you have prepared in the sight of all people, a light of revelation to the Gentiles and the glory to your people Israel."

The child's mother and father marveled at what was said about him. Then Simeon blessed them and said to Mary, his mother: "This child is destined to cause the falling and rising of many in Israel, and to be a sign that will be spoken against, so that the thoughts of many hearts will be revealed. And a sword will pierce your own soul too."

There was also a prophetess, Anna, the daughter of Phanuel, of the tribe of Asher. She was very old; she had lived with her husband seven years after her marriage, and then was a widow until she was eighty-four. She never left the Temple but worshipped night and day, fasting and praying. Coming up to them at that very moment, she gave thanks to God, and spoke about the child to all who were looking forward to the redemption of Jerusalem.

(Matthew 2:1-24)

After Y'shua was born in Bethlehem in Judea, during the time of

King Herod, Magi from the east came to Jerusalem and asked, "Where is he who is born King of the Jews? We saw his star (Jupiter) when it rose in the east (in May, 5 BCE) and have come to worship him."

When King Herod heard this, he was very disturbed, and all Jerusalem with him. When he has called together the all the people's chief priests and teachers of the law, he asked them where the Messiah was to be born. "In Bethlehem, in Judea," they replied, "for this is what the prophet has written: 'But you, Bethlehem, in the land of Judah, are by no means least among the rulers of Judah; for out of you will come a ruler who will be the shepherd of my people Israel.'"

Late October, 5 BCE

Then Herod called the Magi secretly and found out from them the exact time the star appeared (May, 5 BCE), and said, "Go and make a careful search for the child. As soon as you find him, report to me, so that I too may go and worship him."

After they had heard the King, they went on their way, and the star they had seen in the east when it rose went ahead of them until it stopped over the place where the child was. When they saw the star, they were overjoyed. On coming to the house, they saw the child with his mother Mary, and they bowed down and worshipped him. Then they opened their treasures and presented him with gifts of gold and of incense and of myrrh. And having been warned in a dream not to go back to Herod, they returned to their country by another route.

When they had gone, an angel of the LORD appeared to Joseph in a dream. "Get up," he said, "take the child and his mother and escape to Egypt. Stay there until I tell you, for Herod is going to search for the child to kill him."

So he got up, took the child and his mother during the night and left for Egypt, where he stayed until the death of Herod (in March of the following year). And so was fulfilled what the LORD had said through the prophet: "Out of Egypt, I called my son."

When Herod realized that he had been outwitted by the Magi, he was furious, and gave orders to kill all the boys in Bethlehem and its vicinity who were two years old and under, in accordance with the time he had learned from the Magi (May 7 - May 5 BCE). Then what was spoken through the prophet Jeremiah was fulfilled: "A voice is heard in Ramah, weeping and great mourning. Rachel weeping for her children and refusing to be comforted, because they are no more."

After Herod died, an angel of the LORD appeared in a dream to Joseph in Egypt and said, "Get up and take the child and his mother and go to the land of Israel, for those who were trying to take the child's life are dead."

So he got up, took the child and his mother and went to the land of Israel

(Luke 2:39-40)
(after they) had done everything required by the Law of the LORD, (and) they returned to Galilee, to their own town of Nazareth. (Joseph did this because he heard) that Archalaeus was reigning in Judea in place of his father Herod (and) he was afraid to go there. Having been warned in a dream, he returned to his home (district, and because of the town's name) it was fulfilled what was said through the prophets: "He will be called a Nazarene."

(Luke 2:40-52)
And the child grew and became strong; he was filled with wisdom, and the grace of God was upon him.

April, 8 CE
Every year his parents went to Jerusalem for the Feast of the Passover. When Y'shua was twelve years old, they went up to the Feast, according to the custom. After the Feast was over, while the parents were returning home, the boy Y'shua stayed behind in Jerusalem, but they were unaware of it. Thinking he was in their company, they traveled on for a day. Then they began looking for him among their relatives and friends. When they did not find him, they went back to Jerusalem to look for him. After three days they found him in the

Temple courts, sitting among the tea hers, listening to them, and asking them questions. Everyone who heard him was amazed at his understanding and his answers. When his parents saw him, they were astonished and said to him, "Son, why have you treated us like this? Your father and I have been anxiously searching for you."

"Why were you searching for me?" he asked. "Didn't you know I had to be in my Father's house?" But they did not understand what he was saying to them. Then he went down to Nazareth with them and was obedient to them. But his mother treasured all these things in her heart. And Y'shua grew in wisdom and stature, and in favor with God and men."

PART TWO:

THE SIX SIDES OF THE MESSIAH

There is an old saying that states that you must understand where you came from if you are to know where you are going. So, before launching into a full study of Y'shua's life and work, it is critical that prophecies regarding him are carefully evaluated and delineated. Such a study will lay the groundwork for understanding not just what Y'shua believed, but why his adversaries mounted such a fierce opposition.

Not only do I explore linguistic issues in the original Hebrew where appropriate, I also restore traditional Talmudic and rabbinic exegesis to verses which are either downplayed or completely ignored by current Judaism due to their problematic nature.

It therefore should come as no surprise that the Messiah described here is inextricable from his Jewish culture and nature. My purpose is to remove the entire idea of Old/New Testament debate between Jews and Christians per se, to an interpretative case for an entire body of Tenakh writings. In this respect then the identity, circumstances and origin of the Messiah will now shift back to where it has always belonged: as a Jewish debate regarding Jewish Scripture. Anything less will do extreme violence to the unique Hebrew revelation, and encumber it with pagan and Hellenistic influences that dilute its power.

As a final introductory note, I call this section *Six Sides of the Messiah* because I have classified this voluminous data along the simple journalistic lines of *Who, What, When, Where, Why and How.* We begin by asking a very basic question:

Can God Assume Human Form?

> "God is not a man, that He should lie; nor a son of man, that He should change is mind."
>
> Numbers 23:19 (New International Version — NIV)

This verse—and a few others like it— have been the traditional cites against the idea of God uniting with the flesh. We have found opposition not only in the Jewish quarter, but in certain Christian circles as well. The Unitarians, for example, frequently quote this verse to prove that Y'shua was completely human. Similar positions even go back to the apostolic age, with the Gnostics earning a personal rebuke in writing, (1 John 1:7).

However, it takes more than clever editing to "prove" a biblical position. The verse in Numbers is plain enough, for the fact that God is NOT a man is established in the first line of Genesis. On the other hand, Scripture also is adamant that God has unlimited power. How God uses that power is another matter, for He will not do anything that contradicts His will. Therefore, it is God's unchangeable nature (Isaiah 43:13, Malachi 3:6), not His lack of power, which dictates what will happen.

It would then appear to be a spurious—and even dangerous—position to say the God cannot do anything He has not already set His mind to. Or, to put it another way: Just because God is not a man, does not necessarily mean God cannot take on the form of a man if it serves His purpose. For proof of this, we need look no further than the first few chapters of Genesis:

> "Then the man and his wife heard the voice of the

> LORD God as He was walking in the garden in the cool of day."
>
> Genesis 3:8 (NIV)

So here is a record stating that God literally walked with Man as a physical being, and this was hardly confined to just Adam, (Genesis 5:18-24). By the time we get to Abraham, however, the manifestations are getting far more intense and specific:

> "The LORD[80] appeared to Abraham near the great trees of the Mamre while he was sitting at the entrance to his tent in the heat of the day. Abraham looked up and saw three men standing nearby. When he saw them, he hurried from the entrance of his tent to meet them and bowed low to the ground and said, ' If I have found favor in your sight, my LORD, do not pass your servant by. Let a little water be brought, and then you may all wash your feet and rest under this tree. Let me get you something to eat, so you can be refreshed and then go on your way, now that you have come to your servant. 'Very well' they answered, 'do as you say'."
>
> Genesis 18:1-5 (NIV)

So Abraham quickly fetches his wife and makes preparations to receive his guests. However, even though they appear mortal by sharing a meal, it is certain that at least one of them is not:

> "Then the LORD said, 'Shall I hide from Abraham what I am about to do?'"
>
> Genesis 18:17-18 (NIV)

So while it is clear from later information that two of these "men" are actually angels, (Genesis 19:1), ONE OF THEM IS ACTUALLY GOD HIMSELF IN HUMAN FORM. As if to cement the point, the other two "men" continue towards Sodom, while the third one stays behind with Abraham. After a particularly intense "bargaining session", Abraham says:

> "And he said, 'Oh let not the LORD be angry, but let me speak just once more. What if only ten (righteous people) can be found there (in Sodom)? He answered, 'For the sake of ten, I will not destroy it. When the LORD had finished speaking with Abraham, he left and Abraham returned home."
>
> Genesis 18:32-33 (NIV)

There are also two occasions in the Book of Daniel where another manifestation of God appears, but these will be discussed at a later time. The point for now however is that there can be no doubt that God DOES unite with flesh when it suits Him.

THE GLORY OF WHO

The First Titles of Isaiah

We begin with the majestic messianic titles given by the prophet Isaiah, and this time I have two versions of the same verse:

> "For a child is born to us, a son is given to us and the government is upon his shoulder; and his name is called: Pele-joez-el-gibbor-Abiad-sar-shalom (That is, Wonderful in counsel is God the Mighty, the everlasting Father, the Ruler of Peace."[81])
>
> Isaiah 9:5 (JPS 1955)

> "For a child is born, to us a son is given, and the government will be on his shoulders. And he will be called: Wonderful, Counselor, Mighty God, Everlasting Father, Prince of Peace."

Isaiah 9:6 (NIV)

In many ways this verse is a companion piece to Genesis 18, for just as the three visitors there foreshadowed the concept of the triune Deity, Isaiah 9:6 goes an extra step and names each of them in turn.

"Mighty God" and "Everlasting Father" are obviously the First Person of the Godhead (Isaiah 42:8, 44:6) "Prince of Peace" is the Second Person, or the Messiah Himself (Zechariah 9:9), and finally there is the "Wonderful Counselor" or Holy Spirit. Because this last designation is not as obvious as the other two, we need to look at a several verses:

> "And the Spirit of the LORD shall rest upon him—the Spirit of wisdom and understanding, THE SPIRIT OF COUNSEL AND OF MIGHT, the Spirit of knowledge and of fear of the LORD, and His delights shall be in the fear of the LORD."[82]

Isaiah 11:2-3 (JPS 1955)

> "The Spirit of the LORD will come upon you in power, and you will prophesy with them, and will be turned into another person. Once these signs are fulfilled, do whatever your hand finds to do, for God is with you."

1 Samuel 10:6-7 (NIV)

> "Create in me a clean heart, O God, and renew a

steadfast spirit within me. Cast me not away from Thy presence; and take not Thy Holy Spirit away from me."

Psalm 51:10-11 (JPS 1955)

"And it shall come to pass afterward that I will pour out My Spirit upon all flesh. And your sons and daughters shall prophecy. Your old men shall dream dreams. Your young men shall see visions. And also upon the servants and the handmaids. In those days will I pour out My Spirit."

Joel 3:1-2 (JPS 1955)

Finally, we see in Isaiah how God is called "Father" for the first time. When confronted with this evidence, however, some critics allege that God may be called "Father" but that no one, not even the Messiah, could claim to be His Son. Such scriptural contortionists conveniently forget this verse in Proverbs, which is truly devastating to their point of view:

"And I have not learned wisdom, that I should have knowledge of the Holy One. Who hath ascended into heaven and descended? Who hath gathered the winds in his fists? Who hath bound the waters in his garment? Who hath established the ends of the earth? What is his name and what is his son's name, if thou knowest?"

Proverbs 30:3-5 (JPS 1955)

The Son of Adam

From the very beginning, God has been involved in a process of selecting specific people from special families to do His bidding. Starting with Adam, God had to choose one of three sons to pass his Spirit along to. The first, Cain, was cursed and driven from God's presence. The second, Abel, was righteous, but murdered by Cain before he could have children.

This forced Eve to have a third son, Seth, and God rested His favor on him, (Genesis 4:25).

After Seth and Cain developed their own nations, we skip ten generations to a man named Noah. But while Noah's family survives the Deluge, God picks again from three sons. This time it is Shem, from whom we get the term *Semite*.

Ten generations after that, the progenitor of a nation is born.

The Son of Abraham

> "'I swear by Myself,' declares the LORD, 'that because you have done this, and have not withheld your son, your only son, I will surely bless you and make your descendants as numerous as the stars of heaven, and as the sand on the seashore. Your descendants will take possession of the cities of their enemies, and through your offspring all nations on earth will be blessed, because you obeyed me.'"
>
> Genesis 22:16-18 (NIV)

At this point, however, Abraham had two sons. But since God had ordained their separation, only one could be blessed:

> "Then God said, 'Yes, but your wife Sarah will bear

> you a son, and you will call him Isaac; and I will establish My covenant with him as an everlasting covenant for his descendants after him."
>
> Genesis 17:19 (NIV)

Isaac, in turn, also had two sons, but:

> "I see him, but not now. I behold him, but not near. A star will come out of Jacob; a scepter will rise out of Israel . . . A ruler will come out of Jacob."
>
> Numbers 24:17,19a (NIV)

Then, from Jacob's twelve sons we are told:

> "The scepter shall not depart from Judah, nor the ruler's staff from between his feet, until he comes to whom it belongs."
>
> Genesis 49:10 (JPS 1955)[83]

Unfortunately, Judah is by far the largest of the twelve tribes. Of the vast multitudes that will spring from this one son, ONLY ONE DESCENDANT, MORE THAN 800 YEARS REMOVED, WILL BE SELECTED:

> "And there shall come forth a shoot out of the stock of Jesse; and a twig shall grow forth out of his roots."
>
> Isaiah 11:1 (JPS 1955)[84]

The Son of David

Jesse, however, has eight sons (1 Samuel 16:10), and the prophets are unanimous as to which is favored:

> "And of peace there shall be no end, upon the throne of David, and upon his kingdom."
>
> Isaiah 9:6 (JPS 1955)
>
> "Afterward shall the children of Israel return, and seek the LORD their God, and David their king, and shall come trembling unto the LORD and to His goodness in the end of days."
>
> Hosea 3:5 (JPS 1955)
>
> "In that day I will raise up the tabernacle of David that is fallen, and close up the breaches thereof, and I will raise up his ruins, and I will build it as in days of old."
>
> Amos 9:11 (JPS 1955)
>
> "My servant David will be king over them, and they will have one shepherd ... THEY AND THEIR CHILDREN AND THEIR CHILDREN'S CHILDREN WILL LIVE THERE FOREVER AND DAVID MY SERVANT WILL BE THEIR PRINCE FOREVER. I WILL MAKE A COVENANT OF PEACE WITH THEM; IT WILL BE AN EVERLASTING COVENANT."
>
> Ezekiel 37:24, 26 (NIV)

> "For this is what the LORD says, David will never fail to have a man sit on the throne of Israel."

Jeremiah 23:17 (NIV)

Not to be outdone by his ancestors, David provided a long list of potential heirs due to his high number of wives. From all this confusion, we again come down to one son:

> "The LORD declares to you that the LORD Himself will establish a house for you: When your days are over and you rest with your fathers, I WILL RAISE UP YOUR OFFSPRING TO SUCCEED YOU, WHO WILL COME FROM YOUR BODY, AND I WILL ESTABLISH HIS KINGDOM. He is the one who will build a house for my Name, AND I WILL ESTABLISH THE THRONE OF HIS KINGDOM FOREVER."

2 Samuel 7:11-13 (NIV)

And:

> "In the four hundred and eightieth year after the Israelites had come out of Egypt, in the fourth year of Solomon's reign over Israel, in the month of Ziv, the second month, he began to build the temple of the LORD."

1 Kings 6:1 (NIV)

It is therefore no exaggeration to say that God is picking his Messiah from one family in ten thousand!

The "Righteous Branch"

Another common title for the Messiah is "branch":

> "Return to us, O God Almighty. Look down from heaven and see! Watch over this vine, THE BRANCH YOUR RIGHT HAND HAS PLANTED, THE SON YOU HAVE RAISED UP FOR YOURSELF."

> Psalm 80:15 (NIV)

> "In that day the Root of Jesse will stand as a banner for the peoples; the nations will rally to him, and the place of his rest will be glorious."

> Isaiah 11:10 (NIV)

The Branch is Named

Finally from Jeremiah we get this clue:

> "The days are coming, declares the LORD, when I will raise to David a righteous Branch, a king who will reign wisely and do what is just and righteous in the land. In his days Judah will be saved and Israel will live in safety. This is the name he will be called: YHWH OUR RIGHTEOUSNESS."

> Jeremiah 23:5-6, 33:15-16 (NIV)[85]

As a result, Jeremiah is predicting that the Messiah's name will contain part of God's intimate title. Or, to put it another way, HIS

NAME WILL START WITH "YAH"! As for the rest of the name, Zechariah has the answer:

> "Take the silver and gold and make a crown AND SET IT ON THE HEAD OF THE HIGH PRIEST JOSHUA, SON OF JEHOZADAK. Tell him this is what the LORD Almighty says: HERE IS THE MAN WHOSE NAME IS THE BRANCH . . ."
>
> Zechariah 6:11-12 (NIV)

When we look at "Joshua" in Hebrew, we are finally confronted with the Messiah's real name: "YAH-SHUA", which means, "Yah is salvation". "Yahshua the Messiah" then filtered into Greek as Iesous Messiahos, or Y'shua Ha Moshiack

THE MAJESTY OF WHAT

The Universal King

Starting once again with Isaiah, we see two elements of Messiah come together. The first is that he is destined to rule the world. The second is that the king and his throne are immortal:

> "Of the increase of his government there will be no end . . . upholding it with justice and righteousness, FROM THAT TIME ON AND FOREVER. THE ZEAL OF THE LORD ALMIGHTY WILL ACCOMPLISH THIS."
>
> Isaiah 9:7 (NIV)

> " . . . one who will be ruler over Israel, WHOSE

> ORIGINS ARE FROM OLD, FROM ANCIENT TIMES."
>
> Micah 5:2 (NIV)

> "Rejoice greatly, O daughter of Zion! Shout, Daughter of Jerusalem! See your king comes to you . . . He will proclaim peace to the nations. His rule will extend from sea to sea and from the River to the ends of the earth."
>
> Zechariah 9:9a, 10b (NIV)

If there is one common thread that runs through all these prophecies it is simply this: IF EVERYONE TALKS ABOUT A UNIVERSAL AND ETERNAL RULER, THEN BY DEFINITION IT CAN ONLY REFER TO ONE PERSON.

Son of Man and Son of God

By the time we get to Daniel, this same Universal Ruler is clearly identified also. However, the next step Daniel takes is truly startling. He adds two new titles to this king: Son of Man and Son of God and, contrary to other cites in Scripture, neither one of them is mortal:

> "Then King Nebuchadnezzar leaped to his feet in amazement and asked his advisors, Weren't there three men that we tied up and threw into the fire? They replied, Certainly, O King. He said, Look! I see four men walking around in the fire, unbound and unharmed, AND THE FOURTH LOOKS LIKE A SON OF THE GODS."
>
> Daniel 3:24-25 (NIV)

> "In my vision at night I looked, and there before me WAS ONE LIKE A SON OF MAN, COMING WITH THE CLOUDS OF HEAVEN."
>
> Daniel 7:13 (NIV)

And, elsewhere:

> "Your vine is cut down, burned with fire; at your rebuke your people perish. LET YOUR HAND REST ON THE MAN AT YOUR RIGHT HAND, THE SON OF MAN YOU HAVE RAISED UP FOR YOURSELF."
>
> Psalm 80:16-17 (NIV)

Finally, Daniel also leaves no doubt that the "Son of Man" and the Universal King are the same person. Continuing from his introduction" we are also told:

> "His dominion is an everlasting dominion that will not pass away, and his kingdom is one that will never be destroyed."
>
> Daniel 7:15 (NIV)

The Suffering Servant

However, there is a more vulnerable side to the Messiah that seems at odds with these other visions of eternal royal glory. After all, how could an eternal, immortal king also die an ignominious death? Over the centuries, many sages and rabbis have concluded that such contradictions prove that TWO Messiahs were needed. The first was to sacrifice himself, and the second would rule. However, it is equally clear that the prophet who wrote about this more than any other, is in sharp disagreement. We begin with the kingly side:

> "See my servant will act wisely, HE WILL BE RAISED AND LIFTED UP AND HIGHLY EXALTED."
>
> Isaiah 52:13 (NIV)

And yet, this same "exalted one" doesn't look the part:

> "Just as there were many WHO WERE APPALLED AT HIM, HIS APPEARANCE WAS DISFIGURED BEYOND THAT OF ANY MAN, AND HIS FORM MARRED BEYOND HUMAN LIKENESS . . ."
>
> Isaiah 52:14 (NIV)

However, the very next line also leaves no doubt that ugly servant and future king are one and the same:

> "So he will sprinkle many nations AND KINGS WILL SHUT THEIR MOUTHS BECAUSE OF HIM. FOR WHAT THEY WERE NOT TOLD THEY WILL SEE, AND WHAT THEY HAVE NOT HEARD, THEY WILL UNDERSTAND."
>
> Isaiah 52:15 (NIV)

The only other question is: How does a disfigured, suffering servant invoke the humility of kings and become exalted? That answer, which is revealed in Isaiah's next chapter, will have to wait for later.

Andrew Gabriel Roth

THE STRANGENESS OF WHERE

An Uncommon Place

> "Nicodemus, who had gone to Y'shua earlier and who was one of their own number, asked, Does our law condemn anyone without first hearing him to find out what he is doing?
>
> They replied, Are you from Galilee too? Look into it, AND YOU WILL FIND A PROPHET DOES NOT COME OUT OF GALILEE."
>
> John 9:50-52 (NIV)

With the Jewish nation under a constant state of suppression, it became natural for the spiritual leaders to focus their messianic hopes on the kingly Messiah. However, lost in the shuffle was the fact that while the Messiah would save Jerusalem, he would not come from there:

> "But you Bethlehem, Ephrathah, though you are small in the clans of Judah, OUT OF YOU WILL COME FOR ME ONE WHO WILL BE RULER OVER ISRAEL, WHOSE ORIGINS ARE FROM OF OLD, FROM ANCIENT TIMES."
>
> Micah 5:2 (NIV)

As anyone can see, this is another feature of Scripture that must have struck even its writer as bizarre. Jerusalem was, after all, David's city, and since everyone knew the Messiah would sit on the throne of David, it would seem logical to have him come from there and not from some backwater country to the south. Then, in Jeremiah, the bizarre turns into the macabre, as a horrible slaughter of infants points not only to the place, but to the time as well:

> "This is what the LORD says: A voice is heard in Ramah, mourning and great weeping. Rachel weeping for her children and refusing to be comforted, because her children are no more."
>
> Jeremiah 31:15 (NIV)

In the history of the world, no one has ever prophesied the coming of a great king with a massacre of infants. Surely, this would not have been the preferred image Jeremiah would have recorded, HAD NOT GOD COMPELLED HIM TO WRITE IT THAT WAY! The question then arises: Where is Ramah? Joshua gives us the answer:

> "It touched Zebulin on the south, Asher on the west and the Jordan on the East. The fortified cities were Ziddim, Hammath, Kinnereth, Adamah, Ramah..."
>
> Joshua 19:36 (NIV)

Some strange names to be sure, until we combine them once again with Isaiah:

> "Nevertheless there will be no more gloom for those who were in distress. IN THE PAST HE HUMBLED THE LAND OF ZEBULIN AND NAPHTALI, BUT IN THE FUTURE HE WILL HONOR GALILEE OF THE GENTILES BY THE WAY OF THE SEA, ALONG THE JORDAN. The people walking in darkness have seen a great light; on those living in the

land of the shadow of death, a new light has dawned."

Isaiah 9:1-2 (NIV)

Isn't it also interesting that this same section also describes the coming of the Universal King JUST FOUR LINES LATER?

As for Rachel herself, she will bear the child named Naphtali while her sister Leah gives birth to Zebulin, (Genesis 30:7, 19-21).

Interestingly enough, this is also reflected in the ancient Jewish mystical traditions as well:

> "At that time when the dead will be awakened and be in readiness for the resurrection in the Holy Land, LEGIONS UPON LEGIONS WILL ARISE ON THE SOIL OF GALILEE, AS IT IS THERE THAT THE MESSIAH IS DESTINED TO REVEAL HIMSELF. For that is the portion of Joseph (sic), and it was the first part of the Holy Land to be destroyed, and it was thence that the exile of Israel and their dispersion among the nations began."
>
> Zohar Exodus 220a

So, rather than having Galilee denied as the place of a true prophet, IN TRUTH THE GREATEST PROPHET OF THEM ALL COULD COME FROM NOWHERE ELSE!

THE MYSTERY OF WHEN:

The Handwriting on the Wall

Of all the detailed prophecies contained about the Messiah in the OT, only one, Daniel 9:24-27 gives us any precise information about the time of his appearance. Unfortunately, Daniel does not make it easy, choosing to couch this information inside some very figurative language:

> "Seventy sevens are decreed for your people and your holy city to finish transgression, to put an end to sin, to atone for wickedness, to bring in everlasting righteousness, to seal up vision and prophecy, and to anoint the most holy..."
>
> Daniel 9:24 (NIV)

"Your people and your holy city" obviously refers to the Jews and Jerusalem, respectively. The rest of that first line is addressing several issues, such as the end to the old sacrificial system and the true identity of the Messiah. Daniel now moves into giving us some very specific temporal information:

> "Know therefore and understand this. From the issuing of the decree to rebuild Jerusalem, to the coming of the Anointed One, the ruler comes, there will be seven sevens and sixty-two sevens. It will be rebuilt with streets and a trench, but in troubled times..."
>
> Daniel 9:25 (NIV)

Now some scholars point out that "Messiah" as a proper title is not an accurate translation. Rather, it should read "an anointed one" or "an anointed prince" because the definite article "the" (ha) is missing from the word "meshiach", which when translated into Greek becomes "Messiahos". However, "an anointed one" is still an apt title for Messiah, proper or not, as this Psalm clearly shows:

"The LORD swore unto David in truth; He will not turn back from it. 'Of the fruit of thy body I will set upon thy throne. If thy children keep My covenant and My testimony that I shall teach them, their children shall forever sit upon thy throne."

Psalm 135:11-12

Notice first that the Psalm does not apply to David per se' but to his future descendants. Then, it continues this way:

"For the LORD hath chosen Zion; He hath desired it for His habitation. 'This is My resting place forever. Here I will dwell for I have desired it. I will abundantly bless her provision . . . THERE I WILL MAKE A HORN TO SHOOT OUT OF DAVID. THERE I HAVE ORDERED A LAMP OF MINE ANOINTED. HIS ENEMIES I WILL CLOTHE IN SHAME; BUT UPON HIMSELF SHALL HIS CROWN SHINE.'"

Psalm 135:13-15,17-18

So we can see then that this descendant of David, who is given divine status elsewhere in the Hebrew Bible, can still be called "an anointed one."

The other point from Daniel's first line is to understand that in biblical language, a prophetic day equals a year of actual time (Ezekiel 4:4-6).

In this case we are told the total time frame of this prophecy is "seventy sevens" i.e. seventy weeks, or 490 years (7 x 70), starting from the time of "the issuing of the decree to rebuild Jerusalem." Now when did this happen?

King Cyrus of Persia allowed the Jews to return to Jerusalem to rebuild the Temple in 538 BCE.[86] Over the years this legislation got lost until Cyrus' successor Darius found it again. The new king then issued his own version, and advanced funds out of his own treasury to finish the Temple on March 12, 515 BCE.[87]

However, notice that Daniel is not referring to the rebuilding of the Temple alone, **but to all of Jerusalem.**

Since neither Cyrus nor Darius ordered that all of Jerusalem be rebuilt[88], neither king's edict can be the one referred to by Daniel. The correct decree, one which did authorize the total rebuilding of the city, was signed by another Persian King, Artaxerxes, in the year 457 BCE, (Ezra 7:11-26).[89]

Now a common mistake some scholars make is selecting a verse from the second chapter of Nehemiah as the start of Daniel's "clock".[90] In that year, 445 BCE, Nehemiah makes a formal request to return to Jerusalem. Nehemiah also requests various "letters" be granted to him to guarantee his safe passage and to prove he has the authority of the King behind him.

However, these "letters" are not the decree itself. Rather, they are the supporting documentation of that decree. When we look at the historical record, the actual decree was not addressed to Nehemiah at all:

> "Artaxerxes, king of kings, to Ezra the priest, a teacher of the Law of the God of heaven: Greetings. Now I decree that any of the Israelites in my kingdom, including priests and Levites, who wish to go to Jerusalem with you, may go."
>
> Ezra 7:12-13 (NIV)

The king has given his permission by royal decree for the Israelites to go, and Ezra, along with a number of other prominent men and their families, make good on his word and leave. However, when they get to Israel, many problems impede their progress in rebuilding the city. The difficulties become so great that even 12 years later, not much has been done.[91]

Enter Nehemiah, the cup-bearer (or wine taster) to this same king. One day Artaxerxes notices that his valuable servant looks sad, and asks why. Nehemiah responds:

> "If it pleases the king and if your servant has found favor in his sight, let him send me to the city in Judah where my fathers are buried so I can rebuild it."
>
> Nehemiah 2:5 (NIV)

With his decree already in force, Artaxerxes, along with his wife, heartily agree and release Nehemiah from his current duties. When Nehemiah arrives to help Ezra, the city-wide restoration work begins in earnest.

Therefore, 457 BCE is the only date that fits into the strict description in Daniel 9 for two reasons. First, it is the only one that deals with rebuilding of all of Jerusalem and not just the Temple and second, it is the actual year the decree was written, as opposed to the time it was applied in Nehemiah's case. Now that we have the start, we can translate Daniel's time code accurately.

The total years from our start date to the appearance of the Messiah is 69 weeks, or 483 years, which therefore brings us inexorably to the common year 27 as the time that the Messiah makes his debut.

The New Covenant

There are still other signs that will let the believer know, in a general sense, when the Messiah is on his way. Many people mistakenly believe, however, that the "New Covenant" was a wholly Christian invention. The fact is, as early as 629 BCE, Jeremiah knew parts of the old ways were coming to an end:

> "The time is coming, declares the LORD, when I will make a new covenant with the house of Israel and the house of Judah. IT WILL NOT BE LIKE THE COVENANT I MADE WITH THEIR FOREFATHERS when I took them by the hand to lead them out of Egypt..."

Jeremiah 31:31-32a (NIV)

Now let's stop here for just a second and look at two points. First, the "new covenant" is not the same as the one given during the Exodus. Second, even though the fulfillment of the Mosaic Law did not make it obsolete, (Matthew 5:17-20), the very nature of the New Covenant will bring about certain changes. This is not, as Jeremiah clearly states next, because God has changed. Instead, this New Covenant is a contingency set in place WHEN THE ORIGINAL WAS WRITTEN, (Deuteronomy 30:11-20), and the reason for this contingency being triggered, is very clear:

> "... BECAUSE THEY BROKE MY COVENANT, THOUGH I WAS A HUSBAND TO THEM, DECLARES THE LORD..."

Jeremiah 31:32b (NIV)

The consequences of that initial break were the destruction of the First Temple and the Captivity in Babylon. However, God also made it clear He would restore a remnant to Israel once again, and he would give His holy nation another chance:

> "But this is the covenant I will make with Israel at that time. I will put their law in their minds and write it on their hearts. I will be their God and they will be my people. No longer will a man teach his

> neighbor or a man his brother, 'know the LORD', because they will all know Me. From the least of them to the greatest, declares the LORD. FOR I WILL FORGIVE THEIR WICKEDNESS AND WILL REMEMBER THEIR SINS NO MORE."

> Jeremiah 31:33-37 (NIV)

The method that God will "put My Law in their hearts", is obviously by the Counselor, otherwise known as the Holy Spirit. The part of forgiving their sins will, as we will see, become a function of the Messiah himself.

THE WONDER OF HOW

The Ancient of Days

One of the most astonishing aspects of this study is that, in spite of the fact so many details were predicted hundreds of years in advance, many had a hard time accepting the truth when it arrived.[92] Even John the Baptist's father, a learned priest, could not believe it when the angel was right in front of him However, as compelling as the prediction regarding the Messiah's virgin birth is, the answer to the question of HOW does not start here. Rather, we must go back to Daniel again and his Son of Man/Son of God figure.

In what is perhaps one of the most incredible visions of them all, Daniel is actually allowed to view a kind of coronation ceremony that the rest of us could only imagine and tremble at. At the heart of it are two divine beings. Here is how he describes the first, "The Ancient of Days":

> "As I looked, thrones were set in place, and the Ancient of Days took his seat. His clothing was white as snow; and the hair of his head was white

> like wool. His throne was flaming with fire, and its wheels were all ablaze. A river of fire was coming out before him. Thousands upon thousands attended him; ten thousand times ten thousand stood before him. The court was seated and the books were opened."

Daniel 7:9-10 (NIV)

And now, the full verse regarding the "Son of Man" and his relationship to Almighty God:

> "In my vision at night I looked, and there before me was one like a son of man, coming with the clouds of heaven. HE APPROACHED THE ANCIENT OF DAYS AND WAS LED INTO HIS PRESENCE. HE WAS GIVEN AUTHORITY, GLORY AND SOVEREIGN POWER; ALL PEOPLES, NATIONS AND MEN OF EVERY LANGUAGE WORSHIPPED HIM. HIS DOMINION IS AN EVERLASTING DOMINION THAT WILL NOT PASS AWAY, AND HIS KINGDOM IS ONE THAT WILL NEVER BE DESTROYED."

Daniel 7:13-14 (NIV)

Immanuel

So now we are given the additional detail that, even before the Messiah's birth, God had given him power and dominion over the entire world. This inevitably leads us to the next step:

> "Therefore the LORD Himself will give you a sign:

> The young woman will conceive and give birth to a son, and will call him Immanuel."
>
> Isaiah 7:14 (NIV)

The key to this verse is the Hebrew word *almah*, which has been translated as "a young woman of marriageable age". However, if this is correct, a question arises: What is so miraculous about a young woman conceiving a son? The answer comes from a secondary meaning of the same word: "virgin". Proof of this is found in the Greek translation of the Old Testament, or Septuagint. In the two centuries before Messiah when it was written, Jews everywhere understood that *almah* was the Hebrew equivalent to the Greek *parthenos*, which can only mean "virgin".[93] Otherwise, Immanuel is too common a name to be associated with any one man!

The second critical aspect has to do with the name itself. Immanu is the root of the Hebrew word "with us" and "El" is a name for God. Therefore, the name represents a kind of coded message which actually means: "Behold a virgin will conceive and will give birth to a son, who will be called "God with us", or , "who will BE God with us".[94]

The Later Ministry

With all of this evidence so far, it probably is not necessary to be given prophecies regarding the actual ministry itself. Surely having the exact family line, time, place and name of the Messiah centuries in advance is enough. However, even here, God is not finished.

Now we enter an astonishing degree of detail that, in some cases, records the very words of participants yet to be born. The prophetic lens gets particularly sharp regarding the events of Passion Week. We begin with the Messiah's triumphant entry:[95]

> "Rejoice greatly, O daughter of Zion! Shout, Daughter of Jerusalem. See your king comes to you, righ-

teous and having salvation, gentle and riding on a donkey."

> Zechariah 9:9 (comp Matthew 21:1)

However, soon after this, the Messiah will be betrayed by someone close to him:

> "Even my close friend, whom I trusted, has lifted up his heel against me."

> Psalm 41:9 (comp Mark 14:10)

The betrayer also was paid a certain sum for his "service"

> "I told them, If you think it best, give me my pay, but if not, keep it. So they paid me thirty pieces of silver."

> Zechariah 11:12 (comp to Matthew 27:3-10)

After the deed was done, however, the blood money was returned to a very specific place:

> "And the LORD said to me, Throw it to the potter, the handsome price that they had priced me, so I took the thirty pieces of silver and threw them into the house of the LORD to the potter."

> Zechariah 11:13 (comp to Matthew 27:6-7)

Then the betrayer himself is replaced:

> "When he is tried let him be found guilty, and may

his prayer condemn him. May his days be few and may another take his place."

> Psalm 109:7-8 (comp to Acts 1:18-20)

Meanwhile, the Messiah is handed over to false accusers:

> "Do not turn me over to the desires of my foes, for false witnesses rise up against me, breathing violence."

> Psalm 35:11 (comp to Matthew 26:60-61)

And then, after a sham hearing, he is struck and spit on:

> "I offered my back to those who beat me; my cheeks to those who pulled out my beard; I did not hide my face from mocking and spitting."

> Isaiah 50:6 (comp to Mark 14:65)

This is followed by a horrendous execution involving impalement:

> "Dogs have surrounded me; a band of evil men has encircled me. They have pierced my hands and my feet."

> Psalm 22:16 (comp to Mark 15:25)

As the Messiah's enemies watch his torment, even their very insults were recorded in advance:

> "But I am a worm and not a man, scorned by men and despised by the people. All who see me mock

me; they hurl insults, shaking their heads: he trusts in the LORD, let the LORD rescue him. Let Him deliver him, since He delights in him."

Psalm 22:6-8 (comp to Matthew 27:39-40)

After hours of excruciating pain, soldiers gamble for his clothing:

"They divide my garments among them and cast lots for my clothing."

Psalm 22:18 (comp to Mark 15:24)

Then they give him gall and vinegar to drink:

"They put gall in my food and give me vinegar for my thirst."

Psalm 69:21 (comp to John 19:29)

The Messiah then performs the remarkable feat of praying for the welfare of his tormentors:

"In return for my friendship they accuse me, but I am a man of prayer."

Psalm 109:4

Then the suffering Messiah finally dies, and he has his side pierced as well:

"And I will pout out on to the house of David a spirit of grace and supplication. They will look on me, the one they have pierced and they will mourn

> for him as one mourns for an only child, and grieve bitterly for him as one grieves for a firstborn son."
>
> Zechariah 12:10 (comp to John 19:34)

Remarkably, however, his body remains intact after all that trauma:

> "He protects all his bones, not one of them will be broken."
>
> Psalm 34:20

Similarly the length of this period, or the duration of the Messiah's ministry, is also foretold in Daniel:

> "And after the sixty two sevens, the anointed one will be cut off and have nothing..."
>
> Daniel 9:26a

The phrase "cut off" is a popular metaphor for death. In the case of Isaiah 53:8, it specifically applies to the death of the Messiah. Notice that Daniel really means after 69 sevens, since the earlier part talked of seven sevens and then sixty two after it. This part of the prophecy tells us only that the death will occur after 27 CE. At first glance this seems both obvious and redundant, but Daniel gives us a clarification later:

> "He will confirm a covenant with many for one seven, but in the middle of that seven he will put an end to sacrifice and offering..."
>
> Daniel 9:27 (NIV)

This verse then also dovetails with Daniel's earlier statement about "putting an end to transgression" which was to happen also at this same time, the 70th week. Since the death is scheduled for the middle of this same week, we now have the duration of the Messiah's public career from the start of his ministry to the end of his life: 3 and a half years.

If we only include the start of Y'shua's public works, from the Baptism, Daniel hits the year on the nose, and his estimate of the ministry is off by only four months. However, the year 27 begins by Jewish reckoning on the previous August 31st, when the Baptist began "preparing the way for the LORD". In that case, Daniel is now accurate to within a week of the Crucifixion. Either way, it's a pretty incredible estimate; one well beyond the realms of coincidence and luck.

And now we stop here for the present, for our next section will show that, for the Messiah at least, the prophecies don't end with his death.

THE BEAUTY OF WHY

Leader of the Banned

" . . . you will not abandon me to the grave, nor will you let your Holy One see decay."

Psalm 16:10

"When you ascended on high, you led captives in your train; you received gifts from men, even the rebellious—that You, O LORD God, might dwell there."

Psalm 68:18

> "In my vision at night I looked, and there before me was one like a son of man, coming with the clouds of heaven."
>
> Daniel 7:13
>
> "I have not learned wisdom, nor have I knowledge of the Holy One. Who has gone up to heaven and come down? Who has gathered the wind in the hollow of his hands? Who has wrapped up the waters in his cloak? Who has established the ends of the earth? What is his name, and the name of his son? Tell me if you know!"
>
> Proverbs 30:3-4

These previously quoted verses each give a sliver of insight in answering the most vital question of all: Why? However, in all the breadth and depth of the entire Hebrew Bible, only one chapter, Isaiah 53, finally gives us that last piece.

For centuries, rabbis grappled with its implications, attacked it on linguistic grounds, or set up metaphoric facades to explain it away. And yet, in spite of the fact that this verse taken at face value bodes poorly for the conventional Jewish argument, THE VAST MAJORITY OF SAGES AND RABBIS HAVE AFFIRMED IT AS A LITERAL MESSIANIC PROPHECY.

However, because of my exceeding respect and veneration of Hebrew Scripture, as well as for my own people who were inspired to write them, I must do the literary equivalent of bending over backwards to be fair to both sides. No verse in all of Jewish history has ever excited more controversy, and therefore any analysis of its implications must be taken with great care.

First, I will explore the full breadth of the Talmudic debate, BOTH PRO AND CON, regarding it. Next, I will detail how the rabbis deliberated about the verse and provide their own linguistic rules governing it. Additionally, I will not link it to any verse in the New Scriptures, but will allow it to stand on its own, with commentary relating to Hebrew sources only.

My final provision has to do with the translation I have been using. Up until now, I have alternated between the New International Version and the Masoretic Text for the Tenakh quotes. However, because the former is a Christian work, I am fully aware that a few of the Messianic prophecies cited have come under fire as being bad translations.

For example, Psalm 22:16 NIV reads, "they have pierced my hands and my feet". Jewish translators, aware of the crucifixion imagery, have given the verse an alternate, less clear reading: "like a lion they are at my hands and my feet."[96]

Who is right then? Well, here is what one of the world's leading authorities on the Bible and the Dead Sea Scrolls had to say on the issue:

> "Psalm 22 is a favorite among Christians since it is often linked in the New Testament to the death of Y'shua. A well-known and controversial reading is found in verse 16, where the Masoretic Text reads, 'Like a lion they are at my hands and feet,' whereas the Seputagint has, 'they have pierced my hands and my feet'. Among the scrolls the reading in question in found only in the Psalms scroll found at Nahal Hever (abbreviated 5/6HevPs), which reads 'they have pierced my hands and my feet'!

The Dead Sea Scrolls Bible, p. 518-19.

It is also worth noting that both the LXX and the DSS readings are more than 2000 years old, and that the latter collection is considered to be the oldest known source of biblical writings.

However, again I wish to be fair and state clearly that, even if the JPS obscures a few of these Messianic passages, the vast majority of them remain intact with the exception that the NIV takes out "thee, thy, thine" language. In addition, when I quote from Isaiah 53, I will completely defeat the Christian bias charge altogether by quoting from the JPS instead.

The Rabbinic Record Speaks

The following commentaries have been given by great sages and rabbis over the centuries regarding Isaiah 53 and related prophecies:

Abraham Farissol (1451-1526):

"In this chapter (Isaiah 53) there seem to be considerable resemblances and allusions to the work of the Christian Messiah and to the events which are asserted to have happened to Him, so that no other prophecy is to be found the gist and subject of which can be so immediately applied to Him."

Rabbi Moses Alschech (1508-1600):

"Our Rabbis with one voice accept and affirm the opinion that the prophet (Isaiah, in his 53rd chapter) is speaking of the Messiah, and we shall ourselves also adhere to the same view."

Abrabanel (1437-1508):

"This (view on Isaiah 53) is also the opinion of our own learned men in the majority of their Midrashim."

Rabbi Yafeth Ben Ali (10th Century):

"As for myself, I am inclined to regard it as alluding to the Messiah."

Midrash Tanchuma:

"He was more exalted than Abraham, more extolled than Mose, higher than the archangels" (Isa.52:13).

Maimonides (1135-1204) wrote to Rabbi Jacob Alfajumi:

"Likewise said Isaiah that He (Messiah) would appear without acknowledging a father or mother: 'He grew up before him as a tender plant and as a root out of a dry ground' etc. (Isa.53:2)."

Targum Jonathan (4th Century) introduction on Isa. 52:13:

"Behold, my servant the Messiah . . ."[97]

Yalkut Schimeon (ascribed to Rabbi Simeon Kara), 12th Century on Zech.4:7:

"He (the king Messiah) is greater than the patriarchs, as it is said, 'My servant shall be high, and lifted up, and lofty exceedingly' (Isa. 52:13)."

Pesiqta Rabbati (ca.845) on Isa. 61,10:

"The world-fathers (patriarchs) will one day in the month of Nisan arise and say to (the Messiah):

'Ephraim, our righteous Anointed, although we are your grandparents, yet you are greater than we, for you have borne the sins of our children, as it says: 'But surely he has borne our sicknesses and carried our pains; yet we did esteem him stricken, smitten of God and afflicted. But he was pierced because of our transgressions, he was bruised for our iniquities: the chastisement of our peace was laid upon him and through his wounds we are healed (Isa.53,4-5).''

Rabbi Elijah de Vidas (16th. Century):

"The meaning of 'He was wounded for our transgressions, bruised for our iniquities' is, that since the Messiah bears our iniquities which produce the effect of His being bruised, it follows that whoever will not admit that Messiah thus suffers for our iniquities must endure and suffer for them himself."

Siphre:

"Rabbi Jose the Galilean said, 'Come and learn the merits of the King Messiah and the reward of the Just—from the first man who received but one commandment, a prohibition, and transgressed it. Consider how many deaths were inflicted upon himself, upon his own generation, and upon those who followed them, till the end of all generations. Which attribute is greater, the attribute of goodness, or the attribute of vengeance?'-He answered, 'The attribute of goodness is greater, and the attribute of vengeance is the less.'—'How much more then, will the King Messiah, who endures affliction and pains for the transgressions (as it is written, 'He was wounded, etc.), justify all generations. This is the meaning of the word, 'And the LORD made the iniquity of us all to meet upon Him', (Isa.53:6)."

Rabbi Eleazer Kalir (9th.Century) wrote the following Musaf Prayer:

"Our righteous Messiah has departed from us. Horror has seized us and we have no one to justify us. He has borne our transgressions and the yoke of our iniquities, and is wounded because of our transgressions. He bore our sins upon His shoulders that we may find pardon for our iniquity. We shall be healed by His wounds, at the time when the Eternal will recreate Him a new creature. Oh bring Him up from the circle of the earth, raise Him up from Seir, that we may hear Him the second time."

Pesiqta (on Isa. 61:10):

"Great oppressions were laid upon You, as it says: 'By oppression and judgement he was taken away; but who considered in his time, that he was cut off out of the land of the living, that he was stricken because of the sins of our children' (Isa.53:8), as it says: 'But the LORD has laid on him the guilt of us all' (Isa.53:6)."

While this list is fairly comprehensive, that does not mean there were not any dissenters. Rabbis such as Rashi and Ibn Ezra, for example, used linguistic evidence to assert that the Messiah did not bear the diseases of others but suffered from a chronic disease himself. Since Y'shua was healthy, this is used to discredit his claim. However, there are many instances when the key words (makov, choli) are used to invoke images of oppression and slavery and NOT DISEASE, (Ecclesiastes 1:18, Psalm 32:10, Jeremiah 30:15, Lamentations 1:18) or the image these words convey takes on the form of a spiritual dilemma, (Jeremiah 6:7, 10:19).[98]

It was these verses, and many others, that other rabbis used to completely discredit the anti-Messiah argument. They also vigorously opposed another strategy, namely that the Messiah was somehow Israel itself, and that a Messianic Age could be ushered in WITHOUT a Messiah! Here is how these points were met and discredited:

Herz Homberg (1749-1841):

"According to the opinion of Rabbis Rashi and Ibn Ezra, it (Isaiah 53) relates to Israel and the end of their captivity . . . But if so, what can the meaning of the passage, 'he was wounded for our transgressions' be? Who as wounded? Who are the transgressors? Who carried the sickness and bore the pain?"

Rabbi Moses, 'The Preacher' (11th. Century) wrote in his commentary on Genesis (page 660):

"From the beginning God has made a covenant with the Messiah and told Him ,'My righteous Messiah, those who are entrusted to you, their sins will bring you into a heavy yoke '..And He answered, 'I gladly accept all these agonies in order that not one of Israel should be lost.' Immediately, the Messiah accepted all agonies with love, as it is written: 'He was oppressed and he was afflicted'."

Gersonides (1288-1344) on Deut. 18:18:

> "In fact Messiah is such a prophet, as it is stated in the Midrash on the verse, 'Behold, my servant shall prosper . . . ' (Isa. 52:13)."

I would therefore submit respectfully that I affirm the majority opinion of the sages and rabbis regarding their view of the Messiah. The fact is, the view of the Messiah presented here is an Orthodox Jewish one, since all Scriptures are held sacred, their commentaries highly regarded, and an intensive study of the original Hebrew is employed. With all these facts in mind, I now cautiously proceed to Isaiah 53, as translated by the Jewish Publication Society:

> "Who would have believed our report?[99] And to whom hath the arm of the LORD been revealed?[100]
>
> For he shot up right forth as a sapling[101], and as a root out of a dry ground. He had no form or comeliness that we should look upon him, nor beauty that we should delight in him.
>
> He was despised and forsaken of men. A man of pains, and acquainted with disease, and as one from whom men hide their face[102].
>
> He was despised, and we esteemed him not.
>
> Surely our diseases he did bear, and our pains he carried. Whereas we did esteem him stricken, smitten of God, and afflicted.
>
> But he was wounded for our transgressions. He was crushed for our iniquities. The chastisement of our welfare was upon him, and with his stripes we were healed.

All we like sheep did go astray. We turned away everyone to his own way, and the LORD hath made to light on him, the iniquity of us all.[103]

He was oppressed, though he humbled himself and opened not his mouth, as a lamb that is led to slaughter, and as a sheep that before her shearers is dumb.[104]

Yea, he opened not his mouth. By oppression and judgment he was taken away, and with his generation who did reason?

For he was cut off from the land of the living.[105] For the transgression of my people to whom the stroke was due.

And they made his grave with the wicked, and with the rich his tomb[106], although he had done no violence. Neither was any deceit in his mouth.

Yet it pleased the LORD to crush him by disease,[107] to see if his soul would offer itself in restitution.[108] That he might see his seed, prolong his days, and that the purpose of the LORD might prosper by his hand.

Of the travail[109] of his soul he shall see to the full, even My servant, who by his knowledge did justify the Righteous One to the many. And their iniquities he did bear.

Therefore I will divide him a portion among the great, and he shall divide spoil with the mighty,

> because he bared his soul unto death and was numbered with the transgressors.
>
> Yet he bore the sin of many, and made intercession for the transgressors."
>
> Isaiah 53:1-12

At this point I think little else need be said. Isaiah has described the Messiah with far greater passion and grace than I ever could attempt to do. The only thing I would like to add is simply to state the obvious: No one needs get a New Testament to see a clear view of the Messiah. The image presented in the Tenakh is a consistent, shining, faithful mirror of what would later be recorded and grounded in historical fact. Furthermore, none of this should be surprising, since a Hebrew Messiah predicted by Hebrew prophets will find the greatest insights in the language that the revelation sprang from in the first place.

Is There a Seventh Side?

Revisiting the Mystical Tradition

First, it should be noted that there is some controversy as to the origin of the Zohar, The Book of Splendor. Here is what the world's leading authority on Jewish mysticism, Gershom Scholem, had to say on the issue:

> "The most radical opinion was put forth by Heinrich Graetz. He declared that all parts of the Zohar without exception to be the work of Spanish kabbalist Moses de Leon, who died in 1305, and the great historian emptied the vials of an exceedingly vehement wrath over him. Very few reputa-

> tions have come down from the school of Graetz in so battered and pitiable a state as de Leon's... In contrast to this view, the Zohar has been regarded, especially in the preceding generation, as a work altogether without unity, or else one that grew anonymously in the course of time... In either case, Moses de Leon is regarded as the redactor of ancient writings and fragments, to which he may perhaps have added something of his own... THE THEORY THAT "PRIMITIVE" SOURCES AND DOCUMENTS HAVE BEEN PRESERVED IN THE ZOHAR, ALTHOUGH ADMITTEDLY IN A REVISED FORM, IS TODAY WIDESPREAD."
>
> Zohar: The Book of Splendor. Basic Readings from the Kabbalah, p. xiii

Just how much further back these teachings go is almost impossible to determine. Certainly, no serious scholar will accept the fantastic claims that the mystics had recovered secrets from the Garden of Eden[110]. However, other ancient claims do appear more credible, such as linking a small part of the mystical tradition to a much larger body of teachings that became known as the Oral Law, which reportedly originated with Moses at Mount Sinai. Still another scenario sheds almost another millennia off by declaring the prophet Ezekiel as the progenitor of all mystics[111]. What we do know however is that in later centuries the lions' share of torah she'be'al peh ceased being an oral tradition altogether and became compiled into the work we call the Talmud today.

On the other hand, Moses de Leon, the alleged author and certain compiler of the Zohar, himself claimed that his teachings came from an ancient book written by another rabbi who lived in the second century. Additionally, De Leon's rabbi is also accredited with helping compile the Talmud and Mishnah, thus making the case for these other mystical teachings as part of the oral tradition even stronger.

However, in spite of the intense skepticism on the part of Gershom Scholem that Rabbi Simon ben Yonai actually spoke and/or wrote the words attributed to him by de Leon, there are other indications that the mystical tradition stretched back centuries earlier. In particular, another similar collection of writings that held many ideas in common with the Zohar, has been traced between the third and sixth centuries of the common era. Called Sefer Yetzirah, or "Book of Creation", it represents an independent version of the Jewish mystical view, and may even have served as a kind of rough draft for the later and more fully developed works. [112]

To this mix we must also add one more body of Jewish thought that contains an even earlier mystical memory than either the Zohar or the Book of Creation. Unfortunately, no conventional Jewish scholar would include it because, in spite of copious evidence to the contrary, they did not view it as an authentic Semitic document. Today, we know this vessel of proto-mysticism by another name— the New Testament—and the concordance in some cases is striking, as we will show clearly going forward.

In any case, these teachings are of great antiquity, and the evidence suggests that their later suppression by many modern authorities (i.e. since 1600 CE) may have more to do with its agreements with Christian Scriptures as opposed to disagreements with Jewish practice. We will also be able to trace how many of these ideas, admittedly in a more primitive form as Scholem said, have actually been part of the Jewish mindset for thousands of years and are derived from that tradition.

Andrew Gabriel Roth

The Basics of the Mystical Argument
(Ein Sof, Ayin and Sefirot)

With that in mind, let us look at how the basic statements of the mystics concord directly with the Scripture. We'll start with a very unique name for God.

Many of you are certainly aware that several names for God are given in the Hebrew Bible (YHWH, Elohim, Adonai, etc.) and that each one imparts something special about His Being or Nature. However, the mystics employ a name that is found nowhere either in Old or New Testaments. They call Him *Ein Sof*, which literally means "without end", because both His Eternity and Infiniteness are basic to His Nature:

> "The eternal God is your refuge, and underneath are the everlasting arms."

Deuteronomy 33:17

> "But will God really dwell on earth? The heavens, even the highest heavens, cannot contain You, much less the Temple I built!"

1 Kings 8:27

God also possesses infinite Mind and Spirit. Therefore, since we are finite beings, any attempt to define God will inevitably bring about a gap between our vision and the reality. It therefore takes infinity to define infinity.

Nevertheless, ancient Judaism does teach that God's infinity is expressed through the finite via attributes of His being. In other words, the Bible does describe emanations of God that can be quantified in spite of His omnipresence. In particular, many "spirits" of God are given formal titles, while other characteristics are simply named directly. When the mystics looked at these key verses and took them to the sode (secret) level, they gave them the term *sefirot*, and then explained how they came from God during the Creation itself. At that time, there was only God (Ein Sof) and Nothingness (represented by the letter Ayin, which is silent). God had the image of the Universe in His Infinite Mind, but, when He decided to bring it into existence, He spoke, just as Genesis says:

> "And God said, 'Let there be light', and there was light."
>
> Genesis 1:3

So God's Word actually brought about the creation, and there will be much more on this point later on. For now, however, the important thing is that within that divine creative light are these same sefirot, with each of their names also enshrined in the Scripture. In this context, all the mystics did then was look at the Hebrew word that described the sefirot and then used that same word as its name[113]. When all was said and done, ten major groupings of related attributes were identified from various biblical sources. Additionally, each group title was supplemented with minor names, gender identities, and even the names of body parts as their collective linkages formed the image of a mystical man.

Therefore, so that we can better understand the source for these divine attributes, I will present the actual quotes and terms side by side. ALL CAPITAL LETTERS THEN DESIGNATE A MAJOR GROUP TITLE, OR THE MOST COMMON NAME THAT THE SEFIROT GO BY.[114] With that in mind, let us peel back the curtain.

> "The Spirit of the LORD will rest upon him.
>
> The Spirit of WISDOM and of UNDERSTANDING

> The Spirit of . . . POWER
>
> The Spirit of knowledge
>
> The Spirit of fear of the LORD."
>
> Isaiah 11:1-2

This quote alone contains four major sefirot titles:

1) LORD (KETER-"Crown")
2) WISDOM (CHOCKMAH)
3) UNDERSTANDING (BINAH)
4) POWER (GEBURAH)

Additional titles are found here:

> "Yours, O LORD is the . . . GLORY and the VICTORY and the MAJESTY, for all that is in the heaven and in the earth is yours. Yours, O LORD, is the KINGDOM."
>
> 1 Chronicles 29:11

Thus:

6) GLORY (TEFERET)
7) VICTORY (NATZACH)
8) MAJESTY (HOD)
9) KINGDOM (MALKUT)

And the two last sefirot then come from here:

> "Behold I lay in Zion for a FOUNDATION

> (YESOD), a stone; a tried stone, a costly cornerstone of sure foundation."
>
> Isaiah 28:16

And:

> "Give thanks to the LORD, for His MERCY (CHESED) endures forever."
>
> 2 Chronicles 20:21

Gender and Body Types

In addition to the main group titles, each of these names can be classified by gender because:

> "So God created man in his own image; in the image of God he created him; MALE AND FEMALE HE CREATED THEM."
>
> Genesis 1:27

Therefore, since both men and women are created in the image of God, it is also clear that some "images" (or attributes) of God are male and some are female. Here is a potent example of the latter.

> "Wisdom calls aloud in the street, she raises her voice in the public squares; at the head of the noisy streets she cries out, in the gateway of the city she makes her speech."
>
> Proverbs 1:20-21

When we combine this in a drash (comparison) with Isaiah 11:1-2, we can see clearly that WISDOM is a Spirit that comes from God, and this is reflected as an identification of the second sefirot in the mystical tradition. Similarly, the attributes CHESED (Mercy) and NATZACH (Victory) are identified as female, as are all references to the Holy Spirit—Ruach Ha Kodesh—which always appears in feminine grammatical form, (e.g. Psalm 51:13). Other verses showing this gender include:

> "The LORD (says) . . . 'I have a long time held My peace. I have been still and refrained Myself. Now I will cry like a travailing woman, gasping and panting at once."
>
> Isaiah 42:13-14 (JPS 1955)
>
> "But Zion said, 'The LORD hath forgotten me.' Can a woman forget her suckling child, that she should not have compassion on the son of her womb. Yea, these may forget. Yet I will not forget thee."
>
> Isaiah 49:14-15 (JPS 1955)
>
> "For thus saith the LORD: Behold I will extend peace to her like a river, and the wealth of nations like an overflowing stream, and ye shall suck thereof; Ye shall be borne upon the side, and shall be dandled upon the knees. As one whom his mother comforteth, so I will comfort you, and ye shall be comforted in Jerusalem."
>
> Isaiah 66:12-13 (JPS 1955)

Obviously, the male attributes of God are much less subtle, and it should be of no surprise that the Crown (Keter) and the Kingdom (Malkut) of God are linked there. However, what is less well known is that God's maleness can be shown in two forms, Father and Son, thusly:

> "For Thou art our Father, for Abraham knoweth us not, and Israel doth not acknowledge us. Thou, O LORD, art our Father, our Redeemer from everlasting is Thy name."

Isaiah 63:19 (JPS 1955)

> "For thus saith the LORD . . . They shall come with weeping and with supplications will I lead them. I will cause them to walk by rivers of waters, in a straight way wherein they will not stumble. For I am become a father to Israel, and Ephraim is My firstborn."

Jeremiah 31:7,9 (JPS 1955)

> "I will tell of the decree: The LORD said unto me: Thou art my son, this day have I begotten thee. Ask of Me and I will give the nations for thine inheritiance."

Psalm 2:7-8 (JPS 1955)

> "When I behold Thy heavens, the work of Thy fingers, the moon and the stars, which Thou hast established, what is man that Thou art mindful of him? And the son of man, that Thou thinkest of him? Yet Thou has made him but little lower than the angels, and hast crowned him with glory and

> honor. Thou hast made him have dominion over the works of Thy hands; Thou hast put all things under his feet."
>
> Psalm 8:4-7 (JPS 1955)
>
> "Who hath ascended up into heaven and descended? Who hath gathered the wind in his fists? Who hath bound the waters in his garment? Who hath established all the ends of the earth? What is His name, and what is His son's name, if thou knowest?"[115]
>
> Proverbs 30:4 (JPS 1955)

All of these sefirot then lay out beautifully on a chart known as "the tree of life", where each one is given a body part. The Keter, obviously, is the head, while Chokmah and Binah represent the shoulders, Gevurah and Chesed the arms, Tiferet the chest, and Hod and Natzach the legs. Most significantly, Yesod (the foundation of the world), which as we will see represents the Messiah, is the male reproductive organ from which creation comes. The Yesod, also known as "the Son of God", literally stands over the Malkut, the very kingdom of God!

Can Three Be One?

So, how do these concepts of Father, Mother and Son develop over centuries of Jewish study and soul searching? The answer, as alluded to earlier, is to take the mother aspect and identify that as the Holy Spirit, and the son aspect with that of the Messiah, and all of his other biblical titles that we have been discussing. However, if the current state of affairs is not enough to convince the reader that a triune

Godhead, singular and united in will, is deeply enshrined in Jewish thought, the following evidence must be added.

We have already seen that one of the names for God, Elohim, is plural, and that God talks of both men and women being made in His images. Now we turn to the most sacred words any Jew will ever speak:

SHEMA YISRAEL ADONAI ELOHAYNU ADONAI ECHAD.

This passage from Deuteronomy 6:4 is so sacred that Jews around the world are commanded to put it on their doorposts and keep it in front of their eyes through phylacteries. However, what is most significant is that the word for "one" is ECHAD. The reason is that ECHAD means "one" in two ways. The first, is as a singular entity. In Genesis 1:5, the phrase "And there was evening and there was morning DAY ONE", is expressed in Hebrew as "yom echad". [116] However, it is the other meaning that is particularly revealing to our study.

ECHAD also can mean a compound singularity, or how one synagogue may have many members inside it. Thus the sages often refer to ECHAD as a "unity". Another word for one, YACHID, can never be taken in the compound sense, so if the writer wanted to convey that God is exclusively singular in all His manifestations, YACHID would be the better word. The reason that word is not chosen, however, is because it would diminish God's power. Or, to put it another way, if God is YACHID it means He is limited and confined only to one form, and that if He chose to do so, would be unable to alter it. Can God be omnipotent and limited in what He wants to do for and with Himself at the same time? With one voice, all the sages cry out no.

Instead, ECHAD is a beautiful thing to call God, for it says that He can be three in one, or one in three, if His Will chooses it to be so. I liken this type of "contradiction" to how science describes light. Depending on how one looks at it, light can be either a particle or a wave, which are technically mutually exclusive things. And yet, quantum physicists have struggled for more than fifty years to show how the overall structure of the waves are comprised of small particles, even as the particles themselves appear to exhibit separate and exclusive behavior. Perhaps then the apostle John was on to something when he went so far as to say that "God is light", (1 John 1:5).

However, in order to make it clear that such a tri-unity is not representative of three separate beings, the sages point to other verses, like this one:

> "Thus saith the LORD, the King of Israel, and his Redeemer, the LORD of Hosts: I am the first and the last, and beside me there is no God."

> Isaiah 44:6 (JPS 1955)

Now we must take a step beyond these words in English, and go back to the way they appear in Hebrew. As many of you may know, it is the convention of most Bible translations, including this one, to substitute the divine name of YHWH for a euphemism. In the Jewish liturgy, the Holy Name (HaShem) is not pronounced with these letters, but is substituted with the word ADONAI. Furthermore, in terms of the written translations, this trend continues by rendering YHWH as LORD in all capital letters. This divine name also appears as the "LORD" in the "LORD of Hosts" title (YHWH tzvaut), and is rounded out by another name, ELOHIM, which appears as "God" in the last part of the sentence. Therefore, when we restore these divine names as they were originally intended to appear, we get the following:

> "Thus says YHWH, King of Israel, and his redeemer, YHWH of hosts: I am the first and the last. Besides Me there is no Elohim."

> Isaiah 44:6 (Restored Version)

Notice also that there is YHWH, AND THEN YHWH'S REDEEMER

CALLED YHWH OF HOSTS! This is then followed by a singular construct (Me), with the compound word "Elohim", which is again plural. So, what we see is that God is saying is that no "redeemer" can come unless He sent him. Additionally, this same redeemer (YHWH of Hosts) comes from no other ELOHIM, for there is only ECHAD, one, unified Being, manifesting all the attributes according to His Will.

Now let us look at how this same concept of tri-unity is applied in mystical tradition.

Recalling how certain attributes of God are given the identity of Father, Son and Mother, we must now take the matter to the next level. When these terms are expressed in the Kabbalah, the result is a diagram showing all the relationships between the ten sefirot. Now just as this diagram assigns body parts and forms the figure of a man, within the overall scheme is a different internal picture. The sefirot also form three columns (sometimes also called pillars) of the Godhead, and at the head of each is the supreme force of the Father, Son or Mother.

The pillars are also called three tzachtzachot, or "supernal lights", and, as Gershom Scholem explains, even he realizes the obvious Jewish connection to certain Christian beliefs:

> "Above all emanated powers, there exist the root of all roots, three hidden lights which have no beginning, for they are the name and essence of the root of all roots ... It is stressed that these lights constitute one essence and one root which is 'infinitely hidden' (ne'lam ad le-ein sof)—literally hidden until Ein Sof—form a kind of kabbalistic trinity that preceded the emanation of the ten sefirot ... In the terminology of the Kabbalah these three lights are called tzachtzachot (splendors). Christians later found an allusion to their own doctrine of trinity in this theory."

Kabbalah by Scholelm, p. 95

In the Zohar, the three lights/pillars are expressed this way:

> "Thus are YHWH; Elohaynu; YHWH but one unity, three substantive beings which are one; and this is indicated by the voice which a person uses in reading the words, 'Hear O Israel', thereby comprehending the understanding of the most perfect unity of EIN SOF (the boundless one); because all three are read with one voice, which indicated a trinity (t'lita)."

The Zohar, volume 2, p. 43

And, even more remarkably:

> "The prescribed form of daily prayer (a confession of the unity in the Godhead), has for its object, that you will know and comprehend it. We have said in many places that this daily form of prayer is one of those passages concerning unity, which is taught in the Scriptures. In Deuteronomy 6:4 we read fist YHWH, then ELOHAYNU and again YHWH, which together make one unity. But how can their names be one? Are they truly one because we call them one? How can three be one can only be known through the revelation of the Ruach Ha Kodesh (Holy Spirit), and, in fact, with closed eyes. This is also the mystery of the voice. The voice is heard only as one sound, yet it consists of three substances—fire, wind, water—but all three are one, as indicated through the mystery of the voice."

Ibid, p. 43

Finally, for those who continue to assert that all these teachings are medieval in origin, the first century Jewish historian Philo, writing on Abraham's encounter with three heavenly beings, is able to prove otherwise:

> "Now it is very good that these three measures should, as it were, be kneaded together in the soul, and mixed up together, in order that so the soul, having been persuaded that the Supreme Being is God, who has raised his head above all his powers, and who is beheld independently of them and who makes himself visible in them, may receive the character of his power and benificence, and become initiated into the perfect mysteries, may not be too ready to divulge the divine secrets to anyone, but may treasure them up in herself, and keeping a check on her speech, may conceal them in silence; for the words of Scripture are 'to make secret cakes', because the sacred and the mystic statements about the one uncreated Being, and about his powers, ought to be kept secret; since it does not belong to every one to keep the deposit of divine mysteries properly."

The Sacrifices of Abel and Cain, XV, 60

It is therefore ironic that Philo, while trying to encourage keeping the mystical tradition secret, has by his utterances ensured the opposite is the case! Because it is only in his writings that we find a clear Jewish reference to these teachings, which even precedes the "legendary" founding of the Kabbalah by Simon ben Yonai by more than 200 years! As for the tri-une Godhead at the heart of the Kabbalah, Philo even refers to this aspect specifically, and parenthetical additions are my own:

> "It is reasonable for one to be three and for three to be one, for they were one by higher principle . . . he makes the appearance of a trinity (triad) . . . he cannot be seen in his oneness without something else, the chief powers, that exist immediately with him . . . The Creative, which is called ELOHIM, and the Kingly, which is called "LORD" (YHWH) . . . Abraham begins to see the sovereign, holy and divine vision in such a way that single appearance appears as a trinity (triad), and the trinity (triad) as a UNITY (ECHAD).
>
> Questions and Answers on Genesis, IV, 2

The Four Mystical Titles of the Messiah:

Adam Kadmon, Memra, Metatron and Tzaadik

With this very brief tour of the mystical tradition and its origins accomplished, let us now look at the first mystical title: Adam Kadmon:

> . . . the form (image) of G-d in which He created man is actually G-d's blueprint form for man. This "form" or "blueprint" consisted of G-d's first thought in creation, and hence the highest level of creation. This is referred to as 'Adam Kadmon' (Primeval Man).
>
> The Bahir; Kaplan edition p. 95

At that time, again according to the Zohar, the Universe and everything in it only existed in the mind of God. However, once the seifirot appear, they link up and form the image of a man. Then, as Gershom Scholem puts it in two key passages:

> "In His active manifestations, the Godhead appears as the dynamic unity of the Sefiroth, portrayed as the "tree of the Sefiroth," or the mystical human form ('Adam Kadmon), who is none other than the concealed shape of Godhead itself... However, the Sefiroth do not appear only in the shape of the tree. They also appear in the form of Primal Man, ('Adam Kadmon), which corresponds to that of earthly man."
>
> On the Mystical Shape of the Godhead; Basic Concepts in the Kabbalah; p 39, 43

And:

> "God entered into the form of the Adam Kadmon..."
>
> Kabbalah by Gershom Scholem p. 116

So now we see a prototype of the idea of God entering into human form, much the same way Isaiah 9:5-6 calls a certain child "Mighty God, Everlasting Father".

The next step is to see that there were always two forms of the same One God. One is the Spirit (Ruach) or Divine Will, and when God decides to do something, He then speaks the Creative Word, memra[117]. This MEMRA is the second mystical title, and the reason for such a tradition is simple, and has a sound Scriptural source:

> "By the Word of YHWH were the heavens made, and all the hosts of them by the Spirit of His mouth."[118]
>
> Psalm 33:6

This verse, of course, parallels the account in Genesis 1:3, where God pronounced light into existence also with a word.

However, one of the barriers to understanding this concept in the Hebrew Bible has been the consistent "cover up" of the divine name YHWH, which occurs more than six thousand times. Any Jew can easily pronounce these letters properly, but a tradition over the last two millennia has forced most of them to obscure the pronunciation into a less sacred word, "Adonai". If, however, the non-Hebrew reader wants to get some sense of the extent of this substitution, look in any prominent English translation (KJV, NIV, etc), and count the times the word LORD appears in all capital letters. Each one of those LORDs is YHWH in Hebrew!

Therefore, when we restore the divine name, an odd thing happens. In spite of the fact there is clearly only one God, there are more than one YHWHs! Consider:

> And YHWH rained brimstone and fire upon Sodom and upon Gomorrah, from YHWH, from the heavens.
>
> Genesis 19:4 (Original Bible Project preliminary edition)

If this sounds odd, it really shouldn't. The fact is, many ancient commentators were aware of this problem in a wide variety of verses. To explain things a bit better, the great sages of the day worked on a series of Aramaic translations called *targums*, and in those writings they inserted the word MEMRA before YHWH (literally "Word of God") to clarify how one God can have two manifestations of Will and Action. Here is just a sampling of the many times this occurred:

> "And the Word of the YHWH caused to descend upon the peoples of Sodom and Gommorah, brimstone and fire from the YHWH in heaven."

Targum on Genesis 19:4

"And the Word of the LORD spoke all these glorious words..."

Targum on Exodus 20:1

Furthermore, when it came to biblical figures, this was also done frequently, starting with Abraham:

"And Abraham trusted in the Word [Memra] of YHWH, and He counted it to him for righteousness."

Targum Onkelos on Genesis 15:6

"And Abraham worshipped and prayed in the name of the Word [Memra] of YHWH, and said, "You are YHWH who does see, but You cannot be seen."

Jerusalem Targum on Genesis. 22:14

Hagar also does the same thing:

"And Hagar praised and prayed in the name of the Word [Memra] of YHWH who had revealed Himself to her."

Jerusalem Targum Genesis 16:3

It was this Word of YHWH that Jacob also believed in:

"And Jacob vowed a vow, saying, "If the Word

> [Memra] of YHWH will be my support, and will keep me in the way that I go, and will give me bread to eat, and raiment to put on, so that I come again to my father's house in peace; then shall the Word [Memra] of YHWH be my Elohim."
>
> Targum Onkelos on Genesis 28:20-21

Additionally, the same applies to a certain famous ship builder:

> "And YHWH said to Noah, "This is the token of the covenant which I have established between My Word [Memra] and between all flesh that is upon the earth."
>
> Targum Onkelos on Genesis 9:17

And then there are the words of King David, in the Psalms:

> "Trust in the Word (MEMRA) of Yah at all times, O people of the house of Israel! Pour out before Him the sighings of your heart; Say, Elohim is our trust forever."
>
> Targum on Psalm 62:9

Additionally, the Targum of Jonathan brings us back to God, stating that this "Word of YHWH" was the actual Creator:

> "And the Word [Memra] of YHWH created man in his likeness, in the likeness of YHWH, YHWH created, male and female created He them."
>
> Targum Jonathan on Genesis 1:27

And, elsewhere:

> "And the Word [Memra] of YHWH said to Moses: "I am He who said unto the world 'Be!' and it was, and who in the future shall say to it 'Be!' and it shall be." And He said: "Thus you shall say to the children of Israel: 'I Am' has sent me to you."
>
> Jerusalem Targum on Exodus 3:14
>
> "The first night, when the "Word (MEMRA) of YHWH" was revealed to the world in order to create it, the world was desolate and void, and darkness spread over the face of the abyss and the "Word (MEMRA) of the LORD" was bright and illuminating and He called it the first night."
>
> Fragmentary Targum on Exodus 12:42

Finally, all of this specifically applies to the Messiah and the prophecies concerning him:

> "But Israel shall be saved by the Word (MEMRA) of YHWH with an everlasting salvation by the Word of YHWH shall all the seed of Israel be justified."
>
> Targum Jonathan on Isaiah. 45:17, 25
>
> "But I will have mercy upon the house of Judah, and I will save them by the Word (MEMRA) of YHWH, their Elohim."
>
> Targum Jonathan on Hosea 1:7

Having come this far, once again we turn to the words of the expert, Gershom Scholem, to explain further:

> "... the memra—the paraphrase used in the Targumim, the Aramaic Bible translations, to refer to God's word. The memra is not merely a linguistic device for overcoming the problem of biblical anthropomorphisms; it has theological significance in its own right. The memra.... is.... a world-permeating force, a reality in the world of matter or mind, the emmanent aspect of Elohim, holding all things under its ominpresent sway.
>
> On the Mystical Shape of the Godhead: Basic Concepts in the Kabbalah, p. 181-182

To this we must then add the words of another prominent mystic who is completely unknown to conventional Jews. However, his writings most certainly date from a great period of antiquity— more than thirteen centuries removed from the alleged "author" Moses de Leon. Furthermore, this early visionary very eloquently expresses all of these concepts long before they took final shape in the Middle Ages. In Aramaic, this great mystic would be known as Yochanan bar Zawdee, but the rest of the world is more familiar with him as the apostle John. Here is how he said the same thing as all the other great sages:

> "In the beginning was the MEMRA (Word).[119], and the Word was with God, and the Word was God. He was with God in the beginning. THROUGH HIM ALL THINGS WERE MADE. WITHOUT HIM NOTHING WAS MADE THAT HAS BEEN MADE. In him was life, and that life was the light of men.

Signs of the Cross: The Search for the Historical Jesus

> The light shines in the darkness, but the darkness has not understood it."

> John 1:1-5

Such a sweeping statement, was echoed by another early authority unknown to conventional Jewry, Ya'acov Ha Tzaadik:[120]

> "Don't be deceived, my dear brothers. Every good and perfect gift is from above, coming down from the Father of the heavenly lights, who does not change like sifting shadows. He chose to give use birth through the word of truth, that we might be a kind of firstfruits of all he created."

> James 1:16-18

However, getting back to Yochanan, he does not stop with just explaining what the Word did. He tells us the next step, that the Word BECAME flesh, and it is this same being who will judge us all:

> "I saw heaven standing open and there before me was white horse, whose rider was called Faithful and True. With justice he judges and makes war. His eyes are blazing fire and on his head are many crowns. He has a name written on him that no one knows but he himself. He is dressed in a robe dipped in blood, AND HIS NAME IS THE WORD OF GOD[121] . . . ON HIS ROBE AND ON HIS THIGH HE HAS THIS NAME WRITTEN: KING OF KINGS AND LORD OF LORDS."

> Revelation 19:11-13,16

Now let us move on. Our third mystical title, metatron, is a synonym for memra. Again we turn to Gershom Schlolem, who speaks of its origins:

> "The origin of the name Metatron is obscure, it is doubtful whether an etymological explanation can be given. It is possible that the name was intended to be a secret . . . or as a result of glossolalia. . . . Among numerous etymological derivations given three should be mentioned: from [Aramaic] matara, keeper of the watch; from [Aramaic] metator, a guide or messenger . . . from the combination of the two Greek words meta and thronos such as metathronios, in the sense of "one who serves behind the throne." However . . . the Greek word thronos does not appear in Talmudic literature."

Kabbalah; p. 380

However, according to the Zohar, the primary text of Rabbinic Kabbalah, the term "Metatron" points to the "keeper" of Israel from Psalm 121:4:

> What shall I do for him [Metatron]? I will commit my whole house into his hand . . . Henceforth be you [Metatron] a KEEPER as it is written (Psalm 121:4) "The KEEPER of Israel . . ."

Zohar; Amsterdam Ed. vol 2 Ex. p. 51

Furthermore, one prominent tradition is particularly helpful, since it clearly states that "metatron" is the same as "the lesser YHWH", the "Word" or, the first name, "Adam Kadmon". [122] Other verses in the Zohar link "metatron" to God, as well as the messianic "keeper of Israel".

> HaShem said to Moses, "Come up unto YHWH"; this is Metatron. He is called by this name Metatron, because in this name are implied two significant facts which indicate His character.
>
> He is LORD (Adon) and emissary (Shaliach). There is also a third idea implied in the name Metatron: it signifies a "keeper" for in the Aramaic language a keeper (or watchman) is called Materat;" and because He is keeper (or preserver of the world, He is called "The Keeper of Israel" (Psalm 121:4).
>
> From the signification of His name, we learn that He is LORD (Adon) over all which is below; because all the hosts of heaven, and all things upon the earth, are put in His headship and his hand.
>
> Targums on Exodus 20:1, 24:1, p. 114, Col. 1, Amsterdam Edition

However, the most significant aspect of metatron is that the Zohar calls him one of three different manifestations of God. The "middle pillar of the Godhead", as the tradition states, is also called THE SON OF YAH (GOD)! This directly relates also to the way the "tree of life" chart is laid out, from left to right, as Father, Son and Mother (Holy Spirit). Very Jewish, indeed, and here is the proof:

> "The Middle Pillar [of the godhead] is Metatron, Who has accomplished peace above, according to the glorious state there.
>
> Zohar, vol. 3., p. 227, Amsterdam Edition
>
> Better is a neighbor that is near, than a brother far

off. This neighbor is the Middle Pillar in the
godhead, which is the Son of Yah.

> Zohar, vol. ii, p. 115, Amsterdam Edition

The Zohar goes even further with this thought, calling this same entity the "first begotten of all the creatures of Elohim":

> "And Abraham said to his oldest servant of his houses" (Genesis 24:2) Who is this of whom it said "his servant?" In what sense must this be understood? Who is this servant? R. Nehori answered: "It is in no other sense to be understood than expressed in the word "His servant," His servant, the servant of Elohim, the chief to His service. And who is he? Metatron, as said. He is appointed to glorify the bodies which are in the grave. This is the meaning of the words "Abraham said to His servant" that is to the servant of Elohim. The servant is Metatron, the eldest of His [YHWH's] House, who is the first-begotten of all creatures of Elohim, who is the ruler of all He has; because Elohim has committed to Him the government over all His hosts."

> Zohar, Gen. P. 126 Amsterdam Edition

Nor do the remarkable similarities stop there. In language that is clearly reminiscent of Isaiah 53, metatron is also THE ONLY MEDIATOR BETWEEN GOD AND MAN:

> "To keep the way of the tree of life." (Genesis 3:24). Who is the way to the tree of life? It is the great Metatron, for he is the way to that great tree,

to that mighty tree of life. Thus it is written, "The Angel of Elohim, which went before the camp of Israel, removed and went behind them." (Exodus 14:19) And Metatron is called the Angel of Elohim. Come and see, thus says R. Simeon. The holy One, blessed Be He, has prepared for Himself a holy Temple above in the heavens, a holy city, a city in the heavens, and called it Jerusalem, the holy city. Every petition sent to the King, must be through Metatron. Every message and petition from here below, must first go to Metatron, and from thence to the king. Metatron is the Mediator of all that comes from heaven down to the earth, or from the earth up to heaven. And because he is the mediator of all, it is written "And the Angel of Elohim, which went before the camp of Israel, removed; that is, before Israel which is above." (Exodus 14:19).

This Angel of Elohim is the same of whom it is written "And YHWH went before them" (Exodus 13:21) to go by day and by night as the ancients have expounded it. Whoever will speak to me [says Elohim] shall not be able to do so, till he has made it known to Metatron. Thus the holy One, blessed be He, on account of the great love to and mercy with which He has over the Assembly of Israel, commits her (the Assembly) to Metatron's care. What shall I do for Him (Metatron)? I will commit my Whole house into His hand, etc. Henceforth be you a Keeper As it is written "The Keeper of Israel" (Psalm 121:4)."

The Zohar; Amsterdam Edition, volume 2 Ex. P. 51

The fourth and final mystical title dovetails very well with prophecies in Isaiah and Jeremiah of a "righteous branch". In Hebrew, the word for righteous is *tzadik*, and over the centuries this too became a formal name for Messiah:

> "Rabbi Eleazar ben Shammua says [it rests] on one pillar, and its name is "TZADIK" (The Righteous One). For it is said: "And TZADIK is the foundation (YESOD) of the World," (Proverbs 10:25).[123]

b. Hagigah 12b

And from the Rabbinic Kabbalah, we have this:

> "A pillar goes from the earth to the heaven, and its name is TZADIK."

Bahir S 71; M 102

That same pillar, the middle one, is the one previously called "the Son of Yah", which in turn is the same as "metatron", which was established as being the same as "the Word of YHWH" and "Adam Kadmon". Therefore, the only conclusion that is possible is that all these titles refer to the same person, the Messiah, who is described elsewhere in the Talmud with identical language!

For now, let us wrap up the study on TZADIK with another quote from Schlolem:

> "The Tsaddik is understood . . . as a mystical symbol of the LORD of Life . . . The life that flows from the higher Sefiroth is "gathered" into this realm; the positive life force is channeled via this last, passively receptive Sefirah, into all the creatures of the world . . . This Sefirah is the source of the souls

> of all living things . . . Gikatilla knows of two primal sources of living water: one in the highest Sefirah, in the Source called Ein-Sof, the concealed Godhead itself; and the other here, in the realm of Tsaddik. . . . The created world only receives the stream of life within the limits of divine law . . ."
>
> On the Mystical Shape of the Godhead: Basic Concepts in the Kabbalah, p. 103-104

This core concept is also voiced by the great mystic Yochanan bar Zawdee. As stated in the above quote, there are two sources of divine water and, he talks about both. First, from the TZADIK, or the Messiah, we have this:

> "Y'shua answered her, 'If you knew the gift of God and who it is who asks you for a drink, you would have asked him, and he would have given you living water . . . Everyone who drinks this water will thirst again, but whoever drinks the water I will give him will never thirst. Indeed the water I will give him will become in him a spring of water welling up to eternal life."
>
> John 4:10,13-14

And second, from the Ein Sof, also known as the Heavenly Father:

> "And he showed me a pure river of living water, clear as crystal, proceeding out of the throne of God and the Lamb. In the middle of the street of it, and on either side of the river was there the tree of life . . ."
>
> Revelation 22:1-2

Nor is John alone in the New Testament in expressing these views:

> "For in him [Y'shua] is embodied all the fullness of the Godhead."
>
> Colossians 2:9 (The Modern New Testament from the Aramaic)
>
> "For the invisible nature of Him from the creation of the world are clearly seen, being understood by His creations, even His eternal power and Godhead . . ."
>
> Romans 1:20 (The Modern New Testament from the Aramaic)

So we now end, in true mystical fashion, exactly where we began, with the question: Is there a seventh side of the Messiah in the mystical writings? It is an answer that now can only be left up for you, the reader, to answer properly. From where this writer sits, just the processing of this information will prove be as painful as it was insightful to all sides. If the reader is a Jew, the question that must arise is why such writings are seldom discussed openly, even as the Talmud appears to embrace all sorts of divergent views on the same topic? If a Christian, then an honest inquiry must lead to a reevaluation of how divergent aspects of Jewish and Christian thought really are. Is it really Judaism itself that Christianity conflicts with, or merely one of many schools of interpretations about Judaism?

However, the ease at which this mystical material combines so eloquently with the official record cannot be denied, which why so many on the wrong side of this debate have elected to use the strategy of exclusion over that of refutation. This seventh side of the Messiah, if valid, would then assume a most prominent place with its canonical cousins. For just as the first six sides of the Messiah each represent a point from the star of David, so too the mystical piece would, by necessity, radiate out from its hexagonal core, springing from the very essence of the Ein Sof.

Therefore, when the evidence is all put on the table, how different are we?

PART THREE:

RECOVERING THE SEMITIC LINGUISTICS OF THE NEW TESTAMENT

> "But these sectarians . . . did not call themselves Christians, but "Nazarenes," however they are simply complete Jews. They use not only the New Testament but the Old Testament as well, as the Jews do . . . They have the Good News according to Matthew in its entirety in Hebrew. For it is clear they still preserve this, in the Hebrew alphabet, as it was originally written."
>
> Epiphanus; Panarion 29 (fourth century)

Now that we have seen how a great many ideas normally thought of as originating from a Gentile influence in Christianity actually stem from time honored traditions of Jewish thought in the Hebrew Bible, the time has come to look at the other half of the Bible. Just how Semitic is the New Testament itself? In order to answer that question, we will need to look at the core assumptions behind the majority Greek based NT model to see if there is more than one way to interpret the evidence that it presents.

Andrew Gabriel Roth

Answering Ten Challenges from the Greek School

Challenge #1:

Greek was the international language of commerce, and therefore even Jews would have been fluent in it and comfortable enough with it to write the New Testament originally in that language.

"The Greek New Testament has scattered within its pages several Aramaic words. In the Gospel of Mark we find numerous terms. Mark's Gospel is a Greek rendition of Peter's preaching in Aramaic (see Petrine Patriarchates; Alexandria). Y'shua is recorded as saying "Talitha kum!" which means "Little girl, arise!" (Mk 5:41). Y'shua likewise exclaims: "Ephphatha" (Be opened) to the man who was deaf and dumb (Mk 7:32-37). And the blind man of Jericho yells out "Rabbuni" "My master" as Y'shua walked by (Mk 10:51). An Aramaic name for a region Y'shua and his disciples visited is preserved: "Dalmanutha" (Mk 8:10). Some of the terms found in Mark deal with worship such as "qorban" meaning an "offering" dedicated to God (Mk 7:11) and Y'shua addresses God in prayer as "Abba" Father (Mk 14:36). And finally, Mark alone correctly records in Aramaic Y'shua's dying words: "Eloi, Eloi, lama sabachthani?"— My God, my God, why have you forsaken me?" (Mk 15:34). Oddly enough though, Mark doesn't refer to Simon by the Aramaic title Y'shua gave him (Cephas) but employs the Greek translation Peter, meaning rock (Mk 3:16). *(note: not in the Peshitta, which preserves the original 'Keepa'—Paul Younan).*"

Signs of the Cross: The Search for the Historical Jesus

ARAMAIC AND SYRIAC IN THE NEW TESTAMENT—Dr. Daniel F. Stramara, Jr. — Rockhurst University

This first point is by far the most sweeping offered by the Hellenist camp. It rests on the well founded assumptions that Roman dominance of the entire Middle East would have necessitated a fairly sophisticated understanding of Greek and Latin just for even the most pious Jews to get by in the world. Matthew, the tax collector and disciple, is often the prototype example of this line of reasoning. Clearly he would have known Aramaic and would have conversed in that language with people needing to understand provisions in the Roman tax code. On the other hand though, say these scholars, Matthew's books and documentation would most certainly have to be in either Latin or Greek, thus showing the need for those languages in that region also.

Of course, there are an equal amount of adherents that also point to the apostle Paul with the same emphasis. As a Roman citizen by birth, Paul could have had early Greek training just as intensive as his admitted fluency in Hebrew and Aramaic under the tutelage of Rabbi Gamaliel.

However, both of these examples overlook a huge historical issue: *Commercial fluency versus sacred choice.*

Put simply, the fact that Jews in first century Israel had to know some Greek to get by is irrelevant, as is the idea that some might have become quite good at Greek. The Law of Averages certainly suggests that when you have a large sample of people doing the same thing that some will become better at it than others. That is, after all, only common sense, *but it has no bearing on how they viewed the language of sacred scripture!*

For proof of this concept, one need only look at the Jews of today. While a congregation in New York may have their sermons in a different language than say, one in Warsaw, both groups will clearly continue to venerate the Torah exclusively in Hebrew! Therefore, neither the location nor the extent of Greek influence has any bearing on this debate, because the latter clearly stops at the synagogue door. It is what the conventional and early Messianic Jews used in a sacred context, not what they needed secularly, which is the salient issue. And, on that score, the New Testament shows us repeatedly the supremacy of the Hebrew liturgical model.

> "And he said to them, 'These are the words that I spoke with you while I was with you, that it was necessary that all things that were written in the law of Moshe, and in the prophets and in the Psalms concerning me be fulfilled."
>
> Luke 24:44 (Younan Peshitta Interlinear Version)
>
> "That it will be required of this generation of all the blood of the prophets that was shed from the creation of the world. From the blood of Abel to the blood of Zakarya who was killed between the Temple and the altar, yes, I say to you, that it will be required of this generation."
>
> Luke 11:50-51 (Younan Peshitta Interlinear Version)

Both of these citations shed huge light on the Bible that Y'shua knew and read and, by extension, the influence of a given system on first century Israel. In the first case, Y'shua is repeating almost verbatim the division of the Hebrew Tenakh, or first the Torah, then the prophets and finally the other writings which inlcude Psalms.

Similarly, the second citation from Luke reinforces this order. Notice that the generation is "required" (responsible for) the blood shed since the beginning of the world. The first murder victim of course is Abel in the book of Genesis, and the last victim, Zechariah, is the last person murdered in 2 Chronicles (24:20-22), which is the last book of the Hebrew Bible! If they were following the Hellenistic order, with Malachi as the last book, this allusion would make no sense whatsoever. That is why even Greek primacists like Charles Ryrie admit that the allusion is meant to say, "from the first murder mentioned in the Bible to the last."[124]

However, the other side of this debate does bring up at least some intriguing points, which I would like to share at this time. Typically, four lines of evidence are used in assessing the influence of Greek in Israel at the dawn of the Common Era. They are:

1) *Historical:* By the time of the Messiah, the Greek OT had circulated for almost 200 years, and its completion was done by seventy scholars from Jerusalem, who must have, at least tacitly, approved of such an undertaking.

2) *Talmudic:* Even in the Talmud, Torah translations are allowed into Greek.

3) *Cultural:* Prominent Jews—Josephus and Philo are the two most commonly cited—show an incredible mastery of Greek. If they can do it, why not Paul and company?

4) *Archaeological:* Fragments of the Septuagint have even been found at the Qumran Dead Sea Scrolls community, therefore attesting to the acceptance of Greek. Also there is a Greek inscription on the grounds of the former Temple in Jerusalem.

Let us take these core assumptions one at a time.

On the first point, we need to look at the circumstances of the time. This is what Josephus had to say about the compiling of the Septuagint, emphases mine:

"WHEN Alexander had reigned twelve years, and

after him Ptolemy Soter forty years, Philadelphus then took the kingdom of Egypt, and held it forty years within one. He procured the law to be interpreted, and set free those that were come from Jerusalem into Egypt, and were in slavery there, who were a hundred and twenty thousand. The occasion was this: Demetrius Phalerius, who was library keeper to the king, was now endeavoring, if it were possible, to gather together all the books that were in the habitable earth, and buying whatsoever was any where valuable, or agreeable to the king's inclination, (who was very earnestly set upon collecting of books,) to which inclination of his Demetrius was zealously subservient. And when once Ptolemy asked him how many ten thousands of books he had collected, he replied, that he had already about twenty times ten thousand; but that, in a little time, he should have fifty times ten thousand. **But he said he had been informed that there were many books of laws among the Jews worthy of inquiring after, and worthy of the king's library, but which, being written in characters and in a dialect of their own, will cause no small pains in getting them translated into the Greek tongue**; (3) that the character in which they are written seems to be like to that which is the proper character of the Syrians, and that its sound, when pronounced, is like theirs also; and that this sound appears to be peculiar to themselves. **Wherefore he said that nothing hindered why they might not get those books to be translated also; for while nothing is wanting that is necessary for that purpose, we may have their books also in this library.** So the king thought that Demetrius was very zealous to procure him abun-

> dance of books, and that he suggested what was exceeding proper for him to do; and therefore he wrote to the Jewish high priest, that he should act accordingly."

Antiquities, 12.2.1

So let's look at the circumstances of this event again. The Hebrew scholars came from Jerusalem ostensibly because the Seleucid monarch in charge of Israel ordered them to do it! They could have resisted to be sure, but only on pain of death and torture, and what would that accomplish? It would also be well worth pointing out that the translation was *for the king*, and not for the Jews per se. It is true that later Hellenistic Judaism used this as their Bible, but this edition was for the king's library and therefore for his use. Additionally, there is no record of Jews being commanded either in advance of this work or after it to throw out the Hebrew Torah and use this instead. If there were, that would have been a powerful incentive for the Jews to rebel, as they did subsequently against overwhelming odds and at great loss of life with both Seleucid and Roman oppressors who attempted to either dilute their Hebrew faith with pagan trappings or ban it altogether.

Therefore, putting it in context, all these scholars were doing was providing a king with a translation of their Scriptures, the prestige of which could only serve to help the Jewish cause in the long run if the king could understand with little difficulty the culture of his own subjects. Certainly the material benefits in the short term and the prestige, as Josesphus also details, were more than sufficient inducements given the fact that such a work had no bearing on the way they would continue to worship in their homeland.

However, the final nail in the coffin of this argument is to look at the results of this undertaking. It is how this work was received in Israel—not places like Alexandria—which is the material point. For that, two well-established historical indices need to be brought up.

The first has to do with how the rabbis in Israel looked at their own canon. When the time came to decide what books would be considered sacred, and which ones were thrown out, only those books that could show a clear Hebrew pedigree were accepted. In other words, inclusion in the Septuagint collection was not a high enough burden to make it in. The fact that Hellenistic Jews had venerated a collection of apocryphal books for at least two centuries did not matter; having each book exist in Hebrew prior to that compilation did. That fact alone should prove that Hebrew enjoyed (and still enjoys) a sacred status among Jews unmatched by any other language.

The second factor has already been referred to. Put simply, the fact that sermons and siddurs (prayer books) are in English, or even Polish for that matter, is immaterial. The language of the local vernacular is used to explain the faith, but the sacred source that ties them all together is exclusively in Hebrew. The reasons for this, while fairly obvious, are still worth noting—because even when Jews get together and decide to do a translation, it is with deep reservations:

> While Philo and his Alexandrian co-religionists looked upon the translation of the Seventy as the work of inspired men, the Palestinian Rabbis subsequently considered the day on which the Septuagint was composed as one of the most unfortunate in Israel's history, seeing that the Torah could never be adequately translated. And there are indications enough that the consequences of such translations were not all of a desirable nature.
>
> Preface to the 1955 Jewish Publication Society Translation of the Masoretic Text, p. v.

Additionally, here is other evidence from Josephus regarding the lengths that Jews will go through to resist forces of Hellenization:

Now it came to pass, after two years, in the hundred forty and fifth year, on the twenty-fifth day of that month which is by us called Chasleu, and by the Macedonians Apelleus, in the hundred and fifty-third olympiad, that the king came up to Jerusalem, and, pretending peace, he got possession of the city by treachery; at which time he spared not so much as those that admitted him into it, on account of the riches that lay in the temple; but, led by his covetous inclination, (for he saw there was in it a great deal of gold, and many ornaments that had been dedicated to it of very great value,) and in order to plunder its wealth, he ventured to break the league he had made. So he left the temple bare, and took away the golden candlesticks, and the golden altar [of incense], and table [of shew-bread], and the altar [of burnt-offering]; and did not abstain from even the veils, which were made of fine linen and scarlet.

He also emptied it of its secret treasures, and left nothing at all remaining; and by this means cast the Jews into great lamentation, for he forbade them to offer those daily sacrifices which they used to offer to God, according to the law. **And when he had pillaged the whole city, some of the inhabitants he slew, and some he carried captive, together with their wives and children, so that the multitude of those captives that were taken alive amounted to about ten thousand. He also burnt down the finest buildings; and when he had overthrown the city walls, he built a citadel in the lower part of the city, (17) for the place was high, and overlooked the temple; on which account he fortified it with high walls and**

towers, and put into it a garrison of Macedonians. However, in that citadel dwelt the impious and wicked part of the [Jewish] multitude, from whom it proved that the citizens suffered many and sore calamities. And when the king had built an idol altar upon God's altar, he slew swine upon it, and so offered a sacrifice neither according to the law, nor the Jewish religious worship in that country. He also compelled them to forsake the worship which they paid their own God, and to adore those whom he took to be gods; and made them build temples, and raise idol altars in every city and village, and offer swine upon them every day. He also commanded them not to circumcise their sons, and threatened to punish any that should be found to have transgressed his injunction.

He also appointed overseers, who should compel them to do what he commanded. And indeed many Jews there were who complied with the king's commands, either voluntarily, or out of fear of the penalty that was denounced. **But the best men, and those of the noblest souls, did not regard him, but did pay a greater respect to the customs of their country than concern as to the punishment which he threatened to the disobedient; on which account they every day underwent great miseries and bitter torments; for they were whipped with rods, and their bodies were torn to pieces, and were crucified, while they were still alive, and breathed. They also strangled those women and their sons whom they had circumcised, as the king had appointed, hanging their sons about their necks as they were upon the crosses. And if there were any sacred book of**

> the law found, it was destroyed, and those with whom they were found miserably perished also.
>
> Antiquities 12.5.4

Certainly in a situation as grave as this, one could understand if the Jews rejected the Hebrew to survive and adopted—if not pagan practices directly, then a Greek model of Jewish worship with Greek scriptures as a way to stop the slaughter. But, as Josephus indicates, they zealously clung to their original Hebrew culture and scripture even in the face of overwhelming calamity.

However, if that is the case, why does the talmudic work *Midrash Rabbah*—in two places—allow Greek translations of Torah? Consider:

> AND HE SAID: BLESSED BE THE LORD, THE GOD OF SHEM . . . GOD ENLARGE JAPHETH (IX, 26 f.). This alludes to Cyrus who ordered the Temple to be rebuilt; yet even so, AND HE SHALL DWELL IN THE TENTS OF SHEM: the Shechinah dwells only in the tents of Shem. Bar Kappara explained it: Let the words of the Torah be uttered in the language of Japheth [sc. Greek] in the tents of Shem.2 R. Judan said: From this we learn that a translation [of the Bible is permitted].3 Thus it is written, And they read in the book, in the Law of God (Neh. VIII, 8): this refers to Scripture; distinctly (ib.): to a translation; And they gave the sense (ib.)-i.e. the punctuation accents; And caused them to understand the reading (ib.)-this refers to the beginnings of the verses.4 R. Hiyya b. Lulianus said: It refers to the grammatical sequence [of words].5 The Rabbis of Caesarea said: Here we have an allusion to the traditional text.6 R. Zera and R. Hananel said: Even if a man is as well-versed in the

Torah as Ezra, he must not read it from memory and write it.7 But it was taught: It once happened that R. Meir visited Asia Minor,8 and finding there no Scroll of Esther, he read it from memory and wrote it? 10 There [in Babylonia] they say: He wrote two Scrolls, suppressed the first and kept the second as valid [for use].11

Midrash Rabbah—Genesis 36:8

And:

THESE ARE THE WORDS. Halachah1: Is it permissible for a Jew to write a Scroll of the Law in any language, etc.? The Wise have learnt thus2: The difference between [sacred] books and phylacteries and mezuzoth is only that [sacred] books may be written in any language. R. Gamaliel says: With books too [the only other language] in which they permitted them to be written is Greek. And what is R. Gamaliel's reason for saying that a Scroll of the Law may be written in Greek? Our Rabbis have taught thus: Bar Kappara, interpreting the verse, God enlarge Japheth, and he shall dwell in the tents of Shem (Gen. IX, 27), said: This indicates that the words of Shem may be rendered in the languages of Japheth3; therefore have [the Rabbis] permitted [sacred books] to be written in Greek. The Holy One, blessed be He, said: ' See how beloved is the language of the Torah; it is healing for the tongue. '

Midrash Rabbah—Deuteronomy 1:1

Now, in addition to all the reasons previously given on the general hypothesis, the fact remains that the Midrash is being set down no earlier than the third century—and many of the rabbis listed here are commenting significantly later than that—in the Middle Ages! In other words, this ruling is a few centuries too late.

Secondly, there is no mention in the citation at all on the *desirable nature* of the undertaking or that the task in in question wass accepted as a wonderful thing in Israel. In fact, Josephus, who is from the correct time period, says the opposite:

> " . . . for our nation does not encourage those that learn the languages of many nations, and so adorn their discourses with the smoothness of their periods . . ."
>
> Antiquities, 20.11.2

What this amounts to then is a grudging acceptance either from the prism of several centuries after the events when Hebrew culture was at an all time ebb (possibly), or a way of "apologizing" for the few Hellenistic accommodations that were made back in those days (definitely). Between the compiling of the Septuagint and that of the Midrash however, Hellenistic Judaism arose in cities like Antioch and Alexandria and thrived even as their Palestinian counterparts were murdered and suppressed. Is it any wonder then that the rabbis in the first centuries of the common era thought it better to maintain a Jewish presence in these places using this kind of scripture even if they did not accept it as sacred for themselves?

Finally, even the NT records that Greek Jews came to worship at Jerusalem, where the Hebrew liturgy was employed, (John 12:20). Although, once again, allowing something out of necessity and encouraging that same task as some kind of noble act are two completely different issues.

Moving on to the cultural argument, using the historian Philo is a complete red herring that should be utterly thrown out. Philo lived all his life in Alexandria and, like many of his compatriots, had little understanding of Hebrew. Therefore his usefulness in extrapolating to a first century Palestinian paradigm is just about non-existent.

As for Josephus, the previous quote from him (Antiquities 20.1.2) makes it clear that Greek fluency was not encouraged. However, in almost the very next sentence, the Jewish historian makes an even more sweeping statement on the matter:

> But they give him the testimony of being a wise man who is fully acquainted with our laws, and is able to interpret their meaning [in Greek]; on which account, as there have been many who have done their endeavors with great patience to obtain this learning, **there have yet hardly been so many as two or three that have succeeded therein, who were immediately well rewarded for their pains.**
>
> Antiquities 20.11.2

Now this may seem like idle bragging that Josephus puts himself in an elite category, until we put it together with other statements by him that also talk of awkwardness with Greek as well! For example, still sticking to this one crucial paragraph, here is what he had to say about his Greek skills even after living in Rome for almost a quarter of a century:

> I have also taken a great deal of pains to obtain the learning of the Greeks, and understand the elements of the Greek language, although I have so long accustomed myself to speak our own tongue, that I cannot pronounce Greek with sufficient exactness...
>
> Ibid

Signs of the Cross: The Search for the Historical Jesus

Now let us compare and contrast Josephus with another first century Jew, the apostle Paul.

1) *Both Paul and Josephus came from Jewish backgrounds, were native Hebrew and Aramaic speakers, and have a long history of Scriptural study in those languages.*

> "The family from which I am derived is not an ignoble one, but hath descended all along from the priests; and as nobility among several people is of a different origin, so with us to be of the sacerdotal dignity, is an indication of the splendor of a family. Now, I am not only sprung from a sacerdotal family in general, but from the first of the twenty-four courses; and as among us there is not only a considerable difference between one family of each course and another, I am of the chief family of that first course also; nay, further, by my mother I am of the royal blood; for the children of Asamoneus, from whom that family was derived, had both the office of the high priesthood, and the dignity of a king, for a long time together . . . Moreover, when I was a child, and about fourteen years of age, I was commended by all for the love I had to learning; on which account the high priests and principal men of the city came then frequently to me together, in order to know my opinion about the accurate understanding of points of the law. And when I was about sixteen years old, I had a mind to make trim of the several sects that were among us. These sects are three:—The first is that of the Pharisees, the second that Sadducees, and the third that of the Essens, as we have frequently told you; for I thought that by this means I might choose

the best, if I were once acquainted with them all; so I contented myself with hard fare, and underwent great difficulties, and went through them all."

The Life of Flavius Josephus, 1.1-2

When they heard him speak to them in Aramaic, they became very quiet. Then Paul said: 'I am a Jew, born in Tarsus of Cilicia, but brought up in this city (of Jerusalem)[125]. Under (Rabbi) Gamaliel I was thoroughly trained in the law of our fathers and was just as zealous for God as any of you are today."

Acts 22:1-3

2) *Both Josephus and Paul were Roman citizens, which is certainly one possible source of their Greek and Latin knowledge.*[126]

But when Titus had composed the troubles in Judea, and conjectured that the lands which I had in Judea would bring me no profit, because a garrison to guard the country was afterward to pitch there, he gave me another country in the plain. And when he was going away to Rome, he made choice of me to sail along with him, and paid me great respect: and when we were come to Rome, I had great care taken of me by Vespasian; for he gave me an apartment in his own house, which he lived in before he came to the empire. He also honored me with the privilege of a Roman citizen, and gave me an annual pension; and continued to respect me to the end of his life, without any abatement of his

> kindness to me; which very thing made me envied, and brought me into danger.
>
> Life, 1.76
>
> The commander went to Paul and asked, 'Are you a Roman citizen?' 'Yes, I am', he answered. Then the commander said, 'I had to pay a big price for my citizenship.' 'But I was born a citizen,' Paul replied.
>
> Acts 22:27-28

3) *However, in spite of a lifetime of Greek education, both men knew their limitations in that language. (Note the complete quote of Antiquities 20.11.2 on this occasion.)*

> And I am so bold as to say, now I have so completely perfected the work I proposed to myself to do, that no other person, whether he were a Jew or foreigner, had he ever so great an inclination to it, could so accurately deliver these accounts to the Greeks as is done in these books. For those of my own nation freely acknowledge that I far exceed them in the learning belonging to Jews; I have also taken a great deal of pains to obtain the learning of the Greeks, and understand the elements of the Greek language, although I have so long accustomed myself to speak our own tongue, that I cannot pronounce Greek with sufficient exactness; for our nation does not encourage those that learn the languages of many nations, and so adorn their discourses with the smoothness of their periods . . .
>
> Antiquities, 20.11.2

Now before giving Paul's equivalent, let's pause for a moment, and look at this critical statement. Josephus, other than engaging in a bit of *kvelling* (bragging) that he readily acknowledges, has told us that very few first century Jews in Israel (as opposed to Greek speaking Alexandrian Jews like Philo), have mastered the Greek language. Additionally, Josephus' written Greek is as good—if not better—than any shown in the New Testament, although the Gospel of Luke admittedly does gives him a strong run for his money. In any case, the point is that if Josephus is having trouble pronouncing Greek (and by extension understanding it since there are many similar sounding words), we should expect similar problems with his contemporaries, the Jewish writers of the New Testament. This fact is very apparent from the objective view of Peter, who writes about Paul's effectiveness with Greek speaking audiences:

> "Bear in mind that the LORD's patience means salvation, just as our dear brother Paul also wrote you with the wisdom that God gave him. He writes the same way in all his letters, speaking n them of these matters. HIS LETTERS CONTAIN SOME THINGS WHICH ARE HARD TO UNDERSTAND, which ignorant and unstable people distort. As they do the other Scriptures, to their own destruction."

2 Peter 3:15-16

Also, unlike Josephus, Paul needs help *actually writing the Greek letters*, since even his calligraphy leaves something to be desired:

> "I, Tertius, WHO WROTE DOWN THIS LETTER, greet you in the LORD."

Romans 16:22

> "See what large letters I use as I write to you with my own hand!"[127]

> Galatians 6:11

It is now however that we get to the central point of the matter. Josephus, as advanced as his Greek was, still wrote first in his native language!

> "I have proposed to myself, for the sake of such as live under the government of the Romans, to translate those books into the Greek tongue, which I formerly composed in the language of our country, and sent to the Upper Barbarians; Joseph, the son of Matthias, by birth a Hebrew, a priest also, and one who at first fought against the Romans myself, and was forced to be present at what was done afterwards, [am the author of this work]."

> Preface to Wars Against the Jews, 1.1-2

It is also at this point that we see why Josephus' Greek mastery is disadvantageous to the Hellenistic New Testament school. The fact is, Josephus was much more successful than Paul was at thinking as a Gentile. Not only is his Greek is of higher quality, it is written without prior assistance from scribes or translators—a feat neither Peter nor Paul could ever match, (1 Peter 5:12, 1 Thessalonians 1:1, 2 Thessalonians 1:1, Romans 16:22). The former could not even speak in Israel without having his accent detected among Hebrew listeners (Matthew 26:73) and the latter had frequent problems being understood in Greek which are very much reflected in his writings. Josephus' texts, however, are of higher quality—all the more remarkable when we consider that his total output is equal to ten times the material in all four Gospels combined.

What such an analysis does then is completely destroy the argument of "language to fit the occasion". In essence, Josephus made the same decision that the evangelists did. He knew it was a terrific advantage to write in Greek for his Gentile readership, and he did, but not before getting his thoughts down in Hebrew or Aramaic first. It is therefore my position that Paul too, whose Greek was not nearly as accomplished even when he had help, always wrote in his native language first and then had it translated into Greek for churches in Corinth, Ephesus, et. al. In fact, even the Greek copies of these letters bear this scenario out by showing that Paul authenticated his manuscripts in a very special way:

> "I, Paul, write this greeting in my own hand. If anyone does not love the LORD-a curse be on him. Maranatha!"

1 Corinthians 16:21-22

> "I, Paul, write this greeting in my own hand, WHICH IS THE DISTINGUISHING MARK IN ALL MY LETTERS. THIS IS HOW I WRITE."

2 Thessalonians 3:17

The linkage is both obvious and profound. Paul's "distinguishing mark" that is "in all my letters" is an Aramaic phrase! "maranatha"—which means "Our LORD, come"—is by his own testimony attached to all of his original Epistles—and here is the key point—REGARDLESS AS TO THE LANGUAGE OF THE INTENDED CONGREGATION! Even if this interpretation is rejected however, the essential question remains, for why would Paul insert an Aramaic phrase that no one in (Greek) Corinth could possibly understand? The evidence would then strongly suggest, if not prove, that these first congregations knew both original Aramaic copies, as well as early Greek translations of those same copies, circulated regularly and at a very early date. Thus, once again, the Church of the East position is confirmed:

> "The Letters of Paul ... were preserved in the scribal language, the ancient Aramaic. These Letters are highly theological and they are written at a level of scholarship that can only be fully achieved in one language, the ancient Aramaic. Neither the "original Greek" translation, nor the Latin could match that level. As developed and rich as the English language may be, the Scriptures could not be translated any better than the King James Version, because there have never been scholars of both ancient Aramaic and English who discovered the discrepancy and the extent of the distortion."
>
> Victor Alexander, Aramaic Bible Translation Project

Finally, Josephus shares one last thing in common with Paul and the other evangelists. In both cases, it is widely believed that the Aramaic originals these men wrote are forever lost to us. With Josephus, this could very well be true, and it is certainly true of the Aramaic rough drafts of Matthew, John and all the other apostles, with the possible exception of Thomas.[128] However, it is absolutely not true with Paul, because his letters have, as Victor Alexander says, been preserved in their original, scribal Aramaic. The reasons why this fact is not commonly acknowledged is because scholars in the west spent almost sixteen centuries forgetting that these documents existed. Then, even when they "found" them again in the nineteenth century, they were looking at inferior Syriac translations from Greek originals, not the ancient Aramaic documents preserved by the Church of the East. Now, at the dawn of the twenty-first century, the time has come to tell the truth.

The final area of Greek argument on this particular challenge is in the archaeological arena. There have been some significant finds that appear to also favor the Greek cause. We will now discuss the two most important ones.

First, a Greek inscription has been found in an area that was clearly the outer area for the Temple in Jerusalem. Again, this is fluency versus choice. As a matter of necessity, Jews had to inform Gentiles who were ignorant of Hebrew that to progress to the inner courts meant certain death.

The second, and final, piece of evidence, are fragments of the Septuagint that have been found at Qumran. If these caves however were the location of the sacred library of the Essenes, then this could appear to be damning evidence at first glance.

However, that type of alleged "smoking gun" must be tempered with the extremely low amount of Greek mss that have been found when contrasted with the huge caches of Hebrew and Aramaic material. The fact that the Essenes stored these documents in no way proves that they were used liturgically. It may in fact simply be that the Essenes kept a wide variety sources for study as evidenced by the targums, alternate readings and even additional Psalms that have been found there. Finding a "standard" Essene rendering on almost anything is therefore quite elusive. There are also so many marked differences between this tiny desert sect and mainline Judaism as practiced in Jerusalem—which must be our control factor—as to make any extrapolation between the two groups extremely tenuous even if the Greek was highly regarded by them.

Additionally, while there is little doubt that Essenes occupied the area around Khirbet Qumran and stored some of their writings in the nearby caves, it is still by no means certain that every document at Qumran is ipso facto Essene in nature.

In fact, Norman Golb, one of the leading Dead Sea Scrolls scholars in the world, has written a book to suggest the opposite is true. Called *Who Wrote the Dead Sea Scrolls* (New York: Scribner, 1995), Golb very ably points out that many different sects of Judaism—including the Essenes—could have deposited precious documents that, when compared with the finds at Qumran, appear to reflect their diversity. In Golb's scenario, these disparate sects would have fled Jerusalem during its destruction and found sanctuary for their documents in the caves of Qumran. Certainly having a "War Scroll" in one of the caves makes more sense in looking at its connection to the nearby Zealots than the pacifist Essenes. And other problems like having the skeletons of women found in the cemetery of a group that excludes women bring up far more questions than can be answered at present.

However, either way, the paucity of the Greek fragments are certainly not of such a nature to show a universal sacredness of that language, especially when all other aspects point elsewhere.

Challenge #2:

Proof of the NT's origin in Greek is a simple matter. All of the Gospel and epistolary writers used the Septuagint (LXX) version of the OT as quotes, and not the Hebrew Masoretic Text.

Also some detailed treatment should be extended regarding the kind of Scripture used, whether at this early stage or throughout the rest of the process. Much has been made of the fact that Matthew as we now have it quotes from the Septuagint, a Greek translation, and not the original Hebrew Bible. Greek primacists have in fact used this observation to completely divorce the West from the Aramaic phrases and special meanings that form the core evidence of my argument. My response to this theory is in three parts, and the first point is rather simple: Far from disproving a Semitic origin, if Septuagint quotes were actually used in the Greek NT— the opposite conclusion is true!

Also, as we will see, the conclusion of LXX usage in the NT is far from proven. For the moment, however, let us say for the sake of argument that they were. We then should consider the situation this way:

If a translator was going through his original Aramaic sources and trying laboriously to find some bare equivalent in the Greek, translating the Hebrew Old Testament quotes used on his own would most certainly discredit his efforts with his intended audience.

The question then arises, would such Hellenistic Jews, raised their entire lives on the Septuagint, accept anything in Greek other than quotes from that same source? Furthermore, could they possibly believe that any one person, however strong their Greek learning, was able to deliver a superior individual translation from Aramaic into Greek, when an authoritative version had been done and accepted for centuries?

The answer to both questions, as history shows, must be a categorical no, and this is reinforced when we consider that by the time these Gospels reached their final form Jerusalem had been destroyed, and the majority of Palestinian Jews, except for disciples and Nazarenes, had rejected the message. Therefore, the only logical place the apostles could go would be to either Hellenistic Jews or Greek speaking Gentiles, and in both cases the Septuagint was the logical Scripture of choice. Jerome may in fact refer to this very possibility.[129]

The second part of my rebuttal then is largely a repetition of the points in the Greek general influence argument, with those two critical citations in Luke (11:50-51, 24:44).

This use of Hebrew book order however is even more significant when we realize that the revised order in the Greek version had been circulating since 150 BCE . . . at the latest! So, even after nearly 200 years, Y'shua and everyone associated with his movement still used the order of the Hebrew Bible during the time of his ministry. If they did, it is an equally safe bet that Paul was in the same situation. The apostle almost always went to synagogues in every major city he preached in and, even when his main focus was Gentile audiences, used the same Hebrew Bible.

Furthermore, a supporting statement regarding the "Law and Prophets" order is given by the apostle Paul and can be positively dated to the year 54 at the earliest[130]. Therefore, we have clear proof that the use of the Hebrew Scriptures continued well past the point when the Gentile ministry was in full swing. The likelihood is also great that this usage continued at least until the year of Paul's death, 67 CE.

Then, just three years later, Jerusalem and her Temple were destroyed and both Jews and Christians faced heavy persecution by Rome. It was only then, with Jewish culture on the verge of extinction and a Gentile Christian movement eager to separate itself from Judaism so they could also survive, that the use of Greek Gospels— and Greek Old Testament quotes in them—became truly necessary.

By contrast, right up until this time, the New Testament records in several places Greek proselytes ("God fearers") going to the synagogue to hear prayers in Hebrew but also getting them translated into their native tongue. With the Jewish learning structure now destroyed, this was no longer possible, and so Gentile believers needed a Gospel they could understand directly, (Matthew 23:15, Acts 2:10, 14:1, 17:17, 18:4).[131]

Finally, a very interesting possible line of evidence is found in the entire Epistle of James the Just. The apostle, otherwise known by his Hebrew brethren as Ya'acov Ha Tzadik, was the brother of Y'shua and an early leader in the Jerusalem Church. He also headed a Jewish Christian congregation for more than thirty years after the Crucifixion. In his extensive discourse, James very likely has left a historical record of how these early congregations divided up their liturgy.

The epistle begins by drawing from a wide variety of biblical themes in a kind of free form style that can only come from a life long study of the Scriptures. However, once James decides to directly quote from a book, a remarkable structure is revealed.

The direct quoting begins in earnest in 2:8 (comp to Leviticus 19:18, 2:11 comp to Exodus 20:14 and Deuteronomy 5:18, and 2:23 comp to Genesis 15:6). Then James changes abruptly by using an example from the second chapter of Joshua to round out the thought, (2:25).

Two lines later, starting in the third chapter, another quick shift with a discourse on an evil tongue. While the apostle's individual style is very much apparent here, the common imagery between 3:1-

12 and Jeremiah 9:1-16 are quite striking. Both talk about springs of water made bitter by slander, (James 3:10-12, Jeremiah 9:1,16). Both refer to common images of desolation, probably by fire, (James 3:5, Jeremiah 9:10-11). Furthermore both compare slander to a deadly weapon, (James 3:7, Jeremiah 9:3) and, finally, both make mention of animals outliving man because he has an evil tongue and they do not, (James 3:7, Jeremiah 9:10-11).

James then wraps up his teaching with a quote lifted directly out of Proverbs 3:34 (4:6) and a final injunction to his congregation to "sing Psalms", (5:13), and thus retains the Torah-Nebi'im-Ketuvim model.

Such is the case for demonstrating how history proves the Assyrian Church of the East correct.[132] They have claimed that their Aramaic tradition is completely intact from the apostolic age, and that the Scriptures they use are direct descendants of Aramaic originals that were used to help the early Church grow during the first 40 years of its history. The rest, as they say, are just translations.

The third and final part of this analysis then attacks the prejudice inherent at the core of the Greek assumption. Since the Greek texts are assumed by them to be originals, the fact that they use scriptural quotes in that same language is supposed to be powerful evidence. However, I would submit respectfully that their conclusion is already taken as proven simply in the way the question is asked.

Or, to put it another way, if the Aramaic documents were instead the ones shown to have circulated first, whatever quotes the translated Greek mss had would be considered irrelevant. Of course Greek audiences reading Greek translations would want authentic Greek OT quotes! So, in my view, this whole issue is a bit of a smoke screen.

Now let us look at another possibility, namely that the Septuagint was NOT used in the Greek NT. The fact is, if the writers of the Greek NT thought the Septuagint was the sacred writ over the Hebrew, we should expect them to slavishly quote it word for word.

The reality however is quite different, because a bit of a free form style seems to prevail in these quotations that may either represent

Septuagintal influence (at best), or may just be the way the writer decided to set it down in Greek himself (at worst). Here is what I mean.

ISAIAH 7:14

Masoretic Text:

"Therefore the LORD himself shall give you a sign; Behold, a virgin shall conceive, and bear a son, and shall call his name Immanuel."

Septuagint:

"Therefore the LORD himself shall give you a sign; Behold, a virgin shall conceive, and bear a son, and shall call his name Immanuel."

As Quoted by Matthew 1:23:

"Behold, a virgin shall be with child, and shall bring forth a son, and they shall call his name Emmanuel, which being interpreted is, God with us."

Comments:

One important difference: the LXX uses the word "lepsetai" (shall be) while Matthew uses the Greek word "ekzie" (shall be).

ISAIAH 42:1-4

Masoretic Text:

"Behold my servant, whom I uphold; mine elect, in whom my soul delighteth; I have put my spirit upon him: he shall bring forth judgment to the Gentiles. He shall not cry, nor lift up, nor cause his voice to be heard in the street. A bruised reed shall he not break, and the smoking flax shall he not quench: he shall bring forth judgment unto truth. He shall not fail nor be discouraged, till he have set judgment in the earth: and the isles shall wait for his law."

Septuagint:

"Jacob is my servant, I will help him: Israel is my chosen, my soul has accepted him; I have put my Spirit upon him; he shall bring forth judgment to the Gentiles. He shall not cry, nor lift up (his voice), nor shall his voice be heard without. A bruised reed shall he not break, and smoking flax shall he not quench; but he shall bring forth judgment to truth. He shall shine out, and shall not be discouraged, until he have set judgment on the earth: and in his name shall the Gentiles trust."

As Quoted by Matthew 12:18-21:

"Behold my servant, whom I have chosen; my beloved, in whom my soul is well pleased: I will put my spirit upon him, and he shall shew judgment to the Gentiles. He shall not strive, nor cry; neither shall any man hear his voice in the streets. A bruised reed shall he not break, and smoking flax shall he not quench, till he send forth judgment unto victory. And in his name shall the Gentiles trust."

Comments:

With the exception of a word here or there, the only part which matches is the last phrase "And in his name shall the Gentiles trust." One must conclude that Matthew is either taking liberties with the LXX, or taking liberties with his translation of the Hebrew into Greek. Matthew is himself "targuming".

ISAIAH 6:10

Masoretic Text:

"And he said, Go, and tell this people, Hear ye indeed, but understand not; and see ye indeed, but perceive not. Make the heart of this people fat, and make their ears heavy, and shut their eyes; lest they see with their eyes, and hear with their ears, and understand with their heart, and convert, and be healed."

Septuagint:

"Ye shall hear indeed, but ye shall not understand; and ye shall see indeed, but ye shall not perceive. For the heart of this people has become gross, and their ears are dull of hearing, and their eyes have they closed; lest they should see with their eyes, and hear with their ears, and understand with their heart, and be converted, and I should heal them."

As Quoted by Matthew 13:14-15:

"And in them is fulfilled the prophecy of Esaias, which saith, By hearing ye shall hear, and shall not understand; and seeing ye shall see, and shall not perceive: For this people's heart is waxed gross, and their ears are dull of hearing, and their eyes they have closed; lest at any time they should see with their eyes, and hear with their ears, and should understand with their heart, and should be converted, and I should heal them."

Comments:

There is a difference in the Matthew quote between the Greek NT and the Greek OT, and that is that the LXX has the word "auton" (their) after "ears" while the NT has it after "eyes." However, the same passage cited by Mark is quite different.

> "That seeing they may see, and not perceive; and hearing they may hear, and not understand; lest at any time they should be converted, and their sins should be forgiven them."(Mark 4:12) The citation is very free (a "Targum" or "Paraphrase"). Once we interject the usage of freely citing OT passages (as we find many times in the NT), we can no longer be dogmatic that the translation which was used as the base translation was in fact the LXX. It becomes an assumption only.

ISAIAH 29:13

Masoretic Text:

The LORD said: Because these people draw near with their mouths and honor me with their lips, while their hearts are far from me, and their worship of me is a human commandment learned by rote.

Septuagint:

"Wherefore the LORD said, Forasmuch as this people draw near me with their mouth, and with their lips do honour me, but have removed their heart far from me, and their fear toward me is taught by the precept of men:"

As Quoted By Matthew 15:9:

"Ye hypocrites, well did Esaias prophesy of you, saying, This people draweth nigh unto me with their mouth, and honoureth me with their lips; but their heart is far from me. But in vain they do worship me, teaching for doctrines the commandments of men."

Comments:

There are here likewise some differences between the LXX and the Greek NT. The LXX adds "en" (in) before "with their mouth." The NT uses the pharse "me tima" (honours me). The LXX reads, "auton timosi me" (they honour me). The NT has "didaskalias" (doctrines) after "didaskontes" (teaching). The LXX reads "kai didaskalias" (and doctrines) and places it after "anthrpon" (of men).

Mark 7:6-7 "He answered and said unto them, Well hath Esaias prophesied of you hypocrites, as it is written, This people honoureth me with their lips, but their heart is far from me. Howbeit in vain do they worship me, teaching for doctrines the commandments of men."

The literal translation of the LXX reads, "And the LORD has said, This people draw nigh to me with their mouth, and they honour me with their lips, but their heart is far from me: but in vain do they worship me, teaching the commandments and doctrines of men"(Isa. 29:13 LXX). The citation is rather loose if coming from the LXX as we have it.

DEUTERONOMY 18:15,19

Masoretic Text:

The LORD thy God will raise up unto thee a Prophet from the midst of thee, of thy brethren, like unto me; unto him ye shall hearken; . . . 19: And it shall come to pass, that whosoever will not hearken unto my words which he shall speak in my name, I will require it of him."

Septuagint:

The LORD thy God shall raise up to thee a prophet of thy brethren, like me; him shall ye hear: . . . 19: And whatever man shall not hearken to whatsoever words that prophet shall speak in my name, I will take vengeance on him."

As Quoted by Acts 3:23-25:[133]

"For Moses truly said unto the fathers, A prophet shall the LORD your God raise up unto you of your brethren, like unto me; him shall ye hear in all things whatsoever he shall say unto you. And it shall come to pass, that every soul, which will not hear that prophet, shall be destroyed from among the people."

Comments:

Acts 3:22-23 quotes Deuteronomy 18:15 and 19. This is a lengthy portion of Scripture, but demonstrates that Luke was not citing the LXX word for word in Acts chapter 3. While the literal translations may be close, we are here examining the usage of the LXX in the Greek NT. The Greek of both is given below. If Luke were using the LXX we would expect the passage in Acts 3:22-23 to match the passage in Deuteronomy 18:15,19. One does not have to read Greek to see that the two passages are not a perfect match.

EXODUS 9:16

Masoretic Text:

"And in very deed for this cause have I raised thee up, for to shew in thee my power; and that my name may be declared throughout all the earth."

Septuagint:

"And for this purpose hast thou been preserved, that I might display in thee my strength, and that my name might be declared throughout all the earth."

As Quoted by Romans 9:17:

"For the scripture saith unto Pharaoh, Even for this same purpose have I raised thee up, that I might shew my power in thee, and that my name might be declared throughout all the earth."

Comments:

The Greek NT begins with "Oti eis auto touto exegeipa se opos"

(For this purpose have I raised out thee, so that). The LXX begins with "Kai eneken toutou dietepethes, ina" (And for this purpose hast thou been preserved, that). These are two differing readings in both Greek and English. Moreover, the NT uses the Greek word "dunamin" (power), while the LXX uses the Greek word "isxun" (strength).

PSALM 69:22-23:

Masoretic Text:
"Let their table become a snare before them: and that which should have been for their welfare, let it become a trap. Let their eyes be darkened, that they see not; and make their loins continually to shake"

Septuagint:
"Let their table before them be for a snare, and for a recompence, and for a stumbling-block. Let their eyes be darkened that they should not see; and bow down their back continually."

As Quoted by Romans 11:10:
"And David saith, Let their table be made a snare, and a trap, and a stumblingblock, and a recompence unto them: Let their eyes be darkened, that they may not see, and bow down their back always."

Comments:
The NT passage is close to the reading found in the LXX. Yet there are differences. The LXX adds the Greek phrase "enopion auton" (before them) in the first part of the phrase. Also, at the end of verse nine, the NT has the phrase "kai eis antapodoma autois" (and a recompence unto them). However, the LXX places the same phrase in the middle of the verse and not at the end.

PSALM 68:18

Masoretic Text:
You ascended the high mount, leading captives in your train and receiving gifts from people, even from those who rebel against the LORD God's abiding there.

Septuagint:
Thou art gone up high, thou hast led captivity captive, thou hast

received gifts for man, yea, for they were rebellious, that they might dwell among them.

As Quoted by Ephesians 4:8:

Therefore it is said, "When he ascended on high he made captivity itself a captive; he gave gifts to his people."

Comments:

In this verse Paul quotes Psalm 68:18 to support his statement on the grace of Messiah. The quoted words from the Psalms, however, Paul's version of Psalm 68:18 does not come from the Hebrew text, nor from the Septuagint, but from the Aramaic Targums, and this fact even Western Scholars admit (c.f.—Furnish 1971b: 841; Mays 1217; Archer 404)!

Whatever the source, these Greek readings of the OT exist NOWHERE ELSE. Now, to be fair, some Septuagint scholars suggest that there may have been several versions of this work that circulated before the earliest completed mss—which are 600 years after the time of the original. However, if that is the case, it becomes extremely tenuous to show how ANY influence from this collection prevailed upon the Gospel writers. After all, the whole idea is that the Greek Scriptures had such a profound effect on first century Palestinian Jews as to make them want to switch to them for the benefit of their audience in the first place! That having been said then, it seems odd that not a single scrap or fragment of any of these variants has ever been found in the archaeological record, and this even includes versions found at Qumran.

In that case, we now have to postulate as to where these quotes might have come from. Some have suggested that the Gospel writers themselves may have paraphrased them directly, or, when shown that writers like Matthew and Luke sometimes share the same rendering, that some kind of validation process of these paraphrases must have ensued during the compilation process.

Fair enough, but it still does not deal with the issue directly, because it is still important to ask: Where did these Jewish writers learn to do this paraphrasing in the first place, and is there a context from Jewish tradition that can shed light on this process?

The answer to both questions, is YES.

> "The teachers of the law and the Pharisees sit in Moses' seat. So, you must obey them and do everything they tell you. But do not do what they do, for they do not practice what they preach."
>
> Matthew 23:2-3

Now what does, "sitting in Moses' seat" mean? The answer is in the first part of the verse and the phrase, "teachers of the law". As it turns out, the Pharisees are the ones who tell the public what the Scriptures actually mean, and they do so out of oral tradition, as we see here:

> "When Y'shua had finished saying these things, the crowds were amazed at his teaching, because he taught as one who had authority and not as their teachers of the law."
>
> Matthew 7:28-29

This fact is easily shown throughout the entire Sermon. Matthew actually records no fewer than six times where the phrase "You have heard that it was SAID (i.e. spoken by the teachers of the law)" is contrasted with his own interpretation of " . . . but I say to you . . ." (5:21-26, 5:27-30, 5:31-32, 5:33-37, 5:38-42, 5:43-48).

Now let us hear what the great Greek Bible scholar Charles Ryrie had to say about this issue:

> "The scribes had to rely on tradition for authority; Messiah's authority was His own. It disturbed the

Pharisees that he had no 'credentials' as an official teacher in their system."

Ryrie Study Bible (NASV), p. 18

In this context, several curious statements in the Gospels now make a lot more sense:

"Y'shua left there and went to his hometown, accompanied by his disciples. When the Sabbath came, he began to teach in the synagogue, and many who heard him were amazed.

'Where did this man get these things?' they asked. 'What's this wisdom that has been given him, that he even does miracles! Isn't this the carpenter? Isn't this Mary's son and the brother James, Joseph, Judas and Simon? Aren't his sisters here with us?' And they took offense at him."

Mark 6:1-3

" 'Nazareth! Can anything good come from there?' Nathanael asked."

John 1:46

"Not until halfway through the Feast did Y'shua go up to the temple courts and begin to teach. The Jews were amazed and said, 'How did this man get such learning without having studied?'"

John 7:14-15

Now let us look at how such a studying regimen is known to have happened. During this same time period on the Aramaic side, a body of literature had sprung up all over Israel to address a common problem. Deriving their name from the Aramaic phrase "to interpret", the *targumim*—or simply *targums*—were very popular with the common people, and contained a combination of direct translation, local colloquialisms, and some limited free verse.

All these features were of course designed to make it easy for a primarily Aramaic speaker to understand the Hebrew scriptures that were read in the synagogue, but not discussed much outside of it. Additionally their original oral "pedigree", like the Talmud itself claiming to be the Oral Law given at Sinai, went back many centuries before their official compilation. Fragmentary targums of both Job and Leviticus have been found at Qumran[134], and it is certain that other targums—admittedly now lost—must have existed for other books of the Bible as well.

The need for targums arose also out of a situation where differences in local dialect made straight interpretation from Hebrew very difficult, and we see evidences of this throughout the New Testament. In the third chapter of the Gospel of John, for example, Y'shua uses a Galilean idiom, "born again", which his companion Nicodemus does not recognize. This of course necessitates a lengthy reply so he can "get it right". Another instance is actually on the cross in Matthew 27, where Y'shua's cry to God is mistaken for that of "Elijah" by the Hebrew speakers present.

However, from the early centuries of the common era and going forward, only a handful of targums have survived either in early written form or as a later interpolation of oral readings put down into writing during the era of rabbinic Judaism. Furthermore, it seems that most of these surviving interpretations came from the area of Judea. Their northern Galilean counterparts, which are well known as having once existed during the time of Messiah, are completely gone today. Therefore, that is why both Paul Younan and myself postulate that the best candidates for these missing OT quotes are in fact the lost targums of Galilee.

As for the Aramaic NT, their OT quotes do not match any other known collection either. Specifically, not a single one can be shown to have come from Hebrew (Masoretic Text), Aramaic (Peshitta OT—a.k.a. "Peshitta Tenakh") or Greek (Septuagint) sources.

And, since we have seen that the Greek NT fares no better, we must look for a reason for that phenomenon also, and here it is:

> "At Caesarrea there was man named Cornelius, a centurion in what was known as the Italian Regiment. He and all his family were devout and God fearing; he gave generously to those in need and prayed to God regularly."
>
> Acts 10:1-2 (NIV)

Now from the further context of the verse, we know that Cornelius is not a Christian because he gets converted later (Acts 10:44-48), and his ethnicity precludes him from being a Jew by birth, so how is it he "fears God"? The answer, is that he is a proselyte, as Charles Ryrie again explains:

> "Cornelius was a semi-proselyte to Judaism, accepting Jewish beliefs and practices but stopping short of circumcision."
>
> Ryrie Study Bible (NASV), p. 225

For more information on the ramifications of that, let us look elsewhere, emphases mine:

> **Proselyte** is used in the LXX. for "stranger", i.e., a comer to Palestine; a sojourner in the land, and in

the New Testament for a convert to Judaism. There were such converts from early times, (Isa 56:3, Neh 10:28). The law of Moses made specific regulations regarding the admission into the Jewish church of such as were not born Israelites, (Ex 20:10, 23:12, De 5:14). The Kenites, the Gibeonites, the Cherethites, and the Pelethites were thus admitted to the privileges of Israelites. Thus also we hear of individual proselytes who rose to positions of prominence in Israel, as of Doeg the Edomite, Uriah the Hittite, Araunah the Jebusite, Zelek the Ammonite, Ithmah and Ebedmelech the Ethiopians.

In the time of Solomon there were one hundred and fifty-three thousand six hundred strangers in the land of Israel (1 Ch 22:2). Accordingly, in New Testament times, we read of proselytes in the synagogues, (Ac 10:27).. The "religious proselytes" here spoken of were proselytes of righteousness, as distinguished from proselytes of the gate.

The distinction between "proselytes of the gate" (Ex 20:10) and "proselytes of righteousness" originated only with the rabbis. According to them, the "proselytes of the gate" (half proselytes) were not required to be circumcised nor to comply with the Mosaic ceremonial law. They were bound only to conform to the so-called seven precepts of Noah, viz., to abstain from idolatry, blasphemy, bloodshed, uncleaness, the eating of blood, theft, and to yield obedience to the authorities. Besides these laws, however, they were required to abstain from work on the Sabbath, and to refrain from the use of leavened bread during the time of the Passover.

> The "proselytes of righteousness", religious or devout proselytes (Ac 13:43), were bound to all the doctrines and precepts of the Jewish economy, and were members of the synagogue in full communion.
>
> The name "proselyte" occurs in the New Testament only in Matthew 23:15, Acts 2:10, 6:5 and 13:43. The name by which they are commonly designated is that of "devout men," or men "fearing God" or "worshipping God."
>
> Easton's Bible Dictionary, p. 563-564

Now, as it relates to this specific topic, these *proselytes of the gate* were not required to learn Hebrew until they went to the next level, the *proselytes of righteousness*. However, they still had to attend synagogue on the Sabbath and not do any work. So, for these people, *the Pharisees made a provision that they could get the services translated into Greek*. And, as we have seen, another word for interpretation is *targum*.

So, while we may never know for sure, it is very clear that "targumming" in the loose sense of the word, was happening in both Aramaic and Greek. Therefore, whether dealing with the Peshitta or Greek NT versions where these quotes exist, some form of targums must have formed the basis, if not as direct sources, then as a methodology handed down from them, for the earliest believers to record their scriptural paraphrases.

Finally, as Paul Younan also explains, sometimes appearances can be deceiving as to what constitutes an OT quote in the first place:

> It should be realized by now, although Western scholars are stubborn, that not every passage cited as an Old Testament quotation is in fact a quotation. Many times they are allusions or simply a gen-

eral reference, but not an excerpt from an OT passage.

For example, your Acts 7:14 example, in which Stephen says, "Then sent Joseph, and called his father Jacob to him, and all his kindred, threescore and fifteen souls." The number which Stephen gives is 75. However, the passage in Genesis 46:27 totals 70. There we read, "And the sons of Joseph, which were born him in Egypt, were two souls: all the souls of the house of Jacob, which came into Egypt, were threescore and ten."

The Greek LXX agrees with Stephen in Genesis 46:27 and lists the number as 75 souls. This passage is often used as an example of a NT saint citing the LXX. The truth is that Stephen is not quoting anything, he is *referring to something.*

These two texts reflect two ways of numbering Jacob's family. Jacob's children, grandchildren, and great-grandchildren amounted to sixty-six (Gen. 46:8-26). Adding Jacob himself, and Joseph with his two sons, we have seventy.

If to the sixty-six we add the nine wives of Jacob's sons (Judah's and Simeon's wives were dead; Joseph could not be said to call himself, his own wife, or his two sons into Egypt; and Jacob is specified separately by Stephen), we have seventy-five persons, as in Acts."

Therefore the difference in number can be clarified by an examination of the Biblical texts and not referencing the citation to that of the LXX. Further, scrutiny of the passage in Acts clearly shows that Stephen was referring to events in Genesis 46 and not quoting the passage.

And so, in the end, we are back to where we started that neither the use nor disuse of Septuagint quotes impacts on the linguistic primacy issues in any way. If it was used, it was only for the Greek audience of those manuscripts, and if it was not used, it emerged from a cultural milieu of interpreting scripture with some degree of poetic license.

Challenge #3:

Scribal glosses, such as those all over Mark, prove the writer is trying to put Aramaic ideas compositionally into Greek.

First let us define this term. A *scribal gloss* is when there is a break in the narrative that the writer uses to say, "this foreign term REALLY means____". Here is a classic example:

> "After he put them all out, he took the child's father and mother and the disciples who were with him and went where the child was. He took her by the hand and said to her, 'Talitha koum!' (which means, 'Little girl, I say to you, get up!')
>
> Mark 5:40-41 (NIV)[135]

Again, this is an assumption that presupposes the conclusion in its beginning hypothesis. If, as I said before, it is a given that the Greek mss were first, then suggesting that the writer is transliterating Aramaic words into Greek letters and then attaching a note to the reader as to the meaning of that word makes perfect sense.

But do the Aramaic mss reflect such a scenario?

In a word: no. These same scribal glosses are completely missing from the Peshitta.

Now for the Greek school, this too can be explained to their advantage. The Aramaic readers of course knew what those phrases meant, so the translators dropped the explanatory notes going into that language because they were not necessary. So we have oral Aramaic words of Y'shua being compositionally put into Greek for the first time, only to come *translationally back into Aramaic!*

As odd as it sounds, this is the majority view right now, and what I hope to be able to demonstrate is that there is more than one valid way to look at this evidence for glosses of this type. I say "of this type" because other kinds of glosses do not lend themselves at all to such flexible interpretation as we will see in a moment. But for now, let us list the other Aramaic words that Mark uses in the Greek texts.[136] They are:

> Corban (7:11)
> Ephatha (7:34)
> Bar Timaeus (10:46)
> Abba (14:36)
> Golgotha (15:22)

Other scribal glosses in the rest of the Gospels include:

> Immanuel, (Matthew 1:23)
> Raca, (Matthew 5:21)
> Rabbi, (Matthew 26:25, John 1:38)
> Bethesda, (John 5:2)
> Sea of Galilee (John 6:1)
> Siloam (John 9:7)
> Rabboni (John 20:16)

The reality with all of these is, of course, that they are just as likely to be transliterated from Aramaic written sources as they are from oral ones. But, as I also said, there is more than one kind of gloss. Here is another:

> Are you so dull?" he asked. "Don't you see that nothing that enters a man from the outside can make him `unclean'? For it doesn't go into his heart but into his stomach, and then out of his body." (In saying this, Y'shua declared all foods "clean.") He went on: "What comes out of a man is what makes him `unclean.'
>
> Mark 7:18-20 (NIV)[137]

However, in the Aramaic version, the wording is almost identical *except that there is no mention of "Y'shua declaring all foods clean"!* So, if the Peshitta is a translation from the Greek and dates to the fifth century, how is it that this gloss is missing from the text, and yet is present in all the early Greek mss? In other words, how does one phrase translate into NOTHING on the other side?

In such a case then, it is quite possible that the Semitic (read "Jewish") aspects of this verse were altered by Gentiles trying to distance themselves from their own Master's origins and use of kosher dietary laws! And, even if this is not the case, the Peshitta version certainly reflects the more historically accurate portrait of what a first century Jew like Y'shua would have considered fit to consume. Finally, from the context of the verse it is clear that Y'shua was contrasting the clean hands of the Pharisees before a meal and their inner defilement evidenced by them accusing him, and therefore had nothing to do with food at all, (Mark 7:1-15)! It is instead a halachic (legal) point, which basically says, "If you plot great evil, eating pure food will not really matter, because your insides are already UN-KOSHER."

And, finally, there is the explosive example of Mark 3:17, where two disciples are given the title "sons of thunder". In the Greek, this is rendered "Boanerges", but almost all scholars recognize this as a corruption of an Aramaic phrase.

Now here is where it gets interesting. In the Aramaic, that phrase is recorded as "bnai ragshee", but there is a big problem *since bnai ragshee itself has multiple meanings*. In fact, *ragshee* could mean:

1) Enraged, to be in an uproar (used as a metaphor with storms);
2) to feel;
3) to perceive or be conscious of;
4) to rub down;
5) or to be acquainted.

So what does it mean to be sons of *ragshee*? Are they "sons of feeling"? How about "sons of perception" or "sons of acquaintances"? It is even possible to speculate that they just gave great massages! To translate into a language with such a diversity of meaning can hardly be desirable, and would most likely only be done if there were no other alternative, clearer rendering to be made. However, in Aramaic *there is a phrase that only means "thunder"!* So, what happens in this phrase is something very unusual: the Aramaic clarifies itself!

Mark actually puts, "bnai ragshee, D'ATTOHI (that is) BNAI REAMA". The only time then that *reama* has a similar meaning to *ragshee* is in the first definition. Therefore, to go from a Greek original into *ragshee* and then say, "Well, I really meant to use this second definition so forget the first one", is simply preposterous, not to mention awkward in the extreme. Why not simply translate *boanerges* directly into *bnai reama?*

The only other alternative is to affirm the earliest traditions that the second Gospel is an eyewitness account of Peter's being set down by Mark. If so, then Peter must have heard "ragshee" actually said by Y'shua and knew which meaning was appropriate. However, remember that if this proves a clear Aramaic oral layer that both Peter and Mark are native Aramaic speakers! In that case, we could easily imagine Mark taking Aramaic dictation and writing down what Peter said. Then, when *ragshee* comes up, Mark says, "Master, which meaning of that word did you intend?" Peter then responds, "thunder" which prompts Mark to record that answer and, of course, this could not happen in Greek. However, as we will see later on, Mark is actually using a combination of Matthew's Aramaic rough draft and Peter's editorial guidance.

The answer is then one of the most powerful reasons for supposing previous oral and written Aramaic sources in advance of the Greek versions, because only a written source in the same language as its oral predecessor would make such a modification. A translation INTO THAT LANGUAGE, by contrast, would simply pick the most precise term to use there.

Challenge #4:

Greek fragments and mss of the NT are far more numerous and ancient than Aramaic or Hebrew ones.

True, but does that mean it is because the Greek mss came first? Isn't it possible that major social upheavals, wars, and other related events could intervene and cause that situation? We are talking about the Middle East, after all.

To begin with, most New Testament scholars today admit that Aramaic oral sources underlay much of the Gospel record and perhaps a few Epistles as well. We will be getting into the textual evidence in great detail a bit later, so I will not be "proving" this common and widely held position right now, but merely will use it as a launching point.

How these Aramaic oral sources skipped the written phase in that language altogether and ended up in compositional Greek has never been satisfactorily explained, since the assumption that the Greek had to come first anyway is so deeply engrained.

However, from a general historical perspective, there are quite a few examples that argue against this idea or at least raises enough reasonable doubt as to preclude it as the only proper scenario. Of all these, possibly the best one I can sum up in a single word: Tobit.

One of the books of the so-called *Apocrypha,* Tobit was used in the Septuagint collection and became part of the Hellenistic Jewish canon. As recently as the 1940's, the prevailing view was that Tobit was completely compositional Greek and that it never circulated in Israel. Then, in 1947, the Dead Sea Scrolls discovery overturned both assumptions, when the oldest mss of Tobit were found to have been written in Hebrew and stored in Qumran. Apparently good Greek usage did not prove primacy in that case.

And still several others can be called upon as well to bear similar witness. *The Gospel of Thomas,* originally written by the patron saint of Syria, currently only exists in one complete Coptic version and several Greek fragments. In spite of this deficiency however, most scholars accept the idea that the version we now have was tampered with and added to by the Gnostics, and that an original Thomas must have widely circulated in Israel (or Syria), probably in the Aramaic language. As we will see later, certain linkages between Thomas and the Gospels scream at a first century origin, which is why even liberals like the Jesus Seminar postulate that it could date back as far as the 50's. Similarly the famous "Q" document also shows an Aramaic sub-stratum—whether oral or written is in dispute but it is there nevertheless—and even though not a single copy or fragment of Q has been found—it too is believed to have circulated in the 50's.[138] Finally, we have the writings of Josephus which, by his own admission, were written first in Aramaic (or possibly Hebrew) but which have now all perished:

> "I have proposed to myself, for the sake of such as live under the government of the Romans, to translate those books into the Greek tongue, which I formerly composed in the language of our country, and sent to the Upper Barbarians; Joseph, the son of Matthias, by birth a Hebrew, a priest also, and

> one who at first fought against the Romans myself, and was forced to be present at what was done afterwards, [am the author of this work]."

Preface to Wars Against the Jews, 1.1-2

So what happened to them, and how can history shed some light on the reasons behind their fate?

Well, we have to start with the obvious calamity of the destruction of Jerusalem in the year 70. Here are some excerpts from Josephus as to the totality of the destruction:

> And here I cannot but speak my mind, and what the concern I am under dictates to me, and it is this: I suppose, **that had the Romans made any longer delay in coming against these villains, that the city would either have been swallowed up by the ground opening upon them, or been overflowed by water, or else been destroyed by such thunder as the country of Sodom (20) perished by, for it had brought forth a generation of men much more atheistical than were those that suffered such punishments;** for by their madness it was that all the people came to be destroyed.

> And, indeed, why do I relate these particular calamities . . . **no fewer than a hundred and fifteen thousand eight hundred and eighty dead bodies, in the interval between the fourteenth day of the month Xanthieus, [Nisan,] when the Romans pitched their camp by the city, and the first day of the month Panemus [Tamuz]** . . . After this man there ran away to Titus many of the eminent citizens, and told him the entire number of the poor that were dead, and

that no fewer than six hundred thousand were thrown out at the gates, though still the number of the rest could not be discovered; and they told him further, that when they were no longer able to carry out the dead bodies of the poor, they laid their corpses on heaps in very large houses, and shut them up therein . . .

. . . And now the Romans, although they were greatly distressed in getting together their materials, raised their banks in one and twenty days, **after they had cut down all the trees that were in the country that adjoined to the city, and that for ninety furlongs round about, as I have already related. And truly the very view itself of the country was a melancholy thing; for those places which were before adorned with trees and pleasant gardens were now become a desolate country every way, and its trees were all cut down: nor could any foreigner that had formerly seen Judea and the most beautiful suburbs of the city, and now saw it as a desert, but lament and mourn sadly at so great a change: for the war had laid all the signs of beauty quite waste**: nor if any one that had known the place before, had come on a sudden to it now, would he have known it again; but though he were at the city itself, yet would he have inquired for it notwithstanding.

Excerpts from: War, 5.13.6-7; 6.1.1.

We can easily see how this relates to precious manuscripts. The Temple is completely gone, and with it, its archive. People at Qumran, either as Judeans fleeing a wrathful Roman army of near-apocalyptic proportions or concerned Essenes who were probably wiped out two years earlier and took precautions at the beginning of the conflict, had good reasons to fear for themselves and their holy books. Furthermore, if Norman Golb is correct, the calamity was so great that normal sectarian divisions broke down as the Jewish nation gasped for survival and deposited a wide variety of their traditions in the general area.

But at least the Hebrew OT mss had an advantage. They had been circulating for so many centuries and in such great numbers that even this type of catastrophe would not have destroyed them entirely. The Romans, in fact, actually had a copy of the Torah put in one of their own temples, (War 7.5.7)! Also in two cases the Romans allowed prominent Jews to take Hebrew documents out of the city. One, obviously, was Josephus, who tells us in Antiquities several times that he is translating directly from Hebrew sources, and the other is the famous Rabbi Yochanan ben Zakkai, who was allowed to build one Torah academy at Yavneh by the emperor Titus. However, it is also worth noting that the destruction of Jerusalem was still great enough as to cause the Sanhedrin and all Jewish learning to stop there and relocate to Yavneh. But, of course neither Josephus nor Rabbi Yochanan would have made any efforts to save the Hebrew documents written by that *other group* now called "Christians".

Furthermore, the Hebrew NT documents would have almost all been confined to Jerusalem, ground zero of this entire conflagration. Nor could the apostles flee northward to what was, for many of them, their home region. Galilee also suffered horrendous losses during this same time, with estimates of the dead approaching 100,000—and of course the southern end of the Dead Sea, and its calamities at Masada, need hardly be mentioned. Therefore, from one end of the nation to the other, death and destruction were clearly the order of the day and such were the reasons for reducing vast numbers of those early Hebrew witnesses.

Now take that greatly reduced number of remaining mss and add the following disaster to the equation. That next crisis, known as the Bar Kochba Revolt, would have reduced their number even more.

Emerging from the disastrous ashes of defeat six decades before, the second Jewish War proved to be a disaster on a magnitude that easily dwarfed its predecessor—with far greater incentives given to the Romans to "finish the job".

For one thing, the Bar Kochba Revolt was not just a civil uprising. It was a religious one backed up by the Jewish hierarchy, including the great Rabbi Akiba. Bar Kochba (whose name means "son of the star"), was proclaimed the Jewish Messiah and fought the Roman war machine to a standstill for more than three years. His influence was in fact so strong that he was even able to mint coins saying, "year one of the New Israel". So, when he was finally killed, one can imagine how the Roman wrath would turn not just on the infrastructure of the nation, but its faith as well. Here is what the rabbinic record has to say about that issue:

> R. Yochanan said: Rabbi used to expound, "There shall step forth a star (kochav) out of Jacob" (Num. XXIV, 17), thus: read not 'kochav but kozav (lie).
>
> When R. Akiva beheld Bar Koziva he exclaimed, 'This is the king Messiah!'
>
> R. Yochanan b. Torta retorted: 'Akiva, grass will grow in your cheeks and he will still not have come!'
>
> R. Yochanan said: The voice is the voice of Jacob (Gen. XXVII, 22)—the voice [of distress caused by] the Emperor Hadrian, **who slew eighty thousand myriads of human beings at Beitar** (the final battle site of Bar Kochba and his troops).
>
> Eighty thousand vanguard troops besieged Beitar where Bar Koziva was located who had with him

two hundred thousand men with an amputated finger.

The Sages sent him the message, 'How long will you continue to make the men of Israel blemished?'

He asked them, 'How else shall they be tested?'

They answered, 'Let anyone who cannot uproot a cedar from Lebanon be refused enrollment in your army.'

He thereupon had two hundred thousand men of each rank; and when they went forth to battle they cried, '[O God,] neither help us nor discourage us!'

That is what is written, Have you not, O God, cast us off? And go not forth, O God, with our hosts (Ps. LX, 12).

And what did Bar Koziva use to do?

He would catch the missiles from the enemy's catapults on one of his knees and hurl them back, killing many of the foe.

On that account R. Akiva made his remark.

For three and a half years the Emperor Hadrian surrounded Beitar. In the city was R. Eleazar of Modim who continually wore sackcloth and fasted, and he used to pray daily, 'LORD of the Universe, sit not in judgment to-day!' so that [Hadrian] thought of returning home.

A Cuthean (a Samaritan, a sect against the Jews) went and found him and said, 'My LORD, so long as that old rooster wallows in ashes you will not conquer the city. But wait for me, because I will do something which will enable you to subdue it to-day.'

He immediately entered the gate of the city, where he found R. Eleazar standing and praying. He pretended to whisper in the ear of R. Eleazar of Modim.

People went and informed Bar Koziva, 'Your friend, R. Eleazar, wishes to surrender the city to Hadrian.'

He sent and had the Cuthean brought to him and asked, 'What did you say to him?'

He replied, 'If I tell you, the king will kill me; and if I do not tell you, you will kill me. It is better that I should kill myself and the secrets of the government be not divulged.

' Bar Koziva was convinced that R. Eleazar wanted to surrender the city, so when the latter finished his praying he had him brought into his presence and asked him, 'What did the Cuthean tell you?'

He answered,'I do not know what he whispered in my ear, nor did I hear anything, because I was standing in prayer and am unaware what he said.'

Bar Koziva flew into a rage, kicked him with his foot and killed him.

A Bat Kol (a divine voice from heaven) issued forth and proclaimed, 'Woe to the worthless shepherd that leaves the flock! The sword shall be upon his arm, and upon his right eye.' (Zech. 11:17)

It intimated to him, 'You have paralyzed the arm of Israel and blinded their right eye; therefore your arm will wither and your right eye will grow dim!'

At once the sins [of the people] caused Beitar to be captured. Bar Koziva was slain and his head taken to Hadrian.

'Who killed him?' asked Hadrian.

A Cuthean said to him, 'I killed him.'

'Bring his body to me,' he ordered.

He went and found a snake encircling its neck;

so [Hadrian when told of this] exclaimed, 'If his God had not slain him who could have overcome him?'

And there was applied to him the verse, Except their Rock had given them over (Deut. XXXII, 30).

They slew the inhabitants until the horses waded in blood up to their nostrils, and the blood rolled along stones of the size of forty se'ah (71 gallons, the same amount as is needed to make a mikvah kosher. . . .) and flowed into the sea [staining it for] a distance of four miles.

Should you say that [Beitar] is close to the sea; was it not in fact four miles distant from it?

Now Hadrian possessed a large vineyard eighteen miles square, as far as from Tiberias to Sepphoris, and they surrounded it with a fence consisting of the slain at Beitar. Nor was it decreed that they should be buried until a certain king arose and ordered their interment.

R. Huna said: On the day when the slain of Beitar were allowed burial, the benediction 'Who are kind and deals kindly' was instituted

' Who are kind ' because the bodies did not putrefy, 'and deals kindly' because they were allowed burial.

R. Yochanan said: The brains of three hundred children [were dashed] upon one stone, and three hundred baskets of capsules of tefillin were found in Beitar, each basket being of the capacity of three se'ah, so that there was a total of three hundred se'ah.

R. Gamliel said: There were five hundred schools in Beitar, and the smallest of them had not less than three hundred children.

> They used to say, 'If the enemy comes against us, with these styluses we will go out and stab them!'
>
> **When, however, [the people's] sins did cause the enemy to come, they enwrapped each pupil in his book and burned him, so that I alone was left.**
>
> He applied to himself the verse, My eye affected my soul, because of all the daughters [i.e. inhabitants] of my city."
>
> Lamentations Rabba 2:4

The reader should not make any mistake. Those five hundred "schools" were synagogues with their students being burned alive in Torah scrolls—and this is what was done in ONE CITY—let alone the nationwide destruction that came later. Therefore, if this is the fate of the venerable Torah, what would happen if Hebrew NT documents were found by the Romans as well? One thing is certain, it is extremely doubtful they would have cared for the distinction, except that, again, the Hebrew OT mss still had the NT ones greatly outnumbered.

Now we need to look at the Aramaic side of the equation. While the issue of the manuscripts' antiquity will be addressed in the next challenge, no scholar doubts that the Aramaic NT is any younger than the fifth century. Therefore, we can look at what has happened since that time and deal with the half a millennium between that period in history and the apostolic age a bit later on.

Following Constantine's moving of the Empire's capital from Rome to Byzantium, a bitter rivalry arose between him and the Parthian (Persian) Empire, which was the domain of the Church of the East. By the fifth century, bitter divisions threatened to shatter the Christian world, as George Lamsa explains:

> "The Church (of the East) rejected the doctrines advanced at the Council of Ephesus (431 CE) and bitterly opposed the spread of Greek and Monophysite doctrines . . . Then again, Persia, an enemy of the Byzantine Empire, for political reasons was strongly opposed to the introduction of Greek doctrines among the Christians in the East. The Persian kings issued decree to imprison and expel priests and bishops found to be sympathetic to the Byzantine Church."
>
> The Modern New Testament from the Aramaic, p. x

This fact alone should silence anyone who would suggest that the Peshitta was born at this time and was a translation from the Greek, the language of the Assyrian Church of the East's enemies. As time went on, the Church became more isolated from the rest of Christendom, and the Roman Catholics who spread throughout the east managed to get a rival Aramaic group known as the Syrian Orthodox Church to join its rank. This was done, at least partially, so that the SOC could enjoy Roman protection from their increasingly hostile neighbors, but the price for that convenience was quite high. Starting in 508 and again in 616, the SOC revised the original Peshitta NT so that it would be more in line with the more familiar (and by now, popular) Greek texts that had become the standard in the West.

These revisions, both later called the "Peshitto", included five books that the Eastern Church had always rejected but that the Roman Catholics and the rest of the West viewed as canonical. Because no Aramaic versions of these five books were known to exist, they were translated into Aramaic from the Greek. That act, plus the similarity of the names (Peshitta and Peshitto), has confused scholars even to this day. Such a misconception was surely aided in the late nineteenth century, when Protestant missionaries found isolated SOC communities thought lost for seven hundred years. The SOC then brought up THEIR versions to be translated and took the missionaries' money to establish new schools and make their life slightly more bearable. But, the missionaries, while helping these people out quite a bit, nevertheless were misinformed and translated the wrong Aramaic documents into English. The SOC simply did not have the older ones in their possession since they contained ancient theological concepts that they no longer ascribed to.

As for the Church of the East, they too were forgotten by the world and made almost extinct by the hand of one man: Tamerlane.

Tamerlane was a Turk who claimed direct descent from the infamous Genghis Khan, and he is also remembered as one of the most prolific mass murderers in all of history. The scars he left behind in India and the Middle East have yet to heal, for Tamerlane did not even spare his fellow Muslims— let alone the eastern Christians living in his midst or standing in his way. And, remarkably this type of candor about one of their own comes even from Muslim sources:

> "For several years I put off reporting this event. I found it terrifying and felt revulsion at recounting it ... If anyone were to say that at no time since the creation of man by God had the world experienced anything like it, he would only be telling the truth. In fact nothing comparable is reported in the past chronicles. The worst they recall is the treatment of the Israelites and the destruction of Jerusalem by Nebuchadnezzar. But what is Jerusalem compared with the areas destroyed by these monsters? It may well be that the world from now until the end will not experience the like of it again, except for Gog and Magog. The AntiMessiah will at least spare those who adhere to him, and will destroy only his adversaries. The Turks, however, spared none. They killed women, men and chil-

dren, ripped open the bodies of the pregnant and slaughtered the unborn...."

Ibn al-Athir (1160-1234) Muslim chronicler.

And:

"To this ferocity Tamerlane added a taste for religious murder. He killed from piety. He represents a synthesis, probably unprecedented in history, of Mongolic-Turkic barbarity and Muslim fanaticism, and symbolizes that advanced form of primitive slaughter which is murder committed for the sake of abstract ideology, as a duty and a sacred mission."

Rene Grousset, The Empire of the Steppes.

Before this scourge of a man, the Church of the East was a thriving and vibrant Christian sect, with followers as far as China and India. Afterwards, they were little more than a memory—with 99% of their population put to the sword.[139] Tamerlane was equally ruthless in destroying Christian shrines and yes—early Aramaic Christian documents as well. From the time of his death in 1405 until our own day, the eastern Christians have faced a regular and sustained Muslim campaign to wipe them off the face of the earth, with the most recent—and nearly successful—genocide happening in 1915.

Given all this, is it any wonder that many early Aramaic NT mss were either destroyed or yet to be discovered by the West? In fact, in the face of such implacable race hatred from a foe thousands of times more numerous, would it be surprising to find that any surviving Aramaic mss might owe their existence to someone with the foresight to hide them away in Dead Sea Scrolls fashion? Finally, knowing that the difference between Aramaic and Greek—the latter being the consistent language of choice by so many of the Church of the East's foes—is it at all shocking that there are fewer fragments of the former?

Challenge #5:

All Aramaic mss are far later than the Greek (fifth century or later) and are therefore translations from the Greek.

> "Of these Pantaenus was one: it is stated that he went as far as India, where he appears to have found that Matthew's Gospel had arrived before him and was in the hands of some there who had come to know Messiah. Bartholomew, one of the apostles, had preached to them and had left behind Matthew's account **in the actual Aramaic characters**, and it was preserved till the time of Pantaenus's mission."
>
> Pataenus (second century), Book v, Chapter 10. Quoted from the translation by G. A. Williamson, *The History of the Church*, Dorset Press, New York, 1965, pages 213-214.
>
> "Hegesippus, (who lived and wrote about A. D. 188,) made some quotations from the Gospel according to the Hebrews, and from the Syriac Gospel."
>
> Eusebius, Hist. Eccl., iv,22

Actually, it is some of the *revisions of the Peshitta* that are fifth century or later, not the originals. Therefore, it need be little stated that originals then precede their revisions.

As for the comparisons to the Greek collection, they have some additional early fragments—not surprising in the context of the previous point—but in terms of full codices (complete NTs) they date from around the same period as the Aramaic ones!

However, there are differences. Just like the scribal gloss of "In doing so Y'shua declared all foods clean" being not present in the "translated Peshitta", whole sections of what scholars recognize as later additions on the Greek side aren't there either, like John 7:53-8:11. That section, which contains the famous story of the adulteress, is not present in the four earliest COMPLETE Greek NTs, which again go back to the fourth century. Therefore, the assertion that the Peshitta is somehow a translation from Greek texts that came out a century or more later must be viewed as preposterous.

On the other hand, various endings of Mark's Gospel that are all over the place in the Greek texts, are refreshingly unified in the Aramaic with the standard 20 verse sixteenth chapter. That is also why Papias, a disciple of the apostle John who wrote no later than the year 130, talked about Matthew's Gospel being translated from Aramaic and into Greek "as best as they could"—precisely because there was no Greek standard text.

Nor is this even the extent of the differences between the earliest Aramaic and Greek codices. The fact is, there would have been no need to revise the Aramaic—twice!—if it were a translation from the Greek texts.

And, it does not take a lot to prove this absolutely either. Take a standard Greek based translation—any will do—and put it side by side with an original Aramaic one (not Murdock or Jahn, who go from the revised Peshitto texts, but from Paul Younan, Victor Alexander or George Lamsa) and the difference is clear immediately. There are hundreds of instances where the order of sentences—and even paragraphs—are switched around. In fact, these differences were so numerous that Lamsa was not allowed to publish the documentation because A.J. Holman Publishers feared that people raised on the King James Version would be offended! Therefore, if the Peshitta is a translation, it is by far the sloppiest one ever attempted.

Beyond all these evidences, we have the writings of Saint Ephraem who, in 337 quoted a reading that only exists in the Peshitta and made reference to it as the original. Additionally, the ten Church councils that were held in the Persian Empire during the third and fourth centuries never made reference to the need for a translation into Aramaic.

And yet, these same councils debated as late as the year 410 whether Revelation should be included in their pre-existent written canon and had the region as a whole celebrate perennial feast days when the Bible came into the local vernacular of a given segment of the population. Such is the case with the Armenians, various Arab countries, India, and on and on—but nowhere is the feast day for the Aramaic NT recorded because it had been there all along. The liturgy that supports the Peshitta as the original is in fact so strong that even when various eastern Aramaic groups denounced each other and rejected each side's revisions, that they all agree on what came first. Certainly this would not be true either, unless these claims were well established in advance of these early disputes.

Going still further back, we have the case of Tatian to consider. As the Catholic Encyclopedia explains, this Syrian monk did something rather unusual:

> The other extant work [of Tatian's] is the "Diatesseron", a harmony of the four Gospels containing in continuous narrative the principle events in the life of Our LORD. The question regarding the language in which this work was composed is still in dispute. Lightfoot, Hilgenfeld, Bardenhewer, and others contend that the original language was Syriac. Harnack, Burkitt, and others are equally positive that it was composed in Greek and translated into Syriac during the lifetime of Tatian. There are only a few fragments extant in Syriac but a comparatively full reconstruction of the whole has been effected from St. Ephraem's commentary,

the Syriac text of which has been lost, but which exists in an Armenian version.

And the Encyclopedia Brittanica adds:

> (The Diatessaron is a collection of) the four New Testament Gospels compiled as a single narrative by about AD 150. It was the standard Gospel text in the Syrian Middle East until about AD 400, when it was replaced by the four separated Gospels. Quotations from the *Diatessaron* appear in ancient Syriac literature, but no ancient Syriac manuscript now exists.

Now this citation, along with the other, makes reference to a lack of certainty of the original language of this work. However, the Catholic Encyclopedia is equally clear that if the Aramaic was done later it was still before Tatian's death, which was in the year 172. It is therefore likely that Tatian may have been looking at both early Greek and Aramaic mss to do this job, but either way, the fragments that have survived still bear witness to an even older Aramaic source.

From this early time then in the middle of the second century, the liturgy and history takes over. We know absolutely, for example, that the first fifteen patriarchs of the See of Jerusalem, tracing their line from the first century and onwards, were all Semites who wrote, spoke and worshipped exclusively in Aramaic. It is therefore inconceivable that they would not have the basis for that same liturgy—namely the New Testament itself—available to them as well since their own Aramaic prayers quote heavily from it.

It is also at this juncture that it seems advisable to debunk another common misconception. Late in the 19th century, one prominent scholar put forth what he admitted was a "guess", and the ramifications of that musing are still with us today. Dr. F. Crawford Burkitt of the University of Cambridge, a man of great learning and prestige, was the first to suggest that a bishop named Rabbula actually authored the Peshitta.

There were some understandable factors contributing to this assertion. Rabbula was the fifteenth Bishop of the ancient See of Edessa from about the year 412 to 435. He suppressed the Diatessaron of Tatian and replaced the text with four separate Gospels.

Now to be sure, it is therefore easy to see how this act could be misconstrued as Rabbula writing those Gospels in Aramaic himself, but the reality is that Rabbula opposed Tatian's arrogance in thinking that he could pick and choose how to order a combined Gospel.

Another reason for Rabbula's anger must surely have rested on religious grounds. Just prior to his death, Tatian became a member of a heretical sect of Gnosticism. It was these people—also known as the Encraites— that Rabbula despised, and so the bishop separated the Gospels back out again and restored the original Peshitta text that his church still supported at that time.[140]

Additionally two other critical factors need to be considered. First, Rabbula was only the Bishop of Edessa, which meant he did not have the authority to make a change in either his churches' source texts nor their liturgy. So, if he had made his own version, the consent of his superiors would have recorded it as a kind of divine breakthrough. Furthermore, the prestige and ramifications associated with such a work would have been shouted from the rooftops, as the later revisions by this same Christian group later were.

Second, and even more important, is how the Church of the East viewed what Rabbula did. Put simply, Rabbula was a Monophysite that put him in the crosshairs of the COE as a hated enemy and heretic. Therefore, if Rabbula had written the Peshitta, it is virtually impossible that his enemies would have accepted it as authoritative and God-breathed text, just as they rejected the revisions from Rabbula's Church one to two centuries later. In the final analysis then, in spite of whatever credence this theory may find elsewhere, the historical issues absolutely rule against it when they are properly understood.

Challenge #6:

Paul wrote mostly to Greek churches (Galatia, Corinth, Thessally, Collossae, Rome) or to leaders of Greek churches (Timothy, Titus, etc).

In order to look at this assertion and do it justice, the following scriptural survey should prove useful:

And immediately he [Paul] began preaching about Y'shua in the **synagogues**, saying, "He is indeed the Son of God!"

Acts 9:20

There, in the town of Salamis, they went to the Jewish **synagogues** and preached the word of God. (John Mark went with them as their assistant.)

But one day some men from the **Synagogue** of Freed Slaves, as it was called, started to debate with him. They were Jews from Cyrene, Alexandria, Cilicia, and the province of Asia.

Acts 13:5

But Barnabas and Paul traveled inland to Antioch of Pisidia. On the Sabbath they went to the **synagogue** for the services.

Acts 13:14

As Paul and Barnabas left the **synagogue** that day, the people asked them to return again and speak about these things the next week.

Acts 13:42-43

Many Jews and godly converts to Judaism who worshiped at the **synagogue** followed Paul and Barnabas, and the two men urged them, "By God's grace, remain faithful."

In Iconium, Paul and Barnabas went together to the **synagogue** and preached with such power that a great number of both Jews and Gentiles believed.

Acts 14:1

Now Paul and Silas traveled through the towns of Amphipolis and Apollonia and came to Thessalonica, where there was a Jewish **synagogue**. As was Paul's custom, he went to the **synagogue** service, and for three Sabbaths in a row he interpreted the Scriptures to the people.

Acts 17:1-2

That very night the believers sent Paul and Silas to Berea. When they arrived there, they went to the **synagogue**.

Acts 17:10

He went to the **synagogue** to debate with the Jews and the God-fearing Gentiles, and he spoke daily in the public square to all who happened to be there.

Acts 17:17

Each Sabbath found Paul at the **synagogue**, trying to convince the Jews and Greeks alike. After that he stayed with Titius Justus, a Gentile who worshiped God and lived next door to the **synagogue**. Crispus, the leader of the **synagogue**, and all his household believed in the LORD. Many others in Corinth also became believers and were baptized.

Acts 18:4,7-8

The mob had grabbed Sosthenes, the leader of the **synagogue**, and had beaten him right there in the courtroom. But Gallio paid no attention . . . When they arrived at the port of Ephesus, Paul left the others behind. But while he was there, he went to the **synagogue** to debate with the Jews.

Acts 18:17,19

When Priscilla and Aquila heard him preaching boldly in the **synagogue**, they took him aside and explained the way of God more accurately.

Acts 18:26

Then Paul went to the **synagogue** and preached boldly for the next three months, arguing persuasively about the Kingdom of God . . . But some rejected his message and publicly spoke against the Way, so Paul left the **synagogue** and took the believers with him. Then he began preaching daily at the lecture hall of Tyrannus.

Acts 19:8-9

So almost everywhere Paul went, as these verses indicate, he sought out the synagogues first. The question is, were these congregations Hebrew or Hellenistic Jews? To be sure, the answer must be a combination of the two. Verses like Acts 18:4—and elsewhere where a delineation of "Jews and Greeks" is made, would suggest that the Jews themselves were not also of Greek extraction. On the other hand, places like Corinth and Thessaly probably had a Gentile majority and spoke Greek in their synagogues.

However, it doesn't matter how many assemblies fit this description, because the evidence again points to the ethnicity of the audience as being irrelevant. It is the language that Paul felt comfortable communicating in which matters, and the same for Peter, who also needed the same interpreter Paul used, (1 Peter 5:12-13, 1 Thessalonians 1:1, 2 Thessalonians 1:1). However, we will get into this critical evidence in detail later on.

For now though the important point is that both Greek and Hebrew Jews "targummed" extensively, and letters in Aramaic from Paul would have, by long-standing habit, been translated into the local vernacular as a matter of course. Such was the case with both the Jews and the Roman Catholic Church, who put their sacred languages into the words of the people both before and after this apostle's time. It is also a practice continued by the Assyrian Church of the East and modern Jewry, both of whom circulate materials in Aramaic and Hebrew—respectively.

Therefore, all this historical precedent, at a minimum, raises reasonable doubt that Paul wrote compositional Greek epistles to these assemblies, especially when combined with the juxtaposition of Paul and Josephus' situation which was offered in Challenge #1 and will be revisited yet again in a later section.

Meanwhile, I would like to close this line of inquiry with a final question for the reader: If this whole "language to fit the audience" theory is correct, how do its adherents support Greek primacy for the letters of James and Hebrews, which are clearly going to Aramaic Jewish assemblies?

Challenge #7:

The earliest complete Aramaic codices are fourth-fifth century or later.

True ... and so are the Greek ones, but few scholars doubt that the originals of the latter do not go back much further than the earliest codices. The difference is, as we have already seen, that the Greek has more fragments, such as a sliver of John that goes back to 125 CE. Although, once again, that discrepancy is easily accounted for— especially when we consider the historical evidence.

Obviously, there is far more to this issue than simply counting mss and declaring the one with more the winner. The antiquity of the fragments and codices available though is an important point, but it too must be weighed properly in the overall cultural, linguistic and historical paradigms that we have been discussing.

Challenge #8:

Paul was fluent in Greek so why wouldn't he write in that language to a Greek audience?

Neither Paul's fluency in Greek nor the ethnicity of his audience has been established with any degree of certainty. There are in fact real questions raised on both issues with the evidence already presented, which is why I have attempted to show a wider view that represents as many of these combinations as possible.

Once again though it bears repeating: Even if Paul was fluent in Greek, powerful traditions involving translation of Scripture at the assembly level combined with what must have been a clear preference to speak and write in Aramaic make this less likely.

I have two other examples to offer on this point, and firmly believe that if Paul did the translating into Greek of his own Aramaic letters, then the seams of the limits of his understanding clearly show in quite a few places. Either that, or Paul sent his Aramaic letters to the assemblies and someone there did the job and that is why it turned out the way it did.

First, let's look at this verse in Romans:

For when we were still without strength, in due

time Messiah died for the ungodly. **(1) For (2) scarcely (3) for** a **(4) righteous** man will one die; yet perhaps **(5) for** a **(6) good** man someone would even dare to die. But God demonstrates His own love toward us, in that while we were still sinners, Messiah died for us.

Romans 5:6-8 (NKJV)

The bolded and numbered words indicate ones that we need to see in the Greek to understand fully, but before doing that even the English showcases this point to a degree. Almost no one will die for a righteous man, but if he is a good man they will? What does the "good" man have that the "righteous" one does not?

So let us look at how Strong's Exhaustive Concordance defines these key terms as they are in Greek:

(1) #1063-"gar"; a primary particle, conjunction. Definition: 1) "for".

(2) #3433-"molis"; adverb. Definitions: 1) With difficulty, hardly. 2) Not easily, scarcely, very rarely.

(3) #5228-"huper"; primary preposition. Definitions: 1) In behalf of, for the sake of. 2) Over, beyond, more than. 3) More, beyond, over.

(4) #1342-"dikahyos"; adjective. Definitions: 1) Righteous, observing divine laws.

 a. In a wide sense, upright, righteous, virtuous, keeping the commands of God.

1. Of those who seem to themselves to be righteous, who pride themselves in their virtues, whether real or imagined.

2. Innocent, faultless, guiltless.

3. Used of him whose way of thinking, feeling and acting is wholly conformed to will of God, and who therefore needs no rectification in the heart or life.

   a. Only Messiah truly approved of or acceptable of God.

   b. In a narrower sense, rendering to each his due and that in a judicial sense, passing just judgment on others, whether expressed in words or shown by the manner of dealing with them.

(1) Same word as (3)—"huper".

(2) #18-"agathos". A primary word; adjective. Definitions: 1) Of good constitution or nature. 2) Useful, salutary. 3) Good, pleasant, agreeable, joyful, happy. 4) Excellent, distinguished. 5) Upright, honorable.

So let's look at this sentence in detail. It starts with an unambiguous "for" (gar). Then it is followed by "scarcely, very rarely" (molis) and another critical word also translated as "for" (huper) but having the connotation of "in behalf of, for the sake of", etc.

However, the key is contrasting the two adjectives of *dikahayos* and *agathos*. Again the context is "Almost no one will die for *dikahyos* but some MIGHT DIE IN BEHALF OF *agathos*."

The first thing to observe then is simply that there is a middle ground in definitions that the two words share (upright, virtuous, honorable), but if they are interchangeable why the difference in the amount of people willing to die for these two men? It doesn't make sense, therefore, unless we see the DIFFERENCES of the two words, not their similarities.

That being said, logic demands that the person some might be willing to die for IS BETTER than the one hardly anyone would die for, and that means that *agathos*—in all its definitions—must be superior to *dikahyos*, but in fact the OPPOSITE is true. *Dikahyos* can actually be description of the perfect Messiah, whereas *agathos*—while meaning a good person overall—has no such higher level. Therefore, if Paul as a master of Greek wrote this, it is completely illogical and I have much higher regard for him than to suggest this is the case.

The other issue is that if the Peshitta were a translation FROM THIS GREEK SOURCE, we should expect similar words for "righteous" and "good" to appear there, but guess what? They don't! Let's see what it says:

It starts out identically to the Greek, "for hardly/scarcely would anyone die in behalf of", but here is the difference. The word rendered RIGHTEOUS in Greek put down as WICKED in Aramaic! So it really says:

"For hardly anyone would die in behalf of WICKED man, but for a GOOD man, some might die."

Doesn't that make more sense? Isn't a GOOD man better and more worth dying for than a WICKED one?

So how did this happen? The answer is one of the strongest proofs that the translator of Romans looked at an Aramaic written document before doing his work. In Aramaic, the word for "wicked" is *rashiay* (R-Sh-Y-'-A) and the word for "good, blameless" is *rashyin* (R-Sh-Y-'-N). The spelling of these two words is nearly identical and, therefore, if a scribe or translator is not very careful, he can make a wrong choice, which this one obviously did. The alternative, which is even worse, is to suppose that Paul did not know the difference between "good" and "wicked", and I doubt if anyone is going to that extreme.

Finally, while the spelling is similar, the pronunciation is not, and it is therefore almost impossible that this verse was derived from oral Aramaic sources either. This mistake could only come from a physical document.

All right, now on to the second example, and for this we need two translations to make the point:

> For this cause ought the woman to have **power** on her head because of the angels.
>
> 1Corhinthians 11:10 (KJV)

Power on her head? Well maybe another translation will help:

> So a woman should wear a **covering** on her head as a sign of authority because the angels are watching.
>
> 1 Corinthians 11:10 (NLT)

So why would one translator use "power" and the other "covering"? The answer has to do with how the apostle Paul thinks in a semitic framework.

In the Peshitta NT the word used is *sholtana*. In most cases, this word does in fact mean "power", and so we can see how it might be translated as such into Greek. However, *sholtana* also has a secondary meaning of how power is reflected in the person who has or does not have it. So, if the person is a king, his crown is his covering AND his authority/power. For a woman then, in the context of being submissive, her veil—is her sign of authority and her covering as well.

Now, in the Greek, the word for power used in this verse is *exousia*, which did not originally have the secondary meaning of "covering". For proof of this assertion, I turn to what is probably the largest collection of ancient Greek manuscripts and study tools available anywhere, *the Perseus Project* at Tufts University. Their interactive dictionaries show all the shades of meaning of a Greek word wherever it appears in the literature, and not once is this "covering" meaning used:

> **exous-ia**, hê, (exesti) *power, authority* to do a thing, c. inf., chairein kai nosein e. paresti S.*Fr.*88.11 codd.; autôi e. ên saphôs eidenai Antiph. 1.6, cf. Thuc. 7.12; exousian ho nomos dedôke *permission* to do . ., Plat. Sym. 182e; e. poiein Plat. Crito 51d, etc.; e. labein Andoc. 2.28, Xen. Mem. 2.6.24, etc.; labôn e. hôste . . Isoc. 3.45; epi têi tês eirênês e. with the *freedom permitted* by peace, Dem. 18.44: c. gen. objecti, e. echein thanatou *power* of life and death, Poll.8.86; pragma hou tên e. echousin alloi *control* over . ., Diog.Oen.57; e. tinos *power over, licence in* a thing, tou legein Plat. Gorg. 461e; en megalêi e. tou adikein IBID=au=Plat. Gorg. 526a, cf. ti=Plat. Rep. 554c; kata tên ouk e. tês agôniseôs from want of *qualification for* . ., Thuc. 5.50: abs., *power, authority*, E.*Fr.*784.

> **2.** *abuse of authority, licence, arrogance*, hubris kai e. Thuc. 1.38, cf. au=Thuc. 3.45, Dem. 19.200; hê agan e. IBID=au=Dem. 19.272=lr; ametros e. OGI669.51 (i A.D.).

> **3.** Lit. Crit., e. poiêtikê poetic *licence,* Str.1.2.17, Jul.*Or.*1.10b.

II. *office, Magistracy,* archai kai e. Plat. Alc. 1.135b; hoi en tais e. Aristot. Nic. Eth. 1095b21; hoi en e. ontes IDEM=Aristot. Rh. 1384a1; hoi ep' exousiôn LXX*Da*.3.2; hê hupatikê e. the *consulate,* Diod. 14.113, etc.; also hê hupatos e. D.H.7.1; hê tamieutikê e. the *quaestorship,* D.H.8.77; dêmarchikê e., v. dêmarchikos; hê tou thalamou e., in the Roman empire, *LORDship* of the bedchamber, Hdn.1.12.3.

2. concrete, *body of Magistrates,* D.H.11.32; hai e. (as we say) the *authorities,* Ev.Luc.12.11,al., Plu.*Phil.*17.

b. hê e. as an honorary title, POxy.1103 (iv A.D.), etc.

III. *abundance of means, resources,* exousias epideixis Thuc. 6.31; ploutos kai e. Thuc. 1.123, cf. Dem. 21.138; endeesterôs ê pros tên e. Thuc. 4.39; tôn anankaiôn e. Plat. Laws 828d; *excessive wealth,* opp. ousia, Com.Adesp.25a.5D.

IV. *pomp,* Plu.*Aem.*34.

Now the Greek School will counter, "But this is *Koine,* not Classical Greek", and that is my point as well. Koine was born in Alexandria, Egypt, with the translation of the Septuagint FROM HEBREW SOURCES. This secondary meaning was NOWHERE previously, and came from the double meaning of *sholtana.*

"Ah," the Greek School will retort, "but the birth of Koine PRECEDED the NT by 200 years, so this usage could have come in compositionally into Greek at the time Paul wrote it."

Point taken. But, once again the validity of this conclusion is based on the automatic assumption that the Greek mss came first. If all someone knows then is the Greek language and they never study Aramaic, it should not be surprising that Greek patterns will be the only ones that appear relevant to them! By contrast, the point of this entire section has been to show that the evidence suggests more than one answer. So yes, it is possible that Koine Greek absorbed certain minor Semitic eccentricities among its Jewish and Aramean speakers. On the other hand though, it is equally possible to suggest that—just like the Septuagint—that these same eceentricities arise from replicating Semitic patterns of a Hebrew or Aramaic original into the Greek language.

Therefore, to explore another equally valid scenario, I offer the following:

This is clearly a word play rooted in Semitic and not Hellenistic understanding. I say that because another word for "power" also used elsewhere in the Epistles does not have the secondary meaning of "veil" (*#2571-kaluma; see 2 Corinthians 3:13-16),* and vice versa, (*dunatos, hupo, ischus, kratos*). In either case, Paul would have sufficient control in the translation process to pick either an exclusively veil-like or an exclusively power-like word without creating confusion. The reason he did not is because, again, the translator who did it did not have the benefit of this understanding. All he knew was that *sholtana* was staring back at him from the page. A few years later, when the second letter came to his church, either the skill of the translator had improved in the interim or he was replaced with another who had a better of grasp of the language.

There are many more of these examples, but for the sake of keeping the issues to a manageable length I am hopeful these two will suffice.

Challenge #9:

Anyone who studies the structures of NT Greek can tell it is compositional and not translational in nature. Also Koine was so international that what appears to be Semitic influences are actually the original Greek absorbing elements from the native populace.

This is a BIG one folks, and I am going to have to break all the issues into subheadings to deal with it effectively. Although the information is extensive, the strategy is really quite simple.

Put simply, we are going to go full throttle into the best Greek in the entire New Testament, the Gospel of Luke. Luke is the only possible Gentile author here, so if anyone is going to showcase a lack of Semitic patterns in his writing, this is the guy. However, if Luke proves vulnerable to Aramaic primacy then no one else is safe.

Before doing that however, we need to look at the general history of Greek linguistics to put these matters into their proper context.

To koine phrase...

Our story begins about 1400 BCE, when the earliest writing for Aegean peoples such as the Mycenaneans originated. However, the Greek that we know, while having some common characteristics with Linear B, nevertheless derives itself from the Phoenician language.[141] Like Phoenician and, of course, Hebrew and Aramaic, Greek was originally written right to left. Centuries later, the *boustrephon* style came into vogue with letters written up and down, and then alternating from right to left and vice versa. By about 700 BCE however, the left to right convention gained acceptance, and Classical Greek, the language of Socrates and Plato, was born.[142]

About this same time, Etruscan Rome was just getting on its feet, and the native Italians spoke a few minor dialects. A few centuries later however, one of two Classical Greek styles, known as Chalcidian, came in contact with the early Romans, and the result was, albeit with a few changes, the Latin alphabet we know today.[143] Since Latin was then born from Classical Greek, and owing to the fact that all European languages, including English, come from Latin, it is not surprising that the syntactical rules we are familiar with today come from the Greek of this period.

However, by about 330 BCE, the conquering armies of Alexander the Great had spread Greek language and culture from their cradle in south-central Europe all the way across the Middle East and to the gates of India. The enduring result: Another style of Greek more flexible and easier to use than its Classical predecessor, a Greek of the people we now call Koine, and it would remain the standard form of the language well into the fourth century of the common era.[144]

However, it would be a horrendous injustice to pronounce the older form dead. Instead, a divide between the classes occurred, with Classical finding preference in the higher levels of society. To them the common vernacular was just that, common—and crude, when compared with the beauty of the original. Ironically then, this trend is almost identical to one that happened in first century Israel, with Hebrew as the voice of official liturgy and the language of the cultural elite, and Aramaic the lingua franca of the common man.

Therefore, what follows are two types of Semitic patterns in the New Testament. The first, originating from the Greek documents themselves, are those that follow Hebrew and Aramaic syntax, with the difference that an alternate explanation to the Koine Absorption theory is employed.[145] By contrast, the second line of evidence is so deeply and exclusively Semitic that even the foremost Greek authorities posit a previous Aramaic source. However, because they ignore other root trends in the history of first century Jews, I will invalidate the idea that oral Aramaic material did not result in a written counterpart during that time.

Subject-Verb Agreements

It should also be pointed out that cultural influence, wherever it exists, is a two way street. So, if Greek influenced some Jews in Israel, why couldn't Semitic language patterns influence the little Greek that was spoken there? The answer to that question, of course, will be in the evidence that I am about to present. But now it is time to go deeper, into the heart of the Koine Greek itself. And, in order to do that, we must look at what the foremost experts in this language have to say about its syntax. So, while it was well known that Classical Greek follows Latin and English patterns of sentence structure, this is not the case with the Koine:

> "Syntax (as opposed to phonology, morphology and vocabulary) offers more apparent evidence for proposing a special form of 'Jewish Greek' ... The Synoptics, e.g. are translations into Greek of material originally spoken (by Y'shua) in Aramaic or Hebrew. Deisman argues that this cannot be viewed as normative for a description of a living, spoken language in the first century, but in an artificial 'translation Greek.'"
>
> Summary of Deisman, Adolf: "Hellenistic Greek with Special Consideration of the Greek Bible", from *In the Language of the New Testament: Classic Essays.* JSNT supplemental series #60. Stanley Porter, Editor. Sheffield: JSOT Press, 1991, p. 39-59.

And, even more specifically:

> "Biblical Greek is investigated with the same criteria used by the author for the syntax of Biblical Hebrew. Greek marked structures are analyzed having a non-verbal element in the first place of a sentence. As in Hebrew, the non-verbal element is promoted to the role of predicated because it contains the information and is stressed ... These four types of marked structures (clefted, circumstantial, antecedent, and presentative), contrast with the unmarked structure [of classical Greek], or normal independent sentence, having the verb in the

first place. This surprising agreement with the word order of biblical Hebrew poses the problem of biblical Greek in its relationship to classical Greek."

Aliverio Niccacci, Abstract from the paper "Marked Syntactical Structures in Biblical Greek in Comparison with Biblical Hebrew", Liber Annuus (Studium Biblicum Fransiscianum, Jerusalem) 43 (1993), p. 9-69.

And still, to all these things yet more must be added, such as the hundreds of phrases and patterns in the NT that make no sense in Greek to this day.

One of these unique features is actually so prevalent as to appear "normal" to Koine Greek scholars but strikes Classicists as a harsh, or even corrupted, version of how Greek should sound. As a result, from that perspective, there are quite literally hundreds of examples of incorrect sentence structures in the Koine. That is also why my alternative scenario to Koine Absorption focuses on these features primarily coming from the Jews of Alexandria, who translated the LXX word for word from Hebrew. It is therefore no coincidence either that koine is also sometimes referred to as the *Alexandrian dialect*. From there, knowing how all peoples tend to slavishly copy holy words exactly as written, the Semitic word order entered the Koine and remained especially prevalent wherever large Semitic populations undertook the language.

However, in order to explain this, let us look at a very well known verse in Hebrew:

Bereshit bara Elohim et'hashamayim ve'et ha'aretz.

As even a beginning Hebrew school student can tell you, this is the very first line in the Bible, Genesis 1:1, which of course translates as: "In the beginning God created the heavens and the earth." However, the literal order of the actual words is *In the[146] beginning CRE-ATED GOD* or *"bara Elohim"*, and this is significant because all Semitic languages PUT THE VERB FIRST AND THE SUBJECT LAST.[147] By contrast, in all Indo-European languages, of which Greek and English are included, the order is reversed.

Now, looking at a great example in Aramaic, Luke 1:13, we see the same phraseology. The words come out as "was heard your prayer". If the Greek version then was the original, we should expect the opposite in syntax, or "your prayer was heard", but guess what? This Greek, and only this Greek, follows the Aramaic pattern THAT PUTS THE SUBJECT LAST! Therefore, the only way this can happen is if Luke himself, like his Alexandrian Jewish predecessors, is translating in exact word order from Aramaic into Greek.

Such a blatant syntactical reversal by Luke— and in fact most of the other NT writers— not only showcases the Semitic origin of these books, it also speaks volumes as to their reverence for these Aramaic originals. Put simply, *these redactors wanted to show to anyone who reads their work in Greek that they are following the same time honored grammatical conventions that the first sources sprang from!* Nor are these irregularities in Luke's Gospel meant detract from the other wonderful features of his work, because the fact is, both he and the majority of his colleagues are doing this on purpose![148]

Going "towards" the Truth

Nor is this sweeping evidence the extent of Semitic structures in these texts. Another "smoking gun" has to do with a unique use of Jewish prepositions.

Specifically, in Aramaic and Hebrew, the common phrase "to say" or "to speak" translates literally into the English of "to speak towards". However, if this sounds foreign it is because the effect is not apparent in any translation of the Hebrew Bible, but is instead an idiomatic structure that is sacrificed for clarity in the receiving language.

Therefore, once again, if the authors of these works were thinking in Greek, we should expect this feature to be absent in their writing... but it isn't. Just as in the previous example, there are countless phrases in the Greek that have Y'shua or someone else *speaking towards another person, and it is done like that all the time.*

Additionally, we should all understand that the Aramaic writers of the NT are following long established compositional disciplines passed down from their Jewish brethren. Specifically, there are no variations whatsoever in the original Aramaic documents[149], which of course is in sharp contrast to the Greek copies, whose divergences in word choices require extensive harmonization to bring into a cogent form. It is therefore literally the case that no two Greek NT text fragments or documents are exactly alike. Nor should this be surprising, since no two translations from Aramaic into Greek will be alike either! That is also why the Church Father Papias, himself a student of the apostle John, wrote that people translated an Aramaic Gospel of Matthew into Greek, "as best as they could."

Furthermore, again taking a page from the Jews, these authorities followed the same rules of determining the issues of canonicity itself. When the Rabbis sorted through which books should be considered as part of the OT, the single most important factor was whether it had been originally authored in Hebrew. If a given book appeared in the Greek LXX and was without a Hebrew precedent, it was then summarily discarded without a second thought.[150] Similarly, the Church of the East also decided very early on only to accept books originally done in Aramaic, and even then the books also had to have apostolic authority behind them, which is why the West agrees with their inclusion in the first place!

Now, in order to be fair, let me also state that these patterns thus far can be argued to show either: 1) A Semitic influence on original Greek documents or, 2) A tradition which shows the difficulty of putting Semitic thoughts and syntax into Greek during the translation process from Aramaic sources.

However, the next series is intended to show Semticisims that run so deeply beneath the Greek texts as to defy patterns even in the

Signs of the Cross: The Search for the Historical Jesus

Koine itself, and we start with the one man who may have written the best Greek in the entire New Testament: Luke.

The Gentile Who Writes Like a Jew

We begin with an able representative of the Greek School:

> "Luke wrote fine Greek. Of all the authors of the New Testament literature only the author of the Epistle to the Hebrews was in his class as a literary artist and craftsman. The preface to Luke's Gospel contains the best Greek in the entire New Testament.
>
> "That is not to suggest that Luke revived the polished style of composition characteristic of the authors of the Greek classical period such as Homer or Sophocles. Rather, Luke wrote in the popular non-literary Greek in common use in the first century, C.E. But he had a flair of style and a well developed sense of rhetorical sentence structure. He had mastered the rules of grammar and syntax and was proficient in the Greek art of composition."
>
> Keith Nickle, The Synoptic Gospels: An Introduction, p. 128.

However, one particularly glaring error in the Book of Acts may in fact turn this assumption on its head:

> "Now an angel of the LORD said to Philip, "Go south to the road—the desert road—that goes down from Jerusalem to Gaza." So he started out,

> and on his way he met an Ethiopian **eunuch**, an important official in charge of all the treasury of Candace, queen of the Ethiopians. This man had gone to Jerusalem to worship, and on his way home was sitting in his chariot reading the book of Isaiah the prophet."

Acts 8:26-28

Notice how this verse establishes that the Ethiopian is Jewish and went to worship in Jerusalem? The only problem is, eunuchs cannot do this:

> "No one who has been emasculated by crushing or cutting may enter the assembly of the LORD."

Deuteronomy 23:1

Now the word for "assembly" in this verse is *quahawl* (Strong's #6951), and it is used in a variety of ways. Throughout the first five books of Moses, *quahawl* is intended as the group that gathers at the Tent of Meeting or Tabernacle, (Leviticus 16:17, Numbers 10:7,19:20). Later, when the First Temple was built, the word was given the collective usage for the entire nation, (1 Kings 8:4-5, 14, 22, 55, 65, 12:20, 1 Chronicles 13:2, 4, 28:8, 29:1). Additionally, this definition continued throughout the Second Temple period, (Ezra 2:64, 10:1, 8, 12, 14, Nehemiah 5:13, 7:66, 8:2, 17, 13:1, Lamentations 1:10, Joel 2:16, Micah 2:5).

Therefore, under the biblical system, the synagogues would also be included in the term "assembly", so whether this "eunuch" was going to the Temple (most likely) or the synagogues, this prohibition would have applied.

In Aramaic, the word *m'haimna* can mean "eunuch", but it also means "faithful one" or "believer", which is the intended meaning here. [151] Therefore, in this case there is no Greek explanation that can, for lack of a better phrase, *cut it*.

Another great example is in Luke's other work, the Book of Acts:

> "Now at this time some prophets came down from Jerusalem to Antioch. And one of them named Agabus stood up and began to indicate from the Spirit that there would certainly be great famine all over the world. And this took place in the reign of Claudius. And in the proportion that any of the disciples had means, each of them determined to send a contribution for relief of the brethren living in Judea. And this they did, sending it in charge of Barnabbas and Saul to the elders."
>
> Acts 11:27-30[152]

Now this is a curious statement. If the famine is "throughout the world" how is it people in Antioch could send food to those in Judea? Wouldn't the Antiochians also be facing a severe famine?

The Aramaic, of course, resolves this easily.[153] The word for "world" is "a'ra" and is equivalent to the Hebrew term "eretz". The same word means the following depending on context:

> "earth" , Daniel 2:35

> "world", Proverbs 19:4

> "land" Daniel 9:15

Furthermore, the same word is also used frequently as a symbolic name for the land of Israel, and it is this last meaning which is the most appropriate.

Now to be fair, the NIV editors recognize this and use the phrase

"Roman world" to describe the extent of the famine. However, this too is fraught with problems since Antioch was in a Roman province! Furthermore, NASV, KJV and NWT make no such distinction between "roman" and the rest of the world.

However, as to the excellent Greek in Luke being, as Dr. Nickle believes, a clear proof of compositional Greek, the point is at least partially well taken. As a Semiticist, I have no desire to refute a good portion of this assertion for a simple reason: If 22 Aramaic books were, as the Church of the East says, translated into Greek, then by definition some will do a better job of it than others. Luke simply is the best of this group of writers. Although, before getting into the linguistics itself, another question must be asked: Do we know anything about Luke the man that sheds light on his incredible writing talents?

A Sense of Place

> "It is generally held that St. Luke was a native of Antioch. Eusebius (Hist. Eccl. III, iv, 6) has: *Loukas de to men genos on ton ap Antiocheias, ten episteuen iatros, ta pleista suggegonos to Paulo, kai rots laipois de ou parergos ton apostolon homilnkos*—"Lucas vero domo Antiochenus, arte medicus, qui et cum Paulo diu conjunctissime vixit, et cum reliquis Apostolis studiose versatus est." Eusebius has a clearer statement in his "Quæstiones Evangelicæ", IV, i, 270: *ho de Loukas to men genos apo tes Boomenes Antiocheias en*—"Luke was by birth a native of the renowned Antioch" (Schmiedel, "Encyc. Bib.") . . . The writer of Acts took a special interest in Antioch and was well acquainted with it (Acts, xi, 19-27; xiii, 1; xiv, 18-21, 25, xv, 22, 23, 30, 35; xviii, 22)."

> Catholic Encyclopedia, "Biography of Saint Luke"

The tradition of Antioch as the city of his birth is well attested by both Eastern and Western sources. However, the first question that often arises is *which Antioch is intended?* The Bible in fact refers to two cities with this name. The first one, in Syria, is also a Roman provincial capital. The second, which was founded along the Sebaste Road, is called *Pisdian Antioch*. To the uniformed then, Luke is just as likely to have originated from either one.

However, the language is very clear that the correct city is *boomeus Antiochieus en*, or "the Antioch of renown". Of the two cities, Syrian Antioch was far more important. It was many times the size of its Pisdian counterpart and was also the seat of Roman power in the Middle East. Furthermore, it was also a great trading route and center of international commerce. Therefore, there can be little doubt as to which city is intended. The Eastern sources also mention Antioch, and leave no doubt whatsoever that they are also talking about the one in Syria.

With this fact established, we can now turn to what we know about that particular city:

> "Of the vast empire conquered by Alexander the Great many states were formed, one of which comprised Syria and other countries to the east and West of it. This realm fell to the lot of one of the conqueror's generals, Seleucus Nicator, or Seleucus I . . . About the year 300 B. C. he founded a city . . . which was named Antioch, from Antiochus, the father of Seleucus, was meant to be the capital of the new realm . . . When Syria was made a Roman province by Pompey (64 B. C.), Antioch continued to be the metropolis of the East. It also became the residence of the legates, or governors, of Syria. In fact, Antioch, after Rome and Alexandria, was the largest city of the empire, with a population of over half a million. Whenever the emperors came to the East they honoured it with their presence.

The Seleucidæ as well as the Roman rulers vied with one another in adorning and enriching the city with statues, theatres, temples, aqueducts, public baths, gardens, fountains, and cascades; a broad avenue with four rows of columns, forming covered porticoes on each side, traversed the city from east to West, to the length of several miles. Its most attractive pleasure resort was the beautiful grove of laurels and cypresses called Daphne, some four or five miles to the West of the city. It was renowned for its park-like appearance, (and) for its magnificent temple of Apollo . . ."

Catholic Encyclopedia, "The Church at Antioch"

As for the Jewish element in that city, we have this from the historian Josephus:

"For as the Jewish nation is widely dispersed over all the habitable earth among its inhabitants, so it is very much intermingled with Syria by reason of its neighborhood, and had the greatest multitudes in Antioch by reason of the largeness of the city, wherein the kings, after Antiochus, had afforded them a habitation with the most undisturbed tranquillity; for though Antiochus, who was called Epiphanes, laid Jerusalem waste, and spoiled the temple, yet did those that succeeded him in the kingdom restore all the donations that were made of brass to the Jews of Antioch, and dedicated them to their synagogue, and granted them the enjoyment of equal privileges of citizens with the Greeks themselves; and as the succeeding kings treated them after the same manner, they both multiplied to a great number, and adorned their temple gloriously by fine ornaments, and with great magnificence, in the use of what had been given them. They also made proselytes of a great many of the Greeks perpetually, and thereby after a sort brought them to be a portion of their own body."

Wars, 7.3.3

Furthermore, the only reason Syrian overlords who had, under previous leadership, "laid Jerusalem to waste", would later give Jews in Antioch equal status with Greeks, is because of both their number and status as one of the earliest groups to populate that city. Also, we have to remember where Antioch is. Located in the heart of Syria, their native Semitic population has been referred to as "Arameans"—or Aramaic speaking peoples—for thousands of years. In later centuries the Aramaic language itself was mistakenly renamed "Syriac" by the West, because of its linkage to that country.

Therefore, there could hardly have been a city more influential or better situated to produce scholars with fluency in both languages. Western scholars then, while fully cognizant about the level of Greek understanding many of its inhabitants shared, have been ignorant about how those same cosmopolitan qualities fostered the Aramaic side of the equation. That is also why it is also almost a certainty that if anyone could have written both excellent Aramaic and Greek literature, that Antioch was the logical place of their origin. As for Luke, he could either have been an uncircumcised Aramaic speaking Semite, or a Greek proselyte immersed in the Aramaic culture of his hometown since birth. Either way, his fluency in both these languages is more than accounted for.

Andrew Gabriel Roth

Poetry ... in translation?

"The Greeks particularly loved the spoken word, and the quality of their literature stems from it. Their language, with its high proportion of vowel to consonant sounds, lent itself admirably to fluid speech and rich verbal music. Swift movement combined with sober grandeur are the chief characteristics of their arch-poet, Homer. His way with words and images remained the model for subsequent centuries, and his flowing hexameter line was used for subject matter as diverse as Hesiod's homely poems of rural life and the fervent hymns sung at religious festivals as preludes to recitals of passages from the Homeric epics.

"While Homer's influence was supreme, there was still place for the growth of other forms of Greek poetry. One was the choral ode, recited or sung by groups of performers and accompanied by a dance. Each stanza was designed to echo dance movements, and the meters were as complex as the dance rhythms themselves. These odes were originally dedicated to a god or hero; later, ordinary mortals were honored by them. Tragic drama itself arose from festival chants and declamation. Another type of poem was the simple solo song, originating in folksong, which reached sophistication in such hands and Sapho's. Like all Greek poetry, it was sung or recited, not just read, and usually was accompanied by music of the lyre or flute. From these songs derived the love lyric, and also the elegies and epigrams written in honor of the dead, and often inscribed on tombs."

The Horizon Book of Ancient Greece, p. 129.

Signs of the Cross: The Search for the Historical Jesus

As Professor Nickle pointed out at the beginning of this section, Luke shows himself to be a master of Greek composition, following well-established patterns common to his day. In many respects then, this would appear to be evidence of compositional, and not translational Greek. However, while the superb quality of his Greek is undeniable, does it necessarily follow that it is due to it being written first in that language?

In order to answer that question, we need to look at other rules of composition beneath the Greek text, namely that of a poetic nature. That Luke puts poetry throughout his Gospel is beyond dispute. However, Greek poetry had very particular rules and conventions, so we should expect Luke, purportedly a Gentile himself and definitely a master of Greek, to follow those rules.

But, he doesn't.

In fact, "Gentile" Luke doesn't write a single Greek poem! Now how can this be?

First, the reason I put "Gentile" in quotes is because Luke was not your typical *goy*. True, he was born a non-Jew and statements in various NT books indicate that Luke was not circumcised because Paul puts him in a separate group from those who were, (Colossians 4:11-14). However, Luke was most intimately connected with both first century Judaism and the Hebrew Christian movement that grew out of it, because accidents of birth did not prevent someone from becoming a proselyte (convert) to the house of Israel. Nor is it possible to eliminate the strong likelihood that, while not Hebrew, Luke had Semitic blood in him by virtue of being raised in Syria.[154]

Therefore, as was previously explained, Luke is most certainly a *proselyte of the gate,* like Cornelius.[155]

As for his writing, none of the poems that he uses has a single Greek feature, but follows the time honored Semitic system instead.

This system of poetry would, as my dear friend Paul Younan rightly states, take an entire book itself to do justice to. However, a few basic terms will suffice for this limited discussion. Semitic poetry uses two main structures. Similar to a stanza in the West, the first of these is called a *strophe*, which can be thought of as paragraph or main idea. Within each strophe then are smaller verse-like units called *stiches*. The object then is not so much to be a slave to rhyme (although there are many examples when this extra level is employed), but to have the thoughts in the stiches concord with the intent of the adjacent ones and, consequently, with the strophe as a whole.

Now that we have the basics, let's look at one of these poems by Luke, Zacharias' Canticle (Luke 1:67-79). It divides perfectly into 3 strophes with 7 stiches each:

"His father Zechariah was filled with the Holy Spirit
and prophesied:

Strophe 1:
(Stiche 1) "Praise be to the LORD, the God of Israel,
(Stiche 2) Because he has come and has redeemed his people.
(Stiche 3) He has raised up a horn of salvation
(Stiche 4) For us in the house of his servant David
(Stiche 5) As he said through his holy prophets of long ago,
(Stiche 6) Salvation from our enemies
(Stiche 7) And from the hand of all who hate us

Strophe 2:
(Stiche 1) To show mercy to our fathers
(Stiche 2) And to remember his holy covenant,
(Stiche 3) The oath he swore to our father Abraham:
(Stiche 4) To rescue us from the hand of our enemies,
(Stiche 5) And to enable us to serve him without fear
(Stiche 6) In holiness and righteousness
(Stiche 7) Before him all our days.

Strophe 3:
(Stiche 1) And you, my child, will be called a prophet of the Most High;

(Stiche 2) For you will go on before the LORD to prepare the way for him,

(Stiche 3) To give his people the knowledge of salvation through the forgiveness of their sins,

(Stiche 4) Because of the tender mercy of our God,

(Stiche 5) By which the rising sun will come to us from heaven

(Stiche 6) To shine on those living in darkness and in the shadow of death,

(Stiche 7) To guide our feet into the path of peace."

Now here is where we find some incredible poetic patterns that are only apparent in Hebrew or Aramaic. In particular, the second strophe is downright amazing. Starting with stiche 1, the statement "to show mercy" is *khnan*, the Aramaic root of *Yu-khnan* (John). This is followed by stiche 2 and the phrase "he remembers his covenant", and the Hebrew for "he remembers" is *zakhar*, combined with a name for God who does the remembering, or Zakhar-yah. Finally, stiche 3 has "the oath which he swore to our father Abraham", which combines another Hebrew name for "God" (Eli) and "oath" (shaba), to form the name of the Baptist's mother, Eli-shaba (Elizabeth).

Can this be a coincidence that the names of Zacharias, Elizabeth and John are contained beneath the text of a piece of poetry expressly about them? Furthermore, this poem is the exact same type of Hebrew/Aramaic pattern found in both the Hebrew Scriptures and the Aramaic Old Testament, also called Peshitta Tenakh. Another unlikely coincidence, again showing the Semitic rules that the stiches concord, is that the three strophes each deal with the past, present and the future in their proper order.

Our next example, is from the same Aramaic source that was read by Y'shua in the Nazareth synagogue.[156] And, just like Zacharias' Canticle, its strophe is also 7 stiches long. Here then is the Aramaic version of Isaiah 61, which Y'shua proclaimed in Luke 4:18:

(Stiche 1) The Spirit of the LORD is upon me (Rukha d'Maryah Alee)

(Stiche 2) And because of this He has anointed me (w'Mittol Hada Mishkhanee)

(Stiche 3) To declare hope to the poor he has sent me (lam-sabroo l'Miskeeneh Washlakhnee)

(Stiche 4) To heal the brokenhearted (lam-asyo l'Tawryri Liba)

(Stiche 5) And to preach to the captives forgiveness and to the blind sight (w'lam-krazo l'Shawiyeh Shuqana w'Lawayreh Khizya)

(Stiche 6) And to strengthen those who are broken with forgiveness (w'lam-shraro l'Tabireh b'Shuqana)

(Stiche 7) And to preach the acceptable year of the LORD (w'lam-krazo Shintha Maqabiltha l'Marya)

Even for people without Aramaic training, some word plays should just leap off the page. Notice the rhyming words in each line. The first two, of course go together perfectly (Rukha d'Marya Alee/w'Mittol Hada Mishkhane) and then each of the next five stiches also has a rhyming word, such as "to declare" (lam-sabroo), "to heal" (lam-asyo) "to strengthen" (lam-sharo), and finally, "to preach" (lam-krazo), which appears twice. Other poetic patterns are evident in the ending words, such as "alee", "miskhanee" and "washlakhnee" group in lines one through three, and the quadruple rhymes in the remaining lines of "liba", "khizya", "shuquana" and "l'Marya". This is therefore the obvious template for Luke's poetry, a designation that is certainly strengthened by Luke including it in the first place!

Now let's look at another powerful example, the Benediction of Shimon the Priest, (Luke 2:34-35):

(Stiche 1) Behold this one is appointed (Ha ha-na see-ma)

(Stiche 2) For the fall (lam paloo-tha)

(Stiche 3) And for the rise (w'l'aq-ya-ma)

(Stiche 4) Of many in Israel (d'saga-yeh b'Yis-ra-el)

(Stiche 5) And for a sign of dispute (w'l'atta d'kharyana)

(Stiche 6) And in your soul will pass through a spear (w'ba-naw-sha-ki den dee-la-ki ta-bar rum-kha)

(Stiche 7) So that thoughts of many hearts may be revealed (aykh d'nith-ga-leen mikh-sha-wa-tha d'lib-ba-wa-tha sa-ga-yeh)

Could that be *another* seven stiche strophe? What a shock! That's three "sevens" in a row, and all this in the first four chapters. And by the way, in case you are wondering why this particular number is so prevalent, it is because ancient Jews and Arameans considered the number seven as the embodiment of perfection, since that's how many days it took for God to create and rest from His work.

However, the seven-stiche pattern, while very common, is not the only number that Semitic poems relied on. Not surprisingly then, the next most popular number was three. Zacharias' Canticle, as stated earlier, has a 3 strophe-7 stiche pattern. Other poems also have three stophes and, while they vary the number of stiches, the compositional rules are the same. Again, the stiches must match in thought to the others in the strophe, and rhyming, while not required, is very common in sacred poetry.

I have two examples of this three-based poetry in Luke. The first is the most famous teaching Y'shua ever uttered, the *Slotha d'Maran* (Lord's Prayer-Luke 11:2-4, Matthew 6:9-13[157]). It exhibits a 3 strophe-5 stiche pattern, as follows:

Strophe 1
(1) Our Father in Heaven (Aw-an d'wa-shma-ya)
(2) Hallowed be thy Name (Nith-qa-dash shm-akh)
(3) Thy Kingdom come (Tey-tey mal-ku-thakh)
(4) Thy will be done (Neh-weh tsev-ya-nakh)
(5) As in heaven, so on earth (Ay-kan-na d'wa-shma-ya ap b'ar-aa)

Strophe 2
(6) Give us the bread for our need today (Haw-lan lakh-ma d'son-qa-nan yaw-ma-na)

(7) And forgive us our offenses [158] (Wash-wuq-lan khaw-bayn)
(8) As we have also forgiven those who have offended us (Ay-kan-na d'ap akh-nan shwa-qan l'khay-ya-win)
(9) And lead us not into trial (w'la ta-lan l'nis-yo-na)
(10) But deliver us from the evil one (El-la pas-san min bee-sha)

Strophe 3
(11) For Thine is (Mit-tol d'dee-lakh-hee)
(12) The Kingdom (Mal-ku-tha)
(13) And the power (w'khay-la)
(14) And the glory (w'tish-bukh-ta)
(15) Forever and ever, amen (L'a-lam, al-meen, a-meen)

For the sake of simplicity, I have often referred to this as an Aramaic Sonnet because, like its Shakespearean counterpart, it has very specific rules of composition, in spite of the addition of a fifteenth line. However, given the temporal distance between the two, perhaps it might be more accurate to call the Sonnets an English strophe!

Alternatively though, there are far more poetic gems lying below the surface. Just like Zacharias' Canticle and Isaiah 61, the first four lines have rhyming endings of *ah* (dwashmaya, shmakh, malkuthakh, tsevyanakh). The fifth line closes out the thought then with a triple pattern of equal diction (ay-kanna, d'washmaya, aph-bara).

Then, starting in stiche 6, another pattern emerges. Several more rhyming words populate the next three lines (washvoqlan, shawaquan; khaw-bayn, l'khayawin), and these are then followed by two mirror-image rhyming and diction phrases (wela tahlan l'nis-yona, ela pason min bisha).

Finally, the poem ends with two triple treats. The first of these takes up the next three stiches, where kingdom (malkutha) power (w'haila) and glory (w'tishbukhta) all rhyme. The second series, like stiche 5, also divides perfectly as forever (l'ahlam) and ever (al-meen) amen (aw-mayn).

The final three-based poem is the wonderful "Magnificat" of Mary,

(Luke 1:46-55). In a sense, this is a double triple, because there are 6 strophes with 3 stiches each:

Strophe 1
(1) magnifies my soul the LORD
maw-ra-ba nap-shi l'Mar-Yah
(2) and has rejoiced my spirit in God my saviour
w'khad-yat ru-khi b'Al-a-ha makh-ya-ni
(3) because He has looked at the humiliation of His handmaid
d'kha-ar b'am-wak-kha d'am-theh

Strophe 2
(4) for, behold, from now on a blessing will give me all generations
ha ga-yir min ha-sha tu-wa nith-lin ali shar-ba-theh kul-hayn
(5) because he who is mighty has done with me great things
d'awid l'wa-thi rur-ba-theh Haw d'Khay-la-than
(6) and his name is holy
w'qad-dish ash-meh

Strophe 3
(7) and his mercy for ages and generations
w'khna-neh l'da-reh w'shar-ba-theh
(8) is upon those who fear him
al ay-lin d'dikh-lin leh
(9) he has accomplished victory with his arm
awid za-choo-tha b'dar-eh

Strophe 4
(10) He has scattered the proud in the thought of their hearts
w'ba-dar khtee-reh b'tar-ey-tha d'lib-bown
(11) he has cast down the mighty from the seats
sa-khip ta-qyapeh min kor-sa-wa-tha
(12) and he has exalted the humble
w'arim mkee-khe

273

Strophe 5
(13) the hungry he has satisfied with good things
kip-neh saw-aa taw-theh
(14) but the rich he has sent away empty-handed
w'at-ee-reh shara sap-qay-it
(15) he has aided Israel his servant
ad-aar l'Yisrael a-wa-deh

Strophe 6
(16) and he has remembered his mercy
w'ath-dakh-ar kha-na-neh
(17) as he spoke with our forefathers
aykh d'mal-lil am aw-hain
(18) (with) Abraham and with his seed forever
Awraham w'am zar-eh l'alam

Finally, the very short poems do put a greater emphasis on rhyming patterns exclusive to the Aramaic, such as the double strophe-double stiche "Hail Mary", (Luke 1:28):

Strophe 1
(1) Shla-ma La-khi (Hail to you)
(2) Mleet Tay-bu-tha (who is full of grace)

Strophe 2
(3) Mar-an Am-khi (our LORD is with you)
(4) Braykht Be-nish-a (blessed [are you] among women)

As for the Greek poetry, it is just as beautiful and rigorous a discipline as its Semitic counterpart, but is nevertheless quite distinct from it as well. And, the fact is, not even the Greek copies of Luke showcase a single poetic tendency in that language but instead bear testament to the Semitic framework in which they were composed.

Signs of the Cross: The Search for the Historical Jesus

Challenge #10:

It may be that the earliest NT documents draw from Aramaic ORAL sources, but these were quickly written originally in Greek.

In light of all the evidence presented before, little need be said on this point, except what may seem fairly obvious:

This has never happened with any other major religious leader in history—i.e.—where the written stage of the original language of a person is skipped in lieu of composition in a foreign one. Also Greek was the language of the enemy. It was the Romans who burned Jerusalem to the ground, and the later Byzantine Empire that persecuted relentlessly the early Aramaic Christians, who had aligned themselves with the Aramaic speaking Persian Empire, a deadly enemy of Rome. This also goes against everything we know about Semitic people and how they preserve sacred teachings—both Jews and Arabs as well. To give a modern equivalent, it would be like an Orthodox Jew accepting as original and sacred a Torah written in German by Adolph Hitler!

So there you have it. These are the responses to the most frequently cited and most credible points that the Greek School has to offer. In dealing with them in this fashion, it must be conceded that the Law of Averages suggests some of my answers will play better than others and can vary from scholar to scholar and reader to reader. For myself, that is fine and it is an improvement over what has gone before which is a total lack of consideration of these issues. If I can raise reasonable doubt that more than one conclusion can be drawn from the evidence, I will have done well. Or, if I can at least show that the Aramaic is essential to complete understanding—regardless as to how good the Greek is or the talents of the individual Greek scholar who does not know Aramaic—I will be content.

For now however, other evidence that is not directly tied to this particular debate needs to be investigated.

Andrew Gabriel Roth

What the Rest of the World Does NOT Know

Every once in a while someone asks me, "Andrew, all this Aramaic stuff is fine but we have had the Gospels for two thousand years now, so how can your studies add significantly to our body of knowledge?"

This well-intentioned question always brings a smile to my face as I think of them as a Gentile *Tevye* from "Fiddler on the Roof" shouting, "TRADITION!"

Two millennia is an awful long time to develop a structure and a way of thinking, but the rest of Christendom would do well to remember that the Jewish tradition that their faith came from is older still and was the basis for the faith that the Messiah taught. However, before I am accused of dodging the question, I will give a critical insight into the way Y'shua taught that is not only completely foreign to Greek texts, it is even foreign to those who study Jewish culture in light of those texts!

Put simply, Y'shua has a teaching method that has been forgotten since his day and that has, as far as I know, never been written about since. We are about to break startling new ground with one of the oldest languages on the planet.

With that little bit of fanfare accomplished, let me explain. When Y'shua teaches, he employs a number of techniques which cannot be seen in any other language and have therefore been unknown and unappreciated in the West for all this time.

First, he will tend to make two or more key concepts in a teaching rhyme for easy remembrance. The best modern equivalent I can think of is Johnny Cochrane saying, "If it doesn't fit, you must acquit." The second technique is to use the multiple meanings of a single word back to back in a sentence, like when Ben Franklin said, "We must all hang together or, most assuredly, we will all hang separately." And finally, the third technique has no modern equivalent at all. In that method, Y'shua will use one word and follow it up with another one that sounds almost exactly like it but is rarely used in that fashion. In other words, there will be a ton of possible ways that he could make a phrase work, and instead he chooses the most unorthodox option simply because of the way the sound concords with another key part of the teaching.

All of these then, are represented in the following list, which, I might add, is far from exhaustive:

Wide is the door and (rapata ho taraya) . . .

. . . **and broad is the road** (w'arwikha awrkha—Matthew 7:13).[159]

We sang to you **(zamran lakhun)** . . .

. . . **and you did not dance** (w'la raqdithun) . . .

. . . **and we mourned for you** (w'alyan lakhun) . . .

. . . **and you did not cry** (w'la bakhtithun — Luke 7:32; Matthew 11:17).

Ask and shall be given to you (Shalo w'tanihab l'khun) . . .

. . . **seek and you shall find** (balo w'tish khnon) . . .

. . . **knock and it shall be opened to you** (quawsho w'natpakh l'khun—Matthew 7:7).[160]

Foxes have holes (litheleh niqeh ait lhun) . . .

. . . **and for the birds of the sky, a shelter** (w'l'parakhtha d'shmaya mitlileh) . . .

. . . **but the Son of Man has no** (l'breh din d'anasha lith leh) . . .

. . . **place to lay his head** (ayka d'nisamukh resheh—Luke 9:58; Matthew 8:20).

One . . . rejoices (khad . . . kh'da; Luke 15:4-5)[161]

Goods that you have prepared (t'tawatha t'tayawath—Luke 12:19-20)

Brought him . . . crops (alath leh, alaltheh—Luke 12:16)

He lays up treasures (saim leh saimtheh—Luke 12:21)

Crumbs . . . table (parthutha, pathureh—Matthew 15:27, Luke 16:21)[162]

In the BOSOM of his FATHER (b'awba d'Abuhi—John 1:18).

Food . . . kingdom (makultha, malkutha—John 3:3-5, 4:31, 6:26).[163]

In Galilee . . . openly (b'Galeela, b'galeea—John 7:9-10)[164]

Death . . . to come (mawtha, matha—John 8:21)

Gate . . . sheepfold (tara, tyara—John 10:1)

I . . . flock (ena, ana—John 10:7)

> **Shepherd ... pasture** (raya, reya—John 10:2,9)
>
> **Flame (as enlightenment) ... light** (nahira, nuhra—John 11:9-10)[165]
>
> **Sleep (and die) ... sleep** (shkhab, damkha—John 11:11-12)[166]
>
> **It dies ... it produces** (myta, mytya—John 12:24)
>
> **Thomas ... twin** (Tooma, tawma—John 21:2)[167]

However the most interesting of these rhyming pairs for my money is this one in Luke 12:11:

> **Do not be anxious about** (la taspun) ...
>
> **... how should depart your breath** (tapqun rukha) ...
>
> **.... or what you should say** (aw mana tamrun).

This is actually a triple word play and an incredibly strong piece of evidence even on its own. First of all there is the obvious triple rhyme of three words (taspun, tapqun, tamrun). Second it is a clear case of mistranslation the way this appears in the Greek, where Y'shua says, "how you should answer". In Aramaic, this is an expression that has a meaning of "to compose your speech" or "speak properly". It has therefore more to do with how erudite a person is than the simple Greek word "answer" imparts.

Now this may seem a bit nit-picky but it really isn't. If the Greek of this verse was written first, there is only one word in Aramaic that it would be translated into—*inneh*—which means exactly that— "answer", and no connotation or denotation of proper speech is there, just the plain response itself. *Inneh* is also used very frequently throughout the Peshitta NT when this kind of shoot from the hip response is intended. The fact that *inneh* is not used here proves that this extra meaning only exists in the Aramaic.

However, it is the third aspect that is the true mind blower, *because it involves Y'shua using multiple meanings of the same word in Aramaic to make a unified point.* In this case, the word in question is *rukha*.[168] This word (Hebrew *ruach*) has a very powerful double meaning. A look at the Hebrew in Genesis 2:7 reveals this very easily. There, the Spirit (rukha) of God breathes (rukha) into Adam, and he becomes a living being. It is for this reason then that *rukha* has taken on the meanings of spirit, wind, and breath. Luke 12:11 clearly has the "breath" meaning intended, but the very next line has the "spirit" one as in, *for the Holy Spirit (rukha d'qadoosha) will teach you what to say!*

Just a few lines later, another common word that is translated as "spirit/soul" in English is used ... *naphshah* (Hebrew "nephesh"), and the roots of this word are also found in Genesis 2:7. When Adam "becomes a living being/soul", this is the word used[169]. It is this portion of the soul, furthermore, which is mortal, and this gets most telling in Gethsemene when Y'shua talks about HIS SOUL (naphshah) BEING TROUBLED UNTO DEATH. While his *rukha* would continue after death with his spirit and power, his "life force" would die on the cross, only to be resurrected three days later! All of this analysis then is a powerful background for this last example in Luke 12:19 "I will say to myself, 'My soul ... '" because the word "myself" and "soul" is this same *naphshah* which repeats itself to drive the point home.[170] Greek has two separate words for "self" and "soul", but Aramaic has only one.

Therefore, as this teaching unravels in Luke 12, we see Y'shua talking about different parts of the soul and using additional meanings to the words for soul. This facet is simply lost in Greek.

Other Mistranslated Word Pairs

One of the best examples of this phenomenon has already been discussed. The reader will recall how, in Acts 8:27, the Aramaic word *mhaimna* had two meanings, and the wrong one was selected. The proof of the error was that every single Greek mss translated this word as *eunochos* (eunuch).

However, later analysis proved that this *mhaimna* could not be a eunuch because he had attended Temple services which, by definition of his condition, was clearly impossible (Deuteronomy 23:1). Thankfully, the Aramaic word had another well-known meaning that cleared up the matter: "believer". Although, by contrast, the Greek words for "believer"—all deriving from forms of *pistos*, have absolutely no secondary meanings even approaching images of castration. This is just one form of "traps" that await the unsuspecting Greek scholar, and, the fact is, many words in Aramaic have double and triple meanings that can be wrongly applied.

Other eccentricities that would present challenges even for oral Aramaic sources being set down compositionally in Greek include:

1) *Vowel transliteration word pairs: Two words look alike in terms of spelling but because Aramaic has no full vowels, the recovery of their meaning imposes difficulties on the translator. Or, to put it another way, with all the full vowels hidden, one word that appears to mean something can in fact mean the opposite. I have two examples of this problem.*

> "It is easier for a camel to pass through the eye of a needle than for a rich person to enter the kingdom of God."
>
> (Matthew 19:24=Mark 10:25).[171]

Traditional scholars have been aware of the problematic nature of this verse for many years. They have suggested the "eye of the needle" may be a place name, or more specifically, a part of one of Jerusalem's gates that allows a man and a camel to pass, but only in single file. Since this gate has been called "Eye of the Needle", they reason this is what Y'shua meant.

However, this is not the only explanation, and there is no evidence at all that a proper place name was intended either in Aramaic or in Greek. If the "eye of the needle" is literal, then it means no rich people can be saved; bad news for the wealthy followers listed in Luke 8:1-3, as well as two Sanhedrin members, Joseph of Arimathea and Nicodemus.

Fortunately, the Aramaic gives a much clearer image, for while **GAMLA** does mean "camel", **GAMaLA** means "heavy rope"! This would make the statement by Y'shua almost a kind of quick visual metaphor, because it is in an encounter with a rich man that precipitates the comment:

> "If you want to be perfect, go sell your possessions and give them to the poor, and you will have treasure in heaven. Then come; follow me,"

> (Matthew 19:21 = Mark 10:25).

So now we have two images in juxtaposition: a heavy rope (the man's riches) and the needle's eye (the narrow door to salvation). Can a heavy rope pass through such a small opening? The answer is YES, IF IT IS UNDONE ONE SMALL STRAND AT A TIME. The rope "unraveling" would then represent the rich man "unraveling his fortune", so to speak. This is also a great example of Y'shua's sense of humor, because if the question is "Can a rich man enter the kingdom of God", the answer is, "Yes, if he is not so rich by the time he dies"!

Here's another one showcasing the same problem:

> "While Y'shua was in the home of a man known as

Signs of the Cross: The Search for the Historical Jesus

> Simon the Leper, **a woman came to him with an alabaster jar of expensive perfume."**
>
> Matthew 26:6-7a (emphasis mine—NIV)

One detail should leap out at even the casual Bible student: WE HAVE A LEPER LIVING IN A SUBURB OF JERSUALEM ALONG WITH THE REGULAR POPULATION!

Such a situation is clearly impossible:

> "The person who has such an infectious disease must wear torn clothes, let his hair be unkempt, cover the lower part of his face and cry out, 'Unclean! Unclean!' As long as he has the infection he remains unclean. He must live alone; he must live outside the camp."
>
> Leviticus 13:45-46 (NIV)

It also requires very little effort to point out that lepers cannot:

1) Own property.
2) Live in or near Jerusalem, except in a leper colony.
3) Employ servants.
4) Own expensive jars of perfume.
5) Have feasts that Jews will legally be able to attend.

Once again the simplest and most complete answer comes from Aramaic idiom and convention. Two words, each spelled G-R-B-A in the text, have their meanings radically change when the proper vowels are added. "leper" is **GaRBA**, whereas "jar maker" is **GaRaBA**. Obviously then the second choice fits far more easily into the criteria than the first one does.[172]

Furthermore, it simply goes beyond credulity to suggest that a lifelong Aramaic speaker like Matthew could possibly make this mistake in Greek translation, especially since this goes against well known Torah provisions.

Now to be fair, the Greek School has seen the difficulty here and offered up a scenario in response. They say that perhaps the man was no longer a leper because Y'shua cured him and that, like Lazarus in John 12, he was giving a feast in Y'shua's honor to express gratitude for the miracle. "Simon the Leper" would then have been a name that just kind of stuck with him afterwards due to this occasion. There are at least three serious problems however with this suggestion.

First, the text does not tell us this is the case, and the only reason John 12 is compared to it is because such a distinction is made there. Second, lepers, by a matter of law, are never called that again once they are healed. They are always pronounced "clean" by the priests and re-enter society upon recovery, (Leviticus 14:11). Third, consider the ramifications to this man's personal life if he did as these scholars suggest. To keep being referred to as Simon THE LEPER would no doubt drive away business from him and create confusion when other Israelites from outside of his town came to visit there. It would also be considered a legal slander to call someone this if in fact he was not.

Finally, it is also worth noting that because verbal inflections of these word pairs would reveal their different meanings, the likelihood is extremely high that oral sources were not used. The scribe simply looked at the paper and made the wrong choice. So, it would seem then that the simplest explanation that takes into account the most evidence, is in fact the correct one.

2) *Pronunciation "red herrings". Certain letters can have two or even three different ways of pronouncing them depending on context! The letter beyt for example can be a "b", "w" or a "v" sound depending on the word, and there are no hard and fast rules that work all the time. The speaker simply has to "know" what is intended based on living experience with the language.*

Signs of the Cross: The Search for the Historical Jesus

Now before explaining why, a little history is needed. Contrary to the assertions of western scholars who have neither seen nor studied the original Peshitta NT, the dialect of Aramaic that Y'shua spoke is not lost and can be determined with certainty.

Starting in the fifth century, the eastern churches became locked in bitter disputes. The Syrian Orthodox began revising the original Aramaic to reflect their Catholic brethren's reliance on Greek based texts. In fact, the problems of harmonization were so great that they had to do it twice!

Then, when all attempts at getting the Church of the East on board with the Roman Catholics failed, the Syrians wanted to make sure that their texts would never be confused with the ACOE's. To do this, they changed their pronunciation of Aramaic and then, just to make sure everyone knew where they stood with the West, used reversed Greek letters for their vowels. So whereas before the word for "messiah" was "meshikha", which was itself in line with the old Hebrew "moshiack", the Syrians broke with tradition and pronounced it "meshikho". That is also why the original Aramaic NTs are called "Peshit-TA" and the Syrian revised versions are "Peshit-TO". In the West, these two terms are unfortunately still used interchangeably and without any regard for their differences.

As for the Church of the East, they were naturally appalled at what their Syrian counterparts did. Even though the Syrians also made changes in the appearance of the alphabet to distinguish their changed documents from the older ones, the Church of the East knew that the original Aramaic ones could still be in both churches, because it had been used by all eastern Christian groups. With these documents in the older script, the Syrians stood to use their new vowel system to change the way they were pronounced as well. Such a move could then force the original dialect and pronunciation out of existence.

In the end, there was only one solution. The Church of the East kept the original vowel-less script but also began using a different alphabet with dotted vowels to stabilize its pronunciation. That way, with both groups having altered alphabets and vowel systems in place, there would be no doubt and to what belonged to whom. The Syrians could continue with their changes and the Church of the East could preserve their tradition by leaving no doubt as how these words were originally said in the first century. Therefore, the dialect of Y'shua and the dialect of the Peshitta NT are one and the same.

It is also interesting to note that now, with all these disparate Aramaic Christian groups talking again after centuries of hate and mistrust, they have come to a vital agreement on this issue. Currently a group Peshitta version has been developed for all to use regardless of sect, and there is something in it for everybody. For the Syrians and Chaldeans who aligned with the Catholics, their five disputed books are in there, albeit with a note saying that these works were not included in the original canon that they shared at one time. Additionally, these groups got their way with the order of the books reflecting those in the West, so it would look more like a Greek NT. Even certain names of the books were compromised to reflect a pro-Greek stance, such as "Petros" instead of "Keepha" for Peter's epistles.

But there was one thing that Church of the East did get for its efforts, and it is the most important aspect of them all. For the 22 books that they did all agree on as sacred, *their pronunciation was retained as the original!* So now, even COE's former adversaries admit which came first.

The reason then that all this information applies to current Greek NT versions is simply this: Their translators made ANOTHER mistake.

For example, if I was to ask the average Christian, "What is the name of the Apostle John's father?" they would answer "Zebedee" for so the Greek text reads. But that's not how it is pronounced!

"Zebedee" is put in their versions because 90% of the time the letter beyt is the equivalent of "B" in English. However, the way it was pronounced back then, the "W" was used instead and thus it was "Zawdee"! Also notice how the Greek added the vowel "eh" because of this same reasoning, since *beyt* would most certainly have that pronunciation if it were a "B" in that part of the word.

Once again, if this was from an oral Aramaic source, the pronunciation would have guided them to the correct conclusion and it would have been rendered in Greek with a dipthong and spelled *zeta-alpha-epsilon-delta-iota* NOT as it is now with *zeta-epsilon-beta-epsilon-delta-alpha-iota—omicron-sigma* (Zebadios=Zebedee).

When we combine this evidence with other difficulties, the case for written Aramaic primacy becomes very strong indeed. The fact is, a single misread dot completely alters the spelling and meaning of a word (dalet or resh), and, in an overall sense, the right pronunciation was understood only ORALLY by native Aramaic speakers with sufficient experience. By contrast the Greek translators, while adequate in many areas, nevertheless lacked a keen grasp of the finer points which led them into error. However, those errors now end up being a blessing in disguise, since they lead us inexorably to an Aramaic original document done long before their traditional pronunciation was transmitted in a way that the rest of the world could understand.

3) *Areas where rare words in Aramaic throw off the Greek translator.*

There are quite a few examples where the Greek translator simply got confused and decided to "play it safe". Let's look at this moving exchange from the Gospel of John:

> When they had finished eating, Y'shua said to Simon Peter, "Simon son of John, do you truly love me more than these?" "Yes, Lord," he said, "you know that I love you." Y'shua said, "Feed my lambs."
>
> Again Y'shua said, "Simon son of John, do you truly love me?" He answered, "Yes, Lord, you know that I love you." Y'shua said, "Take care of my sheep."

> The third time he said to him, "Simon son of John, do you love me?" Peter was hurt because Y'shua asked him the third time, "Do you love me?" He said, "Lord, you know all things; you know that I love you." Y'shua said, "Feed my sheep."
>
> John 21:15-17 (NIV)

Now for the most part, the Greek translator does a good job. He recognizes that the Aramaic word in 21:15 is best rendered as *arneeon* (little sheep, lamb). In the next line too, the proper word is substituted also in Greek, *probaton*, which is the masculine plural designation for "sheep". So, thus far we have Y'shua saying, "Feed my (baby) lambs and take care of my (adult male) sheep", but the rest of it leaves something seriously lacking. Where, are the "female sheep" for Peter to take care of?

The answer, from the standpoint of the Greek texts, is nowhere. They simply put *probaton* in again, which means that Y'shua told Peter to take care of the children once and the grown men twice!

However, the Peshitta reads differently. In the Aramaic, as I said, the first two words are equivalent. It is the last line that finally clarifies the matter. There the word is *niqui*, which is in the plural feminine. Therefore, only the Aramaic clearly shows this intent that men, women and children are to be taken care of by Peter. By contrast, the reason the Greek does not read this way is because this Aramaic word is extremely rare and only occurs in the Old Testament once. Therefore, understanding the gist of the words is not enough, as the covering over with *probaton* only serves to weaken the excellent point that was there originally.

Therefore, with the linguistic issues thoroughly dealt with, the time has come to lay the foundation for the historical argument.

Signs of the Cross: The Search for the Historical Jesus

The Quick Tour and Outline

Since the mechanics of this theory are so detailed and complex, owing much to the nature of the textual difficulties that it must explain and account for, I have undertaken two basic strategies to make this information accessible to the average lay person.

The first is more of an overview approach, showing how the most important pieces of evidence fit together as a whole. While it represents more of a survey than a formal dissertation, the overview will make reference to certain aspects which are fully discussed elsewhere, and leave it up to the reader to seek out those additional details. In so doing, a person can, with minimal effort, see the full scope and historical structure of the theory, but not get overwhelmed with what seems like a ton of unrelated information.

The second approach is to dive in to the materials presented outside of the summary and take the major topics one at a time and in their full measure. This approach is intended for those people who need direct evidence for every part of the theory and will not look at the overall structure until the details are proven.

So now let us move on to the short version, with the following detailed outline:

APOSTLE Q OUTLINE

(For a thorough review of conventional Q theory and its shortcomings, please see the sections "Q-Tips" and "Mis-Qs")

1) Matthew, part 1.
   A. Claim: Matthew wrote the earliest Gospel. EVIDENCE:
      1) Statements by the early Church Fathers (Papias, Eusebius, etc)
      2) Church of the East traditions (patristic writings, liturgy, order of their holy books reflecting the order they were written in.

B. Claim: Matthew wrote this Gospel in his native language, Aramaic. EVIDENCE:
  1) Same as IA1-2.
  2) Mistranslated word pairs into Greek that could only have been done by a person who has a general understanding of Aramaic, but is not a native speaker. (rope vs. camel, leper vs. jar merchant, misquoting of Psalm 22, etc.)
  3) Mistranslated and mispronounced names that a native Aramaic speaker would not have confused, but a less expert person would have mispronounced due to certain linguistic peculiarities. (Zawdee =Zebedee, etc).
  4) Scribal glosses in Greek texts, but never in the Aramaic Peshitta New Testament, (Talitha cumi, epatha, etc.)

C. Claim: Matthew wrote his gospel no later than the year 49, (a.k.a. "James at 49") EVIDENCE THAT JAMES IS DATED TO THE 40'S:
  1) 2:2 uses the old word for "assembly" (synagogue), not the later and more non-Jewish "church", indicating a split between Jewish and Gentile wings had not happened yet.
  2) James refers to early persecutions happening in the present, and the ones taking place in this period make the most sense.
  3) James makes no mention of the Jerusalem Council, which convened in the year 49, and which he was in charge of. The decisions made there greatly impacted Jewish Christians throughout the Middle East, and since his letter is addressed to these same groups (1:1), it seems very odd that this is not even mentioned. Granted a formal letter was sent in Acts 16 explaining the decision,

but controversy broke out everywhere, and it seems inconceivable that some of that would not have reached James' own church, or that James would not have seen a need to comment on it in this letter. His congregation is very much on "business as usual" mode.

  4) A reference to the "hungry and naked poor of Jerusalem" (2:15), they suffered probably from the famine foretold by Agabus (Acts, 11:28-30), and usually identified with one mentioned by Josephus (Antiquities 20.2.5), which happened in the year 45.

 D. Conclusion to this section: Since James is dated to the 40's and quotes from Matthew, that Gospel must also date from that general time frame.

2) Matthew, part 2: A Tale of Three Copies.

 A. The first copy probably went with the apostle when he did missionary work in Ethiopia. Possible scenarios to explain this journey:

  1) The Candace Scenario:

   a) Candace, the Queen of Ethiopia, is recorded as visiting Jerusalem with a large entourage in the 8th chapter of Acts. At this time I history, Judaism is very influential in Ethiopia, with lore and customs that date back to Solomon. Their national epic, the *Tebra Negast*, identifies their first king (Menelik I) as the child of Solomon and their ruler at the time, the legendary Queen of Sheba. Regardless as to the truth of the legend, Ethiopia's version of Judaism is very ancient and based in traditions surrounding the first Temple, which stood only until 586 BCE. These Jews, both then and now, are known as *falashas,* and they would have been fluent in Hebrew and Aramaic, since these languages were passed down to them by the Jewish priests that came there and spread the faith several centuries before Jews even thought to have their Scripture translated. No one knows for sure why this happened, but the author is persuaded by the argument of Graham Hancock, who believes the priests hid the Ark of the Covenant there to avoid it being defiled by the evil king Manasseh, circa 680 BCE. In any event, the cultural and linguistic linkages between Ethiopia and Israel are beyond dispute, which would explain the Queen's visit.

b) Along with the Queen was her "chief treasurer" who, after a brief respite from his duties, met with the apostle Phillip.[173] After a brief discussion of what is obviously the Hebrew version of Isaiah 53, Phillip converts the chief treasurer to the new faith.

c) At this point, the high official disappears from the text and simply "goes away rejoicing".

d) If, however, the new convert wanted to preach in Jerusalem, then there would be major problem. As chief treasurer, it seems highly unlikely that the Queen would release him from her duties, and she is certainly only abroad for a limited period of time. If she loses one of the key members of her staff while on an official visit, the chance of it becoming an international incident and a diplomatic nightmare seem quite high.

e) The solution then simply could be a matter of trading places. Matthew, having preached to Hebrews in Jerusalem for a number of years (according to Papias and Eusebius), might have desired a change. As a Jew, he would have no difficulty conversing with the falashas, but, even better, his role as a tax collector would have made him a ideal replacement for the chief treasurer who wanted to leave his Queen's service.

f) The incident is dated prior to Paul's conversion, or no later than the year 36. Then, just prior to leaving Matthew would have, like Paul (Galatians 2:7-10) sought Peter's approval for the journey. Peter, reminding Matthew of the danger, probably then suggested that Matthew make a copy of his rough draft for safe keeping. Once this is accomplished, Matthew leaves with his copy, and Peter makes sure his fellow leader, James, also has a copy in his synagogue.

2. The Gradual Return Scenarios:
    a) The tradition is imprecise as to how

long Matthew stayed in Ethiopia, except for the strong inference that it was at least 20 years. Whether that time period was straight through or represented a total amount that involved frequent trips back to Israel is uncertain.

b) However, because there are other traditions that also talk of Matthew preaching in Israel FOR MANY YEARS also, it seems likely that he did shuttle back and forth between the countries, especially since controversies like the Jerusalem Council affected him greatly and probably would have forced his return, if he were included in phrases like "all the brothers" and "the apostles and elders" (Acts 15:4, 6, 22-23).

c) If these assumptions are correct, then Matthew need not have been sent to Ethiopia for the precise reason of replacing the chief treasurer, but could have gone up on his own at a later time, perhaps as late as the year 45. Peter's warnings and precautions however would still have applied.

d) It is also possible that Matthew wrote his rough draft in Ethiopia, brought it back with him to Jerusalem at some point before the year 49, and gave a copy to Peter before returning to Africa. If so, again Peter's reasoning would have applied here, and for the same reasons. Peter does not want this vital source to be lost in case Matthew is killed there, which, as it turns out, is exactly what happened, (New Foxes' Book of Martyrs, p. 6).

e) This copy probably perished around the time of Matthew's martyrdom, between the years 60 and 65. While the place of his death is disputed in the early records, his time in Ethiopia is not, and it is possible that his copy is still preserved somewhere, in one of the alleged cities that the apostle met his end in.

f) Conclusion to this section: Regardless as to the final particulars, the evidence is strong that Matthew did write an early Aramaic rough draft and that James had a copy of it. That being the case, it is inconceivable that James would have such a document without Peter having it first, since the latter man was clearly in charge of things, (Matthew 16:18).

C. James' Copy of Aramaic Matthew.

1) As stated above, James probably got his copy from Peter. Evidence in James' letter shows clearly that he followed the Hebrew pattern of liturgy when leading his congregation, (See "What Scripture Where? Part 2".) First James quotes from the Torah, (Genesis through Deuteronomy), then Joshua is quoted along with and a probable allusion from Jeremiah, and finally there is a direction for his congregation to "sing Psalms" and a line from Proverbs is quoted directly. This three-fold division of

the Old Testament (Torah, Prophets, Writings) is only done with Hebrew-Jewish congregations, whether in Israel or throughout the Diaspora. This is in direct contrast to the Hellenistic Jews, prominent in cities like Alexandria, who only spoke Greek and followed the divisions in the Septuagint, which did not conform to this pattern. Finally, James ends his sermon by quoting directly from Matthew, which may also be a clue that certain early New Testament writings were treated as Scripture and quoted after their Old Testament counterparts. It is certainly the case that these letters, like those of Paul and John, were intended to be read in the early Jewish-Christian and Gentile assemblies, (Colossians 4:16, 2 Corinthians 13:11).

2) James is martyred in the year 62. His copy of Matthew however probably survived a number of years in his synagogue.

3) That same copy then probably perished when Rome destroyed Jerusalem in the year 70. At that time and for several years afterward, a consistent effort was made to track down all Hebrew and Aramaic writings and burn them. The loss to Judaism and early Christianity because of this policy was therefore incalculable. When combined with the destruction of the Royal Library in Alexandria Egypt by Julius Caesar in 47 BCE, no other nation in world history has ever had a more devastating impact on the availability of ancient documents than the Roman Empire. However, while Hebrew copies of Matthew's rough draft (as well as Aramaic notebooks kept by other apostles) are probably lost forever, very early Aramaic completed

Gospels certified by living apostles are still being preserved by the Assyrian Church of the East.

4) Conclusion to this section: While James' copy is most certainly lost forever, it is an act of Providence that the apostle preserved clear cut evidence of its existence in the one piece of writing he did that survived into modern times.

D. Peter's copy of Aramaic Matthew.

1) The remainder of this theory has to do with how this remaining copy was itself copied, used and re-used over a forty-year period, before it either was also destroyed in the First Jewish Revolt, or used as one of the main sources for the final Aramaic copies held by the Church of the East.

2) Starting again with the western patristic tradition, early church documents record that Peter was the main inspiration behind Mark writing his Gospel, that Mark further wrote down "all of Peter's teaching, but not in order", (Catholic Encyclopedia, "Mark, Gospel of"; Eusebius, et. al.).

3) It is also the testimony of both the Gospels and the Church Fathers that Peter and Mark both were native Aramaic speakers, (Matthew 27:73, Eusebius, Jerome) and that Mark performed duties as an interpreter to Peter and (possibly) Paul as well. This may be reflected with the variety of Aramaic phrases that Mark leaves in his Gospel, (5:41, 7:11, 35, 14:36). While the Greek texts contain scribal glosses (helpful notes that say "this word means . . .", none of the Aramaic copies do, since the words are meant to be understood in that language. This is also another proof that the Greek text is relying on an Aramaic original.

4) However, when looking at the big picture, seem-

ingly contradictory lines of evidence present themselves. On the one hand, few facts have greater agreement in the liturgy of both eastern and western churches than the fact that Matthew wrote the first Gospel. However, modern linguists, especially those concerned with the Greek version of a collection of Gospel material called "Q", are equally unanimous that Mark had to come first, because his Greek appears to be both rudimentary and to have undergone significant revision by the other evangelists. The answer to the conundrum however is rather simple: They are both right.

5) Matthew, as we know the work, is not the same thing as the Aramaic rough draft that was early on identified as his Gospel. The proof of this assertion comes from the many bad choices in Greek that result from picking the wrong Aramaic word pair, (see IB2). Therefore, the only way to account for all this information is to say that, for all intents and purposes, *Matthew is Mark!* Or, to put it another way, most of what we know to be Mark's Gospel (less scribal glosses and other later additions) is nothing more than a Greek translation of Matthew's Aramaic Rough Draft. Since Mark was Peter's translator almost exclusively, there can be little doubt as to where Mark's source came from. What follows then is the progression of Mark's rough draft by both the author and the other Gospel writers.

3) Through the eyes of Mark.
   A. Mark's evolution of his own work.
      1. Mark probably begins work on his Gospel in the year 44. At that time (see Acts 12), Peter was put in prison near Jerusalem only to escape a few days

later. Then Peter's first stop on his way home is to a safe house run by Mark's mother Mary. Then, a short time later, (Acts 12:25) Mark leaves from Jerusalem with Barnabbas and Paul to go on a missionary journey. It therefore seems likely that Peter either took Mark with him as a translator or else sent for Mark very soon after his escape.

2. At that point, the work would begin. First, Mark would look at Matthew's Aramaic rough draft and then ask Peter for guidance when several meanings in the text were possible. In the surviving text, this emendation takes the form of details that Matthew—and therefore Luke also— does not record but that Peter apparently remembers. Two examples of this would the designation of James and John as "sons of thunder" and the identification of the blind man as having the name "Bartimaeus". Then, the expanded Aramaic work itself was translated into Greek. A Greek copy of this source would also be useful for evangelizing in the heavily Gentile areas that they were going into, like Cyprus, (Acts 13:4-12). Peter, of course, would also make sure he had a copy of everything Mark did. (While Mark was gone Peter needed another interpreter, but that will be addressed later.)

3. After extensive travels both with and without the apostle Paul, Mark goes to Rome (figuratively called "Babylon" in 1 Peter 5:12) to be with his mentor Peter. It is here, according to Catholic tradition, that Mark began the first revision of his Gospel, circa 60 CE.

4. Then, according to another early tradition (Clement), Mark made a few more changes while assist-

ing a small Christian community in Alexandria, Egypt. It was there, according to the New Foxes Book of Martyrs, that Mark protested against certain festivities of a local deity, Serapis, and was summarily dragged through the streets and murdered. In the earliest Greek and Aramaic copies of Mark there may be a clue about this, because the original narrative stops just prior to the actual resurrection (16:8), which was clearly an event Mark intended to record, if only because he talks about it from a predictive standpoint, (8:31, 10:32-34, 14:62). Therefore, if this most critical piece was missing, it can only be because Mark was killed before he could finish his last chapter, around the year 63.

    5. Subsequently, Mark's writings were smuggled out of Alexandria and made their way back to Peter, who inserted those twelve lines. Now, with the Gospel complete in Aramaic, all the Greek version needed was those few lines also translated there. The rest of the rudimentary Aramaic to Greek work was done entirely by Mark, which was revised and re-edited in the Greek versions of Matthew and Luke.

B. Peter, Silas and Q.

    1. In traditional Q theory, the Mattean Scribe, or the person that edited Greek Matthew into its final form, is a complete unknown. (See IB2 for the reasons why the writer of Greek Matthew cannot be the same person as the actual apostle.) This is also the case with the mysterious "Q" writer himself, and yet both men must somehow be known to us, because they each needed some form of early apostolic accreditation to do what they did. There-

fore, our task, rather than keep such identities a secret, is to search the official record and see if a likely candidate can emerge from the evidence. After more than three years of painstaking research then, this author has come to the conclusion that the Mattean Scribe is otherwise known to us as "Silas" or "Silvanus" in the New Testament. For ease and convenience, we will use only the first version of the name in our discussion.

2. The evidence for Silas as the Mattean Scribe is almost overwhelming. Silas is mentioned in several critical places. In 1 Peter 5:12, the apostle actually gives him credit for translating his first epistle. Then, in the opening statements of both letters to the Thessalonians, Paul gives Silas part credit in writing those letters, which is especially significant since Paul was known to use a scribe quite often, (Romans 16:22).

3. Silas first appears on the scene during the Jerusalem Council in the year 49, where he is hand-picked to deliver (translate?) the Councils' findings to Gentile audiences. Then, in 2 Corinthians 1:19, Paul acknowledges Silas' assistance in helping him preach to Gentiles. While such a quick quote might on the surface seem insignificant, it becomes very important when we consider other statements that Paul could neither communicate in Greek at a high level or even do a decent job in writing out the letters, (see "The Josephus Connection", 2 Peter 3:15-16, Galatians 6:11)!

4. Furthermore, Silas' occasions to help Paul seem oddly convenient. Paul had initially traveled with Mark for almost a year before the young man bolted back to Jerusalem prematurely, (Acts 13:13). For-

tunately for Paul, he was in Pisdian Antioch preaching in synagogues, so he could get by in Aramaic and what little Greek was required.[174] In any case, Paul was able to compensate for Mark's absence because he was focusing on Jewish audiences primarily. Then, when Paul returned to Jerusalem, Mark begged to come with him again, but Paul refused to take him. Then both Paul and Silas leave Jerusalem together, (Acts 15:22). So it seems the apostle finally found Mark's replacement!

5. Then Silas continues his journeys with Paul, and even is imprisoned with him for a short period, (Acts 16:16-40). It is at this point, that Paul and Silas part company. However, that is fine because just prior to this, another interpreter, Luke, enters the scene. Because we know Luke wrote both his Gospel and the Book of Acts, (Luke 1:1-3, Acts 1:1-2), it becomes extremely significant when the pronouns that start as "them" in 16:9 abruptly switch to "we" in 16:10, meaning that Luke is now including himself as part of the traveling party. Such a scenario is further supported by the fact that Paul has just landed in Troas, where Luke works as a physician, and there is an early church tradition that Paul converted Luke while seeking his help for an undisclosed ailment, (Colossians 4:14).

6. Now, with Paul taken care of once again, Silas can continue to shuttle between Peter and Paul, helping when needed as a translator, (1 Peter 5:12).

7. Now, with Mark away frequently on missionary journeys, it is Peter who needs help translating into Greek. The above quote tells us that Peter did

need Silas' help in the year 63, but at this point, almost a decade earlier, with both Mark and Luke otherwise engaged, it is very possible that Silas was called in to help Peter at that time as well. Certainly if Peter needed help with his Greek by the time he wrote his first letter, it would be even more necessary several years earlier. The pattern also shows that Peter would have had a consistent track record of struggling with this language going back more than thirty years before, when his Galilean accent could not even be concealed among his fellow Jews. However, from this point on, the records are silent.

8. Therefore, the scenario which makes the best sense based on our current information would be that Peter, again according to early tradition, would have began to write Aramaic notes of his own, perhaps intended as a way to expand on Aramaic Matthew. Then, when he meets Silas in the early 50's, he would have asked him to translate these notes into Greek, and it is these same translated notes that I believe are known as the Q collection today, thus conferring on Peter the title of Apostle Q.

9. Silas is then given copies of Q, as well as the final Greek version of Mark so he can shuttle them off to Paul's group for evangelizing to Gentiles and helping him communicate better in their language, (2 Peter 3:15-16). Somewhere in this area also Silas would have revised Mark slightly to make it more Greek like, including glosses like 3:17 (boanerges) as well as doing a less than stellar job in transliterating certain Aramaic names

(Zebedee). This version he would have also in time passed on to the apostle Paul.

10. In due time, Paul passes these Greek materials on to Luke, who then goes about inserting phrases first from one and then the other. Luke probably spent a great deal of time doing this, but even though Mark returned to be with him and Paul and brought writing materials and sources to help in the compilation, Mark's Gospel is not with them at that time, (2 Timothy 4:11-13). That final copy will only come after Mark is dead, and is sent to them from Peter and via Silas. Luke also gets access to other material (probably oral stories heard on the missionary journeys, such as the Nativity, the raising of widow's son at Nain, etc.,) and includes them as well. Certainly Luke's extensive use of Semitic poetry throughout his first 6 chapters show a mixture of Aramaic oral and written sources being edited in both languages into a complete form.

12. However, we end this portion with Luke's final Greek Gospel being translated back into Aramaic, and it is this copy that the Church of the East holds, again certified by living apostles, even today.

C. Silas and Greek Matthew.

1. Then Silas finds himself in Rome in the early 60's, and it is not long before chaos breaks out. First Mark leaves to finish his Gospel in Alexandria, forcing Silas to stay behind and help Peter with his epistle. Afterwards, word comes that Mark has been murdered there, which must have been a devastating blow to all present there. Finally, by the year 64 both Peter and Paul are imprisoned. Luke has Paul's writings to be sure, but Peter's

versions are now threatened, so he takes them with him for safe keeping.
2. However, because Silas never saw Luke do any editing of these sources on his own, he must have thought it a good idea to provide his own version, and so the exact same process with splicing Mark and Q happens. Then, also like Luke, Silas has picked up his own oral traditions from Peter and others, and so the unique features of Matthew (another Nativity story, the Sermon on the Mount, etc.) are added also in Greek. The final act is also identical to what happened with the third Gospel as well, as this final Greek Matthew is also translated back into Aramaic, certified by living apostles, and presented to the Church of the East.
3. Conclusion: Thus, all three Gospels are clearly derived from earlier Aramaic written and oral sources and return to the Aramaic language in their final form at the end of the process. From the first century onwards, the Church of the East has an unbroken tradition that stretches into the present day. They declare, quite persuasively, that none of these Aramaic documents have changed the slightest bit since that time. This is a claim also that the Greek manuscripts, where no two versions are identical, are unable to make a credible case for.

The Big Picture

So then, in typical American fashion, let me start with the bottom line: all of the Gospels, in essentially the same forms as we know them[175], stem from the common years 70-100 CE, with other New Testament writings getting even earlier dates. The following list is from *The Complete Gospels*, page 6, and it bears out this principle rather well:

From John the Baptist to Nicea:

Stages in the Development of the early Christian tradition

1-30 CE:

John the Baptist, precursor and mentor of Y'shua[176] (died about 27 CE).

Jesus of Nazareth, traveling sage and wonder worker (died about 30 BCE).[177]

30-60 CE:

Paul of Tarsus, chief founder of Gentile Christianity[178] (letters written about 50-60 CE).

Sayings Gospel Q, (first edition, about 50 CE).

Gospel of Thomas, (first edition, about 50 CE)

60-80 CE:

Signs Gospel (eventually incorporated into John).

Gospel of Mark, the first narrative gospel (first edition, about 70 CE)

Didache, first believers' handbook (first edition).

80-100 CE:

Gospel of Matthew, incorporating Mark and Q (about 80 CE).

Gospel of Luke, incorporating Mark and Q, (about 90 CE).

Dialogue of the Savior (first edition, probably 50-100 CE).

Gospel of Peter[179] (first edition, probably 50-100 CE).[180]

Egerton Gospel (probably 50-100 CE)

Gospel of John, incorporating the Signs Gospel (about 90 CE)

Gospel of Mark, canonical edition (about 100 CE)[181]

100-150 CE

Gospel of John, third edition (insertions and additions).[182]

Secret Book of James, first edition, found at Nag Hammadi.

Jewish Christian Gospels (preserved in patristic quotations)[183]

Didache, second edition (insertions and additions)

Gospel of Thomas, second edition (surviving edition)[184]

Surviving fragment of Gospel of John

Surviving fragments of Egerton Gospel
150-325
Emergence of four "recognized Gospels"
Emergence of an official collection of Christian writings ("New Testament").
Christianity becomes a legal religion (313 CE).
Council of Nicea (325 CE)
First official creeds
First surviving copies of "Bibles" (about 325-350 CE).

As this list also shows, in the last century, we have made great strides in putting these documents into proper historical context. By the early 1900's, an extremely skeptical view that all NT writings were second century or later in origin had taken hold in secular academia. These liberal scholars further asserted, rather confidently, that these same texts had no basis in being attributed to actual apostles. Nowadays however, we find a vastly different scenario, because even in the most recalcitrant liberal circles, is the minimum consensus that these same writings, if not finally edited by the apostles, nevertheless reflect an early teaching that comes from them.

This scholarly about face was the direct result of more detailed studies of the oral traditions of the earliest Christian communities. The similarity in their oral traditions proved, say both liberal and conservative scholars alike, that the original germ, the essential gist of these documents, came from the people tradition claims it does. The fact that many of these same liberal scholars ignore the universal accreditation of the actual Gospels to Matthew, Mark, Luke and John is for the moment irrelevant and will be addressed separately. What is critical at this juncture is that the traditions contained within those documents go back to the very time the events themselves were known to happen. No one now seriously doubts that the apostle Paul wrote the letters that bear his name, and this fact alone gives a stamp of approval to much of the gospel events both in terms of antiquity and reliability.

As a final example, consider Homer's *Iliad*. For many centuries, historians scoffed at the epic as a piece of Hellenic folklore with no basis in fact. They did this because they knew that if the Trojan War happened at all, it must have preceded Homer's time by at least 500 years. Then, toward the end of the nineteenth century, archaeologist Heinrich Schliemann validated the historical aspects of Homer and the oral tradition the poet used to put his work into writing. Yes there were legends added to it about various gods and heroes, but the fact that Troy was burned down completely by an invading Greek army has been turned into a virtual scholarly certainty. If such is the case with Homer, how much more true is it of the Gospels themselves, since there is a minimum 75% reduction in the gap between them and the events they record, as opposed to Homer and Troy? Seventy years is therefore a small enough interval as to ensure the reliability of this sort of transmission, and multiple attestations of these same stories must therefore bring us back to, if not the actual time itself, then a very small handful of years thereafter.

The Three Earliest Sources and "the Apostle's Gate"

> "Many have undertaken to draw up an account of the things that have been fulfilled among us, just as they were handed down to us by those who were eyewitnesses and servants of the word. Therefore, since I have carefully investigated everything from the beginning, it seemed good to me to also write an orderly account for you, most excellent Theophilus, so that you may know the certainty of the things you have been taught."
>
> Luke 1:1-5 (NIV)

According to the vast majority of both liberal and conservative scholars, three sources date back to a written Greek form a mere 20-30 years after the Crucifixion. They are:

Epistles of Paul, James and Peter[185], written between the years 45-66. These letters contain the earliest references to Gospel events, especially the resurrection, which appear 10-20 years before the earliest known narrative Gospel.

Sayings Gospel Q, which is widely believed to have been written and circulated in the 50's, and whose material wound up in Matthew and Luke, but not Mark.

Sayings Gospel Thomas, earliest edition also in the 50's, much of which found its way into the "triple tradition."

However, what is perhaps most interesting is the fact that we know from internal clues that these written traditions existed in earlier forms, in spite of the fact that these original sources have been lost. Such a situation is hardly new to this field, for we know categorically that no original books of the Bible have survived into modern times, only ancient copies of other ancient copies. And yet, we can be sure of the reliability of what we have primarily due to the integrity of oral tradition, as well as the fact that the New Testament has more extant books and fragments (25,000+!) that are in agreement and are sufficiently early enough, as to give it more historical clout than any other ancient book known to survive.

Finally, it should be noted that all these sources share one thing in common. They all had to pass through what I call the *Apostle's Gate*. Stated simply, there were a wide variety of early stories that circulated within 20-30 years of Y'shua's death. However, only those that jibed with the historical record were accepted into the official Gospels, (Luke 1:1-4, John 21:23-24, Galatians 1:6-7, 1 Corinthians 1:11-17, 2 Peter 1:16-17, 2:1-3, 3:14-16, 2 John 1:7, Jude 1:3-4). So whether the sources listed here are in the canon or not, their proximity to the time guarantees that if they are genuine they will pass through the gate and into the Gospels, and if not, they won't.

Andrew Gabriel Roth

It's NOT all Greek to me

" ... The Christian theological establishment has decreed that Greek is the "original" language of the NEW TESTAMENT, despite the existence of voluminous proof that the Gospels were written in Aramaic, the language Jesus spoke and the language of the Biblical lands at the time. My preliminary consideration of this project presents the obvious fact that of the thousands of poetic verses in the Bible, none rhyme in Greek or any other language and yet all rhyme in Aramaic. Surely to consider this coincidence is preposterous."

Victor Alexander, "Aramaic Bible Translation Project", page 2.

What is most revealing about this state of events, however, is the fact that all the major players in the New Testament spoke Aramaic as their native language, and were most comfortable in it, regardless as to their varying competency levels in Greek. Now it is important to note that no serious scholar doubts that Y'shua's teachings were originally delivered in Aramaic, even if translated at the scene into Greek. It is this minimum assertion then, that both Aramaic and Greek understanding are needed to gain a full picture of Y'shua's world, which more than 90% of all scholars agree on.

Therefore, it is one of history's supreme ironies that the language of the most famous man in history is fully understood by less than 1% of these same scholars who profess to study him!

So, let's catch our breath for just a minute. If some of the written Greek dates back to the 50's, it stands to reason that its oral Greek counterpart would be a little earlier, doesn't it? Now with that in mind, another question needs to be asked: How much more early would be the original Aramaic source that version came from?

To answer that question, we must look forward. While the thoroughly Aramaic based poetic forms of the Lords' Prayer have already been discussed, its usage impacts on this point in another way. That prayer, as it turns out, is also part of the Q tradition, or material that is nearly identical in Matthew and Luke (the latter of which adds lines but keeps these as well). As we said, the Q version goes back to the 50's, however, the vast majority of scholars don't put these same versions in the actual Gospels until at least 20-30 years later! Keep this critical thought in mind, because it impacts this discussion in two essential ways.

First, if it takes 20-30 years for Greek stories to go from Q to Gospel, a similar process must, by definition take a sizeable amount of time to have gone from Aramaic to Q! If we even halve the maximum number of years for the previous evolution and calculate it backwards, we have original sources going back to the 30's, the very decade that Y'shua was crucified!

Second, the rule of multiple attestation states that if it takes 20-30 years for a story to circulate from Q into two final Gospels, traditions that made their way into three or four versions must have circulated longer.[186] And yet, as much time as this entire process must have taken, we still have to add another time-consuming step.

The fact is, not only was there enough time in all of this for translation from Aramaic to Greek to happen, *we can even show enough time passed for certain verses to be badly translated into Greek!* In other words, if getting a translation right takes a number of years, allowing for a certain amount of confusion to creep in to get it wrong, must have taken even longer!

Love Letters

The first of our earliest sources, the Epistles of Paul, James and Peter, present many great insights to the careful reader, and have proven extremely useful in rebutting the attacks of many liberal scholars. Nowadays, very few accept the idea, as they once did, that the Gospels are second century documents or later. Part of the credit for this has to go to Paul, whose authorship is almost universally accepted and therefore whose accounts of Gospel facts prove the traditions in those documents go back to the very beginning. Paul has, almost single-handedly, given the Christian historian enough supporting evidence to stand against any assault, linguistic or otherwise.

For example, it used to be said that the original sources never even mentioned a resurrection! Worse still, critics maintained up until recently that the whole issue of Messiah's death was not addressed, or if it was, Mark's Gospel merely showed an empty tomb and had his ending changed, and then copied, into the other Gospels. Setting aside the simple fact that Mark mentions a resurrection from a predictive standpoint, (9:9, 10:34, 14:62), critics instead focused on the last 12 lines, which were apparently added later. However, this fact bolsters rather than degrades the historicity of Mark for three special reasons.

First, these same liberal scholars assert confidently that Mark was written first and then redacted separately by Matthew and Luke. If true, and owing to the part that Q reflects very early statements about the resurrection, (Q = Luke 11:16, 29-32 and Matthew 12:38-42), then the problem of whether Mark just wanted to imply the resurrection in light of the other evidence is very minimal.[187]

Second, another explanation for this same problem is derived from the Church of the East's own traditions. Not only do they present an unbroken line of tradition going back to the apostolic founders of their church, the same tradition exists in their Scripture and liturgy, which has also escaped later revisions. It is therefore very significant that no Aramaic copies lack the 12 lines "added" to Mark 16, since the controversies that split the eastern Churches arose early on, and yet they agree on the same original Scripture. Neither is it viable to suggest that Eastern Aramaic Churches would except Greek versions, when they disputed the validity of versions made in the dialects of their own language. An even worse proposition is to suggest that their traditions about their liturgy, which follow all the accepted rules of oral preservation, are invalid. Such a theory would then have to "prove" that these same people had no Christian Scriptures themselves until the nice Roman Catholic Church gave them Greek "originals" to translate the words of their Savior back into his own native language!

The third reason has to do now with the Pauline Epistles themselves because of their early testimony:

> "Paul, an apostle—sent not from men nor by man, but by Y'shua Ha Moshiack and God the Father, who raised him from the dead."
>
> Galatians 1:1
>
> "They tell how you turned to God from idols to serve the living and true God, and to wait for his Son from heaven, whom He raised from the dead, Y'shua, who rescues us from the coming wrath."
>
> 1 Thessalonians 1:9-10

One of these two quotes is the earliest known reference to the resurrection in written Greek.[188] Some scholars date Galatians to the year 49, which would make it the oldest, or to 55, in which case it's the other.[189]

However, regardless as to which book is the earliest, the fact is that any one of them on their own could easily prove the resurrection as an original idea and not a later addition.

Furthermore, the Epistles also establish what the Gospels say, that eyewitnesses wrote down these events as they saw them:

> "To the elders among you, I appeal as a fellow elder, a witness of Messiah's sufferings and one who will also share in the glory to be revealed."
>
> 1 Peter 5:1

> "For what I received I passed on to you as of first importance: That Messiah died for our sins according to the Scriptures, that he was buried, that he was raised on the third day according to the Scriptures[190] and that he appeared to Peter, and then to the Twelve. After that he appeared to more than five hundred of the brothers at the same time, most of whom are still living[191], though some have fallen asleep. Then he appeared to James, then to all the apostles, and last of all he appeared to me also, as to one abnormally born."
>
> 1 Corinthians 15:3-8

And, my personal favorite:

> "We did not follow cleverly invented stories when we told you about the power and coming of our Lord Y'shua Ha Moshiack, but we were eyewitnesses of his majesty. For he received honor and glory from God the Father when the voice came to him in Majestic Glory, saying, 'This is my Son, whom I love; with him I am well pleased.' We ourselves heard this voice that came down from heaven when we were with him on the sacred mountain."
>
> 2 Peter 1:16-18[192]

Here is Peter's own rebuke to the liberal critics! These were not "cleverly invented stories", as he says, but reports on actual events. What's more, with Peter's writings also dated to the 50s and 60s, we have a clear reference to a supernatural Baptism which is recorded in all four Gospels, (Matthew 3:13-17, Mark 1:9-11, Luke 3:21-22, John

1:29-34[193])! Once again there is proof that a supernatural event can be an original incident that is not reworked later!

The second early tradition is particularly exciting because, even though it did not make it into the Bible officially, it gives us terrific insight into what the original Gospel sources must have looked like.

Thomas' Promises

It turns out that it is entirely possible history owes a far greater debt to one apostle in particular than is commonly known. Peter may have been the designated successor and John the disciple he loved, but Thomas may have done something truly amazing. He may have kept a notebook about original words of Y'shua that actually has survived into modern times.

Unfortunately, as is usually the case in this field, there is a catch involved. The simple reason being that these same early traditions have also been very controversial and presented a number of challenges to secular and religious historians alike. For myself, I must confess that I also fell into a number of traps that this work imposes on the reader, and did not see its full import because of becoming distracted with differences between it and Gospels. Those differences also caused me to ignore its tremendous potential, because I was not looking at how those differences may have been put there to begin with.

However, before we can get into a detailed study of why the Gospel of Thomas is so valuable, it is necessary to look at the controversy it has created, particularly in the fundamentalist community. I will take these points on one at a time.

➢ The Gospel of Thomas is a work of heretical origin belonging to a radical sect known as the "Gnostics".

> "One must assume that as a sayings collection, this text would have enjoyed much greater flexibility of content than is generally due of narrative texts.

> In each new appropriation of the collection, new sayings could easily be added . . ."
>
> The Complete Gospels, p. 302

This is true to a very large extent. The Gnostics no doubt thought they could bolster their viewpoint by showing how their ideology is reflected in apostolic tradition. So, what they did was take an original copy of Thomas and added their own sayings on top of it![194] Even the most liberal proponents of Thomas acknowledge this much, stating that Thomas went through at least three major changes from its now lost original. It probably originally existed in Aramaic[195], was distributed through Syria where he was patron saint, and had an earlier Palestinian version that is almost assumed by most scholars.[196] After this, it was translated next into Greek. Once this was achieved, major additions greatly expanded the work between the second and third centuries.[197] Finally, after this Gnostic fakery was completed, the entire work, old and new, was translated into Coptic, which is the version we now have.

It is these same Gnostic additions which have created such a stir, with statements about women having to become men in order to get into kingdom, reincarnation of men into animals, and other gross errors too numerous to mention. Other differences between Thomas and the Gospels' phraseology have to do with mistranslation problems similar to those discussed earlier, made worse for Thomas because of the paucity of its fragments.

So, even though the current Thomas we have came from a Gnostic library at Nag Hammadi Egypt, that doesn't mean an earlier version of Thomas which is now lost did not exist and that it could not be much more in line with official record.

➢ Thomas is not canonical Scripture.

> "Still, several factors point to a date sometime in the latter decades of the first century, C.E.: First,

> the collection belongs to a time when individual Christian communities were still appealing to the authority of particular apostles (not to "the twelve" as a whole) as the guarantor of their traditions. In this respect it is comparable to Mark, which dates around 70 C.E. Second, the genre of Thomas, the sayings collection, seems to have fallen into disuse among Christians by the end of the first century. Later church fathers revived the form, but always took care to cite the sources for their material, usually the canonical gospels. This is quite different from Thomas, which derives its material not from the canonical gospels, but from the same oral traditions on which these gospels themselves rely. This, in turn, suggests a third factor: Thomas was assembled before Matthew, Mark, Luke and John had attained the ascendancy which the later church codified in the form of a "canon", a process which began in the second century. All of these factors place Thomas approximately in the same period as the canonical gospels (ca. 70-100 C.E.)."
>
> The Complete Gospels, p. 302-3

Certainly the Gnostic additions to Thomas are not inspired, and should be thrown out utterly, to the outside of the Apostle's Gate. However, Thomas does have a great deal in common with material that made it into the canon, with many statements attested to in two, or even three, Gospels. Therefore, if any serious study of the composition of the Gospels is to be undertaken, then we must look again at the strands of early oral and written traditions that were sifted by apostolic discernment under the guidance of God.

Furthermore, if we then throw out all of Thomas, and not just those verses which were added maliciously and without the consent of the original writer, we then throw out the single greatest independent confirmation of vast amounts of material in the Holy Four. It is also very much in keeping God's ways that he should use a heretical sect's library as a method of preserving original Gospel truth, even if we have to work to retrieve it. In that sense, we should remember the admonitions in Thessalonians to test everything, hold on to the good, and avoid all kinds of evil.

> Thomas has an extremely low amount of extant fragments, only a handful in Greek, and just one complete manuscript in Coptic. When we compare this with the 25,000+ fragments of accepted NT books that are out there, there is no way Thomas can compete.

Agreed. However, we need to count the Thomas fragments that match or very closely resemble the Gospels as part of that 25,000 number! Again, those early concordances strengthen the overall proof of the historicity of these events, and the rest should be discarded as later corruptions of record, which is exactly what history tells us they are.

> Thomas material was used by the Gnostics as a thorn in the side of the apostles, and is used by neo-Gnostics and other radicals to attack the traditional Church. To lend credence to Thomas then is to play into our adversaries' clutches.

Also very true. However, it must be fairly pointed out that cults and other non-mainstream organizations don't confine themselves to extra-biblical material! In fact, the bulk of their deceptions come from twisting official records. For example, I once heard a pimp justify his profession on television by saying that his "girls" were "fishers of men"! We don't discard Luke just because someone twists its meaning maliciously, so why discard Thomas when he agrees with Luke? In fact, the very idea that people would pervert the Gospel to their own ends was warned about in advance, (Galatians 1:6-7)! Ignoring historical confirmations of the Gospels contained in Thomas therefore will not stop the enemies of the Word from doing their work, and may in fact advance their cause. The trick is not to do what liberals like the Jesus

Seminar and others have done, which is to say that Thomas is the litmus test for the Gospel's historicity, and the extrapolate that out to force the Gospels into agreement with later, tainted versions of Thomas.

Mutual Validations

Therefore, as a logical extension, it should be apparent that where there is agreement between Thomas and the Gospels, a system of mutual validations arises for both. For the Gospels, to have a story echoed in Thomas brings a whole series statements other than Q into the earlier framework, since Thomas also dates from the 50's. On the other hand, the Gospels return the favor to Thomas by acknowledging that a portion of his sayings were genuine, because they passed through the Apostle's Gate and into legitimacy in the canon.

Thomas' Sermon on the Mount

As an introduction to just how stunning some of these concordances can be[198], let us look at how the apostle Thomas records the essential teachings of the Sermon on the Mount, with words that would also be reflected in both Matthew and Luke's versions[199]:

54 Y'shua said, "Congratulations to the poor, for to you belongs Heaven's kingdom."

58 Y'shua said, "Congratulations to the person who has toiled and has found life."

68 Y'shua said, "Congratulations to you when you are hated and persecuted; and no place will be found, wherever you have been persecuted."

69 Y'shua said, "Congratulations to those who have been persecuted in their hearts: they are the ones who have truly come to know the Father. Congratulations to those who go hungry, so the stomach of the one in want may be filled."

95 [Y'shua said], "If you have money, don't lend it at interest. Rather, give [it] to someone from whom you won't get it back."
32 Y'shua said, "A city built on a high hill and fortified cannot fall, nor can it be hidden."
24 His disciples said, "Show us the place where you are, for we must seek it." He said to them, "Anyone here with two ears had better listen! There is light within a person of light, and it shines on the whole world. If it does not shine, it is dark."
33 Y'shua said, "What you will hear in your ear, in the other ear proclaim from your rooftops. After all, no one lights a lamp and puts it under a basket, nor does one put it in a hidden place. Rather, one puts it on a lampstand so that all who come and go will see its light."
62 Y'shua said, "I disclose my mysteries to those [who are worthy] of [my] mysteries. Do not let your left hand know what your right hand is doing."
104 They said to Y'shua, "Come, let us pray today, and let us fast."[200]
34 Y'shua said, "If a blind person leads a bind person, both of them will fall into a hole."
26 Y'shua said, "You see the sliver in your friend's eye, but you don't see the timber in your own eye. When you take the timber out of your own eye, then you will see well enough to remove the sliver from your friend's eye."
93 "Don't give what is holy to dogs, for they might throw them upon the manure pile. Don't throw pearls [to] pigs, or they might . . . it [. . .]."
94 Y'shua [said], "One who seeks will find, and for [one who knocks] it will be opened."
75 Y'shua said, "There are many standing at the door, but those who are alone will enter the bridal suite."[201]
36 Y'shua said, "Do not fret, from morning to evening and from evening to morning, [about your food—what you're going to eat, or about your clothing—] what you are going to wear. [You're much better than the lilies, which neither card nor spin. As for

you, when you have no garment, what will you put on? Who might add to your stature? That very one will give you your garment.]"

57 Y'shua said, The Father's kingdom is like a person who has [good] seed. His enemy came during the night and sowed weeds among the good seed. The person did not let the workers pull up the weeds, but said to them, "No, otherwise you might go to pull up the weeds and pull up the wheat along with them." For on the day of the harvest the weeds will be conspicuous, and will be pulled up and burned.[202]

76 Y'shua said, The Father's kingdom is like a merchant who had a supply of merchandise and found a pearl. That merchant was prudent; he sold the merchandise and bought the single pearl for himself. So also with you, seek his treasure that is unfailing, that is enduring, where no moth comes to eat and no worm destroys."

45 Y'shua said, "Grapes are not harvested from thorn trees, nor are figs gathered from thistles, for they yield no fruit. Good persons produce good from what they've stored up; bad persons produce evil from the wickedness they've stored up in their hearts, and say evil things. For from the overflow of the heart they produce evil."

47 Y'shua said, "A person cannot mount two horses or bend two bows. And a slave cannot serve two masters, otherwise that slave will honor the one and offend the other. "Nobody drinks aged wine and immediately wants to drink young wine. Young wine is not poured into old wineskins, or they might break, and aged wine is not poured into a new wineskin, or it might spoil. An old patch is not sewn onto a new garment, since it would create a tear."

However, the true extent of shared material between Thomas and the Gospels cannot fully be appreciated until we list all of the similar sayings side by side. The reader is therefore asked to make up his own mind based on the following:

THOMAS:

These are the secret sayings that the living Y'shua spoke and Didymos Judas Thomas recorded.

1 And he said, "Whoever discovers the interpretation of these sayings will not taste death."

GOSPELS:

I tell you the truth, if anyone keeps my word, he shall never see death.

John 8:51

THOMAS:

5 Y'shua said, "Know what is in front of your face, and what is hidden from you will be disclosed to you.

For there is nothing hidden that will not be revealed. [And there is nothing buried that will not be raised."]

6 His disciples asked him and said to him, "Do you want us to fast? How should we pray? Should we give to charity? What diet should we observe?"

Y'shua said, "Don't lie, and don't do what you hate, because all things are disclosed before heaven. After all, there is nothing hidden that will not be revealed, and there is nothing covered up that will remain undisclosed."

GOSPELS:

"So have no fear of them; for nothing is covered that will not be revealed, or hidden that will not be known.

Matthew 10:26, pp. Mark 4:22, Luke 8:17, 12:2

THOMAS:

9 Y'shua said, Look, the sower went out, took a handful (of seeds), and scattered (them). Some fell on the road, and the birds came and gathered them. Others fell on rock, and they didn't take root in the soil and didn't produce heads of grain. Others fell on thorns, and they choked the seeds and worms ate them. And others fell on good soil, and it produced a good crop: it yielded sixty per measure and one hundred twenty per measure.

Signs of the Cross: The Search for the Historical Jesus

GOSPELS:
And he taught them many things in parables, and in his teaching he said to them: "Listen! A sower went out to sow. And as he sowed, some seed fell along the path, and the birds came and devoured it. Other seed fell on rocky ground, where it had not much soil, and immediately it sprang up, since it had no depth of soil; and when the sun rose it was scorched, and since it had no root it withered away. Other seed fell among thorns and the thorns grew up and choked it, and it yielded no grain. And other seeds fell into good soil and brought forth grain, growing up and increasing and yielding thirtyfold and sixtyfold and a hundredfold." And he said, "He who has ears to hear, let him hear."

Mark 4:2-9, pp. Matthew 13:3-9, Luke 8:4-8

THOMAS:
10 Y'shua said, "I have cast fire upon the world, and look, I'm guarding it until it blazes."

GOSPELS:
"I came to cast fire upon the earth; and would that it were already kindled!"

Luke 12:49

THOMAS:
14 Y'shua said to them, "If you fast, you will bring sin upon yourselves, and if you pray, you will be condemned, and if you give to charity, you will harm your spirits. When you go into any region and walk about in the countryside, when people take you in, eat what they serve you and heal the sick among them. After all, what goes into your mouth will not defile you; rather, it's what comes out of your mouth that will defile you."

GOSPELS:
Whenever you enter a town and they receive you, eat what is set before you; heal the sick in it and say to them, 'The kingdom of God has come near to you.'

Luke 10:8-9

And he called the people to him and said to them, "Hear and understand: not what goes into the mouth defiles a man, but what comes out of the mouth, this defiles a man."

Matthew 15:11, Mark 7:15

<u>THOMAS:</u>

16 Y'shua said, "Perhaps people think that I have come to cast peace upon the world. They do not know that I have come to cast conflicts upon the earth: fire, sword, war. For there will be five in a house: there'll be three against two and two against three, father against son and son against father, and they will stand alone.

<u>GOSPELS:</u>

Do you think that I have come to give peace on earth? No, I tell you, but rather division; for henceforth in one house there will be five divided, three against two and two against three; they will be divided, father against son and son against father, mother against daughter and daughter against her mother, mother-in-law against her daughter-in-law and daughter-in-law against her mother-in-law."

Luke 12:50-53, pp. Matthew 10:34-39

<u>THOMAS:</u>

17 Y'shua said, "I will give you what no eye has seen, what no ear has heard, what no hand has touched, what has not arisen in the human heart."

<u>GOSPELS:</u>

Then turning to the disciples he said privately, "Blessed are the eyes which see what you see! For I tell you that many prophets and kings desired to see what you see, and did not see it, and to hear what you hear, and did not hear it."

Luke 10:23-24, pp. Matthew 13:16-17

However, as it is written: No eye has seen, nor ear had heard, no mind has conceived, what God has prepared for those who love Him.

1 Corinthians 2:9

<u>THOMAS:</u>

20 The disciples said to Y'shua, "Tell us what Heaven's kingdom is like."

He said to them, It's like a mustard seed, the smallest of all seeds, but when it falls on prepared soil, it produces a large plant and becomes a shelter for birds of the sky.

GOSPELS:

And he said, "With what can we compare the kingdom of God, or what parable shall we use for it? It is like a grain of mustard seed, which, when sown upon the ground, is the smallest of all the seeds on earth; yet when it is sown it grows up and becomes the greatest of all shrubs, and puts forth large branches, so that the birds of the air can make nests in its shade."

Mark 4 30-32, pp. Matthew 13:31-32, Luke 13:18-19

THOMAS:

21 Mary said to Y'shua, "What are your disciples like?" He said, They are like little children living in a field that is not theirs. When the owners of the field come, they will say, "Give us back our field." They take off their clothes in front of them in order to give it back to them, and they return their field to them.

For this reason I say, if the owners of a house know that a thief is coming, they will be on guard before the thief arrives and will not let the thief break into their house (their domain) and steal their possessions. As for you, then, be on guard against the world. Prepare yourselves with great strength, so the robbers can't find a way to get to you, for the trouble you expect will come.

Let there be among you a person who understands.

When the crop ripened, he came quickly carrying a sickle and harvested it. Anyone here with two good ears had better listen!

GOSPELS:

Watch therefore, for you do not know on what day your LORD is coming. But know this, that if the householder had known in what part of the night the thief was coming, he would have watched and would not have let his house be broken into. Therefore you also must be ready; for the Son of man is coming at an hour you do not expect.

Matthew 24:43, Luke 12:39, Mark 4:29

THOMAS:

24 His disciples said, "Show us the place where you are, for we must seek it." He said to them, "Anyone here with two ears had better listen! There is light within a person of light, and it shines on the whole world. If it does not shine, it is dark."

GOSPELS:

Simon Peter asked him, 'LORD, where are you going?' Y'shua replied, 'Where I am going now you cannot follow now, but you will follow later."

John 13:36

"The eye is the lamp of the body. So, if your eye is sound, your whole body will be full of light; but if your eye is not sound, your whole body will be full of darkness. If then the light in you is darkness, how great is the darkness!

Matthew 6:22-23, Luke 11:34-36

THOMAS:

26 Y'shua said, "You see the sliver in your friend's eye, but you don't see the timber in your own eye. When you take the timber out of your own eye, then you will see well enough to remove the sliver from your friend's eye."

GOSPELS:

Why do you see the speck that is in your brother's eye, but do not notice the log that is in your own eye? Or how can you say to your brother, 'Let me take the speck out of your eye,' when there is the log in your own eye? You hypocrite, first take the log out of your own eye, and then you will see clearly to take the speck out of your brother's eye.

Matthew 7:3-5, Luke 6:41-42

THOMAS:

31 Y'shua said, "No prophet is welcome on his home turf; doctors don't cure those who know them."

GOSPELS:

Now Y'shua himself had pointed out that a prophet has no honor in his own country.

John 4:44, pp. Matthew 13:57-58, Mark 6:4-6, Luke 4:23-24

THOMAS:

32 Y'shua said, "A city built on a high hill and fortified cannot fall, nor can it be hidden."

GOSPELS:

"You are the light of the world. A city set on a hill cannot be hid."
Matthew 5:14.

THOMAS:

33 Y'shua said, "What you will hear in your ear, in the other ear proclaim from your rooftops.

After all, no one lights a lamp and puts it under a basket, nor does one put it in a hidden place. Rather, one puts it on a lampstand so that all who come and go will see its light."

GOSPELS:

What I tell you in the dark, utter in the light; and what you hear whispered, proclaim upon the housetops.
Matthew 10:27

Nor do men light a lamp and put it under a bushel, but on a stand, and it gives light to all in the house.
Matthew 5:15, Mark 4:21, Luke 8:16, 11:33

THOMAS:

34 Y'shua said, "If a blind person leads a blind person, both of them will fall into a hole."

GOSPELS:

Let them alone; they are blind guides. And if a blind man leads a blind man, both will fall into a pit."
Matthew 15:14, Luke 6:39

THOMAS:

35 Y'shua said, "One can't enter a strong person's house and take it by force without tying his hands. Then one can loot his house."

GOSPELS:

But no one can enter a strong man's house and plunder his goods, unless he first binds the strong man; then indeed he may plunder his house.

Mark 3:27, Matthew 12:29, Luke 11:21-22

THOMAS:

36 Y'shua said, "Do not fret, from morning to evening and from evening to morning, [about your food—what you're going to eat, or about your clothing—] what you are going to wear. [You're much better than the lilies, which neither card nor spin.

As for you, when you have no garment, what will you put on? Who might add to your stature? That very one will give you your garment.]"

GOSPELS:

"Therefore I tell you, do not be anxious about your life, what you shall eat or what you shall drink, nor about your body, what you shall put on. Is not life more than food, and the body more than clothing? Look at the birds of the air: they neither sow nor reap nor gather into barns, and yet your heavenly Father feeds them. Are you not of more value than they? And which of you by being anxious can add one cubit to his span of life? And why are you anxious about clothing? Consider the lilies of the field, how they grow; they neither toil nor spin; yet I tell you, even Solomon in all his glory was not arrayed like one of these. But if God so clothes the grass of the field, which today is alive and tomorrow is thrown into the oven, will he not much more clothe you, O men of little faith? Therefore do not be anxious, saying, 'What shall we eat?' or 'What shall we drink?' or 'What shall we wear?'

Matthew 6:25-31, Luke 12:22-30

THOMAS:

38 Y'shua said, "Often you have desired to hear these sayings that I am speaking to you, and you have no one else from whom to hear them. There will be days when you will seek me and you will not find me."

GOSPELS:

Y'shua said, "I am with you a short time only, and then I go to the one who sent me. You will look for me but you will not find me; and where I am, you cannot come.'

John 7:33-36

THOMAS:

39 Y'shua said, "The Pharisees and the scholars have taken the

keys of knowledge and have hidden them. They have not entered nor have they allowed those who want to enter to do so. As for you, be as sly as snakes and as simple as doves."

GOSPELS:

"But woe to you, scribes and Pharisees, hypocrites! because you shut the kingdom of heaven against men; for you neither enter yourselves, nor allow those who would enter to go in.

Matthew 23:13

"Behold, I send you out as sheep in the midst of wolves; so be wise as serpents and innocent as doves.

Matthew 10:16, Luke 11:52

THOMAS:

41 Y'shua said, "Whoever has something in hand will be given more, and whoever has nothing will be deprived of even the little they have."

GOSPELS:

I tell you that for everyone who has, more will be given; but as for the one who has nothing, even what he has will be taken away from him.

Luke 19:26

THOMAS:

44 Y'shua said, "Whoever blasphemes against the Father will be forgiven, and whoever blasphemes against the son will be forgiven, but whoever blasphemes against the holy spirit will not be forgiven, either on earth or in heaven."

GOSPELS:

Therefore I tell you, every sin and blasphemy will be forgiven men, but the blasphemy against the Spirit will not be forgiven. And whoever says a word against the Son of man will be forgiven; but whoever speaks against the Holy Spirit will not be forgiven, either in this age or in the age to come.

Matthew 12:31-32, Mark 3:28-30, Luke 6:43-45

THOMAS:

45 Y'shua said, "Grapes are not harvested from thorn trees, nor

are figs gathered from thistles, for they yield no fruit. Good persons produce good from what they've stored up; bad persons produce evil from the wickedness they've stored up in their hearts, and say evil things. For from the overflow of the heart they produce evil."

GOSPELS:

You will know them by their fruits. Are grapes gathered from thorns, or figs from thistles? So, every sound tree bears good fruit, but the bad tree bears evil fruit. A sound tree cannot bear evil fruit, nor can a bad tree bear good fruit. Every tree that does not bear good fruit is cut down and thrown into the fire. Thus you will know them by their fruits.

Matthew 7:16, 12:33-35, Luke 6:43-45

THOMAS:

46 Y'shua said, "From Adam to John the Baptist, among those born of women, no one is so much greater than John the Baptist that his eyes should not be averted. But I have said that whoever among you becomes a child will recognize the FATHER'S kingdom and will become greater than John."

GOSPELS:

Truly, I say to you, among those born of women there has risen no one greater than John the Baptist; yet he who is least in the kingdom of heaven is greater than he.

Matthew 11:11, Luke 7:28

THOMAS:

47 Y'shua said, "A person cannot mount two horses or bend two bows. And a slave cannot serve two masters, otherwise that slave will honor the one and offend the other. "Nobody drinks aged wine and immediately wants to drink young wine. Young wine is not poured into old wineskins, or they might break, and aged wine is not poured into a new wineskin, or it might spoil. An old patch is not sewn onto a new garment, since it would create a tear."

GOSPELS:

"No one can serve two masters; for either he will hate the one and love the other, or he will be devoted to the one and despise the other. You cannot serve God and mammon.

Matthew 6:24, Luke 16:13

And no one puts a piece of unshrunk cloth on an old garment, for the patch tears away from the garment, and a worse tear is made. Neither is new wine put into old wineskins; if it is, the skins burst, and the wine is spilled, and the skins are destroyed; but new wine is put into fresh wineskins, and so both are preserved."

Matthew 9:16-17, Mark 2:21-22, Luke 5:36-39

THOMAS:

48 Y'shua said, "If two make peace with each other in a single house, they will say to the mountain, 'Move from here!' and it will move."

GOSPELS:

And Y'shua answered them, "Truly, I say to you, if you have faith and never doubt, you will not only do what has been done to the fig tree, but even if you say to this mountain, 'Be taken up and cast into the sea,' it will be done. And whatever you ask in prayer, you will receive, if you have faith."

Mark 11:22-23

THOMAS:

55 Y'shua said, "Whoever does not hate his father and mother cannot be my disciple, and whoever does not hate brothers and sisters, and carry the cross as I do, will not be worthy of me."

GOSPELS:

"If any one comes to me and does not hate his own father and mother and wife and children and brothers and sisters, yes, and even his own life, he cannot be my disciple.

Luke 14:26, Matthew 10:37

THOMAS:

62 Y'shua said, "I disclose my mysteries to those [who are worthy] of [my] mysteries.

Do not let your left hand know what your right hand is doing."

GOSPELS:

And he answered them, "To you it has been given to know the secrets of the kingdom of heaven, but to them it has not been given.

Matthew 13:11, Mark 4:11, Luke 8:10

But when you give alms, do not let your left hand know what your right hand is doing.

Matthew 6:3

THOMAS:

63 Y'shua said, There was a rich person who had a great deal of money. He said, "I shall invest my money so that I may sow, reap, plant, and fill my storehouses with produce, that I may lack nothing." These were the things he was thinking in his heart, but that very night he died. Anyone here with two ears had better listen!

GOSPELS:

And he told them a parable, saying, "The land of a rich man brought forth plentifully; and he thought to himself, 'What shall I do, for I have nowhere to store my crops?' And he said, 'I will do this: I will pull down my barns, and build larger ones; and there I will store all my grain and my goods. And I will say to my soul, Soul, you have ample goods laid up for many years; take your ease, eat, drink, be merry.' But God said to him, 'Fool! This night your soul is required of you; and the things you have prepared, whose will they be?' So is he who lays up treasure for himself, and is not rich toward God."

Luke 12:16-21

THOMAS:

64 Y'shua said, A person was receiving guests. When he had prepared the dinner, he sent his slave to invite the guests. The slave went to the first and said to that one, "My master invites you." That one said, "Some merchants owe me money; they are coming to me tonight. I have to go and give them instructions. Please excuse me from dinner." The slave went to another and said to that one, "My master has invited you." That one said to the slave, "I have bought a house, and I have been called away for a day. I shall have no time." The slave went to another and said to that one, "My master invites you." That one said to the slave, "My friend is to be married, and I am to arrange the banquet. I shall not be able to come. Please excuse me from dinner." The slave went to another and said to that one, "My master invites you." That one said to the slave, "I have bought an estate, and I am going to collect the rent. I shall not be able to come. Please excuse me." The slave returned and said to his master, "Those whom you invited to dinner have asked to be excused." The master said to his slave, "Go out on the streets and bring back whomever you find to have dinner."

Buyers and merchants [will] not enter the places of my Father.

GOSPELS:

And again Y'shua spoke to them in parables, saying, "The kingdom of heaven may be compared to a king who gave a marriage feast for his son, and sent his servants to call those who were invited to the marriage feast; but they would not come. Again he sent other servants, saying, 'Tell those who are invited, Behold, I have made ready my dinner, my oxen and my fat calves are killed, and everything is ready; come to the marriage feast.' But they made light of it and went off, one to his farm, another to his business, while the rest seized his servants, treated them shamefully, and killed them. The king was angry, and he sent his troops and destroyed those murderers and burned their city. Then he said to his servants, 'The wedding is ready, but those invited were not worthy. Go therefore to the thoroughfares, and invite to the marriage feast as many as you find.' And those servants went out into the streets and gathered all whom they found, both bad and good; so the wedding hall was filled with guests.

Matthew 22:1-10, Luke 14:16-24

THOMAS:

65 He said, A [. . .] person owned a vineyard and rented it to some farmers, so they could work it and he could collect its crop from them. He sent his slave so the farmers would give him the vineyard's crop. They grabbed him, beat him, and almost killed him, and the slave returned and told his master. His master said, "Perhaps he didn't know them." He sent another slave, and the farmers beat that one as well. Then the master sent his son and said, "Perhaps they'll show my son some respect." Because the farmers knew that he was the heir to the vineyard, they grabbed him and killed him. Anyone here with two ears had better listen!

GOSPELS:

And he began to speak to them in parables. "A man planted a vineyard, and set a hedge around it, and dug a pit for the wine press, and built a tower, and let it out to tenants, and went into another country. When the time came, he sent a servant to the tenants, to get from them some of the fruit of the vineyard. And they took him and beat him, and sent him away empty-handed. Again he sent to them another servant, and they wounded him in the head, and treated him shamefully. And he sent another, and him they killed; and so with many others, some they beat and some they killed. He had still one other, a beloved son; finally he sent him to them, saying, 'They will respect my son.' But those tenants said to one another, 'This is the heir; come, let us kill him, and the inheritance will be ours.' And they took him and killed him, and cast him out of the vineyard. What will the owner of the vineyard do? He will come and destroy the tenants, and give the vineyard to others.

Mark 12:1-9, Matthew 21:33-41, Luke 20:9-16

THOMAS:

66 Y'shua said, "Show me the stone that the builders rejected: that is the keystone."

GOSPELS:

Have you not read this scripture: 'The very stone which the builders rejected has become the head of the corner; this was the LORD's doing, and it is marvelous in our eyes'?"

Mark 12:10-11, Matthew 21:42-43, Luke 20:17-18

THOMAS:

68 Y'shua said, "Congratulations to you when you are hated and persecuted; and no place will be found, wherever you have been persecuted."

GOSPELS:
"Blessed are you when men revile you and persecute you and utter all kinds of evil against you falsely on my account. Rejoice and be glad, for your reward is great in heaven, for so men persecuted the prophets who were before you.
Matthew 5:11-12, Luke 6:22-23

THOMAS:
69 Y'shua said, "Congratulations to those who have been persecuted in their hearts: they are the ones who have truly come to know the Father.
Congratulations to those who go hungry, so the stomach of the one in want may be filled."

GOSPELS:
"Blessed are the pure in heart, for they shall see God.
Matthew 5:8
"Blessed are those who hunger and thirst for righteousness, for they shall be satisfied.
Matthew 5:6, Luke 6:21

THOMAS:
72 A [person said] to him, "Tell my brothers to divide my father's possessions with me."
He said to the person, "Mister, who made me a divider?" He turned to his disciples and said to them, "I'm not a divider, am I?"

GOSPELS:
One of the multitude said to him, "Teacher, bid my brother divide the inheritance with me." But he said to him, "Man, who made me a judge or divider over you?"
Luke 12:13-14

THOMAS:
73 Y'shua said, "The crop is huge but the workers are few, so beg the harvest boss to dispatch workers to the fields."

GOSPELS:
Then he said to his disciples, "The harvest is plentiful, but the

laborers are few; pray therefore the LORD of the harvest to send out laborers into his harvest."

Matthew 9:37-38, Luke 10:2

THOMAS:

76 Y'shua said, The Father's kingdom is like a merchant who had a supply of merchandise and found a peal. That merchant was prudent; he sold the merchandise and bought the single pearl for himself. So also with you, seek his treasure that is unfailing, that is enduring, where no moth comes to eat and no worm destroys."

GOSPELS:

"Again, the kingdom of heaven is like a merchant in search of fine pearls, who, on finding one pearl of great value, went and sold all that he had and bought it.

Matthew 13:45-46

"Do not lay up for yourselves treasures on earth, where moth and rust consume and where thieves break in and steal, but lay up for yourselves treasures in heaven, where neither moth nor rust consumes and where thieves do not break in and steal. For where your treasure is, there will your heart be also.

Matthew 6:19-21, Luke 12:33

THOMAS:

77 Y'shua said, "I am the light that is over all things. I am all: from me all came forth, and to me all attained. Split a piece of wood; I am there. Lift up the stone, and you will find me there."

GOSPELS:

I am the light of the world. Whoever follows me will never walk in darkness, but will have the light of life."

John 8:12

THOMAS:

79 A woman in the crowd said to him, "Lucky are the womb that bore you and the breasts that fed you." He said to [her], "Lucky are those who have heard the word of the Father and have truly kept it. For there will be days when you will say, 'Lucky are the womb that has not conceived and the breasts that have not given milk.'"

GOSPELS:

As he said this, a woman in the crowd raised her voice and said to him, "Blessed is the womb that bore you, and the breasts that you sucked!" But he said, "Blessed rather are those who hear the word of God and keep it!"

Luke 11:27-28

For behold, the days are coming when they will say, 'Blessed are the barren, and the wombs that never bore, and the breasts that never gave suck!'

Luke 23:29

THOMAS:

86 Y'shua said, "[Foxes have] their dens and birds have their nests, but human beings[203] have no place to lay down and rest."

GOSPELS:

And Y'shua said to him, "Foxes have holes, and birds of the air have nests; but the Son of man has nowhere to lay his head."

Matthew 8:20, Luke 9:58

THOMAS:

89 Y'shua said, "Why do you wash the outside of the cup? Don't you understand that the one who made the inside is also the one who made the outside?"

GOSPELS:

And the LORD said to him, "Now you Pharisees cleanse the outside of the cup and of the dish, but inside you are full of extortion and wickedness. You fools! Did not he who made the outside make the inside also?

Matthew 23:25, Luke 11:39-40

THOMAS:

90 Y'shua said, "Come to me, for my yoke is comfortable and my LORDship is gentle, and you will find rest for yourselves."

GOSPELS:

Come to me, all who labor and are heavy laden, and I will give you rest. Take my yoke upon you, and learn from me; for I am gentle and lowly in heart, and you will find rest for your souls.[204] For my yoke is easy, and my burden is light."

Matthew 11:28-30

THOMAS:

91 They said to him, "Tell us who you are so that we may believe in you." He said to them, "You examine the face of heaven and earth, but you have not come to know the one who is in your presence, and you do not know how to examine the present moment.

GOSPELS:

He also said to the multitudes, "When you see a cloud rising in the west, you say at once, 'A shower is coming'; and so it happens. And when you see the south wind blowing, you say, 'There will be scorching heat'; and it happens. You hypocrites! You know how to interpret the appearance of earth and sky; but why do you not know how to interpret the present time?

Luke 12:54-56

THOMAS:

92 Y'shua said, "Seek and you will find. In the past, however, I did not tell you the things about which you asked me then. Now I am willing to tell them, but you are not seeking them."

GOSPELS:

"Ask, and it will be given you; seek, and you will find; knock, and it will be opened to you. For every one who asks receives, and he who seeks finds, and to him who knocks it will be opened.

Matthew 7:7-8, Luke 11:9-10

THOMAS:

93 "Don't give what is holy to dogs, for they might throw them upon the manure pile. Don't throw pearls [to] pigs, or they might . . . it [. . .]."

GOSPELS:

"Do not give dogs what is holy; and do not throw your pearls before swine, lest they trample them under foot and turn to attack you.

Matthew 7:6

THOMAS:

94 Y'shua [said], "One who seeks will find, and for [one who knocks] it will be opened."

GOSPELS:

Ask, and it will be given you; seek, and you will find; knock, and it will be opened to you. For every one who asks receives, and he who seeks finds, and to him who knocks it will be opened.

Matthew 7:7-8, Luke 11:9-10

THOMAS:

95 [Y'shua said], "If you have money, don't lend it at interest. Rather, give [it] to someone from whom you won't get it back."

GOSPELS:

Give to every one who begs from you; and of him who takes away your goods do not ask them again.

Matthew 5:42, Luke 6:30, 34-35

THOMAS:

99 The disciples said to him, "Your brothers and your mother are standing outside." He said to them, "Those here who do what my Father wants are my brothers and my mother. They are the ones who will enter my Father's kingdom."

GOSPELS:

And his mother and his brothers came; and standing outside they sent to him and called him. And a crowd was sitting about him; and they said to him, "Your mother and your brothers are outside, asking for you." And he replied, "Who are my mother and my brothers?" And looking around on those who sat about him, he said, "Here are my mother and my brothers! Whoever does the will of God is my brother, and sister, and mother."

Mark 3:31-35, Matthew 12:46-50, Luke 8:19-21

THOMAS:

100 They showed Y'shua a gold coin and said to him, "The Roman emperor's people demand taxes from us." He said to them, "Give the emperor what belongs to the emperor, give God what belongs to God, and give me what is mine."

GOSPELS:

And they sent to him some of the Pharisees and some of the Hero'di-ans, to entrap him in his talk. And they came and said to him, "Teacher, we know that you are true, and care for no man; for you do not regard the position of men, but truly teach the way of God. Is it lawful to pay taxes to Caesar, or not? Should we pay them, or should we not?" But knowing their hypocrisy, he said to them, "Why put me to the test? Bring me a coin, and let me look at it." And they brought one. And he said to them, "Whose likeness and inscription is this?" They said to him, "Caesar's." Y'shua said to them, "Render to Caesar the things that are Caesar's, and to God the things that are God's." And they were amazed at him.

Mark 12:13-17, Matthew 22:15-22, Luke 8:19-21

THOMAS:

107 Y'shua said, The FATHER'S kingdom is like a shepherd who had a hundred sheep. One of them, the largest, went astray. He left the ninety-nine and looked for the one until he found it. After he had toiled, he said to the sheep, 'I love you more than the ninety-nine.'

GOSPELS:

What do you think? If a man has a hundred sheep, and one of them has gone astray, does he not leave the ninety-nine on the mountains and go in search of the one that went astray? And if he finds it, truly, I say to you, he rejoices over it more than over the ninety-nine that never went astray.

Matthew 18:12-14, Luke 15:4-7

THOMAS:

109 Y'shua said, The (Father's) kingdom is like a person who had a treasure hidden in his field but did not know it. And [when] he died he left it to his [son]. The son [did] not know about it either. He took over the field and sold it. The buyer went plowing, [discovered] the treasure, and began to lend money at interest to whomever he wished.

GOSPELS:

The kingdom of heaven is like treasure hidden in a field, which a man found and covered up; then in his joy he goes and sells all that he has and buys that field.

Matthew 13:44

Q Tips

The final strand of this earliest tradition comes from a source dubbed "Q", named after the German word "quelle", which means source. As stated several times, Q is a written Greek document that circulated during the 50's, the exact same time Paul was writing his letters and going on missionary journeys. Therefore, the fact that these same letters record some of this material that made it into the Gospel of Mark about 20 years later, can hardly be a coincidence. Neither is it insignificant that many of Paul's letters, just like Q, were also going to Greek speaking Gentiles.

As the theory goes, when Matthew and Luke were written, each writer took two sources to do it. The first, the Gospel of Mark itself, was incorporated nearly intact. However, since both writers also had a better grasp of Greek than Mark did, they revised it into a more polished narrative shell. The second source, Q, was spliced between lines of the improved Markan text. Also, since in many cases these dual versions in Matthew and Luke had a verbal agreement approaching 99%, it was rightly concluded that Q had to be a written Greek source common to both, since two separate translations could not produce such a result.[205]

As it relates to the final stages of Greek editing, this theory is very much on point. However, since we are dealing also with older Aramaic material, the scope of traditional Q theory has proved to be way too narrow, as our next section will explain in detail.

Mis-Qs

In spite of Q-theory's almost universal acceptance, several critical factors are missing from it. In addition to the problem referred to above, we never see the issue of who Q is being addressed, and this is more than a minor oversight. Put simply, Q ignores history.

Nowadays, almost all scholars agree that apostolic traditions sprang up very early in the development of the faith, easily within 10-20 years of the crucifixion. That being the case, it should also be noted that most of the original disciples, those "eyewitnesses of the Word" as Luke says, were still alive and actively sorting out truth from heresy. Here are a few examples from those same early sources:

> "I am astonished that you are so quickly deserting the one who called you by the grace of Messiah and are turning to a different gospel, which is really no Gospel at all. Evidently, some people are throwing you into confusion and are trying to pervert the Gospel of Messiah."
>
> Galatians 1:6-7

> "My brothers, some from Chloe's household have informed me that there are quarrels among you. What I mean is this: One of you says, 'I follow Paul'; another 'I follow Appollos', another, 'I follow Cephas"; still another, 'I follow Messiah.' Is Messiah divided? Was Paul crucified for you? Were you baptized into the name of Paul? . . . For Messiah did not send me to baptize but to preach the gospel—not with words of human wisdom, lest the cross of Messiah be emptied of its power."
>
> 1 Corinthians 1:11-13,17

Signs of the Cross: The Search for the Historical Jesus

> "Bear in mind the Lord's patience means salvation, just as our brother Paul wrote you with the wisdom that God gave him. His letters contain some things that are hard to understand, which ignorant and unstable people distort, as they do the other Scriptures[206], to their own destruction."

2 Peter 3:15-16

With all of these witnesses still alive, it is as close to certainty as history allows for us to say that any material which makes it into the official record has to go through some sort of apostolic accreditation. The earliest centuries of the faith, in fact, show a clear pattern of rooting out not just heresies that developed in the fourth century when the canon became official, but literally from day one, as it spread out of Israel itself.

Therefore, Q does an adequate job of explaining how the writings spread, but leaves the more basic and important issues of who and why to the imagination of the reader. And yet, without the understanding of the who aspect of Q, none of basic mechanics that it so ably describes can possibly move forward at all.

Q also ignores other evidence, both from the Bible and early patristic writings, which can provide this missing piece and give a legitimate historical framework that such an important theory needs. After all, we all know linguistics, like any other human endeavor, does not take place in vacuum. Rather, it is one cultural strand of many, emerging from the welter and din of a greater tapestry. To extricate the linguistic effect alone, while simultaneously ignoring its root causes, is the height of scholarly arrogance and narrow minded thinking.

The fact is, both the Bible and the Church Fathers have a lot to say on this issue, but scholars in the past have focused on a small amount of discrepancies between them which caused their wholesale rejection. However, as we will see, these differences are very slight, and no more serious than any other series of legitimate historians who sometimes find themselves interpreting the same sources a bit differently. Having said that, I will personally make note of all such diversions when they are encountered to let the reader decide how serious they may or may not be.

Introduction to the Apostle Q Scenario

"According to Eusebius (Hist. eccl., 111, xxxix, 16), Papias said that Matthew collected (sunetaxato; or, according to two manuscripts, sunegraphato, composed) ta logia (the oracles or maxims of Y'shua) in the Hebrew (Aramaic) language, and that each one translated them as best he could . . .

Papias says that Matthew wrote the Logia in the Hebrew (Hebraidi) language; St. Irenæus and Eusebius maintain that he wrote his gospel for the Hebrews in their national language, and the same assertion is found in several writers. Matthew would, therefore, seem to have written in modernized Hebrew, the language then used by the scribes for teaching. But, in the time of Messiah, the national language of the Jews was Aramaic, and when, in the New Testament, there is mention of the Hebrew language (Hebrais dialektos), it is Aramaic that is implied . . .

. . . Moreover, Eusebius (Hist. eccl., III, xxiv, 6) tells us that the Gospel of Matthew was a reproduction of his preaching, and this we know, was in Aramaic. An investigation of the Semitic idioms observed in the Gospel does not permit us to conclude as to whether the original was in Hebrew or

> Aramaic, as the two languages are so closely related. Besides, it must be home in mind that the greater part of these Semitisms simply reproduce colloquial Greek and are not of Hebrew or Aramaic origin. However, we believe the second hypothesis to be the more probable, viz., that Matthew wrote his Gospel in Aramaic."
>
> Catholic Encyclopedia (1913)

In order to understand how apostolic history underscores all editing and compilation of the Gospel record, the above information is where we have to start. Our first mystery then is to answer this question:

Is it possible to harmonize two very strong yet seemingly opposite lines of evidence in that linguistics heavily favors Mark as the first Gospel, but the historical record points to Matthew?

As I will hope to show, the answer is yes, and the key to unraveling this seeming contradiction is to make a very odd statement: Matthew is Mark! By that I mean that the original Aramaic Gospel that Matthew wrote was preserved, in Greek translation, by Mark and under the guidance of the apostle Peter who, as we will see, is also history's leading candidate as the author of Q. So now it's time to begin at the beginning.

Early History, 30 to 44

> "The Pauline Epistles were written by Paul to small Christian congregations in Asia Minor, Greece and Rome. These early Christians were mostly Jews of the Dispersion, men and women of Hebrew origin.
>
> "Paul on his journeys always spoke in Jewish synagogues. His first converts were Hebrews. Then came

Arameans as in the case of Timothy and Titus. Their fathers were Aramean and their mothers were Jewish . . .

"Paul was educated in Jewish law in Jerusalem. He was a member of the Jewish Council. His native language was western Aramaic but he acquired his education through Hebrew and Chaldean (or Palestinian) Aramaic, the language which was spoken in Judea. He defended himself when on trial in the Hebrew tongue, Acts 22:2. Paul was converted, healed and baptized in Damascus, Acts 9:17, 18.

"Very early the Epistles were translated into Greek for the use of converts who spoke Greek. Later they were translated into all tongues."

The Modern New Testament from the Aramaic, p. xi, xii

The Messiah is crucified in the year 30. Following this, Peter becomes an early leader of the Jerusalem Church, beginning his missionary activities within that city, (Acts 2:1-4:37). As the movement grows, a powerful preacher named Stephen also emerges. He makes one of the most passionate pleas for Messiah ever recorded, and is stoned to death in the year 33[207].

Present at this execution is a young Pharisee from Tarsus named Shaul, (Acts 8:1). After receiving extensive Jewish training from Rabbi Gamaliel, as well as gaining competency in Greek and Latin from his father, a Roman citizen, Shaul is sent by the Jerusalem Pharisees to nip the Christian movement in the bud. For several years, he was brutally successful. Then, shortly after Stephens' execution, Shaul is himself converted to the Christian cause on the road to Damascus,

(Acts 8:2-9:32). Following this, Shaul takes on his Gentile name, Paul, and sets about beginning his work in earnest.

However, as rumors of Paul's conversion spread, he is met with skepticism from the friends and relatives of those he used to persecute. After being forced to flee first to Arabia and then to Damascus, Paul decides to go to Jerusalem to try and set matters right. There, in the year 36, he is met by Peter and another early leader named Barnabbas. After spending fifteen days receiving oral instructions from Peter, Paul is eventually given the approval to preach the faith, (Galatians 1:16-17, Acts 13:1-3). Furthermore, once Peter imparted his teachings, it was both logical and inevitable that Paul would spread them in his native tongue, Aramaic, where appropriate. In fact, many of Paul's first stops were to Aramaic speaking communities, (Acts 9:19-31, 13:1-3, Galatians 1:17-2:21).

When missionary duties brought Paul to Jerusalem again, his former Jewish colleagues were waiting for their "traitor", and it becomes clear that Paul is in mortal danger, (Acts 9:28-29). Forced again to flee to Syria, Paul then finds himself back in Tarsus, where he remains inactive for 9 years.

During this same period, Peter preaches throughout Israel, Samaria and Syria, to a predominantly Aramaic speaking audience, although it is clear a good number of people in Antioch, a Roman provincial capital, would also have understood Greek. Peter's ministry to a primarily Gentile audience in Corinth may also be alluded to in Paul's letters, (1 Corinthians 1:12).

Then, in the year 44, persecution of the Christians becomes rampant. One of the apostles named James[208] is murdered, and Peter is put in jail by King Agrippa, only to be freed a few days later, (Acts 12:3-12). Then Peter makes his way to a "safe house" run by a woman named Salome. Her son, a talented young man named Yochanan Marcos, would later become known as Peter's traveling companion and write the second canonized Gospel. At any rate, it becomes clear to Peter that the "heat" from his unexpected release, is very much still on, and so he leaves them rather than risk their exposure.

During this same period, the earliest oral traditions about Y'shua emerged, primarily from eyewitness accounts which were later compiled by historians like Luke, (Luke 1:1-3). Some of these could have also come from primitive notebooks kept by apostles, and still others could have been written down by those who heard these same apostles speak. However, regardless as to the actual origin, the core stories about Y'shua—the miracles, crucifixion and resurrection—were attested to very early on by these same living witnesses.

James at 49

> The author is commonly identified with the Lord's brother, the Bishop of Jerusalem . . . Internal evidence (contents of the Epistle, its style, address, date, and place of composition) points unmistakably to James, the Lord's brother, the Bishop of Jerusalem, as the author; he exactly, and he alone, fulfils the conditions required in the writer of the Epistle . . .
>
> The Epistle was probably written about A.D. 47. The reference to the persecutions (ii, 6) is in the present tense, and indicates a stage of suffering which has not yet receded into the past of history. Now, in A.D. 44 the Churches of Judea were exposed to the persecution inflicted by Herod Agrippa, in which James, the son of Zebedee, was murdered (Acts, xii, 1 sqq.). Moreover, the author could not have written after the Council of Jerusalem (A.D. 51[209]), where James acted as president, without some allusion to his decision unanimously accepted (Acts, xv, 4 sqq.). Another indication also derived from indirect internal evidence, is an allusion to the hungry and naked poor (of Jerusalem, ii, 15

> sqq.); they suffered probably from the famine foretold by Agabus (Acts, xi, 28-30), and usually identified with one mentioned by Josephus (Antiq., XX, ii, 5), A.D. 45 . . .
>
> The Epistle was probably written by St. James in Jerusalem; this we may conclude from the study of the life of the author . . . and this opinion finds favour with nearly all its critics.
>
> Catholic Encyclopedia (1913)

Further confirmation of a version of Matthew from this time period is found in the Epistle of James.

However, before explaining that, two critical pieces of evidence need to be offered. First, the absolute latest that this book could have been written is in the year 49. We know this because there is no mention of the famous Jerusalem Council that happened at that time, and James was definitely headquartered in that city, (Acts 12:17).

Additionally, James actually led that conference, and issued the final ruling in behalf of the Jerusalem Church, (Acts 15:13-29).

However, at this point some critics point out that James could have excluded mention of the conference because either the issue had been settled for a number of years or because a letter explaining the Council's findings had already been sent out, so why mention it here?

The answer to both issues however lies in the supporting scriptures, the salient point being that the letter that the Jerusalem Church sent out was to GENTILE BELIEVERS ONLY, (Acts 15:23). Just as important, however, is the fact is that controversies continued between the Jewish and Gentile wings of the church for many years after the conference was over, (Galatians 2:11-21, 3:3, 4:10, 6:12, Hebrews 5:11-12). Where then, is the letter to the Hebrew congregations in and out of Israel for the explanations that relate to their side? After all, now they have to stop pressuring Gentiles to get circumcised, which was certainly a major departure for them. And now, here we have James, author of that same decision, writing a letter to the same side that "lost" the debate, and "forgetting" to mention it at all?

Other internal textual evidence strongly suggests, if not proves, a date this early due to the fact that the term "synagogue" is still being used and not "church" as would have been indicative of later works to describe the community of believers.

Also the importance of the opening line of address, "to the twelve tribes scattered among the nations" cannot be overstated. While many Greek scholars, including Charles Ryrie, believe this letter also was originally authored in Greek, the fact is, there was no reason for this to be the case. James is a native Aramaic speaker writing to other native Aramaic speakers, most of whom have a preference, if not a direct feeling of exclusivity, for studying sacred Scripture only in that language. Not only that, the order of allusions to Old Testament books in James proves his congregation—and their satellites—followed the Palestinian model of liturgy exclusively. [210]

Therefore, if the Greek school can make a claim of primacy in other books (like Ephesians, for example) that the audience dictates the language used, to deny James its Aramaic heritage smacks of the highest form of hypocrisy and scholarly prejudice. Rather, what seems much more likely, is that the excellent Greek used proves the Epistle's early origins, because there was little or no time for the Aramaic to be mistranslated when the actual authorities are practically standing over the shoulders of the writer.

Now we come to the heart of the matter: establishing the fact that James had an early copy of Matthew's Aramaic Gospel. The proof of this assertion comes in four portions. First, there are seventeen clear allusions to the Sermon on the Mount alone, and in one case, he quotes from the same line twice:

> James 1:1 = Matthew 5:12
> James 1:4 = Matthew 5:48
> James 1:5 = Matthew 7:7

James 1:21 = Matthew 5:22
James 1:22 = Matthew 7:24-27
James 1:25 = Matthew 5:17-20
James 2:5 = Matthew 5:3
James 2:8 = Matthew 7:12
James 2:10 = Matthew 5:19
James 2:13 = Matthew 5:7
James 2:18 = Matthew 7:16
James 3:6 = Matthew 5:22
James 3:12 = Matthew 7:16
James 4:4 = Matthew 6:24
James 4:11 = Matthew 7:1
James 5:2 = Matthew 6:19
James 5:10 = Matthew 5:12

Second, James has just as many references to the rest of Matthew:

James 1:6 = Matthew 14:28-31, 21:21
James 1:11 = Matthew 20:12
James 1:27 = Matthew 25:36
James 2:5 = Matthew 25:34
James 2:13 = Matthew 18:32-35
James 2:15 = Matthew 25:35
James 2:18 = Matthew 8:29
James 3:1 = Matthew 23:8
James 3:2 = Matthew 12:34-37
James 3:6 = Matthew 12:36, 15:11,18
James 3:17 = Matthew 4:8
James 4:4 = Matthew 12:39
James 4:6 = Matthew 23:12
James 4:12 = Matthew 10:28
James 5:9 = Matthew 24:33
James 5:13 = Matthew 3:6
James 5:19 = Matthew 18:15

At this point, I can imagine the liberal response: *Well, some of those are Old Testament quotes that both would allude to. Therefore, how can you be sure that James is taking these only from Matthew?*

The answer is contained in the last two steps of this argument. Most scholars would agree that the Sermon on the Mount (Matthew 5:1-7:28) has some of the best examples of Y'shua's original teachings contained in the Gospels. Therefore, our third task is quote these allusions in James and stack them up—word for word—with their equivalents in Matthew. For ease of understanding, I have also arranged the quotes in the order they appear in Matthew, just as I did with the Gospel of Thomas. Here we go:

JAMES:

Listen, my dear brothers: Has not God chosen those who are poor in the eyes of the world to be rich in faith and to inherit the kingdom he promised those who love him?

. . . because judgment without mercy will be shown to anyone who has not been merciful. Mercy triumphs over judgment!

MATTHEW:

"Blessed are the poor in spirit, for theirs is the kingdom of heaven.

Blessed are the merciful, for they will be shown mercy.

JAMES:

Brothers, as an example of patience in the face of suffering, take the prophets who spoke in the name of the LORD.

But the man who looks intently into the perfect law that gives freedom, and continues to do this, not forgetting what he has heard, but doing it—he will be blessed in what he does.

MATTHEW:

Rejoice and be glad, because great is your reward in heaven, for in the same way they persecuted the prophets who were before you.

JAMES:

For whoever keeps the whole law and yet stumbles at just one point is guilty of breaking all of it.

MATTHEW:

"Do not think that I have come to abolish the Law or the Prophets;

Signs of the Cross: The Search for the Historical Jesus

I have not come to abolish them but to fulfill them. I tell you the truth, until heaven and earth disappear, not the smallest letter, not the least stroke of a pen, will by any means disappear from the Law until everything is accomplished. Anyone who breaks one of the least of these commandments and teaches others to do the same will be called least in the kingdom of heaven, but whoever practices and teaches these commands will be called great in the kingdom of heaven. For I tell you that unless your righteousness surpasses that of the Pharisees and the teachers of the law, you will certainly not enter the kingdom of heaven.

JAMES:

The tongue also is a fire, a world of evil among the parts of the body. It corrupts the whole person, sets the whole course of his life on fire, and is itself set on fire by hell.

MATTHEW:

But I tell you that anyone who is angry with his brother will be subject to judgment. Again, anyone who says to his brother, 'Raca,' is answerable to the Sanhedrin. But anyone who says, 'You fool!' will be in danger of the fire of hell.

JAMES:

Perseverance must finish its work so that you may be mature and complete, not lacking anything.

MATTHEW:

Be perfect, therefore, as your heavenly Father is perfect.

JAMES:

Now listen, you rich people, weep and wail because of the misery that is coming upon you. Your wealth has rotted, and moths have eaten your clothes. Your gold and silver are corroded. Their corrosion will testify against you and eat your flesh like fire. You have hoarded wealth in the last days. Look! The wages you failed to pay the workmen who mowed your fields are crying out against you. The cries of the harvesters have reached the ears of the LORD Almighty. You have lived on earth in luxury and self-indulgence. You have fattened yourselves in the day of slaughter.

MATTHEW:

"Do not store up for yourselves treasures on earth, where moth and rust destroy, and where thieves break in and steal.

But store up for yourselves treasures in heaven, where moth and rust do not destroy, and where thieves do not break in and steal.

For where your treasure is, there your heart will be also.

JAMES:

You adulterous people, don't you know that friendship with the world is hatred toward God? Anyone who chooses to be a friend of the world becomes an enemy of God.

Or do you think Scripture says without reason that the spirit he caused to live in us envies intensely?

MATTHEW:

"No one can serve two masters. Either he will hate the one and love the other, or he will be devoted to the one and despise the other. You cannot serve both God and Money.

JAMES:

Don't grumble against each other, brothers, or you will be judged. The Judge is standing at the door!

Brothers, do not slander one another. Anyone who speaks against his brother or judges him speaks against the law and judges it. When you judge the law, you are not keeping it, but sitting in judgment on it.

MATTHEW:

"Do not judge, or you too will be judged. For in the same way you judge others, you will be judged, and with the measure you use, it will be measured to you.

JAMES:

If any of you lacks wisdom, he should ask God, who gives generously to all without finding fault, and it will be given to him.

MATTHEW:

Ask and it will be given to you; seek and you will find; knock and the door will be opened to you.

JAMES:
   If you really keep the royal law found in Scripture, "Love your neighbor as yourself," you are doing right.

MATTHEW:
   So in everything, do to others what you would have them do to you, for this sums up the Law and the Prophets.

JAMES:
   But someone will say, "You have faith; I have deeds." Show me your faith without deeds, and I will show you my faith by what I do.

   My brothers, can a fig tree bear olives, or a grapevine bear figs? Neither can a salt spring produce fresh water. Do not merely listen to the word, and so deceive yourselves. Do what it says. Anyone who listens to the word but does not do what it says is like a man who looks at his face in a mirror and, after looking at himself, goes away and immediately forgets what he looks like. But the man who looks intently into the perfect law that gives freedom, and continues to do this, not forgetting what he heard but doing it, will be blessed in everything he does.

   By their fruit you will recognize them. Do people pick grapes from thornbushes, or figs from thistles? Likewise every good tree bears good fruit, but a bad tree bears bad fruit. A good tree cannot bear bad fruit, and a bad tree cannot bear good fruit. Every tree that does not bear good fruit is cut down and thrown into the fire. Thus by their fruit you will recognize them.

MATTHEW:
   "Therefore everyone who hears these words of mine and puts them into practice is like a wise man who built his house on the rock. The rain came down, the streams rose, and the winds blew and beat against that house; yet it did not fall, because it had its foundation on the rock. But everyone who hears these words of mine and does not put them into practice is like a foolish man who built his house on sand. The rain came down, the streams rose, and the winds blew and beat against that house, and it fell with a great crash."

Fourth, and most importantly, the one time James lists a familiar Gospel quote verbatim, it is exclusive to Matthew, (comp James 5:12 to Matthew 5:37)!

Finally, it is also a very significant and obvious fact that the quotes and references from Matthew that James uses reveal one more great truth to us. Not only do all thirty-five of these parallels prove that some form of the Gospel existed in Jerusalem, they also show an extensive distribution network outside of Israel, to wherever large portions of Jewish Christians congregated throughout the Middle East. They are, after all, the audience that the letter was addressed to in the first place!

The Visiting Scholar Exchange Program

However, as compelling as all this evidence is, the facts may bear out an even earlier composition scenario for the first Gospel. On the other hand, if not, and other factors sent Matthew to Ethiopia, then the overall structure of evidence still points to the former time frame (40-49), for two reasons.

First, Matthew is unanimously attested to as having spent about twenty years there prior to his death sometime in the early to mid 60's. Second, we now know that James had a copy of Matthew's Aramaic Gospel in his possession—probably given to him by Peter—by the end of this same decade.

Be that as it may, whenever the apostle Matthew first set foot in the heart of Africa, it is still well attested to in the patristic writings, and now other factors come into play. Since we know the Church frequently had a say in approving who could go to a certain place on a missionary journey, (Acts 15:1-35, Galatians 2:7-10), it seems likely that Matthew at least advised Peter and other authorities on what he was about to do. At that point, Peter must have reminded Matthew of the extreme danger of this assignment, and a very sensible precaution would have involved Peter making a copy of this same Gospel, lest it or Matthew himself be forever lost. As it turns out, both fears were justified, for that is exactly what happened. Additionally, here is a strong possibility from the official record to explain why Matthew may have left:

> "Now an angel of the LORD said to Philip, "Go south to the road—the desert road—that goes down from Jerusalem to Gaza." So he started out, and on his way he met an Ethiopian eunuch, an important official in charge of all the treasury of Candace, queen of the Ethiopians. This man had gone to Jerusalem to worship, and on his way home was sitting in his chariot reading the book of Isaiah the prophet. The Spirit told Philip, "Go to that chariot and stay near it." Then Philip ran up to the chariot and heard the man reading Isaiah the prophet. "Do you understand what you are reading?" Philip asked. "How can I," he said, "unless someone explains it to me?"
>
> So he invited Philip to come up and sit with him. The eunuch was reading this passage of Scripture: "He was led like a sheep to the slaughter, and as a lamb before the shearer is silent, so he did not open his mouth. In his humiliation he was deprived of justice. Who can speak of his descendants? For his life was taken from the earth." The eunuch asked Philip, "Tell me, please, who is the prophet talking about, himself or someone else?" Then Philip began with that very passage of Scripture and told him the good news about Y'shua. As they traveled along the road, they came to some water and the eunuch said, "Look, here is water. Why shouldn't I be baptized?" And he gave orders to stop the chariot. Then both Philip and the eunuch

> went down into the water and Philip baptized him. When they came up out of the water, the Spirit of the LORD suddenly took Philip away, and the eunuch did not see him again, but went on his way rejoicing. Philip, however, appeared at Azotus and traveled about, preaching the gospel in all the towns until he reached Caesarea.
>
> Acts 8:26-40

Now it seems we have a bit of a problem. This "important official in charge of all the treasury of Candace, the Queen of the Ethiopians", wants to leave his mistress and proclaim the Gospel! How can he do this however without offending her and perhaps creating an international incident?

The answer, it turns out, is simple: Get someone to go back with the Queen in his place. Furthermore, because the Ethiopian is going to be preaching in Jerusalem, why not send an important person from Jerusalem to preach in Ethiopia? It also would not hurt also if the person replacing the treasurer also had a professional background in finance and accounting. Who better to take this job then than a committed apostle who previously had spent many years as a tax collector, like Matthew? Finally, it should be noted that the fact that Matthew was in Ethiopia for this length of time has never been disputed[211], only the place and manner of his death. If the tradition regarding the ministry there at least is unanimous, what better explanation for this missionary journey could there be?

Finally, the most significant aspect of this scenario is the date that it is known to have happened—the year 36[212]—before even Paul was converted to the cause!

Signs of the Cross: The Search for the Historical Jesus

Later Apostolic Development, 45-60

> "... certain linguistic proofs ... seem to show that the Hebrew text (DuTillet) underlies the Greek, and that certain renderings in the Greek may be due to a misread Hebrew original."
>
> Hugh Schonfield, An Old Hebrew Text of Matthew's Gospel (1927)

> "(George) Howard concluded that DuTillet is a revision of an earlier Hebrew Matthew related to the Shem Tob version. Howard elsewhere states his belief that the Shem Tob text is a descendant of a Hebrew text which served as a model for our present Greek text."
>
> The Journal of Biblical Literature (105/1, p. 63, n. 34), 1986

Getting back into the history then, the next step in this process had to do with Peter himself. As stated earlier, Peter was briefly imprisoned around the year 44. After a miraculous escape, the apostle sought temporary refuge in a kind of "safe house" run by an affluent woman known as Salome. Salome, in turn, was assisted by her son, a young man named John-Mark (a.k.a Yochanon Marcos). When it became clear that the authorities were looking to re-incarcerate him, Peter fled back to Jerusalem, and John-Mark followed closely behind him, (Acts 12:1-25).

About a year later, this same John Mark would accompany Paul on the first missionary journey, but would abandon him and return to Jerusalem, (Acts 13:13).

The question is, what happened between these two events? As it stands now, there is every indication that Mark became a student of

Peter's, and other early tradition attests to Mark's role as an interpreter with the apostle:

> "When we turn to tradition, Papias (Eusebius, "Hist. eccl.", III, xxxix) asserts not later than A.D. 130, on the authority of an "elder"[213], that Mark had been the interpreter (hermeneutes) of Peter, and wrote down accurately, though not in order, the teaching of Peter."
>
> Catholic Encyclopedia (1913)

Furthermore, other evidence confirms that Mark received material for his Gospel from Peter, and that, in fact, his Gospel came directly from this apostle:

> "All early tradition connects the Second Gospel with two names, those of St. Mark and St. Peter, Mark being held to have written what Peter had preached. We have just seen that this was the view of Papias and the elder to whom he refers. Papias wrote not later than about A.D. 130, so that the testimony of the elder probably brings us back to the first century, and shows the Second Gospel known in Asia Minor and attributed to St. Mark at that early time. So Irenæus says: "Mark, the disciple and interpreter of Peter, himself also handed down to us in writing what was preached by Peter" ("Adv. Hær.", III, i; ibid., x, 6).
>
> St. Clement of Alexandria, relying on the authority of "the elder presbyters", tells us that, when Peter had publicly preached in Rome, many of those who heard him exhorted Mark, as one who had

long followed Peter and remembered what he had said, to write it down, and that Mark "composed the Gospel and gave it to those who had asked for it" (Euseb., "Hist. Eccl.", VI, xiv).

Origen says (ibid., VI, xxv) that Mark wrote as Peter directed him (os Petros huphegesato auto), and Eusebius himself reports the tradition that Peter approved or authorized Mark's work ("Hist. Eccl.", II, xv). To these early Eastern witnesses may be added, from the West, the author of the Muratorian Fragment, which in its first line almost certainly refers to Mark's presence at Peter's discourses and his composition of the Gospel accordingly (Quibus tamen interfuit et ita posuit); Tertullian, who states: "The Gospel which Mark published (edidit is affirmed to be Peter's, whose interpreter Mark was" ("Contra Marc.", IV, v); St. Jerome, who in one place says that Mark wrote a short Gospel at the request of the brethren at Rome, and that Peter authorized it to be read in the Churches ("De Vir. Ill.", viii), and in another that Mark's Gospel was composed, Peter narrating and Mark writing (Petro narrante et illo scribente— "Ad Hedib.", ep. cxx).

In every one of these ancient authorities Mark is regarded as the writer of the Gospel, which is looked upon at the same time as having Apostolic authority, because substantially at least it had come from St. Peter. In the light of this traditional connection of he Gospel with St. Peter, there can be no doubt that it is to it St. Justin Martyr, writing in the middle of the second century, refers ("Dial.", 106), when he says that Messiah gave the title of "Boanerges" to the sons of Zebedee (a fact mentioned in the New Testament only in Mark, iii, 17), and that this is written in the "memoirs" of Peter (en tois apopnemaneumasin autou—after he had just named Peter). Though St. Justin does not name Mark as the writer of the memoirs, the fact that his disciple Tatian used our present Mark, including even the last twelve verses, in the composition of the "Diatessaron", makes it practically certain that St. Justin knew our present Second Gospel, and like the other Fathers connected it with St. Peter.

If, then, a consistent and widespread early tradition is to count for anything, St. Mark wrote a work based upon St. Peter's preaching. It is absurd to seek to destroy the force of this tradition by suggesting that all the subsequent authorities relied upon Papias, who may have been deceived. Apart from the utter improbability that Papias, who had spoken with many disciples of the Apostles, could have been deceived on such a question, the fact that Irenæus seems to place the composition of Mark's work after Peter's death, while Origen and other represent the Apostle as approving of it (see below, V), shows that all do not draw from the same source. Moreover, Clement of Alexandria mentions as his source, not any single authority, but "the elders from the beginning" (ton anekathen presbuteron—Euseb., "Hist. Eccl.", VI, xiv)."

Catholic Encyclopedia (1913)

The missing piece to all this, however, is to link these teaching sessions with Peter to the other traditions about Matthew. In that case, the logical conclusion is that Peter gave Mark a copy of Matthew's original Aramaic Gospel with the intention of him eventually translating it into Greek. Then, as Mark got into the job, he must have had certain questions about what Matthew was talking about, and sought out Peter for the answers. Those answers, of course, were also translated into Greek and included as part of the overall work. This written document would also have been copied and left in the Jerusalem Church's archives, probably again under the tutelage of Peter. The important point to remember is that, once again, Mark is using an Aramaic source as his guide and adding to it under Peter's direction. The first wave of Peter's additions is in the 15% of additional material that separate Aramaic Matthew and Greek Mark. The second wave, as we will see, is actually Q itself.

Then, picking up the story in Acts 15, the apostle Paul is called back to Jerusalem to attend a major church meeting on circumcision and Gentile conversion, and this happened in the year 49. Now, knowing that Paul was getting ready to preach in Gentile territory where such a Greek source would be needed, and further desiring to be a part of that journey, Mark and Barnabbas sought him out. Paul, however,[214] was still angry at Mark's desertion and was not in a forgiving mood, which forced Mark and his cousin to undertake an impromptu mission of their own to the Greek island of Cyprus. However, Paul, who must have seen the value of such a document, could easily have either relieved Mark of his writings, or else had them copied down before commencing on his journey. A little later on, Paul will pass this same document on to another traveling associate named Luke, the details of which are still to come.

In the meantime, Peter is known to have seen Paul at least once since the Council met, (Galatians 2:11-13). Additionally, on several more occasions another man named Silas traveled between them acting as a kind of courier and, as we will see later, a lot more, (Acts 16:1, 1 Thessalonians 1:1, 2 Thessalonians 1:1,1 Peter 5:12-14[215]).

However, the important point here is that while Paul is preaching and writing his Epistles, Peter is believed to have written a Gospel of his own, and this most probably took the form of added sayings of Y'shua that Mark did not include.

Not only do these same Early Church documents previously quoted also affirm this, even liberal scholars like the *Jesus Seminar* make a similar concession. Their own timeline, that I included earlier, allows for a date as early as the year 50 for such a collection to circulate. The fact that this is the same time that Q also circulated, and that Q is also comprised of these same longer sayings, cannot be coincidental. It is for these reasons that I believe Peter's original sayings Gospel, translated into Greek by Silas, was none other than Q itself. In any event, this is what Peter had say on the subject:

> "With the help of Silas, whom I regard as a faithful brother, I have written you briefly, encouraging you and testifying that this is the true grace of God. Stand fast in it."

1 Peter 5:12

The language could not be clearer. Silas actually helped Peter write his first letter, and if he provided this service at that time, there is every reason to believe this also happened before, since Silas was in Jerusalem during the Council Meeting, (Acts 15:22). Then, a short time later, Silas could have conveyed these same additions to his traveling companion, Paul (Acts 16:1-40)!

So now what we have is a well founded historical mechanism that explains how Paul gets a copy of both Mark's Greek Gospel, and the famous Q source, and additional scriptural evidence will prove easily the circumstances that resulted in their compilation into Luke's Gospel. For now, we must continue with the journeys as recorded in Acts.

From about the mid 50's on, Paul devoted himself almost exclusively to Gentile ministry. Then, early in Acts 16, a very interesting linguistic event occurs. Luke, who works in the city of Troas in Asia

Minor, also happens to be the author of Acts, and he gives us a great clue right here.

It seems that everything from Acts 1:1-16:8 was written later, either as personal remembrances or accounts gathered from Paul and other apostles, (Acts 1:1-2). However, it is in 16:9 that Luke historically enters the story, probably as a physician Paul sought out in that city to treat his exhaustion.[216] Then, in 16:10, the narrative switches from "they and them" to "we and us", indicating that Luke is including himself as part of the "we" for each subsequent event, and Luke's presence is also attested to in other sources, (Colossians 4:14, Philemon 1:24, 2 Timothy 4:11). It is therefore during this period, from 53 to the year of Paul's death in 67, that we need to look for a historical opportunity for Luke to compile his Gospel.

However, for the moment it seems more likely that he began what would later be the last half of Acts first as a kind of missionary journal which he kept as he traveled. Not coincidentally, it is later in this same year that Peter visits Paul, and this could have been the perfect time for Peter's Sayings Gospel, otherwise known as Q, to be given to Paul. However, whether this came from Peter directly or from an intermediary like Silas, it can be said with relative certainty that Paul had both Q and Mark's Gospel in some rough form by this time.

In any event, Paul's evangelizing continues for several years, and survives a number of murder plots, bouts of imprisonment—even a shipwreck—and by the close of the decade Paul finds himself in Rome answering charges. It is at that time that another opportunity to advance the progression of the Gospel record presents itself.

Final Formation Issues, 60-67

Soon after a shipwreck on Malta, around 60 or 61, Paul dutifully returns to Rome to face judgment. However, his accusers fail to appear. In the meantime, Paul is placed under limited house arrest for the next two years, and during this time, Philippians and Ephesians are written, (Philippians 1:12-13, Ephesians 6:19-20). The letters to

Philemon and Colossians also belong to this period, and both of his friends Mark and Luke are with him, (Colossians 4:10-14). This would also appear to be the time when Paul forgives Mark for his earlier mistake, (Philemon 1:24).

In Mark's case, he still does not know about Peter's Q additions. Nor does he know that other Gospels, using his notes as a framework, have probably been circulating for several years before this. As for the charges against Paul, he is freed when the statute of limitations runs out in the year 62.

Mark then returns to Jerusalem to be with Peter again, but Paul goes on his fourth, and final, missionary trip. The first stop is Ephesus, where Timothy is dropped off to head the churches in that area, (1 Timothy 1:3). This is followed by a trip to northern Greece and Macedonia (2 Corinthians 1:16), where Paul pens the first letter to Timothy, and then sails to Crete to drop off his friend Titus with his instructions on how to handle churches there, (Titus 1:4-16). Then it is back to southern Greece (Achaia) and Nicopolis, where he puts his instructions into a formal letter to this same associate, (Titus 3:12). From there, Paul goes to visit Luke in his hometown of Troas[217], but is suddenly arrested and put on a ship to Rome with his companion Luke following a few days behind.

Once Paul arrives in Rome, he finds a city on the brink of anarchy. It is now the year 64. Rome has been devastated by fire, and Emperor Nero has blamed it on the Christians, unleashing a wave of vicious persecution. Paul himself is thrown into prison for the last time. Soon after this, Peter will be arrested and crucified upside down, with Paul languishing in prison for another three years.

However, just prior to this, Peter must have given his assistant Mark all of his writings, which would include Aramaic Matthew.[218] Once again, Q had been given to Paul and circulated elsewhere out of Mark's view, thus explaining all the facets of the traditional theory. Clear textual research also tells us that Matthew did not put his own Gospel into Greek, because certain Aramaic homophonic pairs were mistranslated, and Matthew would know better.

Then, while Luke remains at his side, PAUL COMMANDS THAT MARK BE BROUGHT BACK ALONG WITH SCROLLS, PARCHMENTS AND WRITINGS LEFT BEHIND AT TROAS, (2 Timothy 4:13)![219] It would be at this point then that Luke took Mark and spliced it with Q.

Meanwhile, in a separate location, these same materials found their way into the hands of a man known only as "the Mattean Scribe". While the circumstances behind this compilation are completely unknown, it is more than plausible that he got his materials from the copies that Mark and Peter kept.

Finally, these revised documents, combined with later oral traditions also put down in Greek, would have been very early on translated wholesale back into Aramaic, but with a critical difference apart from the later Aramaic NT documents.

The identity of the person who did this feat is also lost to history. However, it is clear from the Peshitta documents that he had a complicated writing style. On the one hand, he most certainly has a very keen grasp of Aramaic idiom and nuance in most cases. However, this person was still divorced enough from the original composition sources to allow things like the scribal glosses and other translational clues to occur back in that language.

Furthermore, as time went on, the Gentile Christians forgot their Semitic roots, and this was complicated by the fact that the destruction of Jerusalem and the systematic hunting down of Hebrew writings in general, caused the original Aramaic documents to fade from history.[220] Meanwhile, Eastern Christians isolated themselves from the West and retained their original Scripture, which has been mistaken for later Aramaic translations from Greek, especially since five books in the western canon were excluded from their version.

Therefore, at the very least, the fact that these same Eastern Christians still understood the original Aramaic idioms of their Master had an additional effect. It also ensured that their Scripture in terms of word choice and sentence structure would be completely different from the Greek, and yet retain aspects of the Greek at the same time.

In light of all of this evidence then, one final note about the evolution of Mark's gospel is now warranted. Certain irregularities in the Greek have been well-attested to, such as the gloss at 3:17 and the misspelling of Aramaic names like "Zebedee." Since Mark and Peter were native Aramaic speakers and would not make mistakes like this from a written document, the likely scenario is that Silas might have done so and then got this revision also into the hands of Luke.

As for the Gospel of Mark, a recap of the stages of its composition is warranted and goes like this:

1) Mark receives Matthew's Aramaic rough draft from Peter.

2) Mark begins reviewing the manuscript and asks Peter for insights. These are added in Mark's Aramaic composition.

3) Mark then makes a rudimentary translation of his expanded Aramaic version into Greek.

4) Mark and Peter then do some ministry work in Babylon, and still more material is added in Aramaic for the Semitic peoples there.

5) Later, Mark takes his preliminary Greek copy and longer Aramaic version to Rome. Once there, according to Catholic tradition, he revises his Greek copy, but what is not known at the time is that this is done by inserting additional material translated from the Aramaic one.

6) From here, Mark goes to the city of Alexandria, and it is there that Clement claims Mark wrote a "secret Gospel". However, whether or not this version is ever found or not, it seems more than likely that Mark would have also continued revising what Clement considered his official opus for the masses. However, in that case, the work on both the Aramaic and Greek versions literally stopped in mid sentence at a critical juncture. The resurrection, which was

clearly an event Mark intended to record in real time, is mentioned elsewhere frequently from a predictive standpoint, (8:31, 10:32-34, 14:62). Additionally, in both languages, the last word Mark records could never be construed as either a complete thought or a proper sentence. Therefore, if this most critical piece was missing, it can only be because Mark was killed before he could finish his last chapter, around the year 63.

7) The next, and final, logical step then would be that Mark's writings were smuggled out of Alexandria and made their way back to Peter, who inserted those twelve lines. With the Aramaic complete, adding this last material on the Greek side was not difficult, but the earlier variants without those lines on the Greek side were also circulating, being copied, and making their way into the official record. We know this too because the same Catholic sources tell us that Mark himself literally gave his Gospel in Greek to the Romans who asked for it, but both internal evidence and other reliable traditions tell us that other portions had to have been completed posthumously.

Such is the case for explaining the composition of the synoptic Gospels. Now we have to move on to other sections of the New Testament.

The Case for John

> "This is the disciple who testifies to these things and who wrote them down. We know that his testimony is true."
>
> John 21:24

John appears to be in a rather unique situation, and he is not as separate as most have been led to believe. The first critical point to make about John is that there are quite a number of concordances between him and the synoptic authors. This is true even when we exclude obvious agreement points such as the Baptism and Passion Week. Furthermore, while it has been established that some of these incidents occur at different points along the timeline, the fact that they all share a common recording of very similar events is compelling. Consider:

- Moneychangers driven from the Temple, (John 2:12-17, Matthew 21:12-13, Mark 11:12-17, Luke 19:45-46).
- Y'shua returns to Galilee, is rejected by his hometown, and settles in Capernaum, (John 4:43-45, Matthew 4:12-17, Mark 4:14-15,21, Luke 4:14-5:11).
- While in Galilee, Y'shua then makes the specific statement "a prophet has no honor in his hometown", (John 4:43-45, Matthew 4:57, Mark 6:4, Luke 4:24).
- Heals a paralytic with the words, "Arise, take up your bed and walk," (John 5:11, Matthew 9:7-8, Mark 2:11-12, Luke 5:24-25).
- Feeds the 5,000, (John 6:1-15, Matthew 14:13-21, Mark 6:30-44, Luke 9:10-17).
- Walks on water later that night, (John 6:16-24, Matthew 14:22-36, Mark 6:45-56).
- Anointed with oil in "Simon's" house . . . (John 12:1-11, Luke 7:36-50) . . .
- . . . shortly before his death and in Bethany . . . (John 12:1-11, Matthew 26:6-13, Mark 14:1-11).

Such multiple attestations, again, showcase the ancient and original nature of these events, since John is at a minimum drawing from a similar early source. We also cannot deny direct statements of John's qualifications as an eye witness to the events he records, (John 21:24).

Now other aspects of John's development are also very interesting. For example, even liberal critics think John started with a rough draft similar to Thomas, except that it reports only miracles, and not sayings. Dubbed the *Signs Gospel*, liberals like the *Jesus Seminar* think it was so early that it may have predated any other gospel.[221] It is also possible that John, like Thomas and Matthew, had an even earlier version with just sayings and then linked them to these events at a later time.

In any case, John's status as an eyewitness imparts a historical stamp of early authentication to much of his material, and his individual tastes and emphases are very apparent throughout his writings. This is also reinforced by the previous list of Synoptic-John concordances, since all but one of the events listed are shared by Mark, known to have been written decades earlier.

Those facts are also why we can conclude that John is a combination both of oral sources that he shares with the other writers and can validate through his experience, as well as exclusive background material gleaned from his close personal relationship with Y'shua's family.

For proof of the latter, consider that John 7 records a conflict between Y'shua and his brothers during a brief visit back home. Because the other disciples were not with him, the question is, how did John know about it? As it turns out, the answer, is also recorded by him:

> "When Y'shua saw his mother was there, along with the disciple he loved standing nearby, he said to his mother, 'Woman, here is your son.,' and to the disciple, 'Here is your mother." From that time on, this disciple took her into his home."
>
> John 19:26-27

A few years living with Mary, Y'shua's mother, also must have imparted to him certain oral details that other writers were not aware of. This may also be why that, except for the final Passover, the synoptics all but avoid holiday references in their record, because people tended to travel up to the great feasts by family group[222], (Luke 2:41-52, John 7:1-8). That being the case, the other disciples would not have been directly privy to Y'shua's activities at those events, including Purim (5:1), Sukkot (7:1-53) and Hanukkah (10:22-42), which are all exclusively recorded by John. [223] Also the fact that two stepbrothers, James and Jude, would have visited their mother periodically at John's house, didn't hurt matters either. Finally, these people, and other early eyewitnesses, were also responsible for particulars like the Nativity and Genaeology accounts, circulating by word of mouth throughout the last half of the first century.

Finally, John's writing style is replete with Semitic idioms and allusions and, like Mark and Matthew, has certain Aramaic phrases retained even in the Greek. These include:

1) Six occasions where he records Y'shua calling himself "I AM" (YHWH) in Hebrew, (4:24, 26; 8:24, 28, 58; 13:19).

2) Several other more prosaic Aramaic phrases, (3:2, 4:25, 6:25, 7:1, 9:2, 7, 9; 19:17, 20:16).

3) Insights into certain holidays and practices that only a Palestinian Jew would have known, (7:37-39, 10:22-30, 18:28, 38-42).

Additionally, while the proof that the Aramaic version of John came first is partly proven by the lack of 7:53-8:11, one other unique feature in the Gospel deserves special attention for this same reason.

In chapter 11, perhaps Y'shua's most famous miracle is recorded, when he raises Lazarus from the dead. However, for our purposes, the significant fact has to do with Lazarus as a name in Greek texts. It turns out that the original name comes from the Hebrew "Eliezar". However, in Y'shua's particular Aramaic dialect it was common to truncate names. Now here is the odd part. "Eliezar" would have been spelled as "A'lazar" in Aramaic, BUT IT WOULD HAVE BEEN PRONOUNCED WITHOUT THE FIRST 'A'. So while the written name was spelled one way, it was pronounced another, as "LAZAR" which would then have been made into "LAZAR'os" in Greek. Thus, once again we see great attempts being made to take Aramaic original sources and turn them into pale Greek shadows of their former selves.

As for the rest of the NT, the evidence about the Pauline Epistles, James, Peter, and the rest have been dealt with throughout this entire discussion. However, to clarify things, the ending point is simple: 22 books have a clear pedigree of Aramaic primacy. As for the remaining five books (2 and 3 John, 2 Peter, Jude, Revelation), there is not enough evidence to declare that they once existed in Aramaic and now survive as a kind of Semitic memory in Greek, or that they had always existed in Greek. The most that can be said is that these five seem to have less Semitic influences in Greek than the rest of the books in the Christian canon.

In any case, the reader should not be in any doubt as to my views on the subject. In some way that I cannot quantify scientifically, the full 27 book canon (even with the extra verses of John not in the Aramaic), can be verified as the absolute Word of God. God has therefore preserved His Word with both of these languages providing the complete picture. And, because Paul has himself defined faith as the knowledge of that which is unseen and incomplete, I will have to leave this final "proof" in that realm and let the remainder rest at present.

PART FOUR:

Y'SHUA YEAR BY YEAR AND BEYOND

Majority Does Not Rule

Now that issues of authenticity, linguistics and composition have been resolved, the time has come to look at the sources themselves. What do the Gospels say about Y'shua that can be verified and how do we ascertain the actual dates for the events they record? Moreover, can we even figure out the actual combined chronology that these four accounts present to us?

The main rule of thumb for sorting out the proper order of events in the Gospels can be summed up in a sentence: *A single account with valuable and specific information carries more weight than vague multiple accounts.* Or, to put it more succinctly: Majority does not rule; most specific wins. To see why this must be the case, let us look at three versions of the same event:

> "When Y'shua came into Peter's house, he saw Peter's mother-in-law lying in bed with a fever. He touched her hand and the fever left her, and she got up and began to wait on him."
>
> Matthew 8:14-15

"As soon as they left the synagogue, they went with James and John to the home of Simon and Andrew. Simon's mother-in-law was in bed with a fever, and they told Y'shua about her. So he went to her, took her hand, and helped her up. The fever left her and she began to wait on them."

Mark 1:29-31

"Y'shua left the synagogue and went to the home of Simon. Now Simon's mother-in-law was suffering from a high fever, and they asked Y'shua to help her. So he bent over and rebuked the fever, and it left her. She got up at once and began to wait on them."

Luke 4:38-39

In terms of the gist of the event, all three read pretty much the same way. However, Matthew is clearly the poorer for not having more specific information. Matthew's use of the word *when* pervades his entire 8th chapter and gives us no help at all in determining which of the many times Y'shua entered Peter's house that the healing occurred. By contrast, both Mark and Luke tell us clearly that the event took place right after the demon in the Capernaum synagogue was exorcised. However, a final advantage must be extended to Luke alone, because only he says that Y'shua "rebuked the fever", meaning he healed her both by speech and by touch.

Therefore, the point of this should be rather clear. Just because "rebuking the fever" only appears in Luke does not mean that Matthew and Mark are right in omitting it.

Determining the Start of the Ministry

For the start of the Messiah's public debut, the vast majority of scholarship falls into one of two camps: Those who believe Messiah's ministry began 26 or 27 and ended in the common year 30 and those who argue for a later date, a 29/30 start with a year 33 crucifixion.[224]

However, if we turn back to prophecy of Daniel 9 as described in "Six Sides of the Messiah", we see once again that a 483 year period is prophesied from the decree to rebuild all of Jerusalem to the time of the anointed prince's debut. Those numbers, of course, bring us to the year 27. Furthermore, Daniel also describes a "half week" for the Messiah to "declare a covenant with many" before being "cut off"—dying—three and a half years later.

Additionally, further confirmation of this scenario is found in the Gospel of John, which lists at least three Passovers, one Feast of Tabernacles, and one Feast of Dedication (Hanukkah), all of which easily fit into this time frame.

Other evidence in favor of this selection includes the "Sign of Jonah" prophecy (Matthew 12:38-40, comp to Jonah 1:17), which demands a three day period between crucifixion and resurrection, and the listing of Sabbath periods and days of preparations in the Gospels.

Much has been made of the fact that John appears out of step chronologically with the other writers. However, these difficulties are very easily explained when the following facts are considered.

First, we know that there was more than one kind of Sabbath involved during the year of the crucifixion. John calls the day of the crucifixion alternately a "high Sabbath", or "special Sabbath" depending on the translation, and this has often puzzled Christian scholars when certain nuances of Jewish practice are not considered.

Put simply, there were two Sabbaths that week. John is calling the day a "special Sabbath" because the Feast of Unleavened Bread, which starts at sundown, is also considered a Sabbath regardless of the time of week that it occurs and, just as with the weekly Sabbath, no servile work is allowed. Additionally, it is the abstinence from work, not the day itself, which fits this definition. The following day, as recorded in Luke 23:56, is the weekly Sabbath or the one "according to the [fourth] commandment". Only the year 30 has these overlapping Sabbaths, the first running Thursday-Friday and the second Friday-Saturday—both sundown to sundown by the Jewish system. The women would then come to anoint the body at the earliest possible time—Sunday morning.

A second consideration is that John is counting the hours in a day on the Roman clock, whereas the Synoptic authors use Jewish Standard Time. For example, in John's first chapter, the disciples of the Baptist spend "the day" with Y'shua until the "tenth hour", which is four in the afternoon. Similarly, knowing that Y'shua frequently rose at dawn before going on a journey, John 4 describes him thirsty and tired from the journey, and stopping by a well to get something to drink. This, he records, is the sixth hour, which can only be Roman time (noon) and not Jewish (midnight), when no one fetches water from a well or eats!

By contrast, Mark 15 tells us Y'shua died the NINTH HOUR after dawn, which must be three in the afternoon, because the Sabbath is about to begin and the burial would come too late otherwise.

Finally, we notice that Matthew, Mark and Luke have the Last Supper as a Passover meal, but the next day in John's chronology the Pharisees have not eaten the Passover lamb yet! Alfred Edersheim explains why:

> "We have already explained that according to the Rabbis (*Chag.* ii, 1; vi. 2), three things were implied in the festive command to 'appear before the Lord'—'Presence,' the 'Chagigah,' and 'Joyousness.' As specially applied to the Passover, the first of these terms meant, that every one was to come up to Jerusalem and to offer a burnt-offering, if possible on the first, or else on one of the other six

days of the feast. This burnt-offering was to be taken only from 'Cholin' (or profane substance), that is, from such as did not otherwise belong to the Lord, either as tithes, firstlings, or things devoted, etc. **The Chagigah, which was strictly a peace-offering, might be twofold. This first Chagigah was offered on the 14th of Nisan, the day of the Paschal sacrifice, and formed afterwards part of the Paschal Supper. The second Chagigah was offered on the 15th of Nisan, or the first day of the feast of unleavened bread. It is this second Chagigah which the Jews were afraid they might be unable to eat, if they contracted defilement in the judgment-hall of Pilate (John 18:28).** In reference to the first Chagigah, the *Mishnah* lays down the rule, that it was only to be offered if the Paschal day fell on a week-day, not on a Sabbath, and if the Paschal lamb alone would not have been sufficient to give a satisfying supper to the company which gathered around it (*Pes.* vi. 4). As in the case of all other peace-offerings, part of this Chagigah might be kept, though not for longer than one night and two days from its sacrifice. Being a voluntary offering, it was lawful to bring it from sacred things (such as tithes of the flock). But the Chagigah for the 15th of Nisan was obligatory, and had therefore to be brought from 'Cholin.' The third duty incumbent on those who appeared at the feast was 'joyousness.' This expression, as we have seen, simply referred to the fact that, according to their means, all Israel were, during the course of this festival, with joyous heart to offer peace-offerings, which might be chosen from sacred things (Deut 27:7). Thus the sacrifices which every Israelite was to offer at the Passover were, besides his share in the Paschal lamb, a burnt-offering, the Chagigah (one or two), and offerings of joyousness—all as God had blessed each household. As stated in a previous chapter, all the twenty-four courses, into which the priests were arranged, ministered in the temple on this, as on the other great festivals, and they distributed among themselves alike what fell to them of the festive sacrifices and the shewbread. But the course which, in its proper order, was on duty for the week, alone offered all votive, and voluntary, and the public sacrifices for the whole congregation, such as those of the morning and the evening (*Succah* v. 7)."

The Temple: Its Ministry and Services, Chapter 11

Therefore, when all of this evidence is properly understood, we find that the range 27-30 is the only one that fits all these requirements.Additionally, other historical information is found here:

"Now in the fifteenth year of the reign of Tiberius Caesar, when Pontius Pilate was governor of Judea, and Herod was tetrarch of Galilee, and his brother Philip was tetrarch of the region of Ituraea and Trachionitis, Lysanias was tetrarch of Abilene, in the high priesthood of Annas and Caiphas, the Word of God came to John, the son of Zacharias, in the wilderness."

Luke 3:1-2

All eight names can be verified through secular sources as follows:

> *John the Baptist:* Josephus refers to Herod Antipas executing him, and looks at the king's troubles with the King of Arabia as God's judgment against that sin.[225]
>
> *Tiberius Caesar:* Various dating methods, which we shall get into later, put the fifteenth year of his reign somewhere between 26 and 29 CE.[226]
>
> *Pontius Pilate:* According to the eminent historian Josephus and other early authorities, we know that Pontius Pilate ruled Judea from 26-36 CE. In addition, all four gospels, the book of Acts, Josephus and Tacitus (a prominent Roman historian) agree that Y'shua's entire ministry took place during Pilate's tenure.[227] In 1961, archaeologists confirmed this time when they found a plaque commemorating a building he had dedicated.[228]
>
> *Annas and Caiphas:* Caiphas was ruling high priest from the years 18-36 CE. Annas, on the other hand, was the previous high priest, and even though he ruled officially from 6-15 CE, we know he continued to exercise major influence for many years after that (John 18:13, Acts 4:6). In 1990, archaeologists found Caiphas' tomb.[229]
>
> *Herod (Antipas) :* Son of Herod the Great, was tetrarch of Galilee and Perea from 4 BCE-CE 39.[230]

According to Josephus, Philip, another of Herod's sons, became tetrarch of Trachionitis, Gaulonitus and Panaea in 4 BCE. During Messiah's lifetime, he built the city of Caesarea Phillipi., (Matthew 16:13).[231]

> *Lysanias:* This man was tetrarch of Abilene until the first year of the emperor Gaius (Caligula), or 37 CE. Josephus is the sole extrabiblical source for this person and nothing else is known of him. When combined with Luke's assertion, we can infer that he ruled for about eleven years.[232]

To these names we must add one more: Saint Stephen. History shows that he was stoned to death somewhere between the years 30 and 34 CE, and that this was after the crucifixion.[233]

Therefore all the possible dates for Y'shua's ministry and death must fall between 26 and 34 CE.[234] However, those scholars who are in favor of a later ministry insist that since Tiberius did not become Emperor until Augustus' death in the year 14, that the time mentioned in Luke can be no earlier than the year 29.

But is this necessarily the case? Not so when we synchronize it to another clue in John:

> "It has taken forty six years to build this Temple,
> and you are going to rebuild it in three days?"

John 2:20

It is most interesting then that in one place (Antiquities 15.11.1) Josephus tells us the Temple work began in Herod's eighteenth year, which translates to 20 BCE, and took a year and a half to finish (Antiquities 15.11.6)[235].

As for Tiberius, it is also possible to date his reign from the year 12, when he was made co-regent with an ailing Augustus. The Roman historian Seutonius, writing about the year 120, appears to do just that:

> "After two years he returned to the city from Germania [12 A.D.] and celebrated the triumph which he had postponed, accompanied also by his generals, for whom he had obtained the triumphal regalia. And before turning to enter the Capitol, he dismounted from his chariot and fell at the knees of his father, who was presiding over the knees of his father, who was presiding over the ceremonies. He sent Bato, the leader of the

Pannonians, to Ravenna, after presenting him with rich gifts; thus showing his gratitude to him for allowing him to escape when he was trapped with his army in a dangerous place. Then he gave a banquet to the people at a thousand tables, and a largess of three hundred sesterces to every man. With the proceeds of his spoils he restored and dedicated the temple of Concord, as well as that of Pollux and Castor, in his own name and that of his brother.

Since the consuls caused a law to be passed soon after this that he should govern the provinces jointly with Augustus and hold the census with him, he set out for Illyricum on the conclusion of the lustral ceremonies; but he was at once recalled, and finding Augustus in his last illness but still alive, he spent an entire day with him in private."

De Vita Caesarum—Tiberius, XX-XXI—*cited from the Internet Ancient History Sourcebook*

So from 20 BCE, the "forty-sixth year" in John is in fact 27, and the fifteenth year of Tiberius, counting from the year 12, also ends up in exactly the same place.

Finding the Universal Event (Dividing Line)

As I said earlier, vague accounts must give way specific ones and non-linear information is subservient to critical time cues. Sometimes these cues are easy to spot, and other times they require a huge amount of detective work. Because I assume that the Gospels are basically correct, if an event mentioned in all four has a specific time marker in

one, the rest must fall into place based on that information. This is what we need to look for:
- The *Universal Event* must, by definition, appear in all four gospels.
- The *Universal Event* cannot have any significant divergences in details between the four accounts.
- *The Universal Event* must not be an event either from the very beginning (Baptism) or end (Crucifixion) of the ministry, as these have already been dated by more general processes. Ideally, it should happen right in the middle of the three year period.
- Most important of all: *The Universal Event* must have at least one gospel provide conclusive timing information.

There is only one instance where all these criteria converge: The Feeding of the 5,000. We can be certain it is not a separate event from gospel to gospel because other multiple feedings (4,000) are sometimes listed alongside this one, (Matthew 15:29-39, Mark 8:1-13). In addition, all four accounts confirm the event as well as its general time frame and precise location.

As for the actual time, once again it is John to the rescue. He tells us that it happened just before the second to last Passover (or April of 29). *What follows from this fact is the single most important tool for recovering the proper chronology. 95% of all events can be classified as being either before of after this miracle.*

So, from their beginnings to the end of this event, the gospels can be synched accordingly:

Matthew 1:1-13:58, Mark 1:1-6:56, Luke 1:1-9:17, John 1:1-5:47.[236]

Our next four sections will each take one ministry year at a time and recover the detailed chronological information hidden in the Gospel record.

Signs of the Cross: The Search for the Historical Jesus

August 31, 26—December 31, 27

So much has been written about chronological difficulties in the Gospels that it is easy to lose sight of a simple fact: Two thirds of the time and events covered in the Gospels can be assimilated without difficulty. In fact, up until the last year of Messiah's ministry, one can see a clear pattern of the Gospels trading events with another in a systematic, almost graceful manner.

First, Matthew and Luke swap details about the Nativity. Then all four accounts come together for the prologue with the Baptist. After this, the first three Gospels report on the Temptation, and then the focus shifts to John again for the Cana Wedding. John continues until the end of the year, concluding with an 8 month stay in Judea and Samaria.

Our first challenge then is fixing the time of the Cana Wedding as before or after the Temptation. The problem comes about because there is no one Gospel that lists both events in any type of order. Therefore, all of our inferences have to be indirect.

In this case, we have to turn to Mark. He says that Y'shua was tempted "immediately" after the Baptism. Whereas Matthew and Luke are content with the watered down phrase "led" to describe the Spirit of God guiding Messiah to the desert, Mark uses the word "compelled". Since this is the same Spirit present at the Baptism, it seems that Y'shua was literally yanked from the emotional high of the cleansing and deposited instantly to the challenge of the test. Since there is no gap between the Baptism and the Temptation, the Cana Wedding had to happen afterwards.

This also makes sense geographically. John is baptizing in Bethabarah, which is near the Judean desert and the city of Jerusalem, where the full Temptation takes place. Afterwards, Y'shua walks back to Galilee (3-4 days)[237] and meets five men who will later become his disciples. Three days later, they all attend the wedding. Then it's time for a well needed break at Capernaum to rest, and this city is just a few miles to the north of Cana. Following this rest period,

Y'shua once again must go up to Jerusalem for the Passover. Furthermore, the need to "purify" himself, purchase supplies and prepare for the meal is such that he must get there at least a day in advance. Therefore, when you count up all the days between the Baptism and the Passover, this is what emerges:

Baptism to the End of Fasting (in Bethabarah)	40
End of Fasting to Satan's Arrival and Failure (in Jerusalem)	1
Angels minister, help him recover	1
Walks about 20 miles back to Bethabarah and Calls Peter and Andrew	1
Calls Nathanael to follow; Leaves Bethabarah	1
Arrives in Cana (by boat)	2
Turns water into wine at wedding	1
Leaves Cana; arrives in Capernaum	1
Rests in Capernaum with family and disciples	3
Leaves Capernaum; arrives in Jerusalem two days before Passover	3
Passover begins	2
Total Amount of Days	**58**

Therefore, when we subtract 58 days from Passover, the result is a February 9th Baptism. Additionally, having the 40 day Temptation take place and be completed just before Passover (later Easter) is very much in line with the traditional 40 day celebration of *Lent* where Christians give up something they love to commemorate Messiah's sacrifice in the desert.

Other dates need not be stated explicitly here, except for a handful. We now know that the day before— when John the Baptist was questioned by the Pharisees—had to be February 8th. We also know about when the Baptist's solo ministry started and how long it lasted.

With Daniel and the Gospels pointing to the year 27 as the start, we must remember that for the Jewish people the year started during the late summer or early fall. In the case of 27, the first day of Tishri (or New Year's Day) began very early, on August 31. From that date until early February is the maximum period that John could have been preaching in the wilderness and "preparing the way of the Lord". The final piece of information regarding the year is found here:

> "Do you not say, 'There are yet four months and then comes the harvest?' Behold, I say to you, lift up your eyes and look on the fields, that they are white for the harvest."
>
> John 4:35

Before continuing however, it is important to note three things. First, Y'shua followed the Jewish calendar that had two possible new years, roughly in April and September. Second, Y'shua is clearly referring to the start of the harvest and not the end of it in autumn, because, if the latter, the four months prior to that time would also be in harvest season, instead of four months *and then the harvest*. Third, we have to forget that our calendar would have four months prior to the start of harvesting season as a natural byproduct of starting in January. The reason being, if Y'shua followed this convention then it would be very likely he was speaking figuratively, because any year would start this way. Since it did not, the only alternative is that the time reference is literal.

Therefore, since the harvest season in Israel starts in May with the Shavuot holiday, there can be little doubt that subtracting four months from that time brings us to a late December to early January time frame. Then, when combined with the statement in John 3:22 that this began directly after Passover, it is easy to determine that Y'shua's stay in Aenon—and later Samaria—lasted 8 months.

Andrew Gabriel Roth

Gospel Harmony #2: Prelude, Baptism and Temptation:

August 31, 26 through February 7, 27 CE

(Luke 3:1-3)

In the fifteenth year of the reign of Tiberius Caesar — when Pontius Pilate was governor of Judea, Herod tetrarch of Galilee, his brother Philip tetrarch of Iturea and Trachionitis, and Lysanias tetrarch of Abilene— during the high priesthood of Annas and Caiphas, the word of God came to John son of Zacharias in the desert.

(Matthew 3:1)

In those days John the Baptist came preaching in the Desert of Judea saying, 'Repent, for the kingdom of heaven is near,'

(Luke 3:4)

(and) he went into all the country around the Jordan, preaching a baptism of repentance for the forgiveness of sins.

(John 1:6-18)

John was sent by God as a witness to testify concerning the light (of God), so that through him all men might believe. He himself was not the light; he came only as a witness to the light. The true light that gives light to every man was coming into the world. He was in the world, and though the world was made through him, the world did not recognize him. He came to that which was his own, but his own did not receive him. Yet to all who received him, to those who believed in his name, he gave the right to become children of God — children born not of natural descent, nor of human decision or a husband's will, but born of God. The Word became flesh and live for a while among us. We have seen his glory, the glory of the one and only Son, who came from the Father, full of grace and truth. John testifies concerning him. He cries out, saying, "This was he of whom I said, 'He who comes after me has surpassed me because he was before me.'" From the fullness of his grace we have all received one blessing after another. For the law was given through Moses; grace and truth came through Y'shua Ha Moshiack. No one has ever seen God, but God the only Son, who is at the Father's side, has made him known.

(Matthew 3:4-10)
(Now) John's clothes were made of camel's hair and he had a leather belt around his waist. His food was locusts and wild honey. People went out to him from Jerusalem and all of Judea and the whole region of the Jordan. Confessing their sins, they were baptized by him in the Jordan River.

Monday, February 8
But when he saw that many of the Pharisees and Sadducees were coming to where he was baptizing, he said to them: "You brood of vipers! Who warned you to flee from the coming wrath? Produce fruit in keeping with repentance. And do not think you can say to yourselves, 'We have Abraham as our father," I tell you that out of these stones God can raise up children of Abraham. The ax is ready at the root of the trees, and every tree that does not produce good fruit will be cut down and thrown into the fire."

(Luke 3:10-15)
"What should we do then?" the crowd asked.
John answered, "The man with two tunics should share with him who has none, and the one who has food should do the same."
Tax collectors also came to be baptized. "Teacher," they asked, "what should we do?"
"Don't collect more than you are required to," he told them.
Then some soldiers asked him, "And what should we do?"
He replied, "Don't extort money and don't accuse people falsely—be content with your pay."

The people were waiting expectantly and wondering in their hearts if John might possibly be the Messiah.

(John 1:19-23)
(But) this was John's testimony when the Jews of Jerusalem sent priests and Levites to ask him who he was. He did not fail to confess, but confessed freely, "I am not the Messiah."
They asked him, "Then who are you? Are you Elijah?"
He said, "I am not."
"Are you the Prophet?"
He answered, "No."
Finally they said, "Who are you? Give us an answer to take back to those who sent us. What do you say about yourself?"
John replied with the words of Isaiah the prophet: "I am the voice of one calling in the desert, 'Prepare the way of the Lord, make straight paths for him.

(Luke 3:5-6)
"Every valley shall be filled in, every mountain and hill made low. The crooked roads shall become straight, the rough ways smooth. And all mankind will see God's salvation.'"

(John 1:24-25)
Now some Pharisees who had been sent questioned him, "Why then do you baptize if you are not the Messiah, nor Elijah, nor the Prophet?"
"I baptize you with water

(Matthew 4:11)
for repentance,"

(John 1:26) John replied. "But among you stand one you do not know. He is the one who comes after me,

(Matthew 4:11) the thongs of whose sandals I am not worthy to carry

(Luke 3:11 (b)) (or) untie.

(Matthew 3:11 (b)-12)

He is more powerful than I and will baptize you with the Holy Spirit and with fire. His winnowing fork is in his hand, and he will clear the threshing floor, gathering up the wheat into his barn and burning up the chaff with unquenchable fire."And with many other words John exhorted the people and preached the good news to them.

(John 1:28-31)

This all happened in Bethany on the other side of the Jordan, where John was baptizing.

Baptism, Tuesday, February 9

The next day John saw Y'shua coming towards him and said, "A man who comes after me has surpassed me because he was before me. I myself did not know him, but the reason I came baptizing with water was that he might be revealed to Israel."
(Matthew 3:13-16)

Then Y'shua came from Galilee to the Jordan to be baptized by John (along with many others—Luke 3:21). But John tried to deter him, saying, "I need to be baptized by you, and do you come to me?"Y'shua replied, "Let it be so now; it is proper to do this to fulfill all righteousness." Then John consented. As soon as Y'shua was baptized, he went up out of the water, (and during prayer—Luke 3:21), at that moment, heaven was opened and he saw the Spirit of God, (the Holy Spirit—Luke 3:22) descending (in the bodily form of—Luke 3:22) of a dove and lightning on him. And a voice from heaven said, "This is my Son, whom I love; with him I am well pleased." (And the voice said this to Y'shua directly also, "You are my son . . ."—Mark 1:11, Luke 3:22).

(John 1:32-34)

Then John gave this testimony: "I saw the Spirit come down from heaven as a dove and remain on him, except that the one who sent me to baptize with water told me, 'The man on whom you see the Spirit come down on and remain is he who will baptize with the Holy Spirit.' I have seen and I testify that this is the Son of God."

The Temptation, February 9 through March 22
(Mark 1:12)

At once the Spirit sent him out into the desert, and he was in the desert forty days (and forty nights—Matthew 4:2a), being tempted by Satan. He was (also) with the wild animals.

(Matthew 4:2b-8)

(After the forty days and forty nights of fasting) he was hungry. The tempter came to him and said, "If you are the Son of God, tell these stones to become bread.

Y'shua replied, "Man does not live by bread alone, but by every word that comes out of the mouth of God."

Then the devil took him to the holy city and had him stand on the highest point of the temple. "If you are the Son of God," he said, "throw yourself down. For it is written: He will command his angels concerning you, and they will lift you up in their hands, so that you will not strike your foot against a stone."

Y'shua replied, "It is also written: Do not put the Lord your God to the test."

Again, the devil took him to a very high mountain and showed him all the kingdoms of the world and their splendor.

(Luke 4:6-7)

And he said to him, "I will give you all their authority and splendor, for it has been given to me, and I can give it to anyone I want to. So if you worship me, it will all be yours."

(Matthew 4:10-11)

"Y'shua said to him, "Away from me, Satan! For it is written: Worship the Lord your God and serve him only."
Then the devil left him (for an opportune time—Luke 4:13),

(Matthew 4:11 = Mark 1:12b)
and angels came and attended him.

January 1-December 31, 28

Introduction

Once Y'shua returns from Samaria to Galilee, the "real" part of his ministry begins. This is the time when key logistical issues are addressed: more followers are called, a base of operation is set up, and a plan for spreading the message is developed.

It begins with Y'shua leaving Samaria and then arriving in Cana to perform his second miracle, (John 4:43-54). Of particular interest in terms of chronology is this brief statement:

> "After two days he left for Galilee. (Now Y'shua himself had pointed out that a prophet has no honor in his own country.) When he arrived in Galilee, the Galileans welcomed him . . ."

John 4:43-45a

Luke records Y'shua's rejection at Nazareth (Luke 4:14-30) prior to a trip to Capernaum and Matthew tells us Y'shua left Nazareth to settle there after the Baptist had been imprisoned, (Matthew 4:13). From this list of events, it is very easy to reconstruct the full chronology, because it is summarized in John and explained fully in the other three thusly:

1) Y'shua leaves Samaria and returns to Galilee, where he is welcomed, (John 4:43-45).

2) From Galilee, Y'shua travels to the town of Cana and heals a nobleman's son, (John 4:46-54).

3) From Cana, Y'shua arrives in his hometown of Nazareth, but is rejected, (Luke 4:14-30).

4) From Nazareth, Y'shua settles in Capernaum and hears of the Baptist's imprisonment, (Matthew 4:13)

The best time frame would then appear to be from the return of Y'shua to Galilee in January, until the end of March when he had to make a pilgrimage to Jerusalem for the Passover. However, we can do much better than just fix events to a three month period. One of them, *Prophet Without Honor 1*, can be recovered to the exact day, and it is the focus of our next section.

The Isaiah Connection

As he did by mentioning the Abijah division with regards to the birth, Luke again gives us another critical detail for setting a timeline. This time, it is when Y'shua tries to enlighten his hometown of Nazareth but is rejected. Also like Abijah, Luke doesn't make things easy by giving us a firm holiday to pin the date.

But, he does the next best thing.

What Luke tells us is that Y'shua goes up to read in the Nazareth synagogue from the book of Isaiah. More to the point, Luke specifically says *that the scroll was handed to him during the service and that it was part of the custom*. The question that needs determining, however, is what shape did that custom take?

Current Jewry utilizes a one year cycle, with the entire Torah[238] and various prophetic (or *haftarot*) readings. Each section (or *sidrah*) is meant to cover all the Sabbaths and various holiday observances. In all, 54 weekly divisions are used.

So, having grown up in a Jewish home I thought it would be relatively easy to look in my prayer book and find out when that portion of Isaiah was read. However, I soon hit a major snag:

> "The Pentateuch is divided into 54 sections; beginning with the Sabbath following the Feast of Tabernacles, the readings of the Sabbaths of the year are taken in their order from the Five Books of Moses. The readings consist of the whole section or of a selected portion. **There was a variant custom according to which the reading of the Torah extended over a period of three years instead of one year. However, the one year cycle gradually superseded the three year cycle, and has become the universal custom in the Synagogue.**"
>
> *Preface to the Jewish Publication Society 1955 Translation, p. ix*

The critical question then was, of course, *when did the three year cycle disappear?* Of just slightly less importance would also be the factoring in of any regional diversity of worship, as well as how sectarian disputes between the Pharisees and the Sadduccees may have played a role in synagogue worship. Unfortunately, my other resources appeared to contain only bad news:

> "In the early centuries of the Christian era, the Jews of Palestine completed the reading of the entire Torah once in three years.[239] We know, for the most part, how the text was divided into sections for this purpose; but scholars disagree as to when the triennial cycle began and ended . . .

Babylonian congregations, however, read through the entire Torah each year, and their custom ultimately became the standard."

The Torah: A Modern Commentary, p. xxxiv

A Core Argument

However, the roots of this practice of linking scripture with occasion go back much further, even prior to the birth of the synagogue system altogether. In Deuteronomy 31:9-13, Moses is given certain commands which must be read to the congregation of Israel once every seven years. Some time later, Moses' successor Joshua erected an altar on Mount Ebal and renewed the Sinai covenant by reading the entire Book of the Law:

> "Afterward, Joshua read all the words of the law, the blessings and curses, just as it is written in the Book of the Law. There was not a word of all that Moses had commanded that was not read by the whole assembly of Israel, including the women and children, and the aliens who lived among them."
>
> Joshua 8:34-35

In later centuries, Israel frequently alternated between periods of Torah observance and idolatry. In several cases, when the time came to renew their commitment to the former, a prominent leader would once again read the entire Book of the Law, (2 Kings 23:2, Nehemiah 8:3, 13:1). Other occasions had sacred Scripture composed on the spot and read immediately in sacred assemblies, (Deuteronomy 31:30-32:47, Jeremiah 36:1-32).

Therefore, what the evidence suggests apart from one year/three year cycle discussion, is a skeletal linkage of Scripture and occasion, passed down intact regardless as to the system used at that time.

The next step in the process then is to show how this tradition was enshrined and continued, first by the Pharisees and then by today's rabbinic Judaism. As it turns out, a long history of sectarian brinksmanship and rivalry may hold the key to resolving the problem.

Priestly History Revisited

Some time ago, we detailed a general history of the priesthood from Moses all the way through the destruction of the Second Temple. Also as stated before, David took instructions handed down from Aaron and officially divided the priesthood into 24 sections. One of the first priests to serve under this system was a man named *Zadok*, whose name appears to be derived from the word *tzadaak*, or "righteousness." As David's official high priest, Zadok spawned a line that would hold power almost exclusively for more than 800 years, and his followers became known as the *tzadaakim*, better known in English as the Sadduccees.[240]

Then, after the Second Temple was re-dedicated in 165 BCE, another sect began to emerge. After the foreign Syrian rulers had been expelled, Jewish power centered on one family: The Hasmoneans. However, the Sadduccees, who were then in control of the Temple cult, had come under fire from a significant and vocal minority. Distressed that pagan rituals had been allowed to commingle with Temple worship, these group of "rebel priests" called themselves *perushin* ("separate ones"), or "Pharisees" in modern parlance.[241]

The two groups then often fought for dominance amongst the Hasmonean rulers. John Hyrcanus I, for example, started out as a Pharisee but later converted to the Sadduccean cause when the former appeared to turn against him. He later banned most Pharisaic practices from the Temple, and elevated the rival sect.[242]

Some time later, civil war broke out during the reign of King

Jannaeus (103-76 BCE) over conflicting views of Temple practice between these two groups.[243] The price was heavy, costing six years and 50,000 lives. The Pharisees then suffered a devastating loss when, according to Josephus, 800 of them, along with their families, were publicly executed in Jerusalem.[244]

However, the tables would soon turn during the reign of Alexander's daughter, Salome, who was also known as Alexandra, (76-67 BCE). Under the influence of the leader of the Pharisees, who also happened to be her brother, the Sadduccees took the hint and begged not to be slaughtered. Salome acceded to their request, and booted them out of Jerusalem.[245]

Three years later, Rome conquered Syria and Palestine, sweeping the Hasmoneans out of power. Then, in 37 BCE, an Idumean named Herod the Great assumed the Jewish throne as a vassal to Rome. True to his character, Herod was an equal opportunity murderer, and killed Sadduccee and Pharisee alike when it suited his purpose. However, except for some very minor purges at the very beginning and end of his reign, Herod generally elevated the Pharisees and kept their rivals out of power. In particular, Herod saw the Sadduccees as a more direct threat because their family tradition of priests went back eight centuries, and was in direct opposition to Herod's power as king to appoint high priests he felt would keep the tax dollars going to Rome. However, while the high priest was usually a Sadduccee, Herod stealthily made sure that his deputy, also known as a *segan*, was always a Pharisee who had direct control over all the Temple functions, and therefore forced the high priest to follow Pharisaic practice.[246] As Alfred Erdesheim reports, the consequences for defying this tradition were often dangerous:

> "When a Sadduccean high priest, on the Feast of Tabernacles, poured out the water on the ground instead of into the silver funnel of the altar, MACCABBEAN KING THOUGH HE WAS, HE SCARCE ESCAPED WITH HIS LIFE, and ever af-

> terwards the shout resounded from all parts of the Temple, 'Hold up thy hand,' and the priest yearly performed this part of the service. The Sadduccees held, that on the Day of Atonement the high priest should light the incense before he actually entered the Most Holy Place. As this was contrary to the views of the Pharisees, they took care to bind him by an oath to observe their ritual customs before allowing him to officiate at all."
>
> Sketches of Jewish Life, ch. 15, p. 220

Erdesheim would also go on to point out that Pharisaic control was not just confined to major holidays and Great Feasts, but extended into the synagogues as well. This has also been confirmed by more modern scholarship, as British historian Paul Johnson writes:

> "In their battle against Greek education[247], pious Jews began, from the end of the second century BC, to develop a national system of education. To the old scribal schools were gradually added a network of local schools where, in theory at least, all Jewish boys were taught the Torah. This development was of great importance in the spread and consolidation of the synagogue, in the birth of Pharisaism as a movement rooted in popular education, and eventually in rise of the rabbinate."
>
> A History of the Jews, p. 106

Further evidence of Pharisaic dominance existed even at the grass roots level, as Roman domination throughout the time of Messiah fanned the flames of hatred:

> "As a result of their high social status the Sadduccees were dominated by political interests, and in these areas they were rigidly conservative, it naturally being in their best interest to maintain the status quo. Maintaining the status quo necessarily entailed collaboration with the Roman occupiers, by whom their powers were delegated, and for this self serving policy the masses despised the Sadduccees."
>
> The International Standard Bible Encyclopedia, p. 279

With this brief survey of the political and historical conditions of the time accomplished, two decisive facts emerge:

First, the Pharisees emphasized Oral Law[248] and its verbal interpretation, thus agreeing with Luke's portrayal of many scriptural positions being discussed in the synagogue. This was also true of the apostle Paul's preaching more than thirty years later, since he debated the Torah with synagogue officials on many occasions, (Acts 23:6). If the Sadduccees had any say in synagogue services, there is no way oral debate would be encouraged as part of the service.

Second, while the time of the emergence of the three-year cycle is unknown, we can be sure it was in place long before the Pharisees arose. Furthermore, their role in preserving this tradition is far sweeping:

> "The Pharisees maintained their leadership in spiritual matters, especially in urban circles. It is true that the Sadduccean high priests stood at the head of the Sanhedrin. But in fact it was the Pharisees, and not the Sadduccees, who made the greatest impact on the ordinary people ... They held the greatest authorities over the congregations, SO

> THAT EVERYTHING TO DO WITH WORSHIP, PRAYERS AND SACRIFICE TOOK PLACE ACCORDING TO THEIR INSTRUCTIONS. Their popularity is said to have been so high that they were listened to even when they criticized the king or the high priest. They were in consequence able to restrain the king."
>
> Emil Schurer, The History of the Jewish People in the Age of Messiah, 175 BC –AD 135, Volume II, p. 402

Since the rabbinate, once again, derived their model from the Pharisees, it is reasonable to conclude that the system they built either harked back to Pharisaic practice, or was part of the core linkage between occasion and Scripture that was approved and continued by them.[249]

Specifically, the Pharisees had a direct say in the liturgy used at all the Great Feasts, at Rosh Hoshanna and Yom Kippur and the monthly blessing of the moon (Rosh Hodesh). Furthermore, with the Book of Esther dated by even the harshest critics as being written no later than 164 BCE, there was little doubt that the Pharisees also sanctioned its reading in connection with Purim, since this itself in proscribed in Scripture, (Esther 9:18-32).

This umbrella construct would then include all of the special occasions under the present system, less the inclusion of the extra books that had been used before.[250] Once again, even though the timing of the use of these texts is uncertain, we do know that the one year model is simply a reduced version of Pharisaic practice, containing these core linkages which survive to this day. Therefore, despite the fact that the additions to the 54 sidrot system have escaped us, we can nevertheless draw from it that same core practice.

In other words, the occasions and Scriptures associated from then to now match. The only question remaining is how much more Scripture from the third *ketuvim* section was applied, not if the Torah-prophet linkages stayed the same, for they clearly did.

This then brings us back to the main point. In addition to being a Sabbath as Luke says, Isaiah could only be read if one of the following conditions were met:[251]

- If the Sabbath were on the Day of Atonement (Yom Kippur), or whenever this holiday falls during the week. As a fast day, Isaiah's poignant comments about what does and does not constitute a proper "affliction" day for God serve as an annual reminder, (Isaiah 57:14-58:14).
- On the Ninth of Av (Tisha B'Av), a fast which commemorates the day on which both Temples were destroyed.
- Other minor fasts such as the Fast of Esther and the Seventeenth of Tammuz also qualify for Isaiah, but again these days must also fall on a Saturday to be the occasion mentioned by Luke, (Isaiah 55:6-56:8).
- If the Sabbath fell on the 8th day of Passover, then Isaiah would be read, (Isaiah 10:32-12:6).
- Any Sabbath that fell on the new moon was blessed by passages from Isaiah, (Isaiah 66:1-24).

This last point deserves some elaboration. As was discussed earlier, the Jewish calendar is made up of 12 moon based months, with an extra "leap" thrown in once every three years to keep the lunar and solar cycles synchronized.

What I did not emphasize then was the fact that each Jewish month *must begin with the sighting of the new moon.* [252] By our reckoning, this sighting would begin on the evening before the first day of the month, and it would also have to happen on a Friday night to be included in the Sabbath time frame. Therefore, the first day of the month had to be a Saturday which would precipitate the reading from Isaiah.

In looking at how these general rules apply to the actual time frame, the entire year of 27 is out of contention. Put simply, not only are Y'shua's activities well accounted for throughout the year, all four Gospels agree that Y'shua did not return to Galilee prior to the

Baptist's imprisonment, which had not happened yet. As for the year 29, that is out too, since Luke is adamant that this event was before the Feeding of the Five Thousand, which happened in April of that year. Additionally, there are no combined Sabbath/holiday occasions taking place either in 29, or even before the final Passover in the year 30.

That leaves only three possible dates, all in the year 28:

> 1 Shevat/ January 15, Sabbath with a new moon.

> Yom Kippur, 10 Tishri/ 16 September—also a weekly (Saturday) Sabbath.

> 1 Heshvan/ 7 October — Sabbath with new moon.

But which one is correct?

The September 16 date can safely be eliminated because it was Yom Kippur, the holiest day on the Jewish calendar. While it is true that only three feasts (Passover, Shavuot, Sukkot) required attendance in Jerusalem, Yom Kippur came only five days before the last required feast, and between the two extensive preparations and purification rites were necessary. We also have to consider that Y'shua's hometown was at least three days' away from Jerusalem, and because Yom Kippur itself was "the Sabbath of Sabbaths", no one would be allowed to travel. Since we know Y'shua kept every feast required of him, it is quite certain that he would go up when everyone else did, and participated also in the Yom Kippur rites that were held in the Temple.

Finally, if it was Yom Kippur being celebrated at the synagogue, it seems very odd that no mention of its importance is made by Luke or that the Jews, however agitated, would attempt murder on the holiest day of the year!

That leaves two occasions, each a Rosh Hodesh, in January and October.

John 4:45, which is clearly linked to this event in Luke, tells us that the Galileans received him openly because, "they saw all the things that he did in Jerusalem at THE FEAST." Such a vague terminology is rare with John, but the logic is easily understood. Up until now John has only mentioned ONE FEAST—Passover, so there was no need to elaborate. However, if the October Rosh Hodesh is the correct one, A SECOND PASSOVER WOULD HAVE ALREADY HAPPENED, and so the comment by John left intact would make little sense in an overall work filled with precise details. Therefore, the only date left is the first Rosh Hodesh, which happened on January 15th.

Fishers of Men 2, (Matthew 4:18-22, Mark 1:16-20)

Then, with the advent of warmer weather, life returns to one of the many fishing villages nestled along the Sea of Galilee. Our first glimpse of these 4 disciples was in Fishers of Men 1 (John 1:35-42). Originally followers of the Baptist, they seek Y'shua out at their own master's bidding. From that time they apparently alternate between Y'shua and John for a simple reason: They cannot see their original master in jail all the time, (Luke 7:18-24).

Now it's a year later and John's followers are once again intrigued with the new rabbi from Nazareth. The feeling, apparently, is mutual, and so Y'shua gives them a formal invitation to follow him. (We will see how this account is different from the one in Luke 5:1-11 a little later on.)

More Healings in Capernaum, followed by "the tour", (Mark 1:23-39, Luke 4:31-44)

A short time later, perhaps as little as a few days, Y'shua and Company return to Capernaum, staying in or around the area of Peter's house. On the next Sabbath, a demon is expelled from the local synagogue. Maybe two hours after that, Peter's mother in law is healed and serves Y'shua lunch. Finally, after dusk, many more are healed as they crowd outside. The very next morning, Y'shua leaves the relative safety of Capernaum to take his message into the wider world.[253]

When we combine the statements in Mark and Luke, what emerges is a tour that:

- Winds its way through almost every major town in Galilee and Judea.
- Has Y'shua teaching in multiple synagogues on multiple Sabbaths.
- Lasts at least six weeks, bringing Y'shua close to Jerusalem for an unrecorded (and therefore, uneventful) Passover (March 20). Some time later this same tour would bring Y'shua back to Jerusalem again, for the Feast of Weeks celebration recorded in John 5:1-47, (May 20th). It is probably also at this time that Y'shua establishes his second base of operations, this time in Martha's house on the outskirts of Jerusalem.[254] (See next section.)

Assuming that Y'shua also follows his well-established pattern, he will most likely return to Galilee after the Feast of Weeks to be with disciples or family, (John 7:1). Then when the last great feast of the year hits, Y'shua will once again be compelled to up to the Holy City to celebrate Tabernacles, and perhaps also participate in the Jewish New Year festivities which directly precede it, (September 8 though 22).

Whether Y'shua stays in the area for another 6 weeks to attend Hanukkah (November 29 through December 7) or retreats again to Galilee in advance of the rainy season, cannot be determined from the available information.

The Nature of the Feast, or, What was "the Feast of Jews", (John 5:1-47)?

Perhaps the most difficult issue to deal with however is the identification of the "Feast of the Jews" in John 5:1. Traditionally, this occasion has been viewed as a Passover feast. However, several internal textual factors appear to argue against this conclusion.

First of all, John appears to have a very precise and detail-oriented writing style, as evidenced by the fact that he pays far more attention to Jewish holidays and customs than any other Gospel writer. As a Jew himself, John knows all too well that the most important feast of the year is, by far, Passover, and that is also why he lists the holiday BY NAME five times, (2:13, 6:4, 12:1, 13:1, 18:28). Of these, the first three of those citations are obviously separate holidays themselves. Therefore, John shows his reverence for the holiday by always including its title.

John also shows respect by including the names of other feasts as well such as Sukkot (7:2) and even the minor holiday of Hanukkah (10:22). How odd then that this same careful writer would exclude mentioning Passover when he seemed so determined to record it everywhere else!

Another issue has to do with the environment mentioned in the verse. Throngs of disabled people are waiting to dive into a huge pool because a legend promises them a miracle. However, the weather during the early Spring was still chilly enough as to make this unlikely as a Passover. Another main feast, Sukkot, had both aspects against it, since it is mentioned by name elsewhere (John 7:2) and also happens too late in the year, September-October, with the rainy season hard on its heels. A minor feast, Purim, is also eliminated both for reasons of weather and because it never starts on Sabbath, which this clearly was, (John 5:10,17).

The "multitudes" mentioned in 5:3 also impacts our study in another way. Most likely, the feast was of major importance to attract such a large crowd of people to Jerusalem. Certainly, no minor feast would have had the legendary "angel healings" believed to happen at the actual pool. When we combine this data with the fact that it has to take place during the late spring or early summer months, only one candidate remains:

"Eliashib the high priest and his fellow priests went

> to work and rebuilt the Sheep Gate. They dedicated it and set its doors in place."
>
> Nehemiah 3:1

Not only is this Sheep Gate the same one mentioned by the evangelist in John 5:2, it also was part of the overall structure of Jerusalem's walls, and the day it was rebuilt and dedicated is linked to "the Feast of the Jews" this way:

> "And on that day they offered great sacrifices, rejoicing because God had given them great joy. The women and children also rejoiced. The sound of rejoicing in Jerusalem could be heard far away. At that time the men were appointed to be in charge of the firstfruits and tithes. From the fields around the towns they were to bring into the storerooms the portions required by the Law for the priests and Levites."
>
> Nehemiah 12:42-44

From this description then there can be no doubt. The occasion that Nehemiah is referring to must be Shavuot, otherwise known as the Feast of Weeks, since it is only at that time firstfruits are brought up for the priests and Levites.[255] Furthermore, Jewish tradition also tells us that one of the days during this feast, 6 Sivan, is the day Moses received the Ten Commandments. Having all these other events then coincide with the rebuilding of the actual Gate and Pool certainly would also explain why the people thought God blessed that day and ordained miracles on it. Finally, since Shavuot lasts eight days, the healing of the paralytic must have happened on the Saturday encompassed by the occasion.

The only remaining issue then is to figure out the year, and that is relatively simple. John tells us that the feast is before the Feeding of the Five Thousand, the latter event being clearly linked to the second to last Passover in the year 29. Similarly, the year 27 Passover is covered in his second chapter. Then, as was stated earlier, John 4:35 clearly indicates that a winter has taken place between that Passover and this occasion, with Y'shua spending 8 months outside of Jerusalem. Therefore, the only place this feast can possibly fit is in the year 28. Once that is established, we can then state with certainty that the proper date for the healing is on the only Saturday within that feast, or May 20th.

On a final note, it also seems to be the case that John is not mentioning one Passover observance directly. Apparently, this occasion, also in 28, was not witnessed by any of the disciples, and this actually lends credence to the scenario that they did not follow Y'shua full time at that juncture. To be sure, they did travel with him quite extensively, but still kept to their own business, as Mark 1:17 shows. When Y'shua then says "Follow me", it is precisely because he wants that higher commitment from them. On the other hand, Luke's story which is obviously happening later (5:1-11), does not contain this phrase, because all the evidence shows that they were following him already, (5:8).

Without that full time commitment, the most likely scenario is that, just as Luke 2:41 says, that Y'shua went up to that Passover in Jerusalem with his family only. By contrast, John 2:13 has some of Y'shua's disciples tag along because they were all conveniently present at the Cana wedding. However, in the absence of such serendipity, it would appear that going up by family line was the prevalent custom of the day.

The last point then is simply to state that John could only have gained insights into how Y'shua dealt with his family prior to Sukkot (7:1-11) if members of Y'shua's family had told him directly, especially his mother, (John 19:27). Therefore, the evidence most clearly shows that the only reason John did not record this holiday is because either he was not privy to it or because it had gone off without incident. By contrast, the Passovers in 2:13-25, 6:4, and 18:28 were either marked with great controversy or happened around the time of a spectacular miracle, which may explain why the "normal" Passover was assumed to have happened but not singled out directly in writing.

Gospel Harmony #3: Fishers of Men 2 and related events in the year 28

> (NOTE: "Fishers of Men 1" is the incident in John 1:35-42, and "Fishers of Men 3" is Luke 5:1-11. Additionally there is a "Fishers of Men 4" right at the end of John's Gospel.)

Fishers of Men 2, early Spring
(Matthew 4:18-22, Mark 1:16-20)

As Y'shua was walking beside the Sea of Galilee, he saw two brothers, Simon called Peter and his brother Andrew. They were casting a net into the lake, for they were fishermen. "Come follow me," Y'shua said, "and I will make you fishers of men." At once they left their nets and followed him.

Going on from there, he saw two other brothers, James son of Zawdee[256] and his brother John. They were in a boat with their father, Zawdee, preparing their nets. Without delay, Y'shua called them, and they left their father Zawdee in the boat with the hired men and followed him.

Capernaum Demon, Saturday, early Spring (of 28)
(Mark 1:21-28 = Luke 4:31-37)

They went to Capernaum, and when the Sabbath came, Y'shua went into the synagogue and began to preach. The people were amazed at his teaching, because he taught as one who had authority, not as the teachers of the law. Just then a man in the synagogue who was possessed by an evil spirit cried out, "What do you want with us,

Y'shua of Nazareth? Have you come to destroy us? I know who you are—the Holy One of God!"

"Be quiet!" said Y'shua sternly. "Come out of him!" The evil spirit shook the man violently and came out of him with a shriek.

The people were so amazed that they asked each other, "What is this? A new teaching — and with authority! He even gives orders to evil spirits and they obey him." News about him spread quickly over the whole region of Galilee.

(Luke 4:38-39)
Y'shua left the synagogue and went to the home of Simon. Now Simon's mother-in-law was suffering from a high fever, and they asked Y'shua to help her. So he bent over her,

(Mark 1:31)
took her hand and helped her up,

(Luke 4:40-41)
rebuking her fever (which) left her. She got up at once and began to wait on them.

When the sun was setting, the people brought to Y'shua all who had various kinds of sickness, and laying hands on each one, he healed them. Moreover, demons came out of many people shouting, "You are the Son of God!" But he rebuked them and would not allow them to speak, because they knew he was the Messiah.

The Great Tour Begins the Next Day, from early Spring to about May 16
(Mark 1:35-38)
Very early in the morning, while it was still dark, Y'shua got up, left the house and went off to a solitary place, where he prayed. Simon and his companions went to look for him, and when they found him, they exclaimed, "Everyone is looking for you!"
Y'shua replied, "Let us go somewhere else, to the nearby villages, so I can preach there also. That is why I have come."

(Luke 1:42-44)
(But) they tried to keep him from leaving them so (he insisted), saying: "I must preach the good news of the kingdom of God to the other towns also, because that is why I was sent."

(Mark 1:39)
So he traveled throughout Galilee, preaching in their synagogues and driving out demons,

(Luke 4:44)
(even going throughout) Judea (to do so).

(Matthew 4:23—24)
(Then) Y'shua went throughout Galilee, teaching in their synagogues, preaching the good news of the kingdom, and healing every disease and sickness among the people. News about him spread all over Syria, and people brought to him all who were ill with various diseases, those suffering severe pain, the demon possessed, the epileptics and the paralytics, and he healed them.

"I am willing" leper part 1
(Mark 1:40-45)
While he was in one of (these) towns, a man with leprosy came and knelt before him and said, "Lord, if you are willing, you can make me clean."
Y'shua reached out his hand and touched the man. "I am willing," he said. "Be clean!" Immediately he was cured of his leprosy. Then Y'shua said to him, "See that you don't tell anyone. But go, show yourself to the priest and offer the gift Moses commanded, as a testimony to them."
Instead he went out and began to talk freely, spreading the news.

May 20, Arise Pick Up Your Bed and Walk 1
(John 5:1-45)

Some time later, Y'shua went up to Jerusalem for (Shavuot), a feast of the Jews. Now there is in Jerusalem near the Sheep Gate a pool, which in Aramaic is called Bethesda and which is surrounded by five covered colonnades. Here a great number of disabled people used to lie — the blind, the lame, the paralyzed — and they waited for the moving of the water. (From time to time an angel of the Lord would come down and stir the waters. The first one into the pool after each such disturbance would be cured of whatever disease he had.)

One who was there had been an invalid for thirty-eight years. When Y'shua saw him lying there and learned that he had been in this condition for a long time, he asked him, "Do you want to get well?"

"Sir," the invalid replied, "I have no one to help me into the pool when the water is stirred. While I am trying to get in, someone else goes down ahead of me."

Then Y'shua said to him, "Get up! Pick up your mat and walk." At once the man was cured; he picked up his mat and walked. The day on which this took place was a Sabbath, (Saturday, April 1), and so the Jews said to the man who had been healed, "It is the Sabbath; the law forbids you to carry your mat."

But he replied, "The man who made me well said to me, 'Pick up your mat and walk.'"

So they asked him, "Who is this fellow who told you to pick it up and walk?"

The man who was healed had no idea who it was, for Y'shua had slipped away into the crowd that was there.

Later Y'shua found him at the Temple and said to him, "See, you are well again. Stop sinning or something worse may happen to you." The man went away and told the Jews it was Y'shua who made him well.

So, because Y'shua was doing these things on the Sabbath, the Jews persecuted him. Y'shua said to them, "My Father is always at his work to this very day, and I, too, am working." For this reason the Jews tried all the harder to kill him; not only was he breaking the Sabbath, but he was even calling God his own Father, making himself equal with God.

Y'shua gave them this answer: "I tell you the truth, the Son can do nothing by himself; he can do only what he sees his Father doing, because whatever the Father does the Son also does. For the Father loves the Son and shows him all he does. Yes, to tour amazement he will show him even greater things than these. For just as the Father raises the dead and gives them life, even so the Son gives life to whom he is pleased to give it. Moreover, the Father judges no one, but has entrusted all judgment to the Son, that they may honor the Son just as they honor the Father. He who does not honor the Son does not honor the Father who sent him.

"I tell you the truth, whoever hears my word and believes him who sent me has eternal life and will not be condemned; he has crossed over from death to life. I tell you the truth, a time is coming and has now come when the dead will hear the voice of the Son of God and those who hear will live. For as the Father has life in himself, so he has granted the Son to have life in himself. And he has given him the authority to judge because he is the Son of Man.

"Do not be amazed at this, for a time is coming when all who are in their graves will hear his voice and come out—those who have done good will rise to live, and those who have done evil will rise to be condemned. By myself I can do nothing; I judge only as I hear, and my judgment is just, for I seek not to please myself but him who sent me.

"If I testify about myself, my testimony is not valid. There is another who testifies in my favor, and I know that his testimony about me is valid. You have sent to John and he has testified to the truth. Not that I accept human testimony; but I mention it that you may be saved. John was lamp that burned and gave light, and you chose for a time to enjoy his light.

"I have testimony weightier than that of John. For the very work that the Father has given me to finish, and which I am doing, testifies that the Father has sent me. And the Father who sent me has himself testified concerning me. You have never heard his voice nor seen his form, nor does his word dwell in you for you do not believe the one he sent. You diligently study the Scriptures because you think that by them you posses eternal life. These are the Scriptures which testify about me, yet you refuse to come to me to have life.

"I do not accept praise from men, but I know you. I know that you do not have the love of God in your hearts. I have come in my Father's name, and you do not accept me; but if someone else comes in his own name, you will accept him. How can you believe if you accept praise from one another, yet make no effort to obtain the praise that comes from God?

"But do not think I will accuse you before the Father. Your accuser is Moses, on whom your hopes are set. If you believed Moses, you would believe me, for he wrote about me. But since you do not believe what he wrote, how are you going to believe what I say?"

January 1-April 14, 29

The Three Week Blitz

From here John gives us an ending marker of Passover, April 14, which is the Saturday after the multitudes were fed. This then gives us a window of only three weeks.

However during this same period, the following Sabbath events are recorded:

- Y'shua and the disciples pick grain, and this time of year is confirmed by the fact that grain blooms no earlier than March and is harvested no later than June. Also the *Sermon on the Mount* happens around this same time and there Y'shua points to another harbinger of spring: The blooming of the lilies of the field, (Matthew 6:28). An additional seasonal marker is found in Luke 5:1-11, where the weather is sufficiently warm enough to have fishermen stay out all night for a catch.[257]

- On another Sabbath (Luke 6:6-11), Y'shua enters into a Galilean synagogue and heals a man with a shriveled hand.

- Later, after he returns home, Y'shua is once again rejected in the Nazareth synagogue, (*Prophet Without Honor 2*, Matthew 13:53-58, Mark 6:1-6).
- The Passover, which Y'shua must celebrate in Jerusalem (Deuteronomy 16:5) happens also on a Sabbath, April 14. [258] With four Sabbaths (March 24, 31 and April 7, 14) happening in just three weeks, it is not hard to see why many events in this period are recovered to the actual day.[259]

Sermons and Lepers

Perhaps one of the most difficult things to harmonize are two versions of very similar teachings, (Matthew 5:1-7:28; Luke 6:17-49). Many scholars have tried to combine them. However, while this is tempting, specifics in Matthew and Luke prevent this from happening.

Matthew tells us Y'shua was forced *up* a mountain due to pressing crowds and gave these teachings sitting down. Luke tells us Y'shua gave these teachings going *down* to a plain, where he stood up. These are clearly two different places, but did they happen at different times?

For a long time, I thought the answer was no, and had concocted numerous scenarios to explain how Y'shua could have given the Plain Sermon first, been pushed up the mountain by the crowds, taught some more, etc. At the heart of my confusion were three versions of Y'shua healing a leper with the words "I am willing," (Matthew 8:1-4, Mark 1:40-45, Luke 5:12-14).

Matthew appeared to have the advantage, telling us plainly that this leper was healed moments after the long discourse. Mark and Luke however, were more vague, and appeared to agree more with each other than Matthew. They then placed the healing as part of a tour Y'shua made throughout Galilee and Judea, which was definitely BEFORE the Sermon, (Matthew 4:23-25, Mark 1:40-45, Luke 4:44). So, even though my previous harmonization attempts effectively clustered these two great Sermons together with this healing, the resulting problems made the rest of the chronology unworkable.[260]

In the end, there was only one solution which maintained the integrity of the Gospel record, and that was to say that these were two separate lepers.[261] The first one (Mark and Luke) happened during the preaching tour in 28. The second one (Matthew) was a little more than a year later, after the *Sermon on the Mount*. As for Luke's *Sermon on the Plain*, it happens about three days later, after a brief preaching circuit through other local towns.

Minor Problems in Matthew

Additionally, on two occasions, Matthew combines events that are treated as separate in Mark and Luke. The first time is when he pushes together the calling and sending out of the apostles, (Matthew 10:1-43, Mark 3:13-30, 6:7-13, Luke 6:12-17, 9:1-6). The second is when the Grainfields and Withered Hand Sabbaths appear to be linked, but may not be due to the vagueness of his word choices, (Matthew 12:1-14, Mark 2:23-3:6, Luke 6:1-11). None of this is meant to imply of course that Matthew is "wrong". Rather, it is simply a result of different writing styles.

Finally, a brief word should be said regarding the one time when all the Gospels fail to bring up a conclusive date. While the Grainfields and Withered Hand Sabbaths are securely linked to the general time frame of Spring in the year 29, the universal vagueness of Matthew, Mark and Luke make it impossible to determine the exact order with any more precision. In other words, I had to take a guess.

Fishers of Men 3, (Luke 5:1-11)

The next critical event is known as *Fishers of Men 3*, (Luke 5:1-11). In the past many have harmonized this event with similar ones mentioned in Matthew and Mark. However, the differences and details presented in Luke are so profound that this cannot be the case:
- Luke's version happens after the Capernaum Demon is exorcised, whereas Mark, filling in Matthew's details, puts this prior to that same event, (Mark 1:14-20).

- There are certain people present at one event who are not mentioned at the others, (Mark 1:14-20, Luke 5:8-10).
- In one version the fishermen leave their boats at the dock near their home, in another they put out for deep water and land further away, (Mark 1:20, Luke 5:4).

Finally, and most important of all, notice that Y'shua doesn't say "Follow me" in Luke's version BECAUSE THEY ALREADY ARE FOLLOWING WITH PETER CALLING HIM 'MASTER'!

What Y'shua does tell them is "Now you will catch men" as opposed to the other occasion where this is in the future tense: *You will catch men.*

Finally, the last critical fact about this event is that it is the same occasion as *Sower Part 1*. This was not an easy determination to make because, unfortunately, Luke chooses to "bookend" this event between two vague constructs. By that I mean that the end of chapter 4 details a long preaching tour and is followed immediately by 5:1 which only tells us this happened "one day". On the other side of time, this event ends with 5:12, when we are told a healing happens "while Y'shua was in one of the towns".

However, right after the vague start we are given the key to the whole problem:

> "... as Y'shua was standing by the lake of Genessaret, with the people crowding around him and listening to the word of God, he saw at the water's edge two boats. He got into one of the boats, the one belonging to Simon, and asked him to put out a little from the shore. Then he sat down and taught the people from the boat. When he had finished speaking he said to Simon, 'Put out for deep water and let the nets down for a catch.'"
>
> Luke 5:1-4

This discourse that Y'shua delivers first in shallow and then in deeper water is none other than *Sower Part 1*. The details between Luke 5:1-4, Mark 4:1 and Matthew 13:1 demand this unification.

The "Lost Sermon"
(or How Luke Loses Two Chapters and Gives Them to Matthew)

There is one other difficulty with the Sermons in Matthew and Luke, and the chronological ramifications ripple out to effect the strongest anchor we have: *The Universal Event.*

As stated before, the Feeding of the 5,000 is one of the few events that appear in all four Gospels along the same rough time line. For 95% of the events in the Gospels, this dividing line works perfectly. However, even the best rules sometimes need an exception.

The problem arises at the end of Luke 10. It is at that point that Y'shua is in Bethany visiting Martha and Mary and a sibling dispute is resolved. However, there is absolutely no temporal linkage given from there to the opening statement of chapter 11. In fact, Luke 11:1 contains the most vague introduction of any event in any Gospel:

"One day when Y'shua was praying in a certain place..."

Now Matthew 8's attack of the word "when" may have created all sorts of difficulties, but at least he was good enough to tell us *where* these events were happening! Luke doesn't even give us that. We are completely devoid of either geographical or temporal clues. And yet, this discourse has to fit somewhere, doesn't it?

The answer comes from the few textual clues Luke does give us for both this and the following chapter[262]. According to Luke, on one occasion, time and place unknown, a disciple asks Y'shua a very basic question: How should we pray?

Knowing this, it seems extremely unlikely that a disciple would need to ask Y'shua this question twice, and this is how we can fit this section back into its proper place.

The only other time that Y'shua says this prayer is during the Sermon on the Mount, in Matthew! The parallels don't stop there either. We find whole sections of word for word Sermon teachings between Matthew 6-7 and Luke 11-12, just in a slightly different order. We also find other long sections in Luke which could easily serve as introductions for identical sections in Matthew.

For example, almost verbatim teachings are recorded in Matthew 6:25-34 and Luke 12:22-34. However, the long introduction in Luke 12:1-21 also serves as prelude to Matthew 6:25. Then, after Matthew 6:34, Luke 12:35-13:9 very easily snaps into place as closing remarks and events immediately following.

Nor is that even the extent of the concordance. These same long pieces in Luke 11-12 very clearly have expanded teachings and applications omitted by Matthew (comp. Matthew 6:5-15 and Luke 11:1-8)! Right after this Luke 11:9-13 is a perfect match to Matthew 7:7-12. So the question is, what is going on here?

Well, we know that the Mount and Plain Sermons are separate events with similar teachings, but what this analysis also shows is that Luke (and his teacher, Paul) were aware of Matthew's Sermon, but were not sure where to put it since neither was an eyewitness. Therefore Luke does the next best thing: He makes an educated guess.

So where does this leave us? The evidence presented strongly suggests, if not proves, that portions of Luke 11 and 12[263] must be moved and linked with Matthew 5-8 and Matthew 12:22-50. THIS IS THE ONLY TIME WHEN MATERIAL LISTED ON ONE SIDE OF THE UNIVERSAL LINE HAS TO MOVE OVER TO THE OTHER.

Specifically, the order for linking the two parts of the Sermon on the Mount is:

- Introduction—Matthew 5:1-48.
- Prayer Discourse—Matthew 6:1-15, expanded teaching Luke 11:1-8.
- Fasting and Treasures in Heaven—Matthew 6:16-24.
- Do Not Worry Discourse—Introduction (Luke 12:1-21), Main Teaching (Matthew 6:25-34 = Luke 12:22-34), Ending Comments/Surrounding Events (Luke 12:35-13:9).
- Ask, Seek, Knock—Matthew 7:7-12 = Luke 11:9-13.

- Summary Teachings and Conclusion, Matthew 7:13-28.

The only other portion to account for then is Luke 11:14-54 (Sign of Jonah, Lamp Teaching, Various Woes). They each link up (and in effect disappear from Luke chronologically speaking) with their counterparts in Matthew, thusly:
- Luke 11:14-28 merges with Matthew 12:22-37.
- Luke 11:29-32 merges with Matthew 12:38-45.
- Luke 11:33-36 merges with Matthew 5:13-16.
- Luke 11:37-54 is an event only found here, but it moves to after Matthew 12:50 but before 13:1.

Finally, just to close out this section properly, we must deal with Matthew 13:1-52. Here the evangelist is very clear that Y'shua preached his famous *Sower* parable later that day. This teaching must then be combined with Mark 4:1-41 as well as Matthew 8:23-34 and, lastly with another non-linear placement, Luke 8:1-56. A careful reading of all these passages will show a clear harmony and temporal relationship between them.

In closing out this section let me just say that this is by far the most difficult period of the Gospels to recover. It for this reason that I have spent the most time on it detailing the various "traps". Now that it is over, we can heave a collective sigh of relief and move forward.

Now, on Thursday, March 22nd, Y'shua delivered his most important teachings with the "Sermon on the Mount", the complete version of which is below:

Gospel Harmony #4: The Full Sermon:

Sermon on the Mount Part 1, (probably) Thursday, March 22

Matthew 4:25-6:4)
(Now the) large crowds from Galilee, the Decapolis, Jerusalem, Judea and the region across the Jordan followed him. When he saw the crowds, he went up the mountainside and sat down. His disciples came to him, and he began to teach them saying:

"Blessed are the poor in spirit, for theirs is the kingdom of heaven.

Blessed are those who mourn, for they will be comforted.

Blessed are the meek, for they will inherit the earth.

Blessed are those who hunger and thirst for righteousness, for they will be filled.

Blessed are the merciful, for they will be shown mercy.

Blessed are the pure of heart, for they will see God.

Blessed are the peacemakers, for they will be called the sons of God.

Blessed are those who are persecuted because of righteousness, for theirs is the kingdom of heaven.

Blessed are you when people insult you, persecute you and falsely say all kinds of evil against you because of me. Rejoice and be glad, because great is your reward in heaven, for in the same way they persecuted the prophets who were before you.

"You are the salt of the earth. But if the salt loses its saltiness, how can it be made salty again? It is no longer good for anything, except to be thrown out and trampled by men.

"You are the light of the world. A city on a hill cannot be hidden. Neither do people light a lamp and put it under a bowl. Instead they put it on its stand, and it gives light to everyone in the house. In the same way, let your light shine before men, that they may see your good deeds and praise your Father in heaven.

"Do not think I have come to abolish the Law or the Prophets; I have come not to abolish them but to fulfill them. I tell you the truth, until heaven and earth disappear, not the smallest letter, not the least stroke of a pen, will by any means disappear from the Law until all is accomplished. Anyone who breaks one of the least of these commandments and teaches others to do the same will be called least in the kingdom of heaven, but whoever practices and teaches these commands will be called great in the kingdom of heaven. For I tell you that unless your righteousness surpasses that of the Pharisees and the teachers of the Law, you will certainly not enter the kingdom of heaven.

"You have heard that it was said to the people long ago, 'Do not murder, and anyone who murders will be subject to judgment.' But I tell you that anyone who is angry with his brother will be subject to judgment. Again, anyone who says to his brother "Raca (Aramaic: "I spit on you!") is answerable to the Sanhedrin. But anyone who says, 'You fool!' will be in danger of the fire of hell.

"Therefore, if you are offering your gift at the altar and there remember that your brother has something against you, leave your gift there in front of the altar. First go and be reconciled to your brother; then come offer your gift.

"Settle matters quickly with your adversary who is taking you to court. Do it while you are still with him on the way, or he may hand you over to the judge, and the judge may hand you over to the officer, and you may be thrown into prison. I tell you the truth, you will not get out until you have paid the last penny.

"You have heard that it was said, 'Do not commit adultery.' But I tell you that anyone who looks at a woman lustfully has already committed adultery with her in his heart. If your right eye causes you to sin, gouge it out and throw it away. (Aramaic phrase: Remove sinful visions from your eyes or you will be condemned.). It is better to lose one part of your body than for your whole body to be thrown into hell. And if your right hand causes you to sin, cut it off and throw it away. It is better for you to lose one part of your body than for your whole body to go into hell.

"It has been said, 'Anyone who divorces his wife must give her a certificate of divorce.' But I tell you that anyone who divorces his wife, except for marital unfaithfulness, causes her to commit adultery, and anyone who marries a woman so divorced commits adultery.

"Again you have heard it said to the people long ago, 'Do not break your oath, but keep oaths you have made to the Lord.' But I tell you, Do not swear at all: Either by heaven for it is God's throne; nor by the earth, for it is his footstool; nor by Jerusalem, for it is the city of the Great King. And do not swear by your head, for you cannot make one hair white or black. Simply let your 'yes' be 'yes' and your 'no' be 'no'; anything beyond this comes from the evil one.

"You have heard that it was said, 'Eye for eye, tooth for tooth.' But I tell you, Do not resist an evil person. If someone strikes you on the cheek, turn to him the other also. And if someone wants to sue you and take your tunic, let him have your cloak as well. If someone forces you to go one mile, go with him two miles. Give to the one who asks you, and do not turn away from the one who wants to borrow from you."

"He causes the sun to rise on the evil and the good, and sends rain on the righteous and unrighteous. (Again), if you love those who love you, what reward will you get? Are not even tax collectors doing that? And if you greet only your brothers, what are you doing more than others? Do not even pagans do that? Be perfect, therefore, as your heavenly Father is perfect.

"Be careful not to do your 'acts of righteousness' before men, to be seen by them. If you do, you will have no reward from your Father in heaven.

"So when you give to the needy, do not announce it with trumpets, as the hypocrites do in the synagogues and on the streets, to be honored by men. I tell you the truth, they have received their reward in full. But when you give to the needy, do not let your left hand know what your right hand is doing, so that your giving may be in secret. Then your Father, who sees what is done in secret, will reward you.

(Luke 11:1-2)

(Then Y'shua began to pray). When he finished, one of his disciples said to him, "Lord, teach us to pray, just as John taught his disciples."

He said to them, "When you pray,

(Matthew 6:5b-9)

do not be like the hypocrites, for they love to pray standing in the synagogues and on the street corners to be seen by men. I tell you the truth, they have received their reward in full. But when you pray, go into your room, close the door and pray to your Father who is unseen. Then your Father, who sees what is done in secret, will reward you. And when you pray, do not keep on babbling like pagans, for they think they will be heard because of their many words. Do not be like them, for your Father knows what you need before you ask him.

"This is how you should pray:

(Matthew 6:9b-15 = Luke 11:2b-4)
"Our Father in heaven, holy be Your name,
Your kingdom comes,
Your will be done,
As I heaven, so on earth.
Give us this day our daily bread.
Forgive our debts, as we also have forgiven our debtors.
And lead us not into temptation, but deliver us from the evil one.
For Yours is the kingdom, and the power, and the glory,
Forever. Amen.

"For if you forgive men when they sin against you, your heavenly Father will also forgive you. But if you do not forgive men their sins, your Father will not forgive your sins."

(Luke 11:5-8)
Then he said to them, "Suppose one of you has a friend and he goes to him at midnight and says, 'Friend, lend me three loaves of bread, because a friend of mine on a journey has come to me, and I have nothing to set before him.'

Then the one on the inside answers, 'Don't bother me. The door is already locked, and my children are with me in bed. I can't get up and give you anything.' I tell you, though he will not get up to give him the bread because he is his friend, yet because of the man's persistence he will get up and give him as much as he needs."

Signs of the Cross: The Search for the Historical Jesus

(Matthew 6:16-18)

"When you fast, do not look somber as the hypocrites do, for they disfigure their faces to show they are fasting. I tell you the truth, they have received their reward in full. But when you fast, put oil on your head and wash your face, so that it will not be obvious to men that you are fasting, but only to your Father, who is unseen; and your Father, who sees what is done in secret, will reward you.

(Matthew 6:19-20)

"Do not store up for yourselves treasures on earth where moth and rust destroy, and where thieves break in and steal. But store up for yourselves treasures in heaven, where moth and rust do not destroy, and where thieves do not break in and steal.

(Matthew 6:19-21 = Luke 12:22-25)

"Therefore I tell you, do not worry about your life, what you will eat or drink; or about your body, what you will wear. Is not life more important than food, and the body more important than clothes? Look at the (ravens—Luke 12:24) (and other) birds of the air; they do not sow or reap or store away in barns, yet your heavenly Father feeds them. Are you not much more valuable than they? Who of you by worrying can add one single hour to your life?

(Luke 12:26)

Since you cannot do this very little thing, why do you worry about the rest?

(Matthew 6:28-34)

"And why do you worry about clothes? See the lilies of the field grow. They do not labor or spin. Yet I tell you not even Solomon in all his splendor was dressed like one of these. If that is how God clothes the grass of the field, which here today and tomorrow is thrown into the fire, will he not much more clothe you? O you of little faith! So do not worry, saying, 'What shall we eat?' or 'What shall we drink?' or

'What shall we wear?' For the pagans run after all these things, and your heavenly Father knows that you need them.

"But seek first his kingdom and his righteousness, and all these things will be given to you as well. Therefore do not worry about tomorrow, for tomorrow will worry about itself. Each day has enough trouble of its own.

(Luke 12:32-33)

Do not be afraid, little flock, for your Father has been pleased to give you the kingdom. Sell your possessions and give to the poor. Provide purses for yourselves that will not wear out, a treasure in heaven that will not be exhausted, where no thief comes near and no moth destroys.

(Matthew 6:21 = Luke 12:34)

For where your treasure is, there your heart will be also.

(Matthew 6:22-23 = Luke 11:33-36)

(As I said before,) no one lights a lamp and puts it in a place that will be hidden, or under a bowl. Instead he puts it on a stand, so that those who come in may see the light. Your eye is the lamp of the body. When your eyes are good, you whole body also is full of light. But when they are bad, your whole body is full of darkness. If then the light within you is darkness, how great is that darkness! See to it then the light within you is not darkness. Therefore, if your whole body is full of light and no part of it is dark, it will be completely lighted, as when a lamp shines on you.

(Matthew 7:1-6)

"Do not judge, or you too will be judged.

"Do not condemn, and you will not be condemned. Forgive, and you will be forgiven. Give, and it will be given to you. A good measure, pressed down, shaken together and running over, will be poured into your lap. For with the measure you use, it will be measured to you."

He also told them this parable: "Can a blind man lead a blind man? Will they not both fall into a pit? A student is not above his teacher, but everyone who is fully trained will be like his teacher.

"Why do you look at the speck of sawdust in your brother's eye and pay no attention to the plank in your own eye? How can you say to your brother, 'Let me take out the speck out of your eye,' when all the time there is a plank in your own eye? You hypocrite! First take the plank out of your own eye, and then you will see clearly to remove the speck from your brother's eye.

"Do not give to dogs that which is sacred; do not throw your pearls before pigs. If you do, they may trample them under your feet, and then turn and tear you to pieces.

(Matthew 7:7-16 = Luke 11:9-13)

"Ask and it will be given to you. Seek and you will find. Knock and the door will be opened to you. For everyone who asks, receives; he who seeks finds; and to him who knocks, the door will be opened.

"Which of you, if his son asks for bread, will give him a stone? Or if he asks for a fish, will you give him a snake? (How about) an egg? (Will you then) give him a scorpion? If you, then, though you are evil, know how to give good gifts to your children, how much more will your Father in heaven give good gifts to those who ask him? In everything, do to others what you would have them do to you, for this sums up the Law and the Prophets.

"Enter through the narrow gate. For the wide is the gate and broad is the road that leads to destruction, and many enter through it. But small is the gate and narrow the road that leads to life, and only a few find it.

"Watch out for false prophets. They come to you in sheep's clothing, but inwardly they are ferocious wolves. By their fruit you will recognize them. Do people pick grapes from thornbushes, or figs from thistles?

(Matthew 7:17-27)

"Likewise every good tree bears good fruit, but a bad tree bears bad fruit. A good tree cannot bear bad fruit, and a bad tree cannot bear good fruit. Every tree that does not bear good fruit is cut down and thrown into the fire. Thus, by their fruit you will recognize them.

"Not everyone who says to me, 'Lord, Lord,' will enter the kingdom of heaven, but only he who does the will of my Father who is in heaven. Many will say to me on that day, 'Lord, Lord, did we not prophesy in your name and in your name drive out demons and perform many miracles? Then I will tell them plainly, "I never knew you. Away from me, you evildoers!'

"Therefore, I will show you what he is like who comes to me and hears my words and puts them into practice. He is like a wise man building a house, who dug deep and laid the foundation on rock. The rain came down, the streams rose and the winds beat and blew against that house, but the torrent (that) struck the house could not shake it, because it was well built. But the one who hears my words and does not put them into practice is like a man who built a house on the sandy ground without a foundation. The rain came down, the streams rose, and the winds beat against that house, and the moment the torrent struck (it), it collapsed with a loud crash, fell, and its destruction was complete."

Sermon Break: I am willing leper 2, a few minutes after above event (Matthew 8:1-4)

When he came down from the mountainside, large crowds followed him. A man with leprosy came and knelt before him and said, "Lord, if you are willing, you can make me clean."

Y'shua reached out his hand and touched the man. "I am willing," he said. "Be clean!" Immediately he was cured of his leprosy. Then Y'shua said to him, "See that you don't tell anyone. But go, show yourself to the priest and offer the gift Moses commanded, as a testimony to them."

Instead he went out and began to talk freely, spreading the news.

(Later on), as a result, Y'shua could no longer enter a town but stayed in lonely places. Yet people still came to him from everywhere.

(Sermon Break Continues): Lunch Break at a Pharisee's house
(Luke 11:37-53)

(Meanwhile), when Y'shua had finished speaking, a Pharisee invited him to eat with him; so he went in and reclined at the table. But the Pharisee, noticing that Y'shua did not first wash before the meal, was surprised.

Then the Lord said to him, "Now then, you Pharisees clean the outside of the cup and dish, but inside you are full of greed and wickedness. You foolish people! Did not the one who made the outside make the inside also? But give what is inside the dish to the poor, and everything will be clean for you.

"Woe to you Pharisees, because you give God a tenth of your mint, rue and all other kinds of garden herbs, but you neglect justice and the love of God. You should have practiced the latter without leaving the former undone.

"Woe to you Pharisees, because you love the most important seats in the synagogues and greetings in the marketplaces.

"Woe to you, because you are like unmarked graves, which men walk over without knowing it."

One of the experts in the law answered him, "Teacher, when you say these things, you insult us also."

Y'shua replied, "And you experts in the law, woe to you, because you load people down with burdens they can hardly carry, and you yourselves will not lift one finger to help them. Woe to you because you build tombs for the prophets, and it was your forefathers that killed them. So you testify that you approve of what your fathers did; they killed the prophets, and you build their tombs. Because of this, God in his wisdom said, 'I will send them prophets and apostles, some of whom they will kill, some of whom they will persecute.' Therefore this generation will be held responsible for the blood of all the prophets that have been shed since the beginning of the world, from the blood of Abel to the blood of Zechariah, who was killed between the altar and the sanctuary. Yes, I tell you, this generation will be held responsible for it all.

"Woe to you experts in the law, because you have taken away the key to knowledge. You yourselves have not entered, and you have hindered those who were entering."

When Y'shua left there, the Pharisees and the teachers of the law began to oppose him fiercely and to besiege him with questions, waiting to catch him in something he might say.

Sermon on the Mount Part 2, a few minutes after the above event.
(Luke 12:1-13:9)

Meanwhile, when (another) crowd (continued gathering), so that they were trampling on one another, Y'shua began to speak first to his disciples, saying: "Be on your guard against the yeast of the Pharisees, which is hypocrisy. There is nothing concealed which will not be disclosed, or hidden that will not be made known. What you have said in the dark will be heard in the daylight, and what you have whispered in the ear in the inner rooms will be proclaimed from the housetops.

"I tell you, my friends, do not be afraid of those who kill the body and after that can do no more. But I will show you whom you should fear: Fear him who, after killing the body, has the power to throw you into hell. Yes, I tell you, fear him. Are not five sparrows sold for two pennies? Yet not one of them is forgotten by God. Indeed, the very hairs of your head are all numbered. Don't be afraid; you are worth more than many sparrows.

"I tell you, whoever acknowledges me before men, the Son of Man will acknowledge him before the angels of God. But whoever disowns me before men will be disowned before the angels of God. And everyone who speaks a word against the Son of Man will be forgiven, but anyone who blasphemes against the Holy Spirit will not be forgiven.

"When you are brought before the synagogues, rulers and authorities, do not worry about how you will defend yourselves or what you will say, for the Holy Spirit will teach you at that time what you should say.

Someone in the crowd said to him, "Teacher tell my brother to divide the inheritance with me."

Y'shua replied, "Man, who appointed me a judge or an arbiter between you?"

Then he said to them, "Watch out! Be on your guard against all kinds of greed; for life does not consist in the abundance of his possessions."

And he told them this parable: "The ground of a certain rich man produced a good crop. He thought to himself, 'What shall I do? I have no place to store my crops.'

"Then he said, 'This is what I'll do. I will tear down my barns and build bigger ones, and there I will store all my grain and my goods. And I'll say to myself, 'You have plenty of good things laid up for many years. Take life easy; eat, drink and be merry.'

"But God said to him, 'You fool! This very night your life will be demanded from you. Then who will get what you have prepared for yourself?"

"This is how it will be with anyone who stores up things for himself, but is not rich toward God."

"Be dressed and ready for service and keep your lamps burning, like men waiting for their master to return from a wedding banquet, so that when he comes and knocks they can immediately open the door for him. It will be good for those servants whose master finds them watching when he comes, he will dress himself to serve, will have them recline at the table and will come and wait on them. It will be good for those servants whose master finds them ready, even if he comes in the second or third watch of he night. But understand this: If the owner of the house had known at what hour the thief was coming, he would not have let his house be broken into. You also must be ready, because the Son of Man will come at an hour when you do not expect him."

Peter asked, "Lord, are you telling this parable to us, or to everyone?"

The Lord answered, "Who then is the faithful and wise manager, whom the master puts in charge of his servants to give them their food allowance at the proper time? It will be good for that servant whom he master finds doing so when he returns. I tell you the truth, he will put him in charge of all his possessions. But suppose the servant says to himself, 'My master is taking a long time in coming,' and then begins to beat the manservants and womanservants and to eat and drink and get drunk. The master of that servant will come on a day when he does not expect him and at an hour he is not aware of. He will cut him to pieces and assign him a place with the unbelievers.

"That servant who knows his master's will and does not get ready or does not do what his master wants will be beaten with many blows. But the one who does not know and does things deserving of punishment will be beaten with few blows. From everyone who has been given much, much will be demanded; and from the one who has been entrusted with much, much more will be asked.

"I have come to bring fire on the earth, and how I wish it were already kindled! But I have a baptism to undergo, and how distressed I am until it is completed! Do you think I came to bring peace on earth? No, I tell you, but division. From now on there will be five in one family divided against each other, three against two and two against three. They will be divided, father against son and son against father, mother against daughter and daughter against mother, mother in law against daughter in law and daughter in law against mother in law."

He said to the crowd, "When you see a cloud rising in the west, immediately you say, 'It is going to rain,' and it does. And when the south wind blows, you say, 'It's going to be hot,' and it is. Hypocrites! How is it that you do not know how to interpret this present time?

"Why don't you judge for yourselves what is right? As you are going with your adversary to the Magistrate, try hard to be reconciled to him on the way, or he may drag you off to the judge, and the judge turn you over to the officer, and the officer throw you into prison. I tell you, you will not get out until you have paid the last penny."

Now there were some present at that time who told Y'shua about Galileans whose blood Pilate had mixed with their sacrifices.

Y'shua answered them, "Do you think these Galileans were worse sinners than all the other Galileans because they suffered this way? I tell you, no! But, unless you repent, you too will all perish. Or those eighteen who died when the tower in Siloam fell on them — do you think they were more guilty than all the others living in Jerusalem? I tell you, no! But unless you repent, you too will all perish.

Then he told this parable: "A man had a fig tree, planted it in his vineyard, and he went to look for fruit on it, but did not find any. So he said to the man who took care of he vineyard, 'For three years now I've been coming to look for fruit on this fig tree and I haven't found any. Cut it down! Why should it use up the soil?'

'Sir, the man replied, 'leave it alone for one more year, and I'll dig around it and fertilize it. If it bears fruit next year, fine! If not, then cut it down."

(Matthew 7:28)

When Y'shua finished saying these things, the crowds were amazed at his teaching, because he taught as one who had authority, and not as their teachers of the law.

(Mark 4:35-41)

That day, when evening came, he said to his disciples, "Let us go over to the other side." Leaving the crowd behind, they took him along, just as he was, in the boat. There were also other boats with him. A furious squall came up, and the waves broke over the boat, so that it was nearly swamped. Y'shua was in the stern, sleeping on a cushion. The disciples woke him up and said to him, "Teacher, don't you care if we drown? (Lord, save us!)"

He got up, rebuked the wind and said to the waves, "Quiet! Be still!" Then the wind died down and it was completely calm. He said to his disciples, "Why are you so afraid? Do you still have no faith?"

They were terrified and asked each other, "Who is this? Even the wind and the waves obey him!"

Later that same day, Y'shua crossed the lake and healed the man possessed with the Legion demons. (Order of Scripture: Mark 5:1, Luke 8:26b, Matthew 8:28-29, Mark 5:3-20=Luke 8:27-39.) Then, two days later,

The Grainfields Sabbath incident occurs. (Order of Scripture: Matthew 12:1-3, Mark 2:25-26, Matthew 12:5-8, Mark 3:13-19=Luke 6:12-16.)

The following day, Sunday March 25th, saw Y'shua utter a very similar series of teachings contained in Luke 6:17-49, or what many scholars call the "Sermon on the Plain". Shortly after that speech, the crowds force Y'shua to withdraw to the seaside (Mark 3:7-12), which precipitates a lengthy discourse in many famous parables like the Sower (Luke 5:13=Mark 4:1; Mark 4:2-9; Mark 4:10-41=Matthew 13:1-13,18-52). Then, as crowds continue to force Y'shua's boat further out, he advises Peter to put out for deeper water and gives an additional call for the disciples to follow him (Fishers of Men 3—Luke 5:4-11).

This is followed by the Feeding of the Five Thousand, which has an amazing level of detail in unified form:

Gospel Harmony #5: Feeding the Five Thousand and Related Events

About April 6, the Baptist is Gone.
(Matthew 14:1-12)

At that time Herod the tetrarch heard the reports about Y'shua, and he said to his attendants, "This is John the Baptist; he is risen from the dead! That is why miraculous powers are at work in him."

(Others said, "He is Elijah."

And still others claimed, "He is a prophet, like one of the prophets like one of the prophets of long ago." But when Herod heard this, he said, "John, the man I beheaded, has been raised from the dead!—Mark 6:16) (Who, then, is this I hear such things about?" And he tried to see him—Luke 9:9)

Now Herod had arrested John and bound him and put him in prison because of Herodias, his brother Philip's wife, for John had been saying to him: "It is not lawful for you to have her." Herod wanted to kill John, but he was afraid of the people, because they considered him a prophet. (Now) (when Herod heard John he was greatly puzzled; yet he liked to listen to him—Mark 6:20 a).

On Herod's birthday, (he gave a banquet for his high officials and military commanders and

the leading men of Galilee—Mark 6:21) (and) the daughter of Herodias danced for them and pleased Herod so much that he promised with an oath to give her whatever she asked, (even up to half his kingdom, Mark 6:23). Prompted by her mother, she said, "Give me here on a platter the head of John the Baptist." The king was distressed, but because of his oaths and his dinner guests, he ordered that her request be granted and had John beheaded in prison. His head was brought on a platter and given to the girl, who carried it to her mother. John's disciples came and took the body and buried it. Then they went and told Y'shua.

Goes to Mountains to Pray, late evening, followed by designating 12 apostles the next day, between Feeding of the 5,000, April 6-10
(Matthew 14:13 a)

When Y'shua heard what had happened, (his apostles returned).

(Mark 6:30)

The apostles (then) gathered around Y'shua and reported all they had done and taught.

(Mark 6:31)

Then, because so many people were coming and going that they (the disciples) did not even have a chance to eat, he said to them, "Come with me by yourselves to a quiet place and get some rest."

(Matthew 14:13 b-14 = Mark 6:32-33)
So they went away by themselves in a boat to a solitary place (called Bethsaida—Luke 9:10). But many who saw them leaving recognized them and ran on foot from all the towns and got there ahead of them. When Y'shua landed and saw a large crowd, he had compassion on them, because they like lost sheep without a shepherd.

(John 6:3-4)
Then Y'shua went up on a hillside and sat down with his disciples. The Jewish Passover Feast was near.

(Mark 6:34)
(Then) he began teaching them many things,

(Luke 9:11b)
welcom(ing) them, and (speaking) to them about the kingdom of God. (He also) healed those who needed healing.

(John 6:5 b-7)
(Y'shua then) said to Philip, "Where shall we buy bread for these people to eat?" He asked this to test him, for he already had in mind what he was going to do.
Philip answered him, "Eight months' wages would not buy enough bread for each one to have a bite!"

(Mark 6:35-36)
By this time it was late in the day, so his (other) disciples came to him. "This is a remote place," they said, "and it is already very late. Send the people away so they can go into the surrounding countryside and villages and buy themselves something to eat."

(Matthew 14:16)
Y'shua replied, "They do not need to go away. You give them something to eat.

(Mark 6:38)
How many loaves do you have?" he asked. "Go and see."

(John 6:8-9)
Another one of his disciples, Andrew, Simon Peter's brother, spoke up, "Here is a boy with five small barley loaves and two small fish, but how far will they go among so many?

(Luke 9:13b-14)
Unless we go and buy food for all this crowd." About five thousand men were there (besides women and children — Matthew 14:21)

(Matthew 14:18)
(Y'shua said,) "Bring (the food) here to me,

(Luke 9:14b)
(and) have them sit down in groups of about fifty each." The disciples did so, and everybody sat down

(Mark 6:39 b)
in groups of hundreds and fifties.

(John 6:12-13 = Luke 9:14-17= Mark 6:41-44 = Matthew 14:19-23, and then add Mark 6:45 and John 6:14-15)
Y'shua then took the loaves, gave thanks, and distributed to those who were seated as much as they wanted. He did the same with the fish.
When they had all had enough to eat, he said to the disciples, "Gather the pieces that are left over. Let nothing be wasted." So they

gathered them and filled twelve baskets with the pieces of the barley loaves left over by those who had eaten.

Immediately Y'shua made his disciples get into the boat and go ahead of him to Bethsaida, while he dismissed the crowd.

After the people saw the miraculous sign that Y'shua did, they began to say, "Surely this is the Prophet who is to come into the world." Y'shua, knowing that they intended to come and make him king by force, withdrew again into the hills by himself

(Mark 6:46 b)
to pray.

Walks on Water, same evening
(John 6:16-18)
When evening came, his disciples went down to the lake, where they got into a boat and set across the lake for Capernaum. By now it was dark, and Y'shua had not yet joined them. A strong wind was blowing and the waters grew rough.

(Mark 6:47-48 b)
(By this time) the boat was in the middle of the lake, and (Y'shua) was (still) alone on the land. He saw his disciples straining at the oars, because the wind was against them. About the fourth watch of the night (or between 3 and 6 AM),

(John 6:19 a)
when they had rowed three or three and a half miles,

(Mark 6:48b)
he went out to them, walking on the lake.

(Matthew 14:25-26 = Mark 6:48 c-50 = John 6:19b)
He was about to pass by them, but when they saw him walking on

the lake, they thought he was a ghost. They cried out, because they all saw him and were terrified.

(Matthew 14:27 = Mark 6:50 b = John 6:20)

But Y'shua immediately said to them: "Take courage! It is I. Don't be afraid."

(Matthew 14:28-31)

"Lord, if it is you," Peter replied, "tell me to come to you on the water."

"Come," he said.

Then Peter got out of the boat and walked on the water to Y'shua. But when he saw the wind, he was afraid and, beginning to sink, cried out, "Lord, save me!"

Immediately Y'shua reached out his and caught him. "You of little faith," he said. "Why did you doubt?"

And when they climbed into the boat, the wind died down.

(Mark 6:51 b-52)

They were completely amazed, for they had not understood about the loaves; their hearts were hardened.

(Matthew 14:32-36)

Then those who were in the boat worshipped him, saying, "Truly you are the Son of God."

When they had crossed over, they landed at Genesaret. And when the men of the place recognized Y'shua, they sent word to all the surrounding country. People brought all their sick to him and begged him to let the sick touch the edge of his cloak, and all who touched him were healed.

Bread of Life Discourse and Related Events, next day
(John 6:22-59)

The next day the crowd that had stayed on the opposite shore of the lake realized that only one boat had been there, and that Y'shua had not entered it with his disciples, but that they had gone away alone. Then some boats from Tiberias landed near the place where the people had eaten the bread after the Lord had given thanks. Once the crowd realized that neither Y'shua nor his disciples were there, they got into the boats and went to Capernaum in search of Y'shua.

When they found him on the other side of the lake, they asked him, "Rabbi, when did you get here?"

Y'shua answered, "I tell you the truth, you are looking for me, not because you saw miraculous signs but because you ate the loaves and had your fill. Do not work for the food that spoils, but for food that endures to eternal life, which the Son of Man will give you. On him God the Father has placed his seal of approval."

Then they asked him, "What must we do to do the works God requires?"

Y'shua answered, "The work of God is this: to believe in the one he has sent."

So they asked him, "What miraculous sign then will you give that we may see it and believe you? What will you do? Our forefathers ate manna in the desert; as it is written: 'He gave them bread from heaven to eat.'"

Y'shua said to them, "I tell you the truth, it is not Moses who has given you the bread from heaven, but it is my Father who gives you the true bread from heaven. For the bread of God is he who comes down from heaven and gives life to the world."

"Sir," they said, "from now on give us this bread."

Then Y'shua declared, "I am the bread of life. He who comes to me will never go hungry, and he who believes in me will never be thirsty. But as I told you, you have seen me and still you do not believe. All that my Father gives me will come to me, and whoever comes to me I will never drive away. For I have come down from heaven not to do my will but to do the will of him who sent me. And this is the will of him who sent me, that I shall lose none of al the he has given me, but raise them up on the last day."

At this the Jews began to grumble about him because he said, "I am the bread that came down from heaven." They said, "Is this not Y'shua, the son of Joseph, whose father and mother we know? How can he now say, 'I came down from heaven'?"

"Stop grumbling among yourselves," Y'shua answered. "No one came come to me unless the Father who sent me draws him, and I will raise him up on the last day. It is written in the Prophets: 'They will all be taught by God.' Everyone who listens to the Father and learns from him comes to me. No one has seen the Father except the one that is from God; only he has seen the Father. I tell you the truth, he who believes has everlasting life. I am the bread of life. Your forefathers ate manna in the desert, yet they died. But there is the bread that comes down from heaven, which a man may eat and not die. I am the living bread that came down from heaven. If a man eat this bread, he will live forever. The bread is my flesh, which I will give for the life of the world."

Then the Jews began to argue sharply among themselves, "How can this man give us his flesh to eat?"

Y'shua said to them, "I tell you the truth, unless you eat the flesh of the Son of Man and drink his blood, you have no life in you. Whoever eats my flesh and drinks my blood has eternal life, and I will raise him up on the last day. For my flesh is the real food and my blood the true drink. Whoever eats my flesh and drinks my blood remains in me, and I in him. Just as the Living Father sent me and I live because of the Father, so the one who feeds on me will live because of me. This is the bread that came down from heaven. Our forefathers ate manna and died, but he who feeds on this bread will live forever." He said this while teaching in the synagogue in Capernaum.

(John 6:60-71)

On hearing it, many of his disciples said, "This is a hard teaching. Who can accept it?"

Aware that his disciples were grumbling about this, Y'shua said to them, "Does this offend you? What if you see the Son of Man ascend to where he was before! The Spirit gives life; the flesh counts for nothing. The words I have spoken to you are the spirit and they are life. Yet there are some of you who do not believe and who would betray him."
He went on to say, "This is why I told you that no one can come to me unless the Father has enabled him."
From this time, many of his disciples turned back and no longer followed him.
"You do not want to leave too, do you?" Y'shua asked the Twelve.
Simon Peter answered him, "Lord, to whom shall we go? You have the words of eternal life. We believe and know that you re the Holy One of God."
Then Y'shua replied, "Have I not chosen you, the Twelve? Yet one of you is a devil!" He meant Judas, the son of Simon Iscariot, who, though one of the Twelve, was later to betray him.

April 15-December 31, 29

The Rest of the Year

The Passover ended April 22nd. After this, Matthew and Mark both report that Pharisees from Jerusalem came to visit Y'shua. With their emphasis on literal interpretation of the Law, there is no way these teachers would have been anywhere other than the holy city during the Passover, since that was the only acceptable place to keep the holiday, (Deuteronomy 12:11-14, 16:5). Furthermore we also have the Shavuot-Feast of Weeks holiday to deal with, (June 3-10).

Although the text is not precise, it seems logical that Y'shua stayed in and around Jerusalem throughout this time as well, most probably with Martha in Bethany. That would put the visit by the Pharisees sometime between mid June and mid September. The relative paucity of events between now and the late fall also make a later placement more likely.

Those events, primarily from Mark 7–8, include: Healing of a Deaf Man, Feeding of the 4,000, More Pharisees Questions, Peter's Confession (Who Do You Say I am?), and our next topic of discussion, the Transfiguration.

Gimme Shelter

Matthew and Mark say this miracle happens six days after "Who Do You Say I am?" Luke, eight. This is not an insoluble contradiction, since "eight days" is "after six days". Second, it seems likely that Luke is counting both the day Peter confesses his faith and the day it takes Y'shua to arrive in the area and climb up Mount Hermon. Between those two events is therefore a six day interval.

The next question is, when did it happen? Listen to this quote and the detail that is recorded in all three versions:

> "Peter said to Y'shua, 'Lord, it is good for us to be here. If you wish, I will put up three shelters, one for you, one for Moses and one for Elijah."
>
> Matthew 17:4

Now why would Peter say this? Was he just babbling incoherently? It is true that Peter was taken aback by this momentous event. After all, who wouldn't be? But Peter's question does come about for a logical reason:

> "Live in booths for seven days. All native born Israelites are to live in booths, so that your descendants will know that I had the Israelites live in booths when I brought them out of Egypt. I am the LORD your God.
>
> Leviticus 24:42-43

This holiday, otherwise known as the Feast of Tabernacles, now is pregnant with many similarities to the current situation. First, as stated above, it commemorates the Israelites wandering in the wilderness near Mount Sinai, and Moses was there. Second, the Transfiguration is also happening in a wilderness area near a mountain, and Moses is there too! Third, while Moses goes up on the mountain to receive the Law, Y'shua does the same thing to show his power and right to fulfill the Law. Therefore, Peter is offering to build the "shelters" because all his training as a Jew is compelling him to do so.

From about mid September, Y'shua retreats from the northernmost point of his ministry, and goes south into Galilee for the first and only time in his life. Once back in his native area, his brothers chide him for not getting ready to go up to the feast. Y'shua hesitates, but eventually goes up to Jerusalem.

After these events, the rest of the year falls easily into place. From the beginning of chapter 7 the first third of chapter 10, John details with loving precision the religious politics, maneuverings and extensive teachings given during the Feast of Tabernacles and shortly afterwards, to about October 20th. Then, in early December, Y'shua is back in Jerusalem again to celebrate Hanukkah, the last major event of the year.

January 1-May 26, 30

The Implied Return

After being threatened at Hanukkah, Y'shua withdraws to Bethabarah, where the Baptist used to minister, (John 10:40-42). Apparently he had received a warm reception there and felt comfortable staying for some time, probably a few weeks.

However, somewhere during the next month and a half Y'shua would have had to go back to Galilee. We know this because of a statement in Matthew:

> "After Y'shua and his disciples arrived in Capernaum, the collectors of the two-drachma tax came to Peter and asked, 'Doesn't your teacher pay the Temple Tax?"
>
> Matthew 17:24[264]

This occasion was for the "ransom of souls" required of all men age 20 and older in connection with Yom Kippur or the Day of Atonement, (Exodus 30:11-16). Ancient records reveal the exact time of year this tax was collected. According to the Talmud, as well as the book, *The Temple: Its Ministry and Practices* by Alfred Erdesheim, the Temple Tax was collected during the first week of Adar (or Adar Sheni, if a leap year) and was processed no later than the middle of that same month. This would bring us to the week of March 3—10.

A Very Busy March

Just as with the spring of 29, the month of March in the year 30 also looks to be a very busy time. This is now the last month of Y'shua's life. Right after the Temple Tax incident, the first three Gospels record an argument among the disciples about who is the greatest among them.

Then both Matthew and Luke agree that Y'shua's final trip to Jerusalem happened immediately afterwards, (Matthew 19:1, Luke 9:51)[265]. Therefore all the events from Luke 9:46 to 19:28 occur in the month of March.[266] Matthew 19:1-20:29 and Mark 10:1-52 also cover this period.

As for John, he does not directly mention this, but logic demands synching this last Jerusalem trip to the events in Perea as well as the return to Bethany to raise Lazarus, and the brief withdrawal to Ephraim. The beauty of this time period also is that in two cases, (Luke 13:10, 14:1), major events are happening on Sabbaths, and it is possible to date them conclusively to one of two weeks.[267] From this point on, the precision in the Gospels makes dating the rest of the events before, during and after Passion Week a very simple task. Some of the major events break out chronologically this way:

FRIDAY, MARCH 29:

Y'shua Enters Jerusalem. (Order of Scripture: John 12:12, Matthew 21:1-3, Luke 19:32-34, Mark 11:16b, Matthew 21:4, John 12:16-19, Matthew 21:6, Luke 19:37, Matthew 21:7-10, Luke 19:38b-44, Matthew 21:11, Mark 11:11.)

SUNDAY, MARCH 31:

Purging the Temple 2.[268] (Order of Scripture: Mark 11:12-17, Matthew 21:14-16, Mark 11:18-19, Matthew 21:17b, Luke 19:47-48.)

MONDAY, APRIL 1:

Morning:
Cursing the Fig Tree. (Order of Scripture: Mark 11:20-21, Matthew 21:20-22 [with Mark 11:22], Mark 11:24-26.)

Authority Questioned and Various Plots, also Monday morning, April 1. (Order of Scripture: Matthew 21:23-27 = Mark 11:27-33 = Luke 20:1-8; Matthew 21:28-46 = Mark 12:1-12 = Luke 20:9-19; Matthew 22:1-14; Matthew 22:15-22 = Mark 12:13-17 = Luke 20:20-26; Matthew 22:23-33 = Mark 12:18-27 = Luke 20:27-40; Matthew 22:35-40 = Mark 12:28-34; Matthew 22:41-46 = Mark 12:35-40 = Luke 20:41-47; Matthew 23:1-39; Mark 12:41-44 = Luke 21:1-4.)

Afternoon:
Greeks visit Y'shua and the disciples. (Order of Scripture: John 12:20-38.)

Evening:
Various other events. (Order of Scripture: Matthew 26:1-5 = Mark 14:1-2 = Luke 22:1-2; John 12:37-50; [Head Anointing at Bethany[269]]; Mark 14:3-9 = Matthew 26:6-13.)

TUESDAY, APRIL 2:

Morning-Afternoon:
The Betrayal. (Order of Scripture: Luke 22:1-6 = Matthew 26:14-16 = Mark 14:10-1.)

Evening:
Y'shua Washes the Disciples' Feet. (Order of Scripture: John 13:1-17.)
Y'shua Predicts His Betrayal, Part 1. (Order of Scripture: John 13:18-31.)

WEDNESDAY, APRIL 3:

Morning-Afternoon:
Preparations for the Last Supper. (Order of Scripture: Luke 22:7-13 = Mark 14:12-16 = Matthew 26:17-19.)

Evening:
Last Supper; Y'shua Predict His Betrayal, Part 2. (Order of Scripture: Luke 22:14-30= Mark 14:17-31 = Matthew 26:20-35.)
Final Discourse: Sermon on the Mount of Olives. (Order of Scripture: John 14:1-18:1.)
Prayer at Gethsemane. (Order of Scripture: Mark 14:32-42 = Matthew 26:36-46 = Luke 22:39-46.)
The Arrest. (Order of Scripture: John 18:2-3; Mark 14:44-45 = Matthew 26:48-49[with Luke 22:47b-48]; John 18:4-11 [with Luke 22:49

and Matthew 26:52-55]; Luke 22:51-53, Mark 14:50-51, John 18:12-14.)
Peter's first denial. (Order of Scripture: John 18:15-18 = Luke 22:54b-57 = Mark 14:66-68.)
Y'shua is questioned by Annas. (Order of Scripture: John 18:19-24.)

THURSDAY, APRIL 4:

Early morning before dawn:
Peter's Second and Third Denials. (Order of Scripture: Matthew 26:71-72= Mark 14:69-72= Luke 22:58-62= John 18:25-27; Matthew 26:67 = Mark 14:65.)
Y'shua Before Caiphas and the Sanhedrin, Part 1. (Order of Scripture: Matthew 26:57-66 = Mark 14:53-64; Matthew 26:67 = Mark 14:65; Luke 22:65.)

Dawn to 9 AM:
Y'shua Before the Sanhedrin, Part 2. (Order of Scripture: Luke 22:66-71)
Judas Hangs Himself After Returning the Money. (Order of Scripture: Matthew 27:3-10 and Acts 1:18-19.)[270]
Y'shua Sent to Pilate. (Order of Scripture: Luke 23:1-6 = Matthew 27:1-2 and John 18:28-38.)[271]
Pilate Sends Y'shua to Herod. (Order of Scripture: Luke 23:7-10.)
Herod Sends Y'shua Back to Pilate. (Order of Scripture: Luke 23:11-12 = Matthew 27:1-2.)
Y'shua Condemned by Pilate. (Order of Scripture: Matthew 27:11-26 = Mark 15:1-15 = Luke 23:13-25 = John 18:39-19:16)

From here, our final Gospel Harmony showcases what is supposed to be the most difficult event to merge into once account: The period from the Crucifixion to the Resurrection. As we will see, linking this critical interval of time together properly is also quite simple to do:

Gospel Harmony #6: Crucifixion and Resurrection:

The Crucifixion, Thursday, April 4

(Luke 23:26-44 = John 19:16b-27 = Mark 15:21-32 =

As they led him way, they seized Simon from Cyrene, the father of Alexander and Rufus, who was on his way in from the country, and put the cross on him and made him carry it behind Y'shua (while Y'shua carried the front crossbar). A large number of people followed him, including women who mourned and wailed for him. Y'shua turned and said to them, "Daughters of Jerusalem, do not weep for me; weep for yourselves and your children. For the time will come when you will say, 'Blessed are the barren women, the wombs that never bore and the breasts that never nursed!' Then, 'they will say to the mountains, "Fall on us!" And to the hills, "Cover us!" For if men do these things when the tree is green, what will happen when it is dry?"

Two other men, both criminals, were also led out with him to be executed. When they came to the Place of the Skull (or Golgotha), there they crucified him, along with the criminals — one on his right, the other on his left. It was the third hour (by Jewish time) when they crucified him (or 9 AM). Y'shua said, "Father, forgive them, for they do not know what they are doing." Then they offered him wine mixed with myrhh, but he did not take it. And they divided up his clothes into four shares, one for each of them, with the undergarment remaining. This garment was seamless, woven in one piece from top to bottom. "Let's not tear it," they said to one another, "Let's decide by lot who will get it."

This happened that the Scripture might be fulfilled which said: "They divided my garments among them and cast lots for my clothing." So this is what the soldiers did.

Near the cross of Y'shua stood his mother, his mother's sister, Mary the wife of Clopas (and also) the mother of James and Joseph. (Others included Salome, the mother of Zawdee's sons James and John — Matthew 27:55), and Mary of Magdala. In Galilee, these women had followed him and cared for his needs. Many other women who had come up with him to Jerusalem were also there. When Y'shua saw his mother there, and (John) the disciple whom he loved standing nearby, he said to his mother, "Dear mother, here is your son," and to the disciple, "Here is your mother." From then on, this disciple took her into his home.

The people stood watching, and the rulers even sneered at him. They said, "He saved others; let him save himself if he is the Messiah of God, the Chosen One." (Others) who passed by hurled insults at him, shaking their heads and saying, "So! You who are going to destroy the temple in three days, come down from the cross and save yourself!"

In the same way the chief priests and the teachers of the law mocked him among themselves. "Let this Messiah, this King of Israel come down now from the cross, that we may see and believe. He trusts in God. Let God rescue him now, if he wants him, for he said, 'I am the Son of God.'

The soldiers also came up and mocked him. They offered him wine and vinegar and said, "If you are the king of the Jews, save yourself."

There was a written notice above him, which read: THIS IS THE KING OF THE JEWS. Many of the Jews read the sign, for the place where Y'shua was crucified was near the city and the sign was written in Aramaic, Latin and Greek. The chief priests of the Jews protested to Pilate, "Do not write 'King of the Jews,' but that this man claimed to be king of the Jews."

Pilate answered them, "What I have written, I have written."

One of the criminals who hung there hurled insults at him: "Aren't you the Messiah? Save yourself and us!"

But the other criminal rebuked him. "Don't you fear God," he said, "since you are under the same sentence? We are punished justly, for we are getting what our deeds deserve. But this man has done nothing wrong."

Then he said, "Y'shua, remember me when you come into your kingdom."

Y'shua answered him, "I tell you the truth, today you will be with me in paradise."

The Death of Y'shua, 3 PM
(Matthew 27:45-54 = Mark 15:33-41 = Luke 23:44-49 = John 19:28-37)

From the sixth hour until the ninth hour (or from noon to 3 PM), darkness came over all the land.

About the ninth hour Y'shua cried out in a loud voice, "Eloi, Eloi, lemana shawakthani" (Aramaic phrase: "My God, my God, for this I was spared.")

When some of those standing there heard this, they said, "He is calling Elijah."

Later, knowing that all was now completed and so that the Scripture would be fulfilled, Y'shua said, "I am thirsty."

Immediately one of them ran and got a sponge. He filled it with wine vinegar, put it on he stalk of a hyssop plant, and offered it to Y'shua to drink. But the rest said, "Leave him alone. Let's see if Elijah comes to save him and take him down."

(They ignored the crowd and) lifted (the sponge) to Y'shua's lips. Y'shua cried out again in a loud voice (saying), "Father, into your hands I commit my spirit." When he received the drink, Y'shua (then) said, "It is finished." With that, he bowed his head and gave up his spirit.

At that moment, the curtain of the temple was torn in two from top to bottom. The earth shook and the rocks split.

The tombs broke open and the bodies of many holy people who had died were raised to life. They came out of their tombs, and after Y'shua's resurrection they went out into the holy city and appeared to many people.

When the centurion and those with him who were guarding Y'shua saw the earthquake and all that happened, they were terrified and said, "Surely he was the Son of God!"

Now it was the day of Preparation, and the next day was to be a special (annual) Sabbath (for the Feast of Unleavened Bread). Because the Jews did not want the bodies left on the crosses during the Sabbath, they asked Pilate to have the legs broken and the bodies taken down. The soldiers therefore came and broke the legs of the first man who had been crucified with Y'shua, and then those of the other. But wen they came to Y'shua and found he was already dead, they did not break his legs. Instead, one of the soldiers pierced Y'shua's side with a spear, bringing a sudden flow of blood and water. The man who saw it has given testimony, and his testimony is true. He knows that he tells the truth and he testifies so that you may also believe. These things happened so that the Scripture would be fulfilled: "Not one of his bones will be broken," and, as another Scripture says, "they will look on the one they have pierced."

The Burial of Y'shua, from 3 to 6 PM
(Luke 23:50-56 = John 19:38-42 = Mark 15:42-47 = Matthew 27:57-61)

Now there was a man named Joseph, a member of the Council, a good and upright man, who had not consented to the their decision and action. He came from the Judean town of Arimathea and was waiting for the kingdom of God.

Later, Joseph of Arimathea asked Pilate for the body of Y'shua. Now Joseph was a disciple of Y'shua, but secretly, for he feared the Jews. Pilate was surprised to hear that he was already dead. Summoning the centurion, he asked him if Y'shua had already died. When he learned from the centurion that it was so, he gave the body to Joseph.

With Pilate's permission, he came and took the body. He was accompanied by Nicodemus, the man who earlier had visited Y'shua at night. Nicodemus brought a mixture of myrrh and aloes, about seventy-five pounds. Taking Y'shua's body, the two of them wrapped it, with the spices, in strips of linen. This was in accordance with Jewish burial customs. At the place where Y'shua was crucified, there was a garden, and in the garden a new tomb cut in the rock, in which no one had ever been laid. (This was Joseph's own tomb —Matthew 27:60). Because it was the Jewish day of Preparation (with) the Sabbath about to begin, and since the tomb was nearby, they laid Y'shua there. Then he rolled the stone against the entrance of the tomb and went away. Mary Magdalene and the other Mary were sitting there across from the tomb.

The women who had come with Y'shua from Galilee followed (them) and saw the tomb and how his body was laid in it. Then they went home and prepared spices and perfumes. But they rested on the Sabbath is obedience to the commandment.

The Tomb Guarded, Friday, April 5
(Matthew 27:62-66)

The next day, the one after the Preparation Day, the chief priest and the Pharisees went to Pilate. "Sir," they said, "we remember that while he was still alive that deceiver said, 'After three days I will rise again.' So give the order for the tomb to be made secure until the third day. Otherwise his disciples may come and steal the body and tell the people he has been raised from the dead. This last deception will be worse than the first."

"Take a guard," Pilate answered. "Go make the tomb as secure as you know how." So they went and made the tomb secure by putting a seal on the stone and posting the guard.

The Resurrection, Sunday, April 7, 6:01 AM (Jerusalem Standard Time)

The Prelude
(Matthew 28:1 = Mark 16:1-3)

After the Sabbath, at dawn on the first day of the week, Mary Magdalene, and the other Mary went to look at the tomb (along with) Salome, (who) brought spices so that they might go and anoint Y'shua's body. (It was) very early, just after sunrise and they asked each other, "Who will roll the stone away from the entrance of the tomb?"

(Matthew 28:2)
There was a violent earthquake, for an angel of the Lord (had come) down from heaven and, going to the tomb, rolled back the stone and sat on it.

(Mark 16:4a)
But when they looked up, they saw that the stone, which was very large, had been rolled away.

(John 20:2)
So (Mary of Magdala) came running to Simon and the other disciple (John), the one Y'shua loved, and said, "They have taken the Lord out of the tomb, and we don't know where they have put him!"

(Mark 16:4b)
As (the other women) entered the tomb,

(Luke 24:3)
they did not find the body of the Lord Y'shua.

(Mark 16:5)
(Instead), they saw (one) young man dressed in a white robe sitting on the right side and they were alarmed.

(Matthew 28:3-4)
His appearance was like lightning, and his clothes were white as snow. The guards were so afraid of him that they shook and became like dead men.

(Luke 24:4-5)
While they were wondering about this, they suddenly saw (the

second young man). (Now both men were) in clothes that gleamed like lightning (and they) stood before them. In their fright the women bowed down with their faces on the ground, but the men said to them, "Why do you seek the living among the dead?"

(Matthew 28:5 = Mark 16:6)
The (first) angel said to the women, "Do not be afraid or alarmed, for I know you are looking for Y'shua the Nazarene who was crucified."
(Then they both said:) "He is not here; he is risen, just as he said."

(Luke 24:6b-8)
"Remember how he told you, while he was still with you in Galilee: 'The Son of Man must be delivered into the hands of sinful men, be crucified, and on the third day be raised again.'" Then they remembered his words.

(Matthew 28:6 = Mark 16:7)
"Come and see the place where he lay," (the second angel told them). "Then go quickly and tell his disciples and Peter: 'He has risen from the dead and is going ahead of you into Galilee. There you will see him.' Now I have told you."

(Mark 16:8)
Trembling and bewildered, the women went out and fled from the tomb. (At first) they said nothing to anyone, because they were afraid.

(Matthew 28:8-15)
(Then, as) the women hurried away from the tomb (they were) filled with joy and ran to tell his disciples. Suddenly Y'shua met them. "Greetings," he said. They came to him, clasped his feet and worshipped him. Then Y'shua said to them, "Do not be afraid. Go and tell my brothers to go to Galilee; there they will see me."

While the women were on their way, some of the guards went into the city and reported to the chief priest everything that had happened. When the chief priests had met with the elders and devised a plan, they gave the soldiers a large sum of money, telling them, "You are to say, 'His disciples came during the night and stole him away while we were asleep.' If this report gets to the governor, we will satisfy him and keep you out of trouble." So the soldiers took the money and did as they were instructed. And this story has been widely circulated among the Jews to this very day.

(Luke 24:9-11)

When they came back from the tomb, they told all these things to the Eleven and to all the others. It was Joanna, Mary the mother of James, and the others with them who told this to the apostles. But they did not believe the women, because their words seemed to them like nonsense.

(John 20:3-9; summary Luke 24:12)

So Peter and the other disciple started for the tomb. Both were running, but the other disciple outran Peter and reached the tomb first. He bent over and looked in the strips of linen lying there, but did not go in. Then Simon Peter, who was behind him, arrived and went into the tomb. He saw the strips of linen lying there, as well as the burial cloth that had been around Y'shua's head. The cloth was folded up by itself, separate from the linen. Finally, the other disciple, who had reached the tomb first, also went inside. He saw and believed. (They still did not understand from Scripture that Y'shua had to rise from the dead.)

(Mark 16:10)

When Y'shua rose early on the first day of the week, he appeared first to Mary Magdalene, out of whom he had driven seven demons.

First Appearance: Mary Magdalene
(John 20:10-17)

Then the disciples (Peter and John) went back to their homes, but Mary stood outside the tomb crying. As she wept, she bent over to look into the tomb, and saw two angels in white, seated where Y'shua's body had been, one at the head and the other at the foot.

They asked her, "Woman, why are you crying?"

"They have taken my Lord away," she said, and I don't know where they have put him." At this she turned around and saw Y'shua standing there, but she did not realize it was Y'shua.

"Woman," he said, "why are you crying? Who are you looking for?"

Thinking he was the gardener, she said, "Sir, if you have carried him away, tell me where you have put him, and I will get him."

Y'shua said to her, "Mary."

She turned to him and cried out in Aramaic, "Rabboni!" (which means Teacher).

Y'shua said, "Do not hold on to me, for I have not yet returned to the Father. Go instead to my brothers and tell them, 'I am returning to my Father and your Father, to my God and your God.'"

(Mark 16:11 and John 20:18)

Mary of Magdala went to the (nine) disciples with the news: "I have seen the Lord!" And she told those who had been with him and who were mourning and weeping, what he said to her. When they heard that Y'shua was alive and that she had seen him, they did not believe it.

Second Appearance: To Peter
(1 Corinthians 15:5)

(Then) Y'shua appeared to Peter.

Third Appearance: On the Road of Emmaus
(Mark 16:12-14 summary; Luke 24:13-35 full account)

Now that same day two of them were going to a village called

Emmaus, about seven miles from Jerusalem. They were talking with each other about everything that had happened. As they talked and discussed these things with each other, Y'shua himself came up and walked along with them; but they were kept from recognizing him (because) he appeared in a different form to two of them while they were walking in the country.

He asked them, "What are you discussing together as you walk along?"

They stood still, their faces downcast.

One of them, Cleopas, asked him, "Are you the only one living in Jerusalem who does not know the things that have happened there in these days?"

"What things?" he asked.

"About Y'shua of Nazareth," they replied. "He was a prophet, powerful in word and deed before God and all the people. The chief priests and our rulers handed him over to be sentenced to death, and they crucified him, but we had hoped he was the one who was going to redeem Israel. And what is more, it is the third day since all this took place. In addition, some of our women amazed us. They went to the tomb early this morning but didn't find his body. They came and told us that they had seen a vision of angels, who said he was alive. Then some of our companions went to the tomb and found it just as the women had said, but him they did not see."

He said to them, "How foolish you are, and how slow of heart to believe all that the prophets have spoken! Did not the Messiah have to suffer all these things and then enter his glory?" And beginning with Moses and all the Prophets, he explained to them what was said in all the Scriptures concerning himself.

As they approached the village to which they were going, Y'shua acted as if he were going farther. But they urged him strongly, "Stay with us, for it is nearly evening; the day is almost over. So he went in to stay with them.

When he was at the table with them, he took bread, gave thanks, broke it and began to give it to them. Then their eyes were opened and they recognized him, and he disappeared from their sight. They asked each other, "Were not our hearts burning within us while he talked with us on the road and opened the Scriptures to us?"

These (two) returned and reported it to the rest (of their neighbors); but they did not believe them either.

They got up and at once returned to Jerusalem. There they found the Eleven and those with them, assembled together and saying, "It is true! The Lord has risen and has appeared to Simon." Then the two told what had happened on the way, and how Y'shua was recognized when he broke the bread.

Fourth Appearance: To the Ten in Jerusalem (without Thomas)
(Luke 24:36-49 = John 20:19-23, summary: Mark 16:14-18)

While (ten of them) were still talking about this, on the evening of that first day of the week, Y'shua himself stood among them and said, "Peace be with you."

They were startled and frightened, thinking they saw a ghost. He said to them, "Why are you troubled, and why do doubts rise in your minds? Look at my hands and my feet. It is I myself! Touch me and see; a ghost does not have flesh and bones, as you see I have."

When he said this, he showed them his hands and feet. And while they still did not believe it because of joy and amazement, he asked them, "Do you have anything here to eat?" They gave him a piece of broiled fish, and he took it and ate it in their presence.

He said to them, "This is what I told you while I was still with you: Everything must be fulfilled that is written about me in the Law of Moses, the Prophets and the Psalms."

Then he opened their minds so that they could understand the Scriptures. He told them, "This is what was written: The Messiah will suffer and rise from the dead on the third day, and repentance and forgiveness of sins will be preached in his name to all nations, beginning at Jerusalem. You are witnesses of these things. I am going to send you what my Father has promised; but stay in the city until you have been clothed with power from on high."

(Acts 1:4-8)

While he was (still) eating with them he (said), "(I repeat): Do not leave Jerusalem but wait for the gift my Father promised, which you have heard me speak about. For John baptized with water, but in a few days you will be baptized with the Holy Spirit."

(Then) they asked him, "Lord, are you at this time going to restore the kingdom to Israel?"

He said to them, "It is not for you to know the times or the dates my Father has set by his own authority. But you will receive power when the Holy Spirit comes on you; and you will be my witnesses in Jerusalem, and in all Judea and Samaria, and to the ends of the earth."

The disciples were overjoyed when they saw the Lord.

The First Ascension
(Luke 24:50-51)

When he had led them out into the vicinity of Bethany, he lifted up his hands and blessed them. While he was blessing them, he left them and was taken up into heaven

(Acts 1:9-11)
before their very eyes, and a cloud hid him from their sight.

They were looking intently up into the sky as he was going, when suddenly two men dressed in white stood beside them. "Men of Galilee," they said, "why do you stand her looking into the sky? This same Y'shua, who has been taken from you into heaven, will come back in the same way you have seen him go into heaven."

(Luke 24:52-53)

Then they worshipped him and returned to Jerusalem with great joy. And they stayed continually at the temple, praising God.

Fifth Appearance: To the Eleven (Thomas present), April 14
(John 20:24-31)

Now Thomas (called Didymus), one of the Twelve, was not with the disciples when Y'shua came. When the other disciples told him they had seen the Lord, he declared, "Unless I see the nail marks in his hands and put my hand into his side, I will not believe it."

A week later his disciples were in the house again, and Thomas was with them. though the door were locked, Y'shua came and stood among them and said, "Peace be with you!" Then he said to Thomas, "Put your finger here; see my hands. Reach out your hand and put it into my side. Stop doubting and believe."

Thomas said to him, "My Lord and my God!"

Then Y'shua told him, "Because you have seen me, you have believed; but blessed are those who have not seen and yet have believed."

Y'shua did many other miraculous signs in the presence of his disciples, which are not recorded in this book. But these are written so that you may believe Y'shua is the Messiah, the Son of God, and that by believing you may have life in his name.

Second Ascension
(Mark 16:14-20)

Later Y'shua appeared to the Eleven as they were eating; he rebuked them for their lack of faith and for their stubborn refusal to believe those who has seen him after he had risen.

Again Y'shua said, "Peace be with you! As the Father sent me, I am sending you." And with that he breathed on them and said, "Receive the Holy Spirit. If you forgive anyone his sins, they are forgiven; if you do not forgive them, they are not forgiven. (Now) go into all the world and preach the good news to all creation. Whoever believes and is baptized will be saved, but whoever does not believe will be condemned. And these signs will accompany those who believe:) In my name (you) will drive out demons; (and) will speak in new tongues; (Aramaic phrase: You will be able to overcome your enemies and obstacles as if you had) pick(ed) up snakes with (your) hands; and (as if you drank) deadly poison, it will not hurt (you)at all; (and you) will place their hands on sick people, and they will get well."

After the Lord Y'shua had spoken to them, he was taken up into heaven and he sat at the right hand of God. Then his disciples went out and preached everywhere, and the Lord worked with them and confirmed his word by the signs that accompanied it.

Sixth Appearance: By the Sea of Tiberias (Galilee), (Fishers of Men 4), evening of May 16
(John 21:1-14)

Afterward Y'shua appeared again to his disciples by the Sea of Tiberias. It happened this way:

Simon Peter, Thomas (called Didymus), Nathanael (Bartholemew) from Cana in Galilee, the sons of Zawdee (James and John), and two other disciples were together. "I'm going out to fish," Simon Peter told them, and they said, "We'll go with you." So they went out and got into the boat, but that night they caught nothing.

Seventh Appearance, May 17

Early in the morning, Y'shua stood on the shore, but the disciples did not realize tat it was Y'shua.

He called out to them, "Friends, haven't you any fish?"

"No," they answered.

He said, "Throw your net on the right side of the boat and you will find some." When they did, they were unable to haul in the net because of the large number of fish.

Then (John), the disciple whom Y'shua loved said to Peter, "It is the Lord!" As soon as Simon Peter heard him say, "It is the Lord," he wrapped his outer garment around him (for he had taken it off) and jumped into the water. The other disciples followed in the boat, towing the net full of fish, for they were not far from the shore, about a hundred yards. When they landed, they saw a fire of burning coals with fish on it, and some bread.

Y'shua said to them, "Bring some of the fish you have just caught."

Simon Peter climbed aboard and ragged the net ashore. It was full of large fish, 153, but even with so many the net was not torn.

Y'shua said to them, "Come and have breakfast." None of the disciples dared ask him, "Who are you?' They knew it was the Lord. Y'shua came, took the bread and gave it to them, and he did the same with the fish. This was now the third time Y'shua appeared to his disciples after he was raised from the dead.

Peter Reinstated
(John 21:15-23)
   When they had finished eating, Y'shua said to Simon Peter, "Simon, son of John, do you truly love me more than these?"
   "Yes, Lord," he said, "you know that I love you."
   Y'shua said, "Feed my lambs."
   Again Y'shua said, "Simon, son of John, do you truly love me?"
   He answered, "Yes, Lord, you know that I love you."
   Y'shua said, "Take care of my sheep."
   The third time he said to him, "Simon, son of John, do you love me?"
   Peter was hurt because Y'shua asked him the third time, "Do you love me?". He said, "Lord, you know all things; you know that I love you."
   Y'shua said, "Feed my sheep. I tell you the truth, when you were younger you dressed yourself and went where you wanted; but when you are old you will stretch out your hands, and someone else will dress you and lead you to where you do not want to go." Y'shua said this to indicate the kind of death by which Peter would glorify God. Then he said to him, "Follow me!"
   Peter turned and saw that the disciple Y'shua loved (John) was following them. (This was the one who had leaned back against Y'shua at the supper and had said, "Lord, who is going to betray you?")
   When Peter saw him, he said, "Lord, what about him?"
   Y'shua answered, "If I want him to remain alive until I return, what is that to you? You must follow me." Because of this, the rumor spread among the brothers that this disciple would not die. But Y'shua did

not say that he would not die; he only said, "If I want him to remain until I return, what is that to you?"

Eighth and Ninth Appearances
(Matthew 28:16-20)
Then the eleven disciples went to Galilee, to the mountain where Y'shua had told them to go. When they saw him, they worshipped him; but some doubted.

Then Y'shua came to them and said, "All authority in heaven and earth has been given to me. Therefore go and make disciples of all nations, baptizing them is the name of the Father and of the Son and of the Holy Spirit, and teaching them to obey everything I have commanded you. And surely I will be with you always, to the very end of the age."

Tenth Appearance
(1 Corinthians 15:6)
After that (Y'shua) appeared to more than 500 of the brothers at the same time, most of whom are still living, though some have fallen asleep.

Eleventh and Twelfth Appearances
(1 Corinthians 15:7)
Then he appeared to James, and then to all the apostles.

Thirteenth Appearance
(1 Corinthians 15:8)
And lastly he appeared to (Paul) also, as to one abnormally born.

Matthias Chosen to Replace Judas
(Acts 1:12-26)
Then they returned to Jerusalem from the hill called the Mount of Olives, a Sabbath's day walk from the city. When they arrived, they went upstairs to the room where they were staying. Those present

were Peter, John, James and Andrew; Philip and Thomas, Bartholomew (Nathanael) and Matthew; James son of Alphaeus and Simon the Zealot, and Judas son of James. They all joined together constantly in prayer, along with the women and Mary the mother of Y'shua, and his brothers.

In those days Peter stood up among the believers (a group numbering about a hundred and twenty) and said, "Brothers, the Scripture had to be fulfilled which the Holy Spirit spoke long ago through the prophet David concerning Judas, who served as a guide for those who arrested Y'shua —he was one of our number and shared in this ministry. For," said Peter, "it is written in the book of Psalms, 'May his place be deserted; let there be no one to dwell in it,' and, 'May another take his place of leadership.'

Therefore it is necessary to choose one of the men who have been with us the whole time the Lord Y'shua went in and out among us, beginning from John's baptism to the time when Y'shua was taken up from us. For one of these must become a witness with us of his resurrection."

So they proposed two men: Joseph called Barnabbas (also known as Justus) and Matthias. Then they prayed, "Lord, you know everyone's heart. Show us which of these two you have chosen to take over this apostolic ministry, which Judas left to go where he belongs."

Then they drew lots, and the lot fell to Matthias; so he was added to the eleven apostles.

Holy Spirit Comes at Pentecost, May 26
(Acts 2:1-4)

When the day of Pentecost came they were all together in one place. Suddenly a sound like the blowing of a violent wind came from heaven and filled the whole house where they were sitting. They saw what seemed to be tongues of fire that separated and came to rest on each of them. All of them were filled with the Holy Spirit and began to speak in tongues and the Spirit enabled them.

(John 21:24-25)

This is the disciple who testifies to these things and who wrote them down. We know his testimony is true.

Y'shua said and did many other things as well. If every one of them were written down, I suppose that even the whole world would not have room for the books that would be written.

What About "the Lost Years"?

This topic may be the most difficult issue of them all because we have to look at what is not there in the record and somehow extrapolate into the realm of plausible history. However, it should be pointed out that whenever circumstances force an argument from silence, the results are mixed at best. So, I hope that the reader will allow me a bit of a disclaimer when I say that it is far easier to prove what Y'shua did *not* do in the general sense than to make bold statements about specific incidents.

By far then, the most certain and anticlimactic fact that can be determined about Y'shua in this period is a simple one: He never left the Middle East! Here's why:

> "Leaving that place, Y'shua withdrew to the region of Tyre and Sidon. A Canaanite woman from that vicinity came to him, crying out, 'Lord, son of David, have mercy on me! My daughter is suffering terribly from demonic possession.'
>
> "Y'shua did not answer a word, so hid disciples came to him and urged him, 'Send her away, for she keeps crying after us.'
>
> He answered, 'I was sent only to the lost sheep of Israel.'"
>
> Matthew 15:21-24

> "I am not ashamed of the gospel, for it is the power of salvation of everyone who believes; first for the Jew, then for the Gentile."
>
> Romans 1:16

Therefore, the incident in Matthew tells us that right up until the last year of Y'shua's life, the Jewish portion of the divine plan was in full swing. The message was brought first to his hometown, then into the wider areas of the Galilee, and finally, to Jerusalem, where he was rejected again and crucified. Therefore, in spite of the citation in John 21:25 that Y'shua said and did many things not recorded, we can be certain he did not travel more than about 200 miles away from his native soil at any point during his life.

From this point on, the picture gets murky. After the age of twelve he must have continued his apprenticeship with his father. As the eldest son, Y'shua was supposed to inherit the family business. However, what is more remarkable is that there may in fact be ruins still standing that he actually helped build.

Just four miles from Nazareth lay the Roman provincial capita of Sepphoris. While still fundamentally a Jewish city, Sepphoris also had a very cosmopolitan feel to it, and many Romans, Greeks and Syrians either worked there or made it their home. Then, when Y'shua was a teenager, Herod Antipas rebuilt the city and it is well known that he conscripted craftsmen from the local area to help. Therefore, there could hardly have been a more important, lucrative or convenient assignment for Joseph & Son Carpentry.

However, most biblical scholars also believe this success was short lived, with his adopted father Joseph probably passing away sometime in Y'shua's late teen years. At that point, it seems Y'shua probably assumed the role of head of the family for a while, continuing on his father's work. Another fact that many scholars also are relatively certain of is that Y'shua stayed in his home region at least until age twenty, when it was required that he go up to Jerusalem and register for the Temple Tax. The fact that the tax assessors found him so easily is proof enough of this being done. From this point on however, the picture goes completely dim.

So what did he do? Join the Essenes? Possibly, although the way the evidence stacks up it looks like the carpenter just up and left one day to go into the desert. Additionally, he may have simply lived there as a hermit for several years without joining any sect at all!

I say that because all attempts to fit Y'shua's teachings within any accepted Jewish school have all failed. For the most part, he seems to follow the liberal teachings of Hillel when it comes to some applications of Sabbath observance, but other indices exist to show he went further still with what Y'shua believed was appropriate. At the other end of the spectrum, Y'shua's teachings on marriage and divorce are much stricter than either the more conservative school of Shammai or even the Sadduccees.

So where did he get the teachings, even as the Gospel writers tell us he taught with authority and not like the teachers of the Law? Well, since not even his own home town knows the answer to that (Mark 6:1-9), we can only assume it came from elsewhere.

Of course, saying that these teachings came from God is a true, but not wholly satisfactory answer. What I mean is where did Y'shua go to think about these truths, and the answer has to be the desert. Over and over again, we see patterns in the Gospels that Y'shua would withdraw to secluded locales when he needed to think, sometimes getting up at dawn and, on one occasion, deliberately evading his own disciples to do so!

So, like so many prophets did before, Y'shua underwent a spiritual quest, not to find the truth that he had, but to evaluate ways to deliver it to his people when he knew the time was right. That timing, apparently was very important to him, which is why even at the Cana Wedding he said it had not come yet. Then, in between those two events, he must have left the family business behind for two reasons.

First, even though he is from Galilee originally, Mark appears to imply in his first chapter that Y'shua did not settle there until much later, and this may be because he had left on a previous occasion. Second, we see numerous evidences that some of his relatives were hostile— and even angry— towards Y'shua. Mark 2 tells us that some of his family tried having Y'shua locked up in an asylum. Later, John 7 has at least two of Y'shua's brothers dare him to travel into danger, and Y'shua's own comments about houses being divided "two against three and three against two for my sake" could very well be autobiographical.

Was it just that the preaching and odd behavior was embarrassing to them? Certainly comments by Y'shua that his mother and brothers were only those who listened to him did not help the situation, but it seems to me something deeper might be at work.

Y'shua, as the eldest son, was supposed to run the family business. But, if in the course of his stay in the desert his father died, that task would fall on his younger siblings. The whole town would likely wonder "Where is the eldest son?" and "Why isn't he helping out?" And, again, there are concordances in the Gospels, such as when people have to give up their material needs for the sake of the kingdom of God, and when a potential disciple who asked only to bury his father is denied admittance. Such incidents must have hit very close to home indeed.

Now imagine, after all that heartache, he returns like the Prodigal Son, but this time there is no father to help assuage the wounds of the others. And, even upon his return, he is still disappearing for days at a time to think. The frustration on his siblings must have also been aggravated by another factor: There are four of them, a minimum of two other sisters, and a widowed mother to take care of!

So, ironically, to Y'shua the needs of the kingdom and will of his Father are the paramount concerns. But, to everyone else he is neglecting his earthly responsibilities. No wonder then that Y'shua does the same thing with Mary Magdalene by taking her away from chores to preach the kingdom of God to her, even as her sister Martha complains at the lack of help!

Therefore, while I think the evidence is pretty clear that Y'shua went into the desert for a number of years, I can find no other indications as to what he did there.

However, the evidence is much stronger that a close relative of Y'shua, namely John the Baptist, most certainly did have a clear connection to the Essenes.

In accordance with the divine message his father received, John is separated at birth for God according to the Nazirite regulations. A small comparison between Gabriel's message and this requirement will suffice:

> "'Your wife Elizabeth will bear you a son, and you are to give him the name John. He will be a joy and delight to you, and many will rejoice because of his birth, for he will be great in the sight of the Lord. He is never to take any wine or other fermented drink, and he will be filled with the Holy Spirit even from birth.'"

Luke 1:13b-15

> "Speak to the Israelites and say to them: 'If a man or a woman wants to make a special vow, a vow of separation to the Lord as a Nazirite, he must abstain from wine and other fermented drink. He must not drink vinegar made from wine or from other fermented drink. He must not drink grape juice or eat grapes or raisins. As long as he is a Nazirite, he must not eat anything that comes from the grapevine, not even the seeds or skins."

Numbers 6:1-4

And there are striking parallels between Gabriel visiting Zacharias and another angelic visit involving the mother of a famous Nazirite, Samson:

> "The angel of the Lord appeared to her and said, 'You are sterile and childless, but you are going to conceive and bear a son. Now see to it that you drink no wine or other fermented drink and that you do not eat anything unclean, because you will conceive and give birth to a son. No razor may be used on his head, because the boy is to be a Nazirite, set apart by God from birth, and he will begin the deliverance of Israel from the hands of the Philistines.'"
>
> Judges 13:3-5

John was a Nazirite, and even though his beard is not mentioned, he is compared in appearance and message to the prophet Elijah, who most certainly did fit this description, (Matthew 3:4, 2 Kings 1:8). The only other clue about his childhood is a statement in Luke 1:80 that he "lived in the desert until he appeared publicly to Israel."

Now this is a curious statement. Just what is such a young child doing spending the majority of his life in the desert when his father had a respectable living as a priest? Other early (and unofficial) works may provide a clue as to what happened next.

According to the *Infancy Gospel of James*, Herod's campaign against the infants two years old and under extended past Bethlehem and into the area around Jerusalem and other parts of Judea. As a result, the fatal edict applied not just to Y'shua, but to his second cousin John also.

Zacharias, John's father, went to the Temple to administer as normal while his wife Elizabeth took the infant, eventually finding shelter inside a mountain. When Herod's henchman find Zacharias, they give him a horrible choice: Either he tells them where his son is, or he will be killed. Zacharias opts for death and is murdered just a few feet away from the altar.

It is at this point that *Infancy James* ties things together with canonical Gospels in a rather deft manner. First, it identifies John's father as the same Zacharias Y'shua refers to in Luke 11:51, which would seem an obvious and interesting linkage.[272] Then we are told that the man who takes the slain priest's post, Simeon, is the same man mentioned in Luke 1:25-32.

Elizabeth is now elderly and is forced to care for John without a husband or a place to turn to, and here is where early tradition may meet up with a kernel of historical truth. *Infancy James* then goes on to explain that the mountain where Elizabeth lay desperate and prostrate before God suddenly opened up and "an angel in white" took the child inside. As it turns out, the Essenes were known to populate such mountainous areas in the Qumran area, and they also wore white linen robes. This scenario also explains why John, Y'shua's second cousin, says that he never met him before the baptism, (John 1:33).

However, because the Essenes repeatedly emphasize the virtues of community living, John's later lifestyle as a hermit clearly indicates some sort of break had occurred. He then went out on his own but obviously retained a lot of the groups' ire against the rich and corrupt priestly class in Jerusalem. Why else would he call these same teachers a "brood of vipers", (Matthew 3:7)?

Therefore, while there were many other things that Y'shua and his cousin John said and did which were not recorded, the conventions of culture and faith provide subtle yet powerful testimonies as to where they said and did them.

A Final Mystery Solved:

The Apostles' Forgotten Legacy

If there is one part of this work that I truly hope breaks new ground, it is in reassessing the true impact of the original apostles. I say this, not

Signs of the Cross: The Search for the Historical Jesus

as an effort to undermine their contribution but rather, to expand it. Put simply, the world only knows half the story.

In the last two millennia, the story that has taken hold in western consciousness is as follows:

Long ago, in a tiny town called Bethlehem, the man who the world would later call Y'shua of Nazareth was born. He was a pious Jew and a revolutionary teacher. He wrought many great miracles and proved to many that he was the Son of God who had fulfilled the promises in the Torah. However, the Jews, who rejected almost all of his claims, persecuted and intimidated this new group of believers. Subsequently, those "rebels", led most notably by Paul of Tarsus, transformed this small Jewish apocalyptic sect into a worldwide Gentile movement. The Torah had "passed away", and the world moved happily on to the next level of spirituality. Circumcision was replaced by baptism, Saturday Sabbaths by Sunday celebrations of the resurrection, and Passover became Easter, among many other changes.

Am I saying this story is false? Not necessarily, but neither is it wholly true. This tale, like any other, is dependent on the perspective of the storyteller. That person then will, quite obviously, insert some facts that favor their cause and omit others that do not.

However, I also need to be very clear here and say that, while my ideological bent as a Messianic Jew is quite apparent, I am not placing a value judgment on either point of view. Rather, I am restoring a view that has been lost and putting it back into the world of scholarly discourse. In that sense, please allow me to— not discredit this view— but instead put back the pieces that are missing from it. To begin with, once again, we need to turn to the source:

> . . . Tertullus laid charges against Paul in the following address to the governor: "Your Excellency . . . we have found him to be a troublemaker . . . a ringleader of the sect known as the Nazarenes . . .
>
> Paul said . . ."I admit that I follow the Way, which

they call a sect. I worship the God of our ancestors, and I firmly believe the Jewish law and everything written in the books of prophecy. I have hope in God, just as these men do, that he will raise both the righteous and the ungodly."

Acts 24:2,5,11-15 (NLT)

Then Paul, knowing that some of them were Sadducees and the others Pharisees called out in the Sanhedrin, 'My brothers, I am a Pharisee, the son of a Pharisee. I stand on trial because of my hope in the resurrection of the dead.' When he said this, a dispute broke out between the Pharisees and the Sadducees, and the assembly was divided. (The Sadducees say that there is no resurrection, and that there are neither angels nor spirits, but the Pharisees acknowledge them all.)

Acts 23:6-8 (NIV)

So, our first point is that the apostle Paul did not view his group as one separate from Judaism. Instead he declares, like any adherent of a small Jewish sect would at the time, that his group has the true understanding of how perform as a member of that religion:

"I urge you, brothers, to watch out for those who cause divisions and put obstacles in your way that are contrary to the teaching you have learned. Keep away from them. For such people are not serving our Lord Messiah, but their own appetites. By smooth talk and flattery they deceive the minds of naïve people. Everyone has heard about your obedience, so I am full of joy over you; but I want you to be wise about what is good and innocent about what is evil. The God of peace will soon crush Satan under your feet."

Romans 16:17-20 (NIV)

Nor is Paul alone in proclaiming such exclusivity for his own "school":

> [And the Guardian will come] and the elders with him until . . . and they will be introduced into the genealogy . . . And the Guardian will [curse (the unrepentant), saying, 'Be damned without] mercy. [Let him be cur]sed . . .' And he will remove him] from his inheritance for ev[er] . . .
>
> Dead Sea Scrolls 4Q275, quoted from *The Complete Dead Sea Scrolls in English*, p. 592.

This quote from what has become known as a pacifist desert sect we call the Essenes, nevertheless reflects that deeply passionate rhetoric that Jews engage in when they debate. It is therefore very hard, from our more politically correct modern viewpoint, to realize that this was a normal and accepted means of discussion. The New Testament, in spite of all the angry rhetoric it dispenses against the Pharisees, Saduccees and the like, nevertheless also takes great pains to show us when members of those "wrong" sects get something correct. Joseph of Arimathea, for example, was a member of the Sanhedrin[273], which made him most likely a member of the latter group, and the apostle Paul proudly proclaims himself as a "Pharisee and the son of a Pharisee".[274] Furthermore, on one occasion, another group of Pharisees warns Y'shua he is in danger, and a "teacher of the Law" is told he is not far from the kingdom of God.[275]

Thus, for every "Woe unto you, you hypocrites!" that we see come out of Y'shua or the disciple's mouths, we also see a fundamental acceptance of the opposition as fellow Jews. That is also why Y'shua acknowledges that Pharisees "sit in Moses' seat" and that, "unless your righteousness surpasses the teachers of the law" you will not get into the kingdom of heaven". [276]

At the same time, the Pharisees frequently return the favor. They call Y'shua, "Master" and actively engage him in scriptural debate, which is a sign of deep respect. If Y'shua did not have good standing with them, he would simply have been tossed out of the Temple as they did to a certain blind man.[277] Was part of that respect a grudging acceptance of the young rabbi's popularity? Most certainly it was. However, the bigger picture demands that we look at the fact that even the high priest Caiphas had people with him who thought well of the Nazarene prophet.[278]

Therefore, to take this cultural tradition of passionate disputation and somehow turn it into a full scale indictment of all Jews some twenty centuries later, is the height of folly and racial hatred. All of the so-called anti Semitic slurs in the New Testament must then be seen in this light. Terms like "synagogue of Satan", "those who appear to be Jews but are not", and even the very nasty "his blood be on us and our children" are merely the tools that one group uses to prove its case against another. The Essenes condemned the priests in Jerusalem as being consigned to hellfire, and the Pharisees, when not disputing laws among themselves with the competing schools of Hillel and Shammai, slurred the Saduccees as traitors collaborating with Rome. Whether its Moses and Korah or even Maimonides and Rashi, this is what Jews have always done and will continue to do.

Similarly, when we see the apparent fury that is unleashed against Y'shua in the Talmud, the same mechanism is in place. However, the difference is that, while the Jewish Christian contingent was excommunicated from the Pharisaic-Rabbinic system, the real proof of Y'shua's influence lies elsewhere. Judaism, with all its passionate and confrontational style of discourse, nevertheless scrupulously records all sides in the debate. That is, in fact, exactly what the Talmud is; one long, scholarly argument that takes a dozen countries and many centuries to complete, but never resolve.

So, even as the persons themselves may appear vilified and isolated as a form of Jewish heretics in both the New Testament and the Talmud, these documents only represent the partisan forum of each side. Therefore, since this debate started as a Jewish discussion about a Jewish Messiah foretold in Jewish Scripture, I submit the time has come to return to that arena and sort out the rest. However, since we need to see where we came from in order to know where we are going, let us continue with the history:

> "But these sectarians... did not call themselves Christians, but "Nazarenes," however they are simply complete Jews. They use not only the New Testament but the Old Testament as well, as the Jews do... They have no different ideas, but confess everything exactly as the Law proclaims it and in the Jewish fashion, except for their belief in the Messiah, if you please! For they acknowledge both the resurrection of the dead and the divine creation of all things, and declare that God is one, and that His Son is Y'shua the Messiah. They are trained to a nicety in Hebrew. For among them the entire Law, Prophets and the... Writings... are read in Hebrew, as they surely are by the Jews. They are different from the Jews, and different from Christians, only in the following. They disagree with the Jews for they have come to faith in Messiah; but since they are still fettered with the Law—circumcision and the Sabbath, and the rest—they are not in accord with Christians... They have the Good News according to Matthew in its entirety in Hebrew. For it is clear they still preserve

> this, in the Hebrew alphabet, as it was originally written."

Epiphanus; Panarion 29 (fourth century)

And:

> Then Barnabbas went to Tarsus to look for Saul, and when he found him, brought him to Antioch. So for a whole year Barnabbas and Saul met with the church and taught great numbers of people. The disciples were first called Christians at Antioch.

Acts 11:25-26 (NIV)

So what we see then are the beginnings of two ancient groups. The Jewish Messianic believers were first called "Nazarenes" and the Gentiles, following the lead of what the disciples were called in Antioch, began to identify themselves as "Christians". These two, furthermore, were the beginnings of the "sees" that started both in Jerusalem and in that other city. However, in both cases, the final authority was with the former during the first five decades of the faith.[279]

Now, even when scholars do explore the Nazarene-Jerusalem Church and correctly identify it as the same group headed by Peter, Paul, and James the Just, the conventional wisdom is that these Jewish believers faded from view after the destruction of the Temple in the year 70.

The reality, however, is quite different. While it is true that both Jewish Revolts were devastating, the fact is that the Nazarenes continued for several more centuries. The quote used from Epiphanus a short time ago, for example, is from the fourth century.

Another common misconception is that the Nazarenes were the "Judaizers" or "legalists" that are mentioned in a negative light in several places. Here is just one example of many that proves this point:

> Some men came down from Judea to Antioch and were teaching the brothers: 'Unless you are circumcised according to the custom taught by Moses, you cannot be saved. . . .'"
>
> Acts 15:1 (NIV)

So here we begin with an informal group of Jews rendering an opinion. In response to this assertion, the Jerusalem Nazarene Beit Din—their version of the Sanhedrin or "house of judgment"— deliberates on the issue for a time and one of their leaders, James, issues a ruling which is put into a letter this way:

> "We have heard that some went out from us WITHOUT OUR AUTHORIZATION and disturbed you, troubling your minds by what they said . . . Therefore we are sending Judas and Silas to confirm by word of mouth what we are writing."
>
> Acts 15:24,27 (NIV)

Therefore, since it is the Nazarene body that is rebuking these practices, they cannot be the "Judaizers" in question. Furthermore, every decision that is made since then regarding Gentiles goes straight through either the Jerusalem Council or its leadership.

But what happened to the other Jewish Messianics that lost the debate? In their case, they regrouped into a rival sect that we call "Ebionites". The early Church historian Eusebius explains their critical differences from the Nazarenes this way:

> The Heresy of the Ebionites. (1)

The evil demon, however, being unable to tear certain others from their allegiance to the Messiah of God, yet found them susceptible in a different direction, and so brought them over to his own purposes. The ancients quite properly called these men Ebionites, because they held poor and mean opinions concerning Messiah. (2) For they considered him a plain and common man, who was justified only because of his superior virtue, and who was the fruit of the intercourse of a man with Mary. In their opinion the observance of the ceremonial law was altogether necessary, on the ground that they could not be saved by faith in Messiah alone and by a corresponding life. (3) There were others, however, besides them, that were of the same name, (4) but avoided the strange and absurd beliefs of the former, and did not deny that the Lord was born of a virgin and of the Holy Spirit. But nevertheless, inasmuch as they also refused to acknowledge that he pre-existed, being God, Word, and Wisdom, they turned aside into the impiety of the former, especially when they, like them, endeavored to observe strictly the bodily worship of the law. (6) These men, 4 moreover, thought that it was necessary to reject all the epistles of the apostle, whom they called an apostate from the law; (7) and they used only the so-called Gospel according to the Hebrews (8) and made small account of the rest. The Sabbath and the rest of the discipline 5 of the Jews they observed just like them, but at the same time, like us, they celebrated the Lord's days as a memorial of the resurrection of the Saviour. (9) Wherefore, in consequence of such a course they received the name of Ebionites,

> which signified the poverty of their understanding. For this is the name by which a poor man is called among the Hebrews. (10)

Church History of Eusebius, 3:27

And here is additional testimony from Ireneus:

> Those who are called Ebionites agree that the world was made by God; but their opinions with respect to the Lord are similar to those of Cerinthus and Carpocrates. They use the Gospel according to Matthew only, and repudiate the Apostle Paul, maintaining that he was an apostate from the law. As to the prophetical writings, they endeavour to expound them in a somewhat singular manner: they practise circumcision, persevere in the observance of those customs which are enjoined by the law, and are so Judaic in their style of life, that they even adore Jerusalem as if it were the house of God.

Ireneaus of Lyons, Against All Heresies, 1:26.2

So, we now see a number of critical differences between these groups, such as:
- Nazarenes accepted the doctrine of the virgin birth; Ebionites did not.[280]
- Nazarenes affirmed the divinity of the Messiah as God in the flesh in concert with 1 Corinthians 12:3; the Ebionites held that Y'shua was only a man.
- Nazarenes included all the letters of Paul in their canon and in fact kept a full New Testament; Ebionites only venerated Matthew.

- Nazarenes had at one point a full and complete Hebrew version of Matthew; Ebionites possessed a "mutilated and inferior" copy.[281]
- Finally, as stated before, there was the circumcision controversy. While both groups were circumcised, the Nazarenes looked at physical circumcision as going hand in hand with a "circumcised heart". They also believed that a proselyte should learn the Torah and be saved by that effort, which would in turn later lead to physical circumcision. By contrast, the Ebionites as originally mentioned in Acts 15, believed that physical circumcision was required before salvation.

Therefore, what we have seen is that not all Jewish-Christian groups were considered heretical. Rather, both the Nazarene and the Christian groups together rebuked the heresies they found existing within Judaism and Christianity alike.

Then, as a final twist, the original Nazarene movement actually expanded into separate groups. To make this idea a bit easier to understand, consider the fact that so far we have discussed two major ancient assemblies, the See of Jerusalem (Nazarenes) and the See of Antioch (Gentile Christians[282]). Now the time has come to discuss the third, and last, major group:

> "With the help of Silas, whom I consider to be a faithful brother, I have written you briefly, encouraging you and testifying that this is the true grace of God. Stand fast in it. She who is in Babylon, chosen together with you, sends you her greetings, and so does my son Mark."
>
> 1 Peter 5:12-13

Now the official doctrine of the Roman Catholic Church is that "Babylon" is a symbolic code word for Rome, or a way to protect the early believers should this letter fall into the wrong hands. However, when we combine this citation with very early eastern tradition, a very credible case can be made to the contrary.

Although, in fairness to my Catholic brethren, let me just say that I do not dispute the idea that Peter did preach in Rome and helped establish the See of Rome. On the other hand, I am saying that Peter founded more than one group. Several years before his final arrest and crucifixion, the "khugy" or Church of Huts, became a vital force in Babylon. Furthermore they, just like their compatriots in Jerusalem, had their movement gain strength on the backs of a very strong Jewish community. Now, another little known historical fact suddenly becomes relevant: Not all the Jews returned from their captivity there!

Then, sometime before 100 BCE, those Jews translated the Hebrew Scriptures into Aramaic, and the Peshitta Tenkah, or Aramaic OT, was born. As a result, almost two centuries later, Peter was able to preach and debate exclusively in his native language.

At the same time, other apostles sent their Aramaic copies of Gospels and Epistles to the See of Babylon's door, and by the end of the first century, their canon was finished. The original name of this group by the way should also sound familiar: The Assembly of the Nazarenes!

Finally, while one Nazarene leader founded this group in Babylon that would later become known as the Church of the East, the Jerusalem group continued for several hundred years and became a part of the official historical record.

So what happened to the Nazarenes, and where are they now?

To answer that question, we must again go back to the year 70. In the early spring, Rome began to lay siege to Jerusalem. The Nazarenes, rembering the warnings of their Master (Luke 21:20-21), fled to the mountains and settled in a city known as Pella. Once there, the coalition of believers began to fracture under the pressure of the calamities of the day, and the breakaway sect known as the Ebionites was born.

Then the next development, in the year 90, is particularly painful for me to relate for what will become obvious reasons very shortly.

The conventional Jews, unfortunately but understandably, viewed the Nazarenes as traitors. Part of it may have been because the Nazarenes fled early in the conflict with Rome, but surely the majority of the venom came from their continued adherence to belief in Y'shua bar Yosef as Messiah. As a result, they were determined to make sure that none of the "heretics" remained secretly among them, and the task fell to a man known as "Simon the Lesser" to assist that effort in this manner:

> Our Rabbis taught: Simeon ha-Pakuli arranged the eighteen benedictions in order before Rabban Gamaliel in Jabneh. Said Rabban Gamaliel to the Sages: "Can any one among you frame a benediction relating to the Minim?" Samuel the Lesser arose and composed it.
>
> b.Berakot 29a

Now before discussing who the *minim* were, let us show the benediction as it appears today:

> And for slanderers let there be no hope, and let all wickedness perish as in a moment; let all thine enemies be speedily cut off, and the dominion of arrogance do you uproot and crush, cast down and humble speedily in our days. Blessed are you, O L-rd, who breakest the enemies and humbles the arrogant.

Now while this version sounds rather neutral—and even makes sense because of a general injunction against those who would slander Jews—the original benediction was much more specific. Found at the Cairo Genizah, the first "birkhat ha minim" read this way:

> For the renegades let there be no hope, and may the

> arrogant kingdom soon be rooted out in our days, and the Nazarenes and the Minim perish as in a moment and be blotted out from the book of life and with the righteous may they not be inscribed. Blessed are you, O L-rd, who humbles the arrogant.

Sad but true, this was originally a curse specifically against the Nazarenes, and the intent was to eliminate an internal threat by forcing the closet Nazarenes who remained to utter it against themselves. As a result, the Nazarenes were effectively ousted from all synagogues, and as Epiphanus also records, the bitterness was a lingering one:

> Not only do Jewish people have a hatred of them; they even stand up at dawn, at midday, and toward evening, three times a day when they recite their prayers in the synagogues, and curse and anathemize them. Three times a day they say, "G-d curse the Nazarenes." For they harbor an extra grudge against them, if you please, because despite their Jewishness, they proclaim that Y'shua is Messiah . . .
>
> Epiphanius; Panarion 29

Then, in the year 132, the Bar Kochba Revolt began and, for a while, it seemed that the Nazarenes and the Pharisees healed the breach in the face of a common enemy. But while both groups took up arms, the Nazarenes eventually split with the Pharisees again over a very obvious point: They disagreed over who the Messiah was! This was no small contention, primarily because the impetus of the entire revolt rested on the leadership, including the great Rabbi Akiva, proclaiming Bar Kochba as the Messiah. The Nazarenes, of course, looked to their Master, Y'shua bar Yosef, to return and deliver Israel. So, when push came to shove, the Nazarenes again went out on their own, and the ramifications were once again devastating. The Pharisees, now settled comfortably in the new paradigm of Rabbinic Judaism, then labeled the Nazarenes as *meshumeddin* (traitors) in spite of the fact that they too admitted that following Bar Kochba was a grievous error.

On the other hand, it is also quite probable that 99% of today's Orthodox Jewry is not thinking of animosities held sixteen centuries back, but is instead praying for the safety of Israel and her people, as any pious Jew should regardless of denomination. So, while it may have started as a prayer against the Nazarenes back then, chances are they are not being brought to mind in today's version.

Now, getting back to the events happening in the 130's, the Nazarene leadership itself also suffered a terrible blow. Up until then, and dating from the time of James the Just and Peter, all the Bishops of the See of Jerusalem had been Semitic and native Aramaic speakers. But, when Rome conquered Jerusalem again, the last *Nazarene Nasi*, a man named Yehuda, was deposed, and a Gentile named Markus was put in his place.

Then, by the fourth century, Constantine—who was also a rabid anti-Semite— had made a serious attempt to standardize Gentile Christianity, and the Nazarenes were clearly not welcome. From that time forward, Gentiles also declared these Jewish Christians heretical, which is the context of the quote from Epiphanus regarding them. Epiphanus also recorded later on in Panarion 29 that the Nazarenes had settled in places like Beoria and Pella, but that their numbers had dwindled to "insect-like" proportions.

From there however, the picture begins to dim. Certainly some of them would have joined the Church of the East so they could continue to proclaim their faith in the Messiah in their native Aramaic language, and early documents from the COE seem to also bear this scenario out.[283] However, by the rise of Islam in the seventh and eighth centuries, they seem to have ceased altogether. And, even if by some miracle a few survived, Tamerlane most definitely would have fin-

Signs of the Cross: The Search for the Historical Jesus

ished the job by the time his wave of Semitic Christian persecution ended in the Middle Ages.

Nowadays though the clouds from that time do have a few silver linings for us today. For one thing, the fact that Semitic bishops in the See of Jerusalem ceased in the second century virtually guarantees that they used Aramaic New Testament books very early—at least three centuries before many in the West thought the Peshitta was "invented" by Rabbula. Also, this "missing" piece of history fits in perfectly with the rough time (circa 150-170) that Tatian would have begun composing his integrated Aramaic Gospel known as *the Diatessaron*. Now some have disputed the significance of this work based on the probablity that Tatian may have only finished what was begun by his predecessor Justin Martyr, and that his now lost Aramaic text may have been a translation from early Greek mss.

On the other hand though, the circulation of some versions of Aramaic Gospels is reinforced by the testimony of Hegisippius who, around the year 180, specifically refers to quoting from "the Gospel of the Hebrews" and a "Syriac Gospel". In the former case, that title could apply either to either a Nazarene or an Ebionite document. However, since the Ebionites are widely attested to as having a mutilated or inferior version of the former, it seems reasonable to conclude that several Aramaic versions are attested to at this early time, and at least one of those is genuine. Additionally, there is every indication that these works circulated for a considerable period before Heigsippius wrote about them.[284]

As for the Nazarenes, they have made a comeback too, and I am living proof of that fact. We have returned now to take our rightful place also as a kind of missing link between first century Pharisaic-Rabbinic Judaism, Gentile Christianity and mainline Messianic Judaism as well.

And finally, within conventional Judasim as well, there now exists diversity unprecedented since the first century. The fact is, while some may continue to assert that their kind of practice and belief is the one true form, there has been a subtle but profound shift in how the other groups are viewed. Put simply, they may be misled, but they are not traitors to their people. Therefore, tacitly the range of the faith— from Orthodox on the right to Reconstructionists on the left— the contributions of all kinds of Jews are accepted in the Jewish community at large. Now all that remains then is for Nazarenes and other Messianic Jewish groups to finally get to occupy the seats which have been waiting for them for so long. In the end then, the only people who need to be condemned now are those who would oppress and deny any Jew—Messianic or not—their fundamental and inalienable right to exist.

CONCLUSION

As I hope I have shown throughout the course of this book, Jews and Christians share a wonderful tradition. Now, I believe it is time for them to share the future as well. The political choices that forced both sides to put up walls of separation are now, at the beginning of the twenty-first century, no longer viable.

Also, while I believe my point of view has been consistent from the standpoint of Messianic Judaism, my purpose has been to start a dialog and not just provide the answers. I can say this because Jews have always disagreed and yet maintained their cultural identity. In this sense then, I only ask to be allowed to follow in the traditions of my ancestors, whose blood sweat and tears are the greatest source of pride to me personally. So let us talk—kibbitz even—about the Sacred Writ, and leave the politics of personal destruction aside.

Brothers don't always agree on everything, and on some level they should not, for diversity will strengthen their bond. But if Esau can embrace Jacob, can we not then open the door and let everyone come home? Armageddon is coming, and so is the time when every single one of God's people will be needed to fight on the same side.

Come home.

We are stronger with you than without you.

Amen.

Bibliography

(This list is by no means complete.)

BIBLES:

Holy Bible (New International Version). Grand Rapids, Michigan: Zondervan Bible Publishers, 1978.

Brenton, Lancelot, C.L., *The Septuagint with Apocrypha, Greek and English,* The United States of America: Hendrickson Publishers, 1997.

Lamsa, George, *The Modern New Testament from the Aramaic,* San Francisco, California: Harper and Row Publishers, 1997.

Plaut, Gunther, W., *The Torah: A Modern Commentary,* New York: Union of American Hebrew Congregations, 1981.

Ryrie, Charles, Cadwell, Th.D., PH D, *The Ryrie Study Bible, New Testament (New American Standard Version).* Chicago, Illinois: Moody Press, 1976.

Thompson, Frank, Charles, D.D., PH D., *The New Chain Reference Bible (King James Version), Fourth Edition.* Indianapolis, Indiana: B.B. Kirkbride Bible Company, Inc, 1964.

Thompson, Frank Charles, D.D., PHD., *The Thompson Chain Reference Bible, Second Improved Edition (New International Version)*. Indianapolis, Indiana: B.B. Krikbride Bible Company, Inc, 1994.

The Holy Scriptures According to the Masoretic Text. Philadelphia, Pennsylvania: The Jewish Publication Society of Amerca, 1955.

The New Covenant Aramaic Peshitta Text with Hebrew Translation, Jerusalem: The Aramaic Scriptures Research Society in Israel, 1986.

Ktaba d'diteequa yedata d'Maran Eshooa Meshikha (Book of the New Covenant of the Lord Jesus the Messiah), New York: B'shanta Meshikhata Aplar, 1982.

BIBLE REFERENCE:

Catholic Encylcopedia, Encylcopedia Press, Inc., 1913.

The Story of the Bible Volumes I & II, New York: Wm. H. Wise and Company, 1952.

Ausebel, Nathan, *Pictorial History of the Jewish People*, New York: Crown Publishers, 1953.

Easton, M.G., *Illustrated Bible Dictionary*, New York, New York: Crescent Books, 1989.

Foxe, John, *The New Foxe's Book of Martyrs*, North Brunswick, NJ: Bridge Logos Publishers, 1997.

Strong, James, *Strong's Exhaustive Concordance of the Bible*, Nashville, Tennessee: Thomas Nelson Publishers, 1995.

Wright, Ernest, G., *Great People of the Bible and How They Lived*, Pleasantville, New York: The Readers Digest Association, 1974.

OTHER BOOKS, MAGAZINES AND JOURNALS:

Anderson, Robert, *The Coming Prince*, Grand Rapids, Michigan: Kregel Publications, 1954.

Bainton, Roland, H., *The Horizon History of Christianity*, New York: American Heritage Publishing Company, Inc., 1964.

Baltsan, Hayim, *Webster's New World Hebrew Dictionary*, New York, New York: Simon and Schuster, 1992.

Bettenson, H., *The Early Christian Fathers, Eleventh Edition*, London: Oxford University Press, 1991.

Borg, Marcus, J., *Meeting Jesus Again for the First Time: The Historic Jesus and the Heart of Contemporary Faith*. New York, New York: Harper Collins, 1994.

Bulmer-Thomas, Ivor, *The Quarterly Journal of the Royal Astronomical Society*, Vol 33, p.363, 1992.

Burke-Gafney, W. "Kepler and the Star of Bethlehem," *Journal of the Royal Astronomical Society of Canada*, p. 417-25, December 1937.

Chester, Craig, "The Star of Bethlehem," *IMPRIMIS: The Monthly Journal of Hillsdale College*, Vol 22, Number 12. Hillsdale College, Michigan, 1993.

Chua-Eoan, Howard, "The Secret Lives of Jesus Christ," *Time Magazine*, April 8, 1996.

Ciotti, Joseph, "The Magi's Star: Misconceptions and New Suggestions," *Gtiffith Observer*, 42, p. 2-14, December, 1978.

Clark, David, H., Parkinson, John, H., and Stephenson, F., Richard, *Quarterly Journal of the Royal Astronomical Society*, Vol. 32, 1977, p. 443.

Davis, Avram, Dr., and Mascetti, Manuella, D., *Judaic Mysticism*, New York: Hyperion Publishers, 1997.

Davidson, Marshall, B., *The Horizon Book of Christianity*, New York: The American Heritage Publishing Company, Inc., 1964.

Elson, John, "Eyewitnesses to Jesus? A German Scholar Argues that Three Bits of Papyrus Are the Oldest Fragments of St. Matthew's Gospel," *Time Magazine*, April 8, 1996.

Elson, John, "The New Testament's Unsolved Mysteries," *Time Magazine*, December 18, 1995.

Epstein, Morris, *All About Jewish Holidays and Customs, Revised Edition*. New York, New York: Ktav Publishing House, 1970.

Errico, Rocco, A. and Bazzi, Michael, J., *Classical Aramaic Book 1*, Irvine, California: Noohra Foundation Publishers, 1992.

Federer, C., "Rambling Through December Skies," *Sky & Telescope*, p. 394-6, December, 1968.

Finegan, Jack, *Handbook of Biblical Chronology*. Princeton, New Jersey: Princeton University Press, 1964.

Golb, Norman, *Who Wrote the Dead Sea Scrolls? The Search for the Secret of Qumran*, New York: Simon and Schuster, 1995.

Hale, William, *The Horizon Book of Ancient Greece*, New York: The American Heritage Publishing Company, Inc., 1965.

Heslop, W.G., *Diamonds from Daniel*, Grand Rapids, Michigan: Kregel Publications, 1976.

Hughes, David, W., *Nature*, Vol 264, 1976, p. 513.

Hughes, David, W., *The Star of Bethlehem: An Astronomer's Confirmation*, New York, New York: Walker and Company, 1979.

Humphreys, Colin, J., *Quarterly Journal of the Royal Astronomical Society*, Vol 32, 1991, p. 389.

Jacobs, Louis, *The Schocken Book of Jewish Mystical Testimonies*, New York: Schocken Press, 1997.

Jeremiah, David with Carlson, C.C., *The Handwriting on the Wall: Secrets from the Prophecies of Daniel*. Dallas, Texas: Word Publishing, 1992.

Jerome, *Commentary on Daniel*. Translated by Gleason L. Archer, Jr. Grand Rapids, Michigan: Baker Books, 1959.

Johnson, Luke Timothy, *The Real Jesus: The Misguided Quest for the Historical Jesus and the Truth of the Traditional Gospels.* San Francisco, California: Harper Collins, 1996.

Josephus, Flavius, *The Works of Flavius Josephus Translated by William Whiston, A..M..* Philadelphia, Pennsylvania: The International Press and the John C. Winston Company, 1730.

Kelley, Page, H., *Biblical Hebrew: An Introductory Grammar,* Grand Rapids, MI: Wm. B. Eerdmans Publishing Company, 1992.

Kelley, Page, H., *A Handbook to Biblical Hebrew,* Grand Rapids, MI: Wm. B. Eerdmans Publishing Company, 1992.

King, Geoffrey, *Daniel, A Detailed Explanation of the Book,* London, England: Henry Walter, 1966.

Kittio, John, D.D., *Palestine From the Patriarchal Age to the Present,* New York: Peter Fenelon Collier, 1899.

Keller, Werner (translated by William Neil), *The Bible as History: A Confirmation of the Book of Books,* New York: William Morrow and Company Publishers, 1956.

La Sor, William, Sanford, Hubbard, David, Allen and Bush, Frederick, William, *Old Testament Survey,* Grand Rapids, Michigan: William B. Eerdman's Publishing Company, 1982.

Liddell, H.G. and Scott, R., *Greek—English Lexicon.*

Marshall, Roy, "The Star of Bethlehem," The Morehead Planetarium, Chapel Hill, North Carolina, 1949.

Martin, Ernest, *The Birth of Christ Recalculated, Second Edition*. Pasadena, California: The Foundation for Biblical Research, 1980.

Martin, Ernest, *The Star that Astonished the World*. Pasadena, California: The Foundation for Biblical Research, 1994.

Matt, Daniel, C., *The Essential Kabballah: The Heart of Jewish Mysticism*, San Francisco: Harper Collins Publishers, 1996.

McClaren, Alexander, *Expositions of Holy Scripture*, London, England: Hodder and Stroughton, 1908.

McDowell, Josh, *Evidence That Demands a Verdict, Volume II*, Nashville, Tennessee: Thomas Nelson Publishers, 1993.

Meier, John, P., *A Marginal Jew: Rethinking the Historical Jesus, Volume 1*. New York, New York: Doubleday, 1991.

Miller, Robert, J., *The Complete Gospels Annotated Scholars Version*. San Francisco, California: Harper Collins, 1992.

Mosely, John, "Common Errors in Star of Bethlehem Planetarium Shows," *The Planetarian*, Third Quarter, 1981.

Nickel, Keith, F., *The Synoptic Gospels: An Introduction*. Atlanta: John Knox Press, 1980.

Ostling, Richard, N., "Jesus Christ: Plain and Simple," *Time Magazine*, January 10, 1994.

Payne, Robert, *The Horizon Book of Ancient Rome*, New York: The American Heritage Publishing Company, Inc., 1965.

Rodman, Robert, "A Linguistic Note on the Christmas Star," *Griffith Observer*, 40, p. 89, December, 1976.

Schiffman, Lawrence, *Reclaiming the Dead Sea Scrolls*, Philadelphia and Jerusalem: Jewish Publication Society, 1994.

Scholem, Gershom, *Zohar, the Book of Splendor: Basic Readings from the Kabbalah*, New York: Schocken Books, 1949.

Scholem, Gershom, *Major Trends in Jewish Mysticism, 3rd Revised Edition*, New York: Schocken Books, 1961.

Seiss, Joseph, A., *Voices from Babylon*, Philadelphia, Pennsylvania: Castle Press, 1879.

Sheler, Jeffrey, L., "In Search of Christmas," *U.S. News and World Report*, December 23, 1996.

Sheler, Jeffrey, L., "Who Was Jesus?," *U.S. News and World Report*, December 20, 1993.

Sheler, Jeffrey, L., with Seider, Jill and Tharp, Mike., "In Search of Jesus: Scholars Seek the Answers in History," *U.S. News and World Report*, April 8, 1996.

Sheler, Jeffrey, L., "Mysteries of the Bible," *U.S. News and World Report*, April 17, 1995.

Strobel, Nick, *The Star of Bethlehem: An Astronomical Perspective*, Seattle, Washington: Astronomy Department of the University of Washington, December, 1995.

Templeton, Charles, B., with Freedman, David Noel, Gill, Theodore, Summercales, William, and Harpur, Charles, *Jesus*, New York, New York: Simon and Schuster, 1973.

Tuckerman, Bryant, *Planetary, Lunar and Solar Positions, 601 B.C. to 1 A.D.* Philadelphia, Pennsylvania: Memoirs of the American Philosophical Society, X62, 1962.

Van Biema, David, "The Gospel Truth?," *Time Magazine,* April 8, 1996.

Vardaman, Jerry, "A New Inscription Which Mentions Pilate as 'Prefect', *Journal of Biblical Literature,* 81, 1962.

Vermes, Geza, *The Complete Dead Sea Scrolls in English,* New York, NewYork: The Penguin Press, 1997.

Walvoord, John, *Daniel, Key to Prophetic Revelation,* Chicago, Illinois: Moody Press, 1971.

Wigoder, Geoffrey, *Illustrated Dictionary and Concordance of the Bible.* Pleasantville, New York: G.G. The Jerusalem Publishing House Ltd. in association with Reader's Digest Association, Inc., 1986.

Yonge, C.D., *The Works of Philo,* The United States of America: Hendrickson Publishers, 1993.

PICTURE CREDITS:

Reliquary of the True Cross, Anonymous (ninth century), Milan: Brea Milan Musuem.

Adoration of the Trinity, attributed to Albrecht Durer (1471-1528), Milan: Brea Milan Museum.

Head of Christ, attributed to Rembrandt Van Rijn (1606-1669), New York: Metropolitan Museum of Art.

The Supper at Emmaus, attributed to Michaelangelo Merisi de Carvaggio (1573-1610), London: National Gallery.

ENDNOTES

1 Scriptures references are NIV, adapted from Jesus to Y'shua. Mishnah Translation by Jacob Neusner

2 b. Shabbat 31a.

3 The author is indebted to Dr. James Trimm, who wrote up a similar study on this same topic.

4 <u>The Complete Dead Sea Scrolls in English</u>, p. 38-9; 139-141.

5 Notice here a technique within a technique, for this short sentence is actually a kol v'khomer!

6 In Hebrew, "righteous" and "just" are the same word, *tzaadak*.

7<u>All About Jewish Holidays and Customs</u>, p.2.

8<u>Illustrated Bible Dictionary</u>, p. 588 and <u>The Horizon Book of Ancient Rome</u>, p. 38. Although most historians today dismiss the legend of Romulus, Remus and the founding of Rome as having happened on April 21, 753 BCE, the fact remains that the Romans certainly believed it. Whether myth or not, the *Anno Urbis* still stands as the defining event in Rome's emergence, and all of their history is dated from that reference.

9 <u>Thompson Chain Reference Bible (King James Version)</u>, p. 245; Illustrated Dictionary and Concordance of the Bible.

10 Such a designation started in Jewish circles as a way to downplay Gentile influence. Jewish authorities already had to accept a Gentile calendar in addition to their own, but to have the system actually named after the Messiah was too much for them. They therefore talk about "eras in common" with the Christian world. In this century, such a practice has become standard in higher academic circles.

11 Since 1,334 years separate Diacletion and Pope Gregory, the actual amount of time lost was approximately 10 days, 9 hours, and 40 minutes, thus necessitating the full "eleventh" day. Superstition abounded in Gregory's day that the days were "stolen" from the lives of the people, when in reality they only "lost" about fifteen hours. If Gregory had waited until the 12th day was perfectly in synch with the loss, it could only have been done about 45 years later!

12 <u>The Case for Christ</u>, p.101. Author Lee Strobel interviews the prominent archaeologist John McKay ("Archaeology and the New Testament"—Grand Rapids, 1991) about the work of his colleague Jerry Vardaman, who found the coin. While McKay thinks there could be two men named Quirinius and Luke is simply writing about the first one in 7 BCE, I am more inclined to the position of Walter Liefeld, who wrote in *The Expositors Bible Commentary*, p. 9:

> "Quirinius had a government assignment in Syria at this time and conducted a census in his official capacity. Details of this census may have been common knowledge in Luke's time but are

505

now lost to us (cf. E.M. Blaiklock, "Quirinius," ZPEB, 5:56). An incomplete MS describes the career of an officer whose name is not preserved but whose actions sound as if he might have been Quirinius. He became imperial "legate of Syria" for the "second time." While this is ambiguous, it may be a clue that Quirinius served both at the time of Y'shua'ss birth and a few years later."

Either way, however, there is more than enough historical evidence for a Quirinius led census in 7 BCE.

13 Antiquities, 18.2.1

14 As James Kiefer correctly points out in Infancy Narratives in Matthew and Luke, Apamea, a city-state in Syria was granted "autonomy" but was still subject to census and taxation. The same was true of Nabatean kingdom of Petra, and yet it had more rights than the "friend" Herod did, since it was allowed to mint silver coins, and Herod only copper.

15 Antiquities, 17.11.3.

16 This is very consistent with Herod's previous behavior. Before Cleopatra and Marc Anthony's defeat at Actium (31 BCE), Herod rebuffed the Egyptian Queen and only attempted reconciliation when it was clear he was in danger. Towards the end of his life, Herod killed his own son, because he thought it would strengthen his position with Rome. See Antiquities, 15.4.1-4, 17.7.1.

17 Smith's Bible Dictionary, "Money, coined".

18 Ethelbert Stauffer, *Jesus and His Story* (New York: Alfred Knopf, 1960) p. 23. Silver coins in fact seem the norm for Nabatea, (K.

Schmitt-Korte and Michael Cowell, 'Nabataean Coinage- Part I. The Silver Content Measured by X-Ray Fluorescence Analysis', *NC*: 33-58). Nabatea is also a great example of how the whole "independence" game worked in the Middle East with respect to Rome. In Antiquities 14.5.1, King Aretas is forced to pay 300 talents at the behest of Rome. Additionally, even though in terms of governance this kingdom is independent, the last king made an interesting deal with the Romans that showed the true situation. Aretas IV promised, in exchange for Roman "protection" from attack, to give the kingdom over to them after his death. When this happened in 106 CE, it was annexed directly, but there is every indication that the Nabateans paid taxes to Rome well in advance of this time. It is also worth pointing out that Apamea, as previously stated, proves that "autonomy" does not mean "tax free".

19 In fact this minority view is not the sole domain of the Orthodox Church. Scholar Ernest Martin is probably the best representative of this revised orthodoxy. In his two books *The Birth of Christ Recalculated* and the more recent *Star that Astonished the World*, a respectable attempt is made to combine the astronomical data of the 1 BCE lunar eclipse along with his own new translation of relevant texts to bolster the later death date. Martin's point is that the 4 BCE eclipse was only a partial one whereas the 1 BCE eclipse was total, making the former very difficult to detect with the human eye. However, as Craig Chester and John Meier point out, ancient authorities made no distinction between partial and total lunar eclipses and it was certainly possible to predict the eclipse and have Josephus insert it as a valuable time marker later. Also, Martin's translation of the key text on which his entire argument rests has been almost universally rejected.

20 It is the author's contention that, while the logistical statement is correct, the year it happened is not.

21 Antiquities, 17.6.4.

22 Illustrated Dictionary and Concordance of the Bible.

23 Antiquities, 17.8.1.

24 Perhaps the most intriguing aspect of this event is that it had to take place in April, the month Rome was founded. It may in fact also be the case that all official censuses followed this pattern of celebration through taxation. If so, it would also go a long way to reinforcing the position that Rome conducted the start of these registrations—which required massive migrations of the populace—during the spring to fall season, when the weather was good.

25 Antiquities, 17.6.5 - 17.8.1; Wars of the Jews, 1.23.8.

26 The Star of Bethlehem, p.1. See also The Star that Astonished the World for a thorough treatment of the two lunar eclipses.

27 Antiquities, 17.9.1-3, Wars Against the Jews, 1.23.1-8. Translator William Whiston points out that the next cite in Josephus, a sedition occurring before Passover, happened 13 months after the lunar eclipse (March 13th, 4 BCE) and not the following month. In my view, Whiston is incorrect, as a careful reading of the same account in *Wars Against the Jews* clearly states that the sedition was stirred up *during the actual funeral*, and that "the Passover...was *now at hand*".

28 During biblical times, a month could not officially start until the new moon was sighted. A series of guideposts were set up by the Levites, and when one group saw the new moon, a lantern would be lighted. When the next nearest group saw this, they too would light a lantern, until word of the new month had reached all of Israel. It is also interesting to note that sometime Israel's enemies

also lit premature month fires, in an attempt to spread chaos. See All About Jewish Holidays and Customs, p. 8.

29 The Star of Bethlehem: An Astronomical Perspective, p. 4. Of the two locations, Babylon appears to the preferred choice of most scholars, many of whom point out that the finest observatory in ancient world, Sippar, is from that country. Also see The Bible as History, p. 351. On the other hand, Persia is also suggested on occasion because of a legend that the Persian prophet Zoroaster would be reincarnated in a manger. Therefore, the Magi could have followed the sign searching for their returning prophet and were led to Israel because of the unique celestial symbolism we have been discussing. However, it is also fair to point out that the traditions about the Magi imply they did not all come from the same place (hence "we three kings of Orient are..."). In the final analysis then, I would favor a scenario where at least one Magi was from Babylon), and one of the two others came from Persia. They could have met on trade routes that both countries use and that lead straight into Israel. The last Magi, if the lore is correct, probably came from yet another country, perhaps Syria, who also uses those trade routes and would have an acute interest also, since the Pisces sign covered them as well as the Jews in Israel. Their nationality however is secondary to the main point, which is that the celestial phenomena and the cultural and geographical features of the Middle East make for a very plausible scenario regarding the Magi's precise arrival in Jerusalem.

30 An excellent source for study is Mary Boyce's landmark book "Zoroastrians" (London: Routledge & Kegan Paul, 1979.) Also the "Arabian Infancy Gospel" 7:1 relates how the Magi arrived in Jerusalem in accordance with this same prophecy.

31 The Histories of Tacitus, 5.4. Also see The Bible as History, p. 350. In December of 1999, a new wrinkle was added to this discussion,

when Michael Molnar found Roman coins that commemorated the annexation of Judea (Israel). Dated to around 5 CE, the coins depict a ram looking backward to a star. Molnar immediately concluded then that the sign of the Jews in ancient times was Aries, and not Pisces.

However, I contend that this is a premature conclusion, primarily because no other cites in ancient literature make this designation. Furthermore, the rabbinic writer Abrabanel clearly referred to more ancient traditions that has Pisces as the Jewish sign. Abrabanel and his predecessors surely knew that that the word "fish" in Greek was used as the earliest sign of the Christian church, and also that the very word for fish in Greek, "icthys", became an acrostic which spelled out the phrase "Jesus Christ, Son of God, Savior". Therefore, if there was ancient knowledge that Pisces was not the sign of his own people, it is virtually certain that Abrabanel would not only have said so, but that such a fierce rejection of this designation would have almost universally reflected in the record of the Talmud. However, no such discussion in the Talmud was ever recorded which, when we consider that almost every other aspect of the Christian story was attacked in polemics like the *Toledoth Yeshu*, is extremely significant.

Finally, an alternate explanation for the ram being on the coin is found in the writings of Tacitus, a Roman historian, who wrote at the end of the first century. According to the Histories 5.4, the Romans believed that the Jews sacrificed rams as a way of defying authority:

> "They (the Jews) slay the ram in derision of Hammon, and they sacrifice the ox, because the Egyptians worship it as Apis."

The rest of the chapter also relates other astrological information, including the association of the planet Saturn with the Jews. It is therefore likely that the Romans put the ram on the coin as a way to remind the Jews that they could not defy them as they did their previous opponents. Furthermore such a coin would also play the same role that Roman eagle over the Temple arch did, which was to prove that they existed at Rome's pleasure.

See the 12/20/99 article *Finding the Christmas Star*, by Jennifer Viegas, available at www.abcnews.com. Molnar also details the theory in his book, *The Star of Bethlehem: Tthe Legacy of the Magi*.

32 <u>The Bible as History</u>, p. 349.

33 <u>Infancy Narratives in Matthew and Luke</u>, p. 3.

34 The Yom Kippur conjunction may in fact foretell the exact day of the birth two years later. It would also clarify the angel's comment, "You shall name him Yah-shua (The LORD Yah will Save) for he shall save Yah's people from their sins." Sins cannot be forgiven on any other day of the year in Jewish thought. Also see <u>The Bible as History</u>, p. 351.

35 In fact, early December was the worst time the Magi could have left. With a projected travel time of about four months, the Magi's entire trip would have been done during the rainy season. See <u>The Bible as History</u>, p. 353-4.

36 <u>The Star of Bethlehem: An Astronomical Perspective</u>, p. 4. We should also consider how frequently both the conjunction and the massing would occur so closely together. Such a confluence is more than likely unique in all of human history.

37 <u>Quarterly Journal of the Royal Astronomical Society</u>, Volume 33, p. 363.

38 <u>Quarterly Journal of the Royal Astronomical Society</u>, Volume 33, p. 363.

39 The Star of Bethlehem: An Astronomical Perspective, p. 4-5. Also, a bit closer to home, Josephus (Antiquities, 2.9.2), talks of an Egyptian "sacred scribe" foretelling doom to the kingdom if an Israelite child is not found and killed. While Josephus does not mention a predictive astronomical event, it was well known that such sacred scribes based their pronouncements on the movements of the heavens. Therefore, since Josephus only refers to astronomical phenomena once in his entire body of writings, it should not be surprising that he would de-emphasize the possible celestial portent surrounding Moses' birth.

40 Quarterly Journal of the Royal Astronomical Society, Volume 33, p.363.

41 The Star of Bethlehem: An Astronomical Perspective, p. 4.

42 The same pattern can be found in the Aramaic as well. The "star"(kawkwa) is definitely a singular entity. Plural Aramaic words are indicated by the use of two distinctive dots above the word called a *syame*, and no such mark appears in the text. Leaving the issue of which language came first in the New Testament aside for the moment, the fact that both Aramaic and Greek have distinct singular and plural terms for words like star/stars, constellation, heavens, and so on, should effectively put to rest any idea of the triple conjunction being intended as the celestial event happening on the night of the birth. The more familiar Greek terms are used here only as a matter of convenience. Also see Classical Aramaic, Volume 1, p. 20.

43 *A Linguistic Note on the Christmas Star,* Griffith Observer, December, 1976.

44 *A Linguistic Note on the Christmas Star,* Griffith Observer, December, 1976.

45 <u>Greek - English Lexicon</u>.

46 <u>Greek - English Lexicon.</u>

47 NIV footnote. Recent linguistic studies have also leaned toward this conclusion. Scholars have pointed out that this verse in Greek uses the singular form (*en te'anatole'*) and not the more familiar plural (*anatolai*) which appears everywhere else in the NT. The singular is, according to these same scholars, closely associated with astronomy and the early (heliacal) rising of a star, whereas the plural never is. Also see <u>The Bible as History</u>, p. 350. As for Aramaic sources, translations by George Lamsa and Victor Alexander also support this scenario, with "rising" implied in the text.

48 While it is true other stars "move" in the sense that most "rise and set", this is not all the action that Matthew has described. Yes, the king's star did rise, but it also tracked itself across the heavens, sped up, slowed down and then paused. Normal "stars", as we understand the term today, simply do not do this.

49 Further confirmation of a four month journey from Babylon to Jerusalem is found in Ezra 7:8-9: "Ezra arrived in Jerusalem in the fifth month of the seventh year of the king. He had begun his journey from Babylon on the first day of the first month, and arrived in Jerusalem of the first day of the fifth month, for the good hand of his God was on him." This journey is taking place in the Spring months, and we can also gather by the statement, "for the good hand of his God was on him", that Ezra made pretty decent time. Certainly Ezra had tremendous motivation to get there as fast as possible! Also, when we consider that Ezra is carrying out instructions from a king, it is almost certain that he traveled in some measure of style, at least with some camels, (Ezra 7:14-16). Similarly, the Magi were already laden with expensive gifts, which

may have put them on a similar status with Ezra, especially since they were so well received by Herod. Finally, the extravagance and wealth of these astrologers from the East might also explain why the idea of them as "we three kings of Orient are" took hold so early in Christian folk imagination.

50 Notice that Kepler isn't viewing the triple conjunction, but a singular one of Jupiter and Saturn in Pisces, which reminded him of the triple conjunction referred to by Abrabanel. The actual triple conjunction of these same planets had happened a few centuries before this, around 1364.

51 Again, the same holds true for *kawkwa*, the Aramaic equivalent to *aster.*

52 Once again, this is assuming a Greek primacist model. It is however the author's contention that Matthew originally composed his Gospel in Aramaic, or possibly Hebrew, and that "aster" would simply represent the best Greek equivalent for *kawkwa*, the term used in the Peshitta Gospels. In that case, Matthew is drawing not from Septuagint tradition, but from longstanding Semitic conventions.

53 "Septuagint" was the title given to the first translation of the OT. Written in Koine Greek and compiled roughly between 250 and 200 BCE, this version is one of the most vital tools biblical scholars have. In some cases, (i.e. Exodus 12:40), an entire phrase which has been omitted in the traditional Masoretic Hebrew is restored in the Greek. The word "septuagint" means "seventy", and is derived from the number of translators traditionally ascribed to its production.

54 *Common Errors in Star of Bethlehem Planetarium Shows*, <u>Planetarian</u>, Third Quarter, 1981.

55 The Bible as History, p. 350

56 The Aramaic phrasing here is not as strong as the Greek, but neither does it contradict the Greek reading of "abiding" in the fields. Certainly no fixed structures or shelters are even hinted at in the Peshitta, and so there is no reason to overturn the traditional reading.

57 Herod, while pretending to be Jewish, was actually of Idumanean (Edomite) descent. He was therefore Semitic, but not specifically Hebrew.

58 We must consider the fact that, as rare as the triple conjunction itself is, the chances of it hitting the singular day of Yom Kippur are unprecedented, happening last perhaps millions—or even billions—of years ago. Furthermore, even if the triple conjunction had an exact yearly cycle, like Halley's Comet, the number of years between happenings (1400) times the number of days in the year (365), would guarantee that one conjunction in the set would not hit that day again for at least 170,333.3 years. Certainly this is more than rare enough to answer Herod's question!

59 Of course, the same applies in Aramaic, where we can tell if the star/planet is singular or plural.

60 Certainly not during the Feast itself, because then all the Jews had to be in Jerusalem. Rather, what I am suggesting is that the census was scheduled about a month before. In so doing, Roman troops and administrators could be dispatched to throughout the province and then gathered very efficiently into Bethlehem/Jerusalem to provide security for the Feast. This arrangement also made sense for pilgrims, as they could register while they were on their way.

61 To see just how unpleasant Jerusalem could be during the rainy season, see Ezra 10:9-13, where the rains impede the Jews from venturing outside at all. Ezra also names the time of year, the first day of the tenth month, which would correspond to about two months before Passover, or January-February. The Nisan to Nisan cycle is clearly intended for two reasons: 1) Ezra 6:19 puts Passover in the first, not seventh, month and thus sets the cycle for the book and, 2) If it ran on a Tishri to Tishri cycle, this weather would not have been occurring, for then it would take us to about two months before Tabernacles, or July-August.

The most ironic thing about using this verse for this purpose however, is that Ezra imposes the same sanction on Jews to appear that Caesar and his census did, that is, to either make the trip or lose their property, (Ezra 10:7). However, there are a few marked differences between this and the Roman situation. First of all, the edict applied only to Jerusalem and the surrounding area, and the fact that only three days were given to get there proves this could not be far reaching. Second, Ezra is trying to make a moral and spiritual point by forcing the journey and wants the other Jews inconvenienced. Third, the amount of people in Judah/Jerusalem at this time is fairly low (under 50,000 total—2:64-65) and out of this number, only a fraction would have to appear. Once there, however, the weather still proved to be a major impediment and had to be reckoned with. In that sense, I have no doubt that if the Romans imposed a census for all the outlying areas to be on the move to their ancestral homes regardless of distance, that the condition of the roads would be such that even those with good intentions would have great difficulties getting through. All that aside, the Romans also would have trouble traveling to various places to administer the census as well.

62 On the PBS Frontline program *From Jesus to Christ* (broadcast April 7-8, 1998), one scholar noted how the Romans had an active dislike for governing the contentious Jews. She cites as an example

the fact that Pilate was much happier in his pagan palace at Caesarea and dreaded having to return to Jerusalem during the Passover to ensure proper security. Even the Temple itself had a tower called the Antonia from which Roman soldiers could look down on the throngs of pilgrims which packed the narrow streets during the Three Great Feasts. Josephus also records, cited elsewhere, that rioting had been known to break out amongst Jews during the census. Although I point out this was more likely to occur during the *apotimosis*, not the *apographe* that Joseph was going up for, one could easily see how the Romans would not take any chances. Furthermore, since the Romans tried to limit their contact with the Jerusalem populace, it would make sense to hold the census around the same time as a great feast and thus "kill two birds with one stone".

63 See Charles Ryrie's notes on Luke 2:7, even though he leans to a different setting in his conclusion, the linguistics used are the same. Also see Easton's Bible Dictionary, p. 443, and Great People of the Bible and How They Lived, p. 320.

64 Webster's New World Hebrew Dictionary, p. 73, 796. The word *evoos* is also rendered as "stall, crib or feeding trough". In fact the English word "manger" is also derived, like the Greek, from a root word of "to eat". This manifests in the Latin/Italian "mangia".

65 Great People of the Bible and How They Lived, p. 320.

66 The Complete Gospels, p. 392.

67 This range is assuming Joseph built the sukkah himself, which is very likely given his profession. If however Joseph did not build it, but appropriated someone else's, like the innkeeper's, then he

would have had to give it up before the holiday started, thus cutting the range to four days.

68 This is also recorded in the pseudo-epigraphic work *Infancy James* (The Complete Gospels, p. 392).

69 See Ezekiel 16:4 and Job 38:9 which detail this process. Also consult Illustrated Bible Dictionary, p. 100 and Great People of the Bible and How They Lived, p. 320.

70 The Horizon Book of Ancient Rome, p. 75, 349.

71 The Martyrdom of Polycarp or the Letter of the Smyrnaens, p.1. As Richard Neil Shrout points out in his revision of an older translation, Polycarp was actually executed as an atheist by his Roman tormentors! Apparently, by denying Jupiter, Polycarp was seen as possessing no spiritual value whatsoever by the Emperor when in reality he had "served the LORD for eighty six years".

72 It's very convenient for us two millennia later to look at ancient polytheists as a kind of intellectual curiosity. However, we would do well to remember that the term "paganism" was a definition that applied to more than 90% of the world's population at that time. In this light, we can understand how the Jew's insistence on only one God must have struck the rest of the world as very odd. For example, it was common practice for the gods of one country to be "co-opted" by another. What the Egyptians called Isis, the Canaanites knew as Astarte, Marduk of Babylon was equivalent to Zeus in Greece, and so on. Therefore, it should not be surprising that Greco-Roman pagans would try to incorporate the "Jewish God" into their pantheon, and many identified Him, ironically, with Dionysus, the god of wine! Also the Roman Emperor Caligula, driven mad by disease and already believing himself to be Jupiter, also gave himself the title of Hebrew Messiah! The only people

not doing this kind of divine cross-pollenization were the Jews, and this gave rise to much suspicion from their enemies since they didn't "play the game".

73 It is therefore one of the most ironic twists of history that when the Hebrew "I AM" name was rendered into the Greek NT, the Greeks chose the word "Kurios" ("LORD") which up until then had been applied to Zeus, the Greek name for Jupiter! Nor are Hebrew sources immune from this translational problem. The phrase 'The LORD" in Hebrew is *baalim*, and is derived directly from the Canaanite deity Baal. Dutillett (Hebrew) Matthew restores the proper usage.

74 That is to say it started out as seven days. By the time the Empire fell in the fifth century it had been extended to 27 days, and has been cited by many historians as a prime factor in Rome's downfall.

75 The Bible as History, p. 353.

76 Clement of Alexandria: The Original Christian Philosopher, p. 1.

77 *In Search of Christmas,* U.S. News and World Report, December 23, 1996.

78 *In Search of Christmas,* U.S. News and World Report, December 23, 1996.

79 *In Search of Christmas,* U.S. News and World Report, December 23, 1996.

80 That is, YHWH appeared.

81 Notice that whether it is rendered "Wonderful Counselor, the

Mighty God" or "Wonderful in counsel is the Mighty God", the meaning is the same. The "counsel" is clearly coming from God, and therefore so would the "Counselor", necessitating its proper name. Other verses (Isaiah 11:1-3, Psalm 51:10-11), name the "Spirit of Counsel" (Holy Spirit) directly and give the additional title, "Spirit of the LORD".

82 There seems to be a recurring pattern throughout this translation that whenever divine aspects are expressed in human terms, they are never capitalized. However, the descriptions make it clear that long standing English conventions regarding capitalization of divine manifestations be respected.

83 The decision to use the NIV or the Masoretic Translation has more to do with personal taste than concerns for accuracy. Where the MT deliberately obscures meanings ("thrust though" instead of "pierce" in Zechariah 12:10, "pit" instead of "grave" in Psalm 16:9) it is carefully noted with original Hebrew meanings restored. Otherwise, a secondary concern has to do with the cumbersome nature of "thee, thou, thine" in the MT, and in cases where it is particularly vexing I have turned to the NIV. The NIV is also consulted when certain idioms are not clear enough in the MT. Most us know what "seed" means in Genesis 22:18, but "descendants" really brings the point home better in modern parlance.

84 "twig" the same Hebrew word is translated "branch" by the NIV. Also another English word "shoot" is rendered elsewhere (Jeremiah 23:5) by this same word.

85 The divine name (YHWH) is restored by the author to make a linguistic point. It is not written as such in the NIV, although the NIV reflects the original Hebrew text by rendering it "LORD" is all capital letters.

86 Old Testament Survey, p. 662.

87 Old Testament Survey, p. 640.

88 In fact, Samaritans protested to the king that the Jews were in effect "taking advantage" by also trying to rebuild the city walls. This is further evidence of the limited nature of that particular decree, (Ezra 4:1-16).

89 Old Testament Survey, p. 644.
  NOTE: Artaxerxes came to power in the year 465 and Ezra 7:8-10 clearly states that Ezra received this decree from the king in the seventh year and fifth month of his reign, or 457 BC.

90 Handwriting on the Wall, p. 195. See also The Coming Prince by Robert Anderson for an even more detailed treatment of this point of view.

91 Also see Haggai 1:1-2:19 for a compact, yet thorough treatment of the problems Ezra and Nehemiah faced.

92 However, even this was predicted in advance. The introduction to Isaiah 53:1 is typical: "Who would have believed our report?"

93 Matthew 1:18, Luke 1:26-38.

94 John 1:14.

95 All of the following cites are NIV.

96 The determination as to who is right may rest upon if one takes a literal or figurative view of the verse. This particular word for "pierce" (*ariyeh*—Strong's #736, New World Hebrew Dictionary p. 17) occurs nowhere else in Scripture. Its literal meaning is that of

"lion". However, Strong's adds that it is used as a metaphor for violence, hence the rendering "pierce". In such a case, rules laid down by the great rabbi Hillel will resolve the intent. In the *drash* discipline (the second of four progressively difficult levels), a verse is compared with another of similar meaning or subject. So therefore, what is needed is to find another Messianic prophecy that talks about how the Anointed One dies, and see if a literal or figurative meaning is to be preferred. Such a verse is found in Zechariah 12:10, "they will look upon me, the one they have **pierced** and they will mourn for him as they would an only son." In this case the word for pierce is *dakar*, which both Strong's (1856) and New World Hebrew Dictionary p. 52 render as "to stab, pierce, thrust through." Also, the metaphoric intent of the verse is clear even in Masoretic English translation: "**like a lion** they are at my hands and my feet."

97 A careful reading reveals that Isaiah 52:13 is the true introduction to Isaiah 53:1. We also must remember that when the prophet originally wrote his book, no numbers were used for chapters or verses, and thus the original Hebrew phraseology sometimes gets obscured for the sake of modern conveniences.

98 Also the commentary from *Rabbi Simeon Ben Jochai* makes it clear the Messiah is "diseased" or acquainted with disease" because he has traveled into the "palace of the sons of sickness" where he redeems the world. Disease is also frequently listed as the consequence of transgressing God's law, (Deuteronomy 28:20-22), and therefore the phrases "surely our diseases he did bear" (Isaiah 53:4) and "The LORD hath made to light on him the iniquity of us all" (Isaiah 53:6) are two ways of expressing the same effect of this singular propitiation. Or, to put it another way, TO CARRY AWAY SIN IS THE SAME AS CARRYING AWAY DISEASE.

99 "who would have believed…" is a fascinating beginning because

the prophet knows as he writes this that it won't be a "popular" vision to rally the people to. In fact, Isaiah is clear that most will reject the suffering servant.

100 "arm of the LORD" appears several times in Isaiah, and is usually associated with manifestations of God, (Isaiah 43:13, 48:13, 51:5). Therefore if the Messiah is "revealed by the arm of God" he must be from God as well. Isaiah 43:10 is particularly revealing, since it seems to put the Messiah, at the very least, as the perfect embodiment of God on earth.

101 "sapling" , another way of saying "branch, shoot" (Jeremiah 23:5).

102 In spite of all the kingly aspects, the Messiah here is again depicted as ugly, again, not a way to foster a popular image.

103 These lines establish once and for all the divine aspects of the Messiah, for no man could bear the sin of the human race.

104 The image of the suffering servant Messiah as a sacrifice is striking. Isaiah makes the point repeatedly that he did not cry out or protest. He also comes very close to calling the Messiah "the lamb of God", proving this was not a Christian invention.

105 "cut off from the land of the living" is the clearest indication that the Messiah was alive literally after his death, as the last four verses show him doing other things. It also dovetails well with the "son of man" prophecy (Daniel 9:24-27) which talks about him being "cut off" when the half week ends.

106 These are very specific statements. One would not expect a kingly Messiah to be executed with criminals. It is also amazing that the detail about the Messiah being laid in a rich man's tomb is also picked up on, (Matthew 27:38, 57).

107 "crush him by disease" is rendered because of the Hebrew word *makov*. Also please see the rabbinic commentary from Talmud Sanhedrin 98b which calls the Messiah "the leprous one" but doesn't make the "crushed by disease" interpretation. Rather, these rabbis focused on the Messiah's "affliction" by his enemies.

108 "to see if his soul would offer itself in restitution" is perhaps the most cogent explanation for why the Messiah had to die.

109 "travail" = suffering. These last four lines prove that the concept of John 3:16 was foretold well in advance in Jewish Scripture. To try and divorce Jewish tradition from it now is a bit disingenuous to say the least.

110 See The Essential Kabbalah: The Heart of Jewish Mysticism by Daniel Matt, p. 2.

111 See The Schocken Book of Jewish Mystical Testimonies, by Louis Jacobs, p. 8. The vision of Ezekiel is also one the most precisely dated events in the Bible, having happened on July 28, 593 BCE.

112 The Essential Kabbalah, p. 4,

113 The following is derived from the preface of The Essential Kabbalah.

114 For the purposes of a basic exercise, this is a bit overly simplistic. Each title has many different sub classifications and interlocking terms, depending on the aspect the scholar wishes to bring out. Therefore this is just the smallest taste of the full sea of titles contained in the Bible and expressed by the mystics. The grouping of the totality of this however into ten broad categories is accurate.

115 What is significant about the Proverbs 30:4 quote is that, unlike many others that talk of David or Israel as God's "son", this particular offspring has divine properties. The concept is further developed in Daniel 7:13-15 as a "son of man" who also descended from heaven. This is exactly the kind of detailed comparison of Scripture (drash) that the mystics used to develop their ideas about the sefirot, which can also be classified as belonging to Father, Son or Mother groups. The final development of this sode teaching takes the mother aspect and relates it to the Holy Spirit, which is always in feminine form in Hebrew. The son aspect also undergoes a similar transformation, into that of the Messiah. Thus we see a legitimate Jewish origin of a triune Godhead that is still one being manifesting in different forms.

116 But even here notice that ECHAD is used in a compound sense also. It describes two things (and there was evening AND there was morning) and puts them under the umbrella of ONE defintion, "day".

117 The equivalent word in Aramaic is *milta* and it is used in the Aramaic version of the Gospel of John.

118 In fairness to the Kabbalah's critics, *memra* is not the Hebrew word used in the Psalm. In that case, the word is *dabar*. However, there can be little doubt that both can be used in this same context. Another way to look at *memra* is that it can also mean "fulfillment", which is the same as manifesting will through a creative word. Also, it is certain that the targum writers, circa 150 BCE, intended *memra* to have the same meaning as *dabar* when they inserted it as "word of God". Finally, it is also true that Psalm 33:6, regardless as to the word used, did form the basis for the mystical concept of *memra*.

119 Remember that John is a native Hebrew speaker, so he would use

"memra" and not the more familiar Greek term "logos", which is what most Gentile Christians know. The Peshitta uses the Aramaic equivalent "miltha", but if an original Hebrew John were found, it would probably say "memra".

120 Better known in the west as "James the Just", apostle and author of the Epistle that bears his name. Interestingly enough, his Aramaic name is actually closer to "Jacob" than "James" in English.

121 The Aramaic sources prove particularly useful here. In the Peshitta New Testament, the "word of God" is clearly spelled out as "miltha d'Alaha". "miltha" is also used as this same term in John 1:1-4, and is the Aramaic equivalent of "memra". It is also worth noting that since "metatron" is given as the only mediator between God and man, this divine "memra" judge must therefore refer to the same being. Other clues in the mystical titles certainly support such a conclusion.

122 This is not the only possibility. A second tradition links him with Enoch, but this is discredited, as James Trimm explains:

"The other tradition has it that Metatron is just a name for Enoch. How did the two become confused?
The answer lies in the Book of Enoch.
The earliest extra-biblical Ma'aseh Merkavah account is found in the Book of Enoch Chapter 14. Here Enoch comes before the figure on the throne and comes near to the "Holy Word". The setting is that Enoch has been attempting to intrecede for the fallen angels. Enoch passes through the worlds and comes before the throne and before the Word. Enoch is then given a message of judgement to take back to the fallen angels (1Enoch 13-15)
Now the "Word" (Memra) is Metatron and it was this Word (Metatron) who gave Enoch a message to take back to the fallen

angels. In a much later Rabbinic document the Midrash of Shemichazah and Aza'el we read:

> Forthwith Metatron sent a messenger to Shemichaza and said to him: "The Holy One is about to destroy His world and bring upon it a flood.

> This parallels 1Enoch 13-15 exactly only Enoch has simply become "a messenger" for Metatron, his name (Enoch) has been dropped. (Shemichazah and Aza'el were the leaders of the Fallen angels (1En. 6; 10))

I think that from this we can see how eventually Metatron (Adam Kadmon; the Lesser YHWH; the Word) became confused with his messenger Enoch."

123 Proverbs 10:26 in non-Jewish versions.

124 <u>The Ryrie Study Bible</u>, p. 50.

125 See Acts 21:17.

126 However, Josephus also goes to great lengths to praise his level of both Greek and Hebrew learning, long before he became a formal citizen of Rome. Paul very likely received an early Greek education from the time of his infancy, as Josephus most certainly did, based on his autobiography.

127 This may not seem an admission of weak writing on the surface, but the fact is that scribes of all types in the ancient world were trained to make the most effective use of space possible. Hence, the production of large letters shows that Paul did not have this

ability. Furthermore, even though Romans is the only letter that directly names a scribe writing the entire work, the many other references that Paul makes to "writing in my own hand" contrast with the balance of those letters. Otherwise we would assume Paul wrote them all the way through, which he did only if they were short enough! Compare Romans 16:22, 1 Corinthians 16:21, Galatians 6:11 and Colossians 4:18 with Philemon 1:19-21.

128 I hold out a little hope for Thomas because parts of his Gospel survive in Coptic, an Egyptian dialect with some Semitic features, and because Thomas was the patron saint of Syria. Many scholars therefore believe it is likely, or even certain, that Thomas' work was composed in Aramaic also, and it may be that proof of it could be found someday, just as the Greek and Coptic copies shook the world when they were discovered.

129 Jerome, *On Famous Men 3*.

130 When Paul is confused with an Egyptian terrorist in Acts 21:38, the event he is accused of causing is also recorded by Josephus, who dates it to the year 54. Also keep in mind that the Roman questioning Paul uses the phrase "some time ago" to describe the event in question, meaning it could easily be a few years later.

131 Acts 18:4 is particularly interesting with its references to "Jews and Greeks"—indicating clearly that the Jews there were not Hellenistic.

132 As we will also see later, the Epistle of James also lends critical evidence to at least some rough draft of Matthew circulating more than 30 years before most liberal scholars believe the Greek version was written.

133 LXX (Deut. 18:)"15: Propheten ek ton adelphon sou, os eme,

anastnsei soi Kupios o Theos sou: autou akousesthe: . . .19:Kai o anthropos os ean me akouse osa an lalese o prophetes ekeivos epi to onomati mon, ego ekdiknso ek autou."

Greek NT (Acts 3:)"22: Oti propheten umin anastesei kupios o Theos umon ek ton adelphon umon, os eme: autou akousesthe kata panta osa an lalese pros umas. 23: estai de pasa psuxe etes an me akouse tou prophetou ekeinou exolothpeuthesetai ek tou laou."

For those who wish a literal translation of each Greek word, the following is provided:

LXX (Deut. 18:)"15: Propheten(Prophet) ek(out) ton adelphon sou(the brethren of you), os eme(like me), anastnsei soi(shall raise up) Kupios o Theos(the LORD God) sou(of you): autou(him) akousesthe(shall ye hear): . . .19:Kai(And) o anthropos(the man) os ean me akouse(if he shall not hear) osa an(whatsoever) lalese(he may say) o prophetes(the prophet) ekeivos(that person) epi to onomati mon(in the name of me), ego(I) ekdiknso(vengeance) ek autou(out of him)."

Greek NT (Acts 3:)"22: Oti propheten(A prophet) umin(to you) anastesei(will raise up) kupios o Theos(the LORD God) umon(your) ek(out of) ton adelphon(the brethren) umon(of you), os eme(like me): autou(him) akousesthe(shall ye hear) kata(in) panta(all things) osa an(whatsoever) lalese(he may say) pros(to) umas(you). 23: estai de(and it shall be) pasa(every) psuxe(soul) etes(which) an me akouse(may not hear) tou prophetou ekeinou (of that prophet) exolothpeuthesetai(shall be destoryed) ek(out) tou laou(of the people)."

134 The Complete Dead Sea Scrolls in English, p.431-439.

135 Note the use of NIV in this case because, as I said, the Aramaic sources do not have the gloss and so I must use a competent Greek based text to make the point.

136 One example which is excluded is Mark 15:34 (Eli, Eli, lama sabachthani) which is actually a mistranslation from the Aramaic. This issue will be addressed in detail later on.

137 This example, and a few others in Mark, will impact on the compositional theory to be laid out later on. In that scenario, Mark took an Aramaic copy of Matthew's rough draft and put it into Greek. This Greek version then went through several editing phases, including one revision by Mark and another one done by Peter after Mark's death, until it reached final form by the end of the first century. Since it is highly unlikely that either Mark or Peter would make these mistakes in Semitic understanding, the most likely culprit is the Mattean Scribe who put Greek Matthew into final form. In that process, he very likely made a copy of Mark with these changes that also ended up in Luke's hands, and since Silas traveled between both groups frequently, he is the best choice for this designation.

138 We will be going into a tremendous amount of detail about the impact of Q on NT composition later. For now, however, the salient point is that Q is a reconstruction based on common material now enshrined in Matthew and Luke. It is therefore those pieces from Matthew and Luke that I am addressing in terms of Aramaic underpinnings, at least at the oral level.

139 The Horizon Book of Christianity, p.106-107.

140 The Modern New Testament from the Aramaic, p. viii-ix. A clarification here is in order. While Rabulla's church at the time accepted the eastern Peshitta, he had a radically different way of interpreting it with regards to Christ's nature that set him against the COE. The two groups therefore had a major dotrinal dispute *about* Scripture as opposed to one about that same Scripture's authenticity.

141 Phoenician is a Semitic tongue widely believed to be an ancestor of Aramaic and Hebrew. The three languages appear to share the same 22-letter alphabet as well as being read from right to left. However, there may be even more interesting scholarly trends on the horizon. Cyrus Gordon, one of the world's leading Semiticists who is hailed for his authoritative work on Ugaritic grammar, has taken on a rather controversial position. While most scholars focus on the Minoan use of Linear B as an early form of Greek, Gordon is one the very few scholars convinced that its cousin— Linear A—is actually Semitic. Gordon even goes so far as to claim that the Philistines spoke a Semitic tongue when they first landed in Palestine in about 1500 BCE, and notes that Samson and the Philistines did not need an interpreter to speak, whereas other biblical incidents go out of their way to list such arrangements. While at this time the full extent of Semitic languages and their influences in what became the Greek world later are uncertain, it is safe to assert that between Phoenician and possibly Linear A combined, that a case can be made for early and pervasive Semitic patterns in that part of the world.

For more information, please see the November/December 2000 edition of <u>Biblical Archaeology Review.</u>

142 <u>The Horizon Book of Ancient Greece</u>, p.34.

143 <u>The Horizon Book of Ancient Rome</u>, p. 145.

144 Deisman, Adolf. "Hellenistic Greek with Special Consideration of the Greek Bible", p. 39-59.(Summary given by Rodney Decker, Assistant Professor of Greek and Theology, Calvary Theological Seminary.)

145 That alternative is, put simply, that koine Greek originated (or at least reached its final form) with the translation of the LXX. The Hebrew scholars, determined to stick to the original as much as

possible, did not follow Greek word order but retained the verb-subject-object sentence structure which is found only in Semitic languages. It is therefore the author's contention that writers like Luke also followed this strategy by taking their Aramaic original writings and making them sound more Semitic in the translated Greek on purpose.

146 Technically, the first definite article of a Hebrew sentence is dropped. In other words, if it were English, the word *ve* (the) would appear between the preposition *b'* (in) and *reshit* (literally "head [of things]"). Greek also, like English, retains this first definite article, EXCEPT OF COURSE AGAIN IN THESE 22 GREEK NT BOOKS, where it is dropped in Semitic fashion. This tactic, like the two others, is also a consistent pattern throughout the Greek translations of the Peshitta canon, and is again conspicuously absent in the five disputed books that were compositionally made in Greek. When we combine all three occurrences together, the number of Semiticisms apparent probably reaches about six hundred.

147 Of course, both systems put the object last, so Indo-European would have it as "Y'shua spoke to the disciples", whereas Semitic languages render it "Spoke Y'shua to the disciples".

148 The fact is also that these deliberate linguistic manipulations are far from uncommon in Luke's writings. One blatant example is in his third chapter, where the genealogy of the Messiah is given. For the scores of names in the past, the definite article (*the* in English) is put between father and son, such as "THE son of David." However, when we get to Joseph, THE is missing, which on the surface appears to be bad grammar by an otherwise excellent Greek writer like Luke. The reason then that Luke appears to break the rules, however, is simply due to his assertion that Joseph is not Y'shua's natural father. Similarly, Matthew appears

to also break with convention by saying, "Take the child AND HIS MOTHER", which also appears incorrect when the intent is not considered. Therefore, precedent such as these examples and others lays a solid foundation for other "clues" in Koine Greek being left to testify to the language of the original sources, especially in light of statements like Luke 1:1-5.

149 That is, among the original Peshit-TA documents held by the Church of the East. These should not be confused with the later Peshit-TO revisions.

150 However, it should be noted that not all Hebrew books were necessarily given a free pass either. Song of Songs and Esther, for example, had other issues that made them very controversial as well.

151 Furthermore, the reason behind this word choice is probably due to the man's nationality. Even though Ethiopian Jewry has a very credible claim to dating their conversion to as far back as Solomon's time, it is also obvious that the man in question did not look like a typical Jew in Israel. In that sense, and owing to the certainty that he was also circumcised, he is not being viewed as a proselyte in the typical sense because he can point to generations observant Jews in his lineage. Knowing that, Luke is then going out of his way to say, "he is a true one, a real believer and a son of Israel." Such a distinction also goes back to the two levels of proselytes ("gerim"). The "proselyte of the gate" was not circumcised and was getting Jewish services in his native language while being expected to learn Hebrew in the future. It is also these people that probably served as the model for James' decision at the Jerusalem Council regarding Gentile believers (Acts 15-16). However, a "proselyte of righteousness" was circumcised and kept the whole Torah. So, whether this man came from a family of righteous proselytes or converted on his own, the Torah made no distinc-

tion between him and those jews who were born in Israel, and this is what Luke is referring to.

152 James Trimm uses this as an example of Aramaisms in Luke's writings. Unfortunately at this point, most scholars and myself lean towards the idea that Luke's Greek is consistently compositional, and not a translation. On the other hand, the Book of Acts also appears to be written backwards in that 1:1-16:8 use the terms "they, them" and 16:9 onwards it is "we" "us". In that very same verse, Paul is in Troas, Luke's hometown, and so many have come to the conclusion that Luke began a journal starting from that time, when he was asked to go on a missionary journey with Paul. Then, perhaps a few years later, Luke compiles materials from Paul and his other traveling companion, Mark, and these will form the basis of both his Gospel and the first fifteen chapter of Acts that he did not witness. The same Aramaisms then may have come from Paul and/or Mark's slightly off translations that Luke copied down.

153 Even though Luke, who wrote Acts, was probably not Aramaic competent, his discussions with Paul in Greek could have resulted in this piece of evidence.

154 In fact, this may be one of the reasons, admittedly speculative, behind why Luke does not include the story of the Syrio-Phoenician woman, (Matthew 15:21-28, Mark 7:24-30). In particular, Y'shua's statement that he was "sent only to the lost sheep of the House of Israel", as well as the disciples' own lack of regard for her, may have given Luke serious pause. Certainly many Greeks from Antioch might not have liked the account and Luke is, after all, also Syrian. Matthew and Mark, on the other hand, as Palestinian Jews, would have had no such concerns in relating the tale.

155 Again, whether Luke was of Greek or Aramean blood, the rules

for both kinds of proselytes were the same in Israel. Although, if he was the latter, it must be conceded that an extra reason for his Semitic skills is clearly warranted.

156 Actually the scroll Y'shua read from was in Hebrew, however the source that Luke writes down is from a now lost Galilean Aramaic targum of the same verse.

157 The version in Matthew is the more complete, with "kingdom-power-glory"…it is put here with the smaller Lukan version for the sake of convenience. Interestingly enough, not all Greek mss have this longer ending, while all Aramaic one do.

158 Yet another mistranslation of Aramaic sources occurs here, where the Greek reads "forgive our debts as we forgive our debtors", when in Aramaic the words for "debt" and "offense" are very similar.

159 In both parts of this example, the rhymes are with different parts of speech at the end of each phrase, proving that these features are far more extensive than the mere propensity of rhyming possessive suffixes that Aramaic allows.

160 These last few examples rhyme partly due to the addition of pronoun suffixes (e.g. "lkhon")—equivalent to terms like "them" and "they" in English. However, even taking this aspect into consideration, the words which are not conjugated also rhyme (such as ask-seek-knock) and the diction rates also go together. It is also worth pointing out that Y'shua very well could have chosen these words precisely because when conjugated they would come out in such a memorable pattern.

161 The abbreviation of this saying is for convenience sake, but the concept is the same. Y'shua is telling people that even a man with

one hundred sheep will leave the remainder to go off in search of a single lamb. When he finds the one lamb, he "rejoices" greater than the does in the ninety-nine he left behind. Therefore the them is "rejoicing in the one", and in this case "rejoice" and "one", while not a pure rhyme, nevertheless have the same effect as one since the similarity between the words will stick in the hearer's mind as a kind of alliterated double shot. It is also a Messianic pun, because "rejoicing in the one"—particularly a lamb is a very strong Jewish and eastern Christian concept. It is referred to in fact in John's first chapter with the phrase, *b'reh eykhadiyah nitil* (only begotten son) or as "THE ONE" (eykhadiya).

162 In the case of Matthew, the speaker is not Y'shua, but a Syrio-Phoenician woman. However, this is still an important one because it shows the Semitic mindset to use rhymes in order to make a more forceful point. On the other hand, Luke's cite uses the same words coming out of Y'shua's mouth.

163 While these two words do not appear together in the same sentence, it is clear that Y'shua is playing off of their similar sounds by switching their definitions. His "food" is to do the will of the Heavenly Father who sent him...which is the same definition of the Kingdom of God. The use of "makultha" is definitely awkward in Aramaic if this extra allegory was not beneath it, because in John 4:9 the preferred term of "sebartha" (food) is used instead of the rarely used "makultha" (nourishment). It is the same in English, where we would say, "Let's eat", instead of, "Let us consume nutrients."

164 Technically this is a word play used by the narrator and not Y'shua, but the use of this device is equally effective irrespective as to who is employing it. It is a bit on the ironic side as well, because he was "in Galilee", his home region, and yet felt the need NOT to go to the Feast openly (b'galeea) but in secret. The word play is also

intentional on John's part because he could have more easily said, "He went up in secret" and not used the word "openly" at all. The only reason to do the additional work then was to drive this point home. It may also be an allusion to the fact that the one from Galilee has all the secrets!

165 *Nahira* literally means "flame" but, as Paul Younan points out, it is used as an idiomatic expression in the sentence as meaning, "he has no enlightenment". It is a wordplay with verse 9, where the word *nuhra* (light) is used.

166 While these words do not rhyme, they illustrate a rarer type of word play. The second word refers to regular sleep, as does the first one in most situations. However, here the pun is that the first word (shkhab) also can mean idiomatically, "to take rest of this world"—or literally to die. So, while both words can superficially mean "sleep" and are translated as such in Greek and—by extension—English, the switching of synonyms by Y'shua indicates that his disciples did not understand that Lazarus was actually dead.

167 Exactly who Thomas looked like may never be known, but regardless of that, the true nature of the title is in its sonic characteristics. "tooma" (Thomas) can be slurred or altered slightly into "tawma" which means "twin". So, in effect, "tooma" sounds like "tawma" in the same way that Thomas looks like...? This happens to be beautiful touch in Aramaic, where the sounds are used as a kind of mimic of the images.

168 The same word play with "rukha" can also be found in John 3:8-9.

169 The Aramaic reads, "naphshah khayva" with the second word modifying the word "soul" with the adjective "living". It is also fair to point out that Genesis 1 and 2 are full of these double meanings. The first man is named "Man" (Adam) and the first woman

"Living". (Khayva- Eve). Adam becomes a living soul and his wife, also named "Living" is a part of him, bone of his bone and flesh of his flesh. However, even if "khayva" was not there to modify "naphshah", it would be implied. Ezekiel is referring to this word when he says "the soul that sins, it shall die", and Y'shua himself also uses it when he says, "My soul is troubled to the point of death."

170 Technically speaking, the words appear as *naphshi* in the text, because the last letter (I), is used as the first person possessive "my", but as a suffix. The same construction is found in Thomas' exclamation "My LORD and my God!" (Mari w'Alahi).

171 The common cites of these word pairs in both Matthew and Mark proves that an Aramaic editing process between them occurred before their compilation, insertion or translation in the more familiar Greek.

172 The first "ah" sound that is understood in words like GAHR-ah-BAH are due to the way the consonant before them is pronounced, whereas in the middle of the word the syllable could stop abruptly (GAHM-LA) without needing another vowel. More often than not, deciding if a vowel goes there or not is a leading cause of mistranslation.

173 In yet another instance of mistranslation, the Greek shows its inferiority. It renders the word "eunuch", when in Aramaic a word pair exists giving almost the same pronunciation and identical spelling to the words "eunuch" and "chamberlain/high official". It is this latter meaning which is intended, since eunuchs, by virtue of the fact that they cannot be circumcised, would not be allowed to worship in the Temple.

174 The fact that these synagogues followed Hebrew and not Helle-

nistic conventions is strongly suggested by a statement a few lines later, WHERE THE TORAH AND THEN THE PROPHETS WERE READ IN THE SERVICE. While Greek Jews did read from Scripture in their services also, this formal division did not exist as a rule. Then Paul follows the exact same pattern James did, quoting from Torah first, then switching to the "writings" portion, namely the Psalms. Furthermore, Paul's reference to "God fearing Gentiles" also points to this conclusion, since it was well known that people with this title listened to sermons in Hebrew while having interpreters translate them into Greek. Greek Gentiles who attended services in their own language, would not have been called this.

175 The chart shown can also be a bit misleading in that it declares that some fragments of John may have been assembled as late as the year 150, and that "the emergence of four recognized Gospels" could date between 150 and 325. However, while certain issues of canonicity did not get resolved until this time, to automatically say that the traditions which comprise said canon are not more correctly attributed to the apostolic age, is narrow minded an prejudicial in the extreme. It is therefore patently unfair to throw out the best linguistic and historical evidence simply because certain controversies were long standing in the Early Church.

176 Right away the prejudice of the Jesus Seminar is apparent. See how quickly they discount the universally accepted notion in all four Gospels, and therefore the earliest notion, that the Baptist was forerunner of Christ, but not his "mentor", as the Baptist himself eagerly points out.

177 Notice how they are so willing to admit that the miracles happened, and yet deny the purpose for which they happened, (John 10:36-38)? We will see this pattern a bit later, in the form of the

Jewish response to Y'shua, which in spite of its intention adds much credibility to the Gospel record.

178 We'll see just how "Gentile" Paul was later on. In the meantime, just another manifestation of their prejudice, is clearly shown, (Acts 22:1, 23:6).

179 Pay attention to this designation, as it will be critical later.

180 Peter himself was dead by the year 67, which would tend to support an earlier date in this range!

181 This designation is one I heartily disagree with. Too much of Mark was incorporated and spliced with Q and also redacted by Matthew and Luke to justify such a later final edition. This also jibes against the best historical evidence which is unanimous in the fact that Mark wrote all of his Gospel, revised it once in Rome, and possibly a second time in Alexandria, the place of his martyrdom, in about the year 68.

182 In this case the authors are probably referring to part of chapter 8, since the story of the woman caught in adultery ("He who is without sin...") is not in some of the earliest manuscripts. However, reliable oral tradition from John (and possibly Mary, whom he lived with—John 19:26-27) could still be had at the close of the first century, since John himself was alive at least until the year 96. Furthermore, the earliest manuscripts do have a critical detail in them which would tend validate final insertions if not in John's life then very shortly thereafter. The Gospel itself makes a reference to other living witnesses working in tandem with John: "This is the disciple who testifies to these things AND WHO WROTE THEM DOWN. WE KNOW his testimony is true." (John 21:24). It seems then very likely that even if John died before finishing the Gospel, that others who were witnesses to what he said wrote

that down and testified to it also, which could only be done just after he passed away. On the other hand, there is very strong evidence that John wrote his Gospel first, then his letters, and finally Revelation itself (John 1:1-5, 1 John 1:1-7, Revelation 1:1-3, 9, 19). In that case, the attestation of these other witnesses need not be posthumous, but rather a way to add strength to the document itself.

183 These fragments, which were preserved by the Church Fathers, show a very early Jewish belief in Y'shua as the Messiah quite separate from the Gentile version that superseded it. These fragments also represent, if not the actual texts themselves, then later "memories" of what may have been in the original Aramaic Gospel of Matthew, which Jerome associates these with. The date here is probably very conservative, as Jewish Christian (Nazarene) traditions go back much further than this. In fact, the apostle Paul, who called himself also a Nazarene "which you call a sect", clearly did not believe it was anything other than an extension of Jewish practice, (Acts 24:5,14-16.)

184 "second edition" is a very minimal and almost prejudicial assertion. We must remember that the fragments of Thomas in Greek were *themselves subject to Gnostic alteration by this time*, then subsequently translated into Coptic, which itself had at least one saying (114) added to it. Other sayings from the Greek fragments which match up to the Coptic show later revision in the latter language, (Gr. Thomas 37) and some of the Coptic may have in fact deleted portions from the Greek, (Gr. Thomas 30, comp to Coptic saying 77). While debate still rages on as to which came first, these features leave precious little doubt of the fact that the original Thomas, very much in line with the Gospel tradition, had plenty of time to redone and added to by the Gnostics. Fortunately, as the section "Thomas' Promises" explains in detail, the editing seams of the original are still apparent.

185 The Complete Gospels, p. 6. Robert Funk is a lot more sure of Paul's ancient character than Peter's. Still, he doesn't discount Peter's possible contribution altogether either. He puts on the same chart a possible early edition of Peter's Gospel also dated to 50, and no later than 100 CE. What is interesting here is that since Funk does not directly attack the authenticity of many writings that could be ascribed to the apostle, who is known to have been killed by the year 67 (64 is more likely). If extra-canonical works can be ascribed to Peter in the first century, then I see no reason why the better established Petrine Epistles, to whom these other sources are constantly compared with (see p. 400), should not be accorded the same privilege. As for the other two, both Paul and James the Just were killed in 60's as well.

186 That is, with the normal triple tradition, or *synoptic* (Matthew, Mark and Luke) triples. The exception to this is what I call "odd triples", or stories not in Mark but ascribed to Matthew, Luke and John. In those cases it seems a separate editing process after the famous Q redactions occurred, which would put the material in the 70's, or after Mark was composed. There are no Mark-Luke-John triples in the Gospels.

187 The Complete Gospels, p. 274. Although in the introduction to the section the authors state Q has no resurrection statements or narratives, that supposition is disproved by including the Sign of Jonah prophecies in the Q collection, to which it clearly belongs. The fact is, whoever Q was, he must have known that Jonah survived the whale, and so the statement about the Son of Man being inside the earth for three days and nights as being analogous to this story is proof of early symbolism and allusions to resurrection even in this collection.

188 Another early indirect reference to the resurrection may be in the book of James, dated to no later than the year 49, and possibly

to a few years before. While James does not state the resurrection directly, he does explicitly refer to Christ as returning, (5:7), judging (5:8-9) and raising the dead, (5:15).

189 The author holds to the view that Galatians is from the year 49 and applies to the cities in southern Galatia which were founded on the first missionary journey. In support of this evidence, as noted biblicist Charles Ryrie states, is the fact that the book shows that in the time it was written that the circumcision issue had not yet been settled by the Jerusalem Council, which met in 49. In the author's view, this fact is more critical than the one used to support a Northern Galatian address, mainly that Luke (Acts 16:6, 18:23) appears to only "count" the north in his references to the region. Whether this was Luke's intention or not as Paul's chronicler, the fact remains that it is overly simplistic to assume one's geographical predilection would be identical to another's from a different background, especially when the historical evidence on the other side is so strong. See The Ryrie Study Bible, p. 331.

190 "raised from the dead according to the Scriptures" can either mean the OT, in which case labeling Q's recording of the Sign of Jonah as a resurrection statement is correct, as again Jonah is being used to predict a return after three days, or it may mean some form of other Epistles or rough Gospels to this effect. Either way, it proves these stories came very early indeed! Furthermore, Paul's reference to the appearances, in the right order, gives earlier dates to both the Gospels and the Book of Acts, as far as preserving tradition is concerned.

191 Again, why would Paul appeal to 500 witnesses, most of whom were still alive, if they could not substantiate what they saw?

192 Even though the Assyrian Church of the East does not include

this book in the canon, the author nevertheless believes the book to be authentic and supports a full 27-book canon.

193 John may not record the actual voice that the others do, but does reveal that Spirit told him he was the Son of God, which is essentially the same thing.

194 This is certainly the case with saying 114, which is acknowledged also in <u>The Complete Gospels</u>. Other sayings such as 21, 56, 49, 50 and 80 are tagged by the editor as showing heavy Gnostic influences.

195 Robert Miller, editor of <u>The Complete Gospels</u>, disagrees on page 301, however, it is fair to point out that the sayings which Thomas and the Gospels have in common are some of the same ones which have shown an Aramaic substratum. Whether this reflects oral or written Aramaicisms no one is certain, but its probable origins in Syria certainly make the latter very plausible in a general sense. And then we have this comment from p. 302: "It is noteworthy, however, that the opening line of the gospel reads, 'These are the secret sayings the the living Y'shua spoke and Didymos Judas Thomas recorded.' Didymos Judas Thomas seems to have been a popular legendary figure from apostolic times, especially in Syria. IN FACT, IT IS ONLY IN EASTERN SYRIA THAT WE FIND PRECISELY THIS FORM OF THE NAME, WHERE IT OCCURS IN THE ACTS OF THOMAS…Thomas, or Didymos Judas Thomas, was apparently the patron apostle for Syria. As such, most scholars now assume that the Gospel of Thomas, in more or less its present form, originally came out of Syria. IT IS CERTAINLY POSSIBLE, HOWEVER, THAT AN EARLIER VERSION MAY HAVE ORIGINIATED IN PALESTINE. Saying 12 in this gospel, after all, appeals not tot he authority of Thomas, but to that of James, who is associated in early Christianity with the Jerusalem Church (see Galatians 1:19)."

196 The Complete Gospels, p. 302.

197 It is also possible that some Gnostic additions started in the first century itself, in which case so much the better. The Gnostics certainly began their theological attacks at an early stage. If this is so, then we can obviously see how the same early source was applied by both traditional Christians and Gnostics, as they developed along different paths. Either way, we can still see the traces of the original tradition that did make it into the official record.

198 The Complete Gospels, p.305-322, is the source for this translation.

199 While both versions share common material, Luke and Thomas appear to share far more of a rough order of sayings in common than either do with Matthew, (see Matthew 5:1-7:28 and Luke 6:17-49). This leads me to believe that Luke actually had earlier material than the Mattean Scribe did.

200 A good place for the Lord's Prayer to happen?

201 A very interesting quote, as it appears to act both as a metaphor for the wide and narrow gates, (Matthew 7:13-14) and also serve as a reminder of a longer parable regarding ten virgins waiting for their groom, (Matthew 25:1-13).

202 This is an interesting possible variation on either the grass which is here today and tomorrow thrown in the fire, (Matthew 6:30), or even the salt of the earth that is only good for trampling on, (Matthew 5:13).

203 The Coptic translation reads, as the Gospels do, "son of man". The Jesus Seminar people are simply letting their anti-Christian bias show through in their word choices, since the Semitic idiom

for son of man (bar'nasha), can be literally rendered as human beings. While the roots of the word support this, it ignores the tradition as to how this came to mean "son of man", such as in Daniel 7:13.

204 Note that in Aramaic the word *naphshah* can be rendered either as "self" or "soul".

205 Another version of Q theory is the so-called "Four Source Theory". In it the same two sources are employed by Matthew and Luke, but the particulars in Luke came from a separate oral source named "L", and those from Matthew are called "M". This version is actually closer to my conclusions, in that I also agree that particulars in these two Gospel are in fact later oral traditions unique to that particular writer. However, since all this again only took 70 years to finalize, the term "late" is a bit of a misnomer, and is only applied in the relative sense. In either case it does not matter, as the patterns between Matthew, Luke and Q are the same, and are equally explained by my theory no matter the number of sources. See The Complete Gospels, p. 54, for more information.

206 "other Scriptures" is very significant since it contrasts Paul's letters with the Old Testament. That means that during the first thirty years after the crucifixion, the earliest Churches had both Epistles and the Torah. That being the case, they would have, within 10-20 years of the event had Greek writings that deal with the words and deeds of Y'shua, his resurrection being the most critical part of the early liturgy. Other points in the Epistles appear to be direct quotes from what must have been a very early written source incorporated later into the Gospels, if not a full narrative Gospel in and of itself.

207 The actual dates for these events are derived from *The Illustrated Dictionary and Concordance of the Bible,* subject heading: "Paul".

Signs of the Cross: The Search for the Historical Jesus

Some traditional information regarding the Gospel writers is derived from *The New Foxe's Book of Martyrs* and data regarding possible early composition dates and accompanying apostolic evidence from notes in *The Ryrie Study Bible*.

208 This James, the brother John and son of Zebedee, is not to be confused with another prominent James, who was the step-brother of Y'shua and known as Ya'acov Ha Tzadik ("James the Just"). The former, the one under discussion, was killed in the year 44, whereas the latter survived until the year 62. Also the second person's name in Hebrew is not "James" as we would know it, but is closer to "Jacob". The duality of names may be the result of many Semites holding dual Gentile appellations, or it may have more to do with Greek translators making the names of the disciples more palatable to a Gentile audience. I tend to lean toward the former explanation, since it has copious examples in the NT record with Kepha (Simon), Shaul (Paul), Nathanael (Batholomew), Levi (Matthew), and many others.

209 The Catholic Encyclopedia was written in 1913, and depending upon how one counts up the time, it is possible to have a two year window regarding these events. However, most scholars today agree with the 49 date for the conference, and so this is what the author is going with.

210 See "What Scripture Where? Part 2."

211 New Foxe's Book of Martyrs, p. 6. See also "Catholic Encyclopedia: Matthew, Apostle", for a fuller listing of the various theories regarding his death. The author however, leans towards the former explanation, that Matthew died in the Ethiopian village of Naddabah, and hopes that his Aramaic Gospel may still lie there, waiting to be discovered even now.

212 On the other hand, the Church fathers talk of Matthew "preaching to the Hebrews" in Jerusalem for "years", and if the implication is that this happened for "many years" then Matthew could not have left that early. Other traditions talk of the Ethiopian official going back to his country and winning many converts there, so Matthew could have been sent down later to help him. Either way, Matthew is definitely evangelizing in that territory no later than the year 45, which is more than enough time for his Gospel to be given to the apostle James by the time he quotes from it five years later.

213 "on the authority of an elder" is an extremely significant statement. Even though Papias is being quoted by Eusebius, it is very well known that he was a student of the apostle John, the son of Zebedee. Since most scholars agree that the writer behind the Gospel of John is the same as the one who did the three additional letters that bear this name and Revelation, it is almost certain that "the elder" is also this same apostle, since this was another title used by him, (2 John 1:1).

214 A careful reading of Acts 15 shows that the Jerusalem Council met prior to Peter and Paul arguing in Antioch, and this links well with the statements in the second chapter of Galatians.

215 Notice in this verse that Mark is also with Peter and Silas.

216 The Illustrated Bible Dictionary, p. 429-430.

217 "hometown" is a bit of a misnomer, since early tradition attests to Luke being born in Syrian Antioch. Troas, where Paul found him practicing medicine, is merely the place Luke moved to as an adult. Ironically, this same city is located near another city also named Antioch, in Turkey. See Eusebius (Hist. Eccl. III, iv, 6), which has: "Loukas de to men genos on ton ap Antiocheias, ten

episteuen iatros, ta pleista suggegonos to Paulo, kai rots laipois de ou parergos ton apostolon homilnkos—"Lucas vero domo Antiochenus, arte medicus, qui et cum Paulo diu conjunctissime vixit, et cum reliquis Apostolis studiose versatus est." And, elsewhere a clearer statement by the Church father says, in "Quæstiones Evangelicæ", IV, i, 270: "ho de Loukas to men genos apo tes Boomenes Antiocheias en—", which means "Luke was by birth a native of the renowned Antioch" (Schmiedel, "Encyc. Bib."). As Paul Younan further points out:

"Antioch in Syria would be the only renowned Antioch, since the one in Psydia was little more than a stopping point for soldiers in Roman times. "

218 According to the Catholic Encylcopedia, while there is some controversy, most authorities (Jerome, Tertullian, Clement and Origen) have concluded that Mark's Gospel was written before Peter's death in 67 CE.

219 However, Mark does not provide his final draft of his Gospel, which is finished by Peter after Mark dies in the year 63. It is possible though that Mark might have left some rough draft with Luke at this stage, although if true, Luke, being the careful historian that he was, probably waited until the final version of Mark's Gospel was conveyed by Silas before pronouncing his work completed.

220 That is, the original "autograph" Scriptures penned by apostles. There is a strong claim from the Assyrian Church of the East that nearly identical copies of those originals are preserved in their liturgy.

221 The Complete Gospels, p. 177.

222 The second chapter of John appears to record a Passover when

the family and the disciples went up to Jerusalem together, but a careful reading disproves this, since it says Y'shua went up to Jerusalem, and not in conjunction with these others. It is also possible that in that one instance everyone left from Capernaum at the same time and on the same road.

223 Granted Purim and Hanukkah are minor and optional feasts. However that fact bolsters my position. Since they were optional, it is even less likely that all of them would go to the trouble of a Jerusalem pilgrimage, especially Hanukkah, which was in the middle of the rainy season. The Gospels also do not record the disciples being present at either holiday.

224 This is not to say there are not minor variations on the two main themes. John Meier, for example is clearly in the year 30 camp for Christ's death. However, he also argues for reasons we will get into later for a year 28 start. Similarly, others have suggested a 2-year ministry for the 33 death date. It is my view that any period less than 3 years and an odd amount of months contradicts clear evidence in the Gospels and Daniel and should therefore not be considered.

Finally, a misguided and very small minority propose the year 32 as a death date, regardless of the start date, which is all over the place. They make this proposition solely on a misunderstanding of the years referred to in Daniel 9:24-27.

225 <u>Antiquities</u>, 18.5.2.

226 <u>A Marginal Jew</u>, p. 374.

227 <u>Antiquities,</u> 18.3.2-3; <u>The Annals of Tacitus,</u> 15.44.

228 <u>Journal of Biblical Literature,</u> 81, 1962, p.70-71.

229 *The New Testament's Unsolved Mysteries,* Time Magazine, December 18, 1995.

230 Illustrated Dictionary and Concordance of the Bible.

231 Illustrated Dictionary and Concordance of the Bible.

232 Antiquities, 18.6.10.

233 Illustrated Dictionary and Concordance of the Bible.

234 A Marginal Jew, p. 374. Meier's time frame is even more stringent than my own. He contends that the entire range of Y'shua's ministry and death is only from 28 - 33 CE.

235 Less the outer courts and other expansions, which continued until about the year 63.

236 The one exception, Luke 11:1-13:9, and how it is actually part of Matthew's Sermon (5:1-7:28), will be fully discussed at a later time. Even taking this into account, however, the rule still applies to more than 95% of the combined Gospel record.

237 This assumption is well established in the scholarly community. Because Y'shua and his followers are young, they most likely walk at a vigorous pace, say about 5 miles and hour. If this figure is multiplied by 7 hours, not including rests and meal periods, the total distance comes to between 30-35 miles a day. At that pace, Y'shua and his disciples would be in the vicinity of Jerusalem well into the third day, and might perhaps require a fourth if either bad weather or a slower pace prevailed during their journey.

The BBC documentary *Jesus: The Conspiracy* (broadcast on PBS April 2, 1999), also confirmed this assumption.

238 That is, the first five books of the Bible, or Pentateuch.

239 However, one of the main keys to this mystery is understanding the phrase "entire Torah". In its narrowest sense, the word "Torah" means just the Five Books of Moses, also known as the Pentateuch. Additionally, even though a specific Hebrew word—*tenakh*—is the technically correct term for the whole Hebrew Bible, "Torah" also took on this more expansive meaning. Therefore, "entire Torah" refers not just to the Five Books, but to the remainder as well.

240 Some scholars allege that the Sadduccees took their name from another Zadok who lived during the second century BCE, however this has not found widespread acceptance. Furthermore, the fact that the Sadduccees preceded the Pharisees is well established and at the core of this argument.

241 Eminent Bible scholar Lawrence Schiffman even goes so far as to postulate that during this time some of the Sadduccees themselves were disgusted by these practices. Believing that their Temple had been defiled, they soon settled in the desert, and started a monastic sect we know better as the Essenes.

242 Antiquities, 13.10.5-7.

243 Antiquities, 13.13.5.

244 Antiquities, 13.14.2.

245 Antiquities, 13.16.1-3.

246 See Antiquities, 18.1.4., and Lawrence Schiffman's New Light on the Pharisees: Insights from the Dead Sea Scrolls, *Bible Review*,

Signs of the Cross: The Search for the Historical Jesus

June 1992, p. 54. Also Emil Schurer's <u>History of the Jewish People in the Age of Christ</u>, p. 402, is very instructive on the matter.

247 Which, unfortunately, included the Sadduccees, who had become Hellenized enough to neglect Temple duties to compete in the Olympic games...naked! Some even went so far as to have an operation that appeared to re-stretch the foreskin, making them appear uncircumcized! See *The Second Book of the Maccabbees*, 4:14.

248 By contrast, the Sadduccees only relied on the written Torah and kept slavishly to interpretations of it listed in their *Book of Decrees*. Josephus, in Antiquities 13.10.5 explains: "What I would now explain is this, that the Pharisees have delivered to the people a great many observances by succession from their fathers, which are not written in the laws of Moses; and for that reason it is that the Sadducees reject them, and say that we are to esteem those observances to be obligatory which are in the written word, but are not to observe what are derived from the tradition of our forefathers. And concerning these things it is that great disputes and differences have arisen among them, while the Sadducees are able to persuade none but the rich, and have not the populace obsequious to them, but the Pharisees have the multitude on their side. But about these two sects, and that of the Essens, I have treated accurately in the second book of Jewish affairs."

249 Both early Jewish tradition and the historian Josephus in fact record that the continuation of Pharisaic practices after the First Jewish Revolt (66-73 CE) was due to one man, Rabbi Yochanan ben Zakkai, the last disciple of Hillel. That is why Hillel's particular flavor of Pharisaism was the only one to survive, since his student would not have acknowledged any other school.

250 According to <u>The Holy Scriptures According to the Masoretic</u>

Text, p. ix, the third division of books (ketuvim or writings) was used extensively in the Synagogue system many centuries ago but fell into disuse. Now only a much reduced collection from this section remains in the liturgy, although it is still well represented.

251 <u>The Holy Scriptures According to the Masoretic Text,</u> p. xiii-xv.

252 <u>All About Jewish Holidays and Customs,</u> p. 8.

253 "relative safety" is not a misnomer, especially when we remember that the first Nazareth crowd tried to kill him and that even members of his own family tried to either have Y'shua committed to an asylum or put into deadly situations, (Luke 4:14-30, Mark 3:20-21, John 7:1-10).

254 This may also explain where some of Y'shua's female followers came from. Mary Magdalene could have been healed close to her house in Bethany. And Joanna, the wife of Herod's accountant, also lived nearby in Bethlehem, and could have come into contact with Y'shua at that time, (Luke 8:1-3).

255 The reason for this certainty is because the Law clearly required that the very first bits of the harvest be dedicated to this Feast, hence the term "firstfruits". So, if this dedication of the wall was a separate occasion, then it happening either before of after Shavuot is a direct violation of the Torah. If it's before, then Shavuot is not the first time in the year the produce is being used, and if after, you could not call it firstfruits, since the official holiday for using them had passed.

256 This name is not rendered as written in the NIV. Original Aramaic and Peshitta usage is retained.

257 While the ground in Jerusalem never really froze much during

winter, the heavy and incessant freezing rains made life very unpleasant, (Ezra 10:9, Song of Songs 2:11, Matthew 24:20). Furthermore according to *Kittio's Palestine* (1899) p. 23, certain areas of Israel were very prone to heavy snowfall in January or February, even as much as a foot or more. Such conditions around a seaside area would make work very difficult and, even if the fishermen still were able to put in a regular day's work, the odds of them being willing to stay out all night would be slim.

258 The timing for this miracle is particularly tight. John 6:1-4 tell us "the Passover was near", most likely about a week away. However, the following also as to happen: the next day, Y'shua is still in Bethsaida, giving the "Bread of Life" discourse, (John 7). Then he has to travel at least 3 days to get to Jerusalem and getting there one day early to "purify" himself, purchase supplies, and make meal preparations, (John 11:55).

259 This is not to say this period is without its difficulties, far from it! In many cases, confining an event to this time frame is the best we can do. Also many similar events are happening in a short period, making for certain chronological problems. For example, Y'shua is in and out of boats so often, that it is hard to determine when he healed the paralytic, conquered the Legion demons, etc.

260 It should not be surprising that Y'shua would use the same admonition ("Go show yourself to the priest..." on both occasions, since their circumstance was the same. Nor is it surprising that both lepers would bow before Y'shua and beg for mercy or that Y'shua would respond to their pleas with the same words, "I am willing".

261 It is all too easy, and unfortunate, to apply our cultural standards to the distant and diverse past. In a country where more than 95% of the adult population is literate, it is easy to forget that Y'shua is

from a time and place which placed a much heavier emphasis on oral teaching and repetition. As such, these similar sermons in Matthew and Luke are only one series of many instances where Y'shua repeats himself. Two other instances which bear mentioning are the "Foxes Have Holes" events (Matthew 8:18-22, Luke 9:51-62) and the four places (only two separate events, however) where "The Lamp On a Stand" teaching is recorded, (Matthew 5:14-16 with pp. in Luke 11:33-36 and Mark 4:21-22 with pp. in Luke 8:16-17).

262 In particular, Luke 12:1 makes it clear that many thousands were present for this teaching, which once again is the same event as Matthew 5:1-7:28.

263 Also to be included in the move are the first nine verses of chapter 13.

264 This is also implied in John 11:7. At that time Y'shua is not in Judea, but has probably returned to Galilee when he hears that his friend Lazarus is ill.

265 In fact Luke 9:51 is perhaps the strongest indication that this is shortly before the Crucifixion: "As the time approached for him to be taken up to heaven, Y'shua resolutely set out for Jerusalem."

266 This is, of course, excepting the repetition of Matthew's Sermon and surrounding events found in Luke 11:1-13:9.

267 This is primarily because Lazarus must be raised from the dead about the middle of March to accommodate: 1) the withdrawal to Ephraim, and 2) Y'shua's return to Bethany six days before the Passover, or March 28, (John 12:1).

268 The first purging, in John, is actually a separate event and not a

misplaced memory of this one as has often been supposed. John's version is well before the Feeding of the Five Thousand whereas the Synoptics are unanimous that their purge comes later.

269 There are several anointings throughout the Gospels and they are all individual events with their onwn significance. The anointing in Luke 7:36-50 is done to certifiy Y'shua's claim as Messiah. The fact that it is sone by a sinful woman and not a priest is also significant, because it shows that, unlike David, Y'shua's righteousness came from within himself, and was not conferred by a mediator. This is also along the same lines of the Baptism, where John is clearly the one who should be baptized by Y'shua, but Y'shua says to so anyway to "fulfill all righteousness". Near the end of his life however, the two other anointings are done to prepare him for burial, because Jewish custom required that both the feet (John 12:1-11) and the head (Mark 14:1-11). This fact is confirmed in Mark 14:8 directly, and proof that they are two separate occasions is that one is "six days before the Passover" (John 12:1) and the other "two days before the Passover" (Mark 14:1).

A final bit of confusion that needs to be addressed is that there are TWO men named 'Simon" who have Y'shua dine with him during these various anointings. The first, in Luke 7, is Simon the Pharisee. The second, erroneously called "Simon the Leper" but truly identified in Aramaic as "Simon the Jar Maker", is depicted in Matthew 26:6-7 and Mark 14:1-11.

270 Notice that both versions could have happened. Judas could have been hanging from a tree on high, the rope could have snapped, and his innards could have spilled out as a result.

271 In this case the Pharisees are celebrating their Passover a day later, or doing the "second chagigah", as is related in Succah v, 7. Galileans and Judeans slaughtered the lambs over a two-day period to avoid congestion, so that is why Y'shua's Passover meal is a

day earlier than when the Pharisees desire to "eat the Passover. Other alleged time clues are resolved by looking at the differences between Synoptic and Johanine mehtods of time keeping. The former relies on the Jewish method and the latter, Roman.

272 Obvious and interesting, yes, but not necessarily accurate. As was clearly shown earlier, the Zechariah referred to in this quote is the same as the one in 2 Chronicles 24:20-22, not John the Baptist's father, who came seven centuries later.

273 Mark 15:43.

274 Acts 23:6.

275 Luke 13:31, Mark 12:34.

276 Matthew 23:1-3, 5:20. Notice also how, even as he acknowledges their authority, he still separates that power from whether they are right or wrong. Very Jewish indeed!

277 Matthew 22:17, John 9:34-38. While it is true that the Pharisees are using flattery in the first case to trap Y'shua, they also use the title of "Rabbi" even when no such artifice is intended, such as in Matthew 17:24.

278 John 7:45-52, 10:19-21, 11:45-57. Notice that Nicodemus, in addition to being a disciple of Y'shua, is also a member of the Sanhedrin which is headed by the high priest Caiphas.

279 See Galatians, chapters 1 and 2. Paul had to get permission to preach from the Jerusalem Church. Furthermore, in spite of Paul's bombastic style of "opposing Peter to his face", he never records the outcome of the dispute, probably because he still lost the argument with the people in charge! Finally, a lot of the disputes

between the Jewish and Gentile wings would not be resolved until the Jerusalem contingent issued what we call in rabbinic parlance, a ruling from their "beit din", or house of judgment, (Acts 15:1-41).

280 Ireneus tells us of another group of the same name that did accept the virgin birth but maintained all the other heresies of the first group. However, the Ebionites I am referring to are the majority sect that denied the former concept.

281 Epiphanus, Heresies 30. Also see The Complete Gospels, p. 437.

282 Also the Syrian Orthodox Church, a Semitic and Aramaic speaking group, traces their lineage to Antioch as well.

283 Dr. Trimm makes the point that the Nazarenes would have probably migrated into the COE extensively in the fourth-sixth centuries. Although, from the COE side, their documents suggest the genesis of such an event began much earlier and at a very high level. In fact, there are two Patriarchs of the See of Babylon who, in addition to being from the See of Jerusalem, are actually related to the Messiah directly. The sixth Patriarch, Mar Abris (ruled 90-107), was a descendant of the Virgin Mary and the eighth, Mar Yakub Ha Rishon (the First—ruled 172-190), claimed Joseph as his ancestor. There can also be little doubt that when these individuals ascended to the Patriarchate, that significant numbers of members from their old See would have joined them. Finally, the Jewish leaders who were in large numbers from both Sees would have ensured that Aramaic NT books circulated among their members well before Rabbula's—or even Tatian's—birth.

284 See Eusebius; Hist. Eccl., iv, 22, and also the testimony of Pantaeus from second century, which again reads from book v, chapter 10:

"Of these Pantaenus was one: it is stated that he went as far as India, where he appears to have found that Matthew's Gospel had arrived before him and was in the hands of some there who had come to know Christ. Bartholomew, one of the apostles, had preached to them and had left behind Matthew's account **in the actual Aramaic characters**, and it was preserved till the time of Pantaenus's mission."

Quoted from the translation by G. A. Williamson, *The History of the Church*, Dorset Press, New York, 1965, pages 213-214.